A·N·N·U·A·L E·D·I·T·I·O·N·S

Public Administration 04/05

Eighth Edition

EDITOR

Howard R. Balanoff

Texas State University

Dr. Howard R. Balanoff is the William P. Hobby Professor of Public Service at Texas State University at San Marcos. He is also the director of the university's William P. Hobby Center for Public Service and serves as the director of the Texas Certified Public Manager (CPM) Program. Having taught at Texas State University for more than 28 years, he has also served as an adjunct professor of public affairs and educational administration and has taught at the University of Texas at Austin. Dr. Balanoff received a bachelor of arts in political science and history from Hunter College of the City University of New York. He received his master's and doctorate in urban and regional planning from Texas A&M University. He is the author of numerous articles in the area of public administration and planning and is the editor of the textbook *Public Administration*. He is a former member of the National Council of the American Society for Public Administration (ASPA) and past-president of the National Certified Public Manager (CPM) Consortium. He has also served as the chair of ASPA's Professional Development and International Affairs Committee. His specialty areas are personnel administration, public policy, and professional development and education in the public sector. Dr. Balanoff also teaches courses and conducts research in the area of international and comparative public administration. For 7 years he served on active duty as a communications-electronics officer and missile combat crew commander in the U.S. Air Force and for 13 years as a member of the Air Force Reserves. He holds the rank of Major USAF-Retired.

McGraw-Hill/Dushkin

530 Old Whitfield Street, Guilford, Connecticut 06437

Visit us on the Internet

http://www.dushkin.com

Credits

1. **Introduction and Overview of Administration**
   Unit photo—© 2004 by PhotoDisc, Inc.
2. **Governmental and Organizational Behavior**
   Unit photo—© 2004 by PhotoDisc, Inc.
3. **Human Resources Administration**
   Unit photo—TRW Inc. photo.
4. **Finance and Budgeting**
   Unit photo—© 2004 by PhotoDisc, Inc.
5. **Technology and Information Systems**
   Unit photo—© 2004 by PhotoDisc, Inc.
6. **Public Policy, Planning, Intergovernmental Relations, and the Law**
   Unit photo—© 2004 by Sweet By & By/Cindy Brown.
7. **International and Comparative Public Administration and Policy**
   Unit photo—© 2004 by Sweet By & By/Cindy Brown.

Copyright

Cataloging in Publication Data
Main entry under title: Annual Editions: Public Administration. 2004/2005.
1. Public Administration—Periodicals. I. Balanoff, Howard R., *comp.* II. Title: Public Administration.
ISBN 0-07-294953-8 658'.05 ISSN 1052-7532

Eighth Edition

Cover image © 2004 PhotoDisc, Inc.
Printed in the United States of America 1234567890BAHBAH54 Printed on Recycled Paper

Editors/Advisory Board

Members of the Advisory Board are instrumental in the final selection of articles for each edition of ANNUAL EDITIONS. Their review of articles for content, level, currentness, and appropriateness provides critical direction to the editor and staff. We think that you will find their careful consideration well reflected in this volume.

To the Reader

In publishing ANNUAL EDITIONS we recognize the enormous role played by the magazines, newspapers, and journals of the public press in providing current, first-rate educational information in a broad spectrum of interest areas. Many of these articles are appropriate for students, researchers, and professionals seeking accurate, current material to help bridge the gap between principles and theories and the real world. These articles, however, become more useful for study when those of lasting value are carefully collected, organized, indexed, and reproduced in a low-cost format, which provides easy and permanent access when the material is needed. That is the role played by ANNUAL EDITIONS.

September 11, 2001, was a "watershed" for the United States in general and for our public service in particular. The world has changed dramatically, and I strongly believe that Americans must now view public administration and public policy differently than we did before September 11.

As I was getting ready to do the research for the eighth edition of *Annual Editions: Public Administration*, I found myself focusing on articles that revolved around disaster, chaos, and uncertainty. I was drawn to articles that would help public administrators and public servants cope with the problems of our modern world. Therefore this edition of the book contains articles not only about 9/11 but also about other disasters.

I would like to dedicate *Annual Editions: Public Administration 04/05* to David O. "Doc" Cooke for his 50+ years of outstanding service to the Pentagon and to public service. At the time of his passing, Doc was a senior public servant who had been a mentor for hundreds if not thousands of career and noncareer civil servants including numerous secretaries of defense. Public administrators in the federal civil service and the American Society for Public Administration miss Doc, but he will certainly not be forgotten.

Special thanks go to Astrid Merget whose Donald Stone Lecture at the 2002 American Society for Public Administration (ASPA) Conference helped frame the organization and structure of this edition of *Annual Editions: Public Administration*. With a view toward the future, this edition includes all new articles. Not a single article was retained from the last edition.

It should also be mentioned that the depth and complexity of the public administration discipline is barely touched in this volume. The 7 units and 38 articles in this edition have, however, been selected to provide an insight into a very sophisticated and challenging field of study.

Each unit begins with an overview that provides an introduction to the articles that follow. The units and subunits in this book reflect many of the traditional subject areas of public administration, such as organizational behavior, human resources administration, public finance and budgeting, technology and information systems, public policy, and international and comparative public administration. In addition, as mentioned previously, special emphasis has been placed on coping in an era of disaster, chaos, and uncertainty.

Articles have been selected from a variety of leading public administration journals such as *Public Administration Review*, *Public Finance & Budgeting*, *Journal of the American Planning Association*, *Governing*, *Public Management*, *Planning*, and the *Review of Public Personnel Administration*.

I would like to express my appreciation to those who have helped me prepare this book for publication. I would like to thank the members of the McGraw Hill/Dushkin Advisory Board for their assistance and to express my appreciation to colleagues, staff, public administration students, and alumni at Texas State University for their friendship and support.

I would also like to recognize my friend and colleague, Rice University professor and former Texas Lt. Governor, William P. "Bill" Hobby. *Texas Monthly* editor Paul Burka once said that Bill Hobby has done more for public and higher education than any individual in Texas history. I agree with that assessment, and I'm extremely proud to hold the William P. Hobby Professorship in Public Service at Texas State University.

Special thanks go to my wife, Marilyn, and my daughters, Emily and Amy, for assisting me and providing me with continuous moral support and encouragement. Emily, a Ph.D. student in Political Rhetoric at the University of Texas at Austin, was especially helpful, assisting me with my research in finding and evaluating articles for this edition.

This is the eighth edition of *Annual Editions: Public Administration*, and we would like to know what you think of it. Please take a few minutes to complete and return the *article rating form* at the back of the volume. Anything can be improved, and we need your help in order to publish future volumes of the highest quality.

Howard R. Balanoff

Howard R. Balanoff
Editor

Contents

UNIT 1
Introduction and Overview of Administration

The four articles in this section are designed to provide insight into the field of public administration and identify some of the big questions and challenges that public administration will face in the twenty-first century.

The concepts in bold italics are developed in the article. For further expansion, please refer to the Topic Guide and the Index.

UNIT 2
Governmental and Organizational Behavior

The six articles in this unit focus on the major areas of organizational behavior, including productivity and performance, organizational communication, and ethics in public sector organizations.

The concepts in bold italics are developed in the article. For further expansion, please refer to the Topic Guide and the Index.

UNIT 3
Human Resources Administration

UNIT 4
Finance and Budgeting

The concepts in bold italics are developed in the article. For further expansion, please refer to the Topic Guide and the Index.

UNIT 5
Technology and Information Systems

The five selections in this section review the latest trends in public management practices and how they can improve operations of organizations in the public sector.

The concepts in bold italics are developed in the article. For further expansion, please refer to the Topic Guide and the Index.

UNIT 6
Public Policy, Planning, Intergovernmental Relations, and the Law

Nine articles in this unit focus on public policy issues, regional planning concerns, and the impact of governmental decisions on public law.

The concepts in bold italics are developed in the article. For further expansion, please refer to the Topic Guide and the Index.

Part C. Intergovernmental Relations and Public Law

UNIT 7
International and Comparative Public Administration and Policy

The five selections in this section consider some of the differences between the public administration policy in the United States and abroad. What can be learned from these differences is examined.

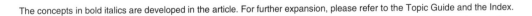

The concepts in bold italics are developed in the article. For further expansion, please refer to the Topic Guide and the Index.

Topic Guide

This topic guide suggests how the selections in this book relate to the subjects covered in your course. You may want to use the topics listed on these pages to search the Web more easily.

On the following pages a number of Web sites have been gathered specifically for this book. They are arranged to reflect the units of this *Annual Edition*. You can link to these sites by going to the DUSHKIN ONLINE support site at *http://www.dushkin.com/online/*.

ALL THE ARTICLES THAT RELATE TO EACH TOPIC ARE LISTED BELOW THE BOLD-FACED TERM.

World Wide Web Sites

The following World Wide Web sites have been carefully researched and selected to support the articles found in this reader. The easiest way to access these selected sites is to go to our DUSHKIN ONLINE support site at *http://www.dushkin.com/online/*.

AE: Public Administration 04/05

The following sites were available at the time of publication. Visit our Web site—we update DUSHKIN ONLINE regularly to reflect any changes.

General Sources

Council for Excellence in Government

http://www.excelgov.org

The Council for Excellence in Government works to improve the performance of government at all levels as well as to better govenment's place in the lives and esteem of citizens.

Federal Web Locator

http://www.infoctr.edu/fwl/

A one-stop shopping center for federal government information, this site includes government agencies, up-to-date public and private links, and a search mechanism.

Gateway to State and Local Government Information

http://stateandlocalgateway.rockinst.org

Hosted by the Rockefeller Institute of Government, this gateway provides news, data, and analysis on the finances and employment of state and local governements.

ICMA: International City/County Management Association

http://www.iclei.org/LA21/map/ICMA.htm

The list of Web sites offered here by ICMA may be of interest to local public administrators. Included subjects are Community and Economic Development, Personnel and Human Resources, Public Safety, and Public Works.

Library of Congress

http://www.loc.gov

The nation's oldest federal cultural institution, the Library of Congress serves as the research arm of Congress. It is also the largest library in the world, with more than 126 million items on approximately 530 miles of bookshelves.

National Academy of Public Administration

http://www.napawash.org

Public policy and administration links at this site include Homeland Security, Government, Public Policy and Analysis, and Public Administration.

National Certified Public Manager Consortium

http://www.cpmconsortium.org

This consortium is the national organization responsible for setting standards and accrediting public sector management training programs across the United States.

New Federalism Home Page

http://newfederalism.urban.org

This site, dedicated to exploring the return of power to the individual states, discusses the federal budget, the Welfare Reform Bill, and the results of federal devolution. See also *http://www.mncn.org/newfed/states.htm.*

State and Local Government on the Net

http://www.statelocalgov.net/index.cfm

Search individual states for elected officials, state government jobs, state organizations, and other links to local government sites.

UNIT 1: Introduction and Overview of Administration

American Society for Public Administration (ASPA)

http://www.aspanet.org

The ASPA is the focal point for intellectual and professional interaction, and its Web site is a rich source of information.

***Public Administration Review* (PAR)**

http://www.aspanet.org/publications/par/index.html

The PAR, a major journal for those interested in public sector management, presents this Web page that contains book reviews, archives, a search mechanism, and related links.

UNIT 2: Governmental and Organizational Behavior

Government Accounting Standards Board (GASB)

http://www.gasb.org

The mission of the GASB is to establish and improve standards of state and local governmental accounting and financaial reporting that will result in useful information for users of financial reports and also guide and educate the public, including issuers and auditors.

National Academy of Public Administration (NAPA)

http://www.napawash.org

NAPA is an independent, nonprofit organization chartered by Congress that responds to specific requests from public agencies and nongovernmental organizations.

National Center for Public Productivity

http:/newark.rutgers.edu/~ncpp/

The National Center for Public Productivity is a research and public service organization devoted to improving productivity in the public sector.

Partnership for Public Service (PPS)

http://www.ourpublicservice.org

The PPS is a nonpartisan organization dedicated to revitalizing public service. It seeks to restore public confidence in and prestige of the federal civil service through an aggressive campaign of public-private partnerships as well as focused research and educational efforts.

Public Sector Continuous Improvement Site

http://curiouscat.com/psci/index.html

John Hunter's site, which aims to help public sector employees improve their organizations, includes online resources, lists of organizations, and important links, plus an online guide, a reading list, and a search capability.

Stateline.org

http://www.stateline.org

Stateline.org was founded to help journalists, policy makers, and engaged citizens become better informed about innovative policies.

UNIT 3: Human Resources Administration

Sexual Harassment in the Workplace: A Primer

http://www.uakron.edu/lawrev/robert1.html

This article is a very complete discussion of the subject, including statistics, tables, federal laws, case studies, employer liability, and guidelines for a sexual harassment policy.

Skill-Based Pay

http://www.bizcenter.com/skillpay.htm

The material at this site has been reproduced from the book, *Designing Skill-Based Pay,* by Donald F. Barkman.

U.S. Department of Labor

http://www.dol.gov/index.htm

This document, "Working Together for Public Service," is the report of the Secretary of Labor's Task Force on Excellence in State and Local Government Through Labor-Management Cooperation.

Zigon Performance Group

http://www.zigonperf.com

This commercial company specializes in performance appraisal, management, and measurement systems for teams and hard-to-measure employees. The Web site offers measurement resources, performance measurement examples, publications, and how-to workshops.

UNIT 4: Finance and Budgeting

FirstGov

http://www.firstgov.gov

The official U.S. gateway to all government information, FirstGov.gov is the catalyst for a growing electronic government.

Giving Federal Workers the Tools They Need to Do Their Jobs

http://acts.poly.edu/cd/npr/npr-3-3.htm

This paper lays out what the federal government is doing, can do, and must do in the future to provide more responsive and more humane government that costs less by recasting what people do as they work.

Performance Measurement Page (City of Grand Prairie)

http://www.cityofgp.com/citygov/bettergov/perform/perform.htm

This Grand Prairie, Alberta, Canada, Web page provides definitions and principles of performance measurement.

The U.S. Chief Financial Officers Council

http://www.cfoc.gov

CFOC is the organization of the CFOs and Deputy CFOs of the largest federal agencies and senior officials of the Office of Management and Budget and the Department of the Treasury who work collaboratively to improve financial management in the U.S. government. Events, links, documents, and initiatives can be found here.

UNIT 5: Technology and Information Systems

Activity-Based Costing (ABC)

http://www.esc-brest.fr/cg/cgkiosk3.htm

Created in France, this site leads to everything you might want to know about activity-based costing.

Alliance for Redesigning Government

http://www.napawash.org/pc_local_state/about.html

This site allows the visitor to hypothetically reinvent federal, state, and local government by using basic concepts, actual cases, available resources, and contacts with practitioners.

American Capital Strategies

http://www.americancapital.com/news/press_releases/pr/pr19961024.html

Malon Wilkus's article "ESOP Privatization," which is the historic account of the federal government's Office of Personnel Management's privatization of its Office of Federal Investigations, makes fascinating reading. It is the first privatization in the United States that transferred majority ownership to its employees through the use of an ESOP.

Brookings Institution

http://www.brook.edu

The Brookings Institution, a private, independent, nonprofit research organization, seeks to improve the performance of American institutions, the effectiveness of government programs, and the quality of U.S. public policies. Through its Web site, explore the Centers on Social and Economic Dynamics and on Urban and Metropolitan Policy.

Center for Policy Research on Science and Technology (CPROST)

http://edie.cprost.sfu.ca

CPROST at Simon Fraser University in Vancouver, BC, Canada, was established with a primary focus of improving public policy and private decision-making processes by increasing public participation and promoting sound methodologies for the implementation of technological change. Click on Management of Technological Change and A Roadmap to the Internet to explore on your own.

Economic Development Administration

http://12.39.209.165/xp/EDAPublic/Home/EDAHomePage.xml

This Department of Commerce site links to current fact sheets, regulations and notices, and contacts and resources, all helpful to understanding economic development issues.

Putting Technology to Work for America's Future

http://sunsite.unc.edu/darlene/tech/report3.html

Here is an excellent paper on the technology policy issued on February 22, 1998, by the Clinton administration, entitled "Technology for America's Economic Growth."

Reason Foundation

http://www.reason.org/privatizationctr.html

The Reason Public Policy Institute's Privatization Center has been at the center of the debate on streamlining government. Their Web site is filled with interesting information.

UNIT 6: Public Policy, Planning, Intergovernmental Relations, and the Law

Capitol Reports: Environmental News Link

http://www.caprep.com

This excellent source of environmental news links to federal and state agencies, courts, Congress, state legislatures, and federal regulations.

Hopwood Reactions and Commentary

http://www.law.utexas.edu/hopwood/reaction.html

This page provides links to press releases, news articles, and other materials offering many opinions about this important affirmative action case. Additional material is also available at *http://www.law.utexas.edu/hopwood/.*

Innovation Groups (IG)

http://www.ig.org

IG is a network of city, town, and county government leaders that provides support for pioneering new approaches to managing cities. The group provides networking, research, and training opportunities to local government administrators.

National Association of Counties

http://www.naco.org/counties/index.cfm

The National Association of Counties offers this entry into county government sites by state.

National League of Cities

http://www.nlc.org

The NLC Web site leads to Legislative Priorities, Local Government Access, Policy Process, News and Events, Other Resources, and a search capability.

UNIT 7: International and Comparative Public Administration and Policy

Division for Public Administration and Development Management

http://www.unpan.org/dpepa.asp

This United Nations site is a source for international information on management innovation and development, public economics, public policy, and public and private parnerships.

European Group of Public Administration (EGPA)

http://www.iiasiisa.be/egpa/agacc.htm

EGPA's page leads to study groups on personnel policies, productivity and quality in the public sector, and the development of contracting in the public sector.

Governments on the WWW

http://www.gksoft.com/govt/en/

This site offers access links to government Web sites throughout the world.

Institute of Public Administration of Canada (IPAC)

http://www.ipaciapc.ca

IPAC is a national bilingual (English/French) nonprofit organization that is concerned with the theory and practice of public management.

Latin American Center for Development Administration (CLAD)

http://www.clad.org.ve/siare/index.htm

CLAD hosts an online database containing thousands of public administration documents and resources. Although the site is written in Spanish, many of the resources contained within the database are in English.

Section on International and Comparative Administration (SICA)

http://www.uncc.edu/stwalker/sica/

SICA, a division of ASPA, specifically aims to facilitate professional networking globally through a series of programs.

UNPAN

http://www.unpan.org

The mission of UNPAN is to promote the sharing of knowledge, experiences, and best practices throughout the world in sound public policies, effective public administration, and efficient civil services through capacity-building and cooperation among member states, with emphasis on south-south cooperation and UNPAN's commitment to integrity and excellence.

We highly recommend that you review our Web site for expanded information and our other product lines. We are continually updating and adding links to our Web site in order to offer you the most usable and useful information that will support and expand the value of your Annual Editions. You can reach us at: *http://www.dushkin.com/annualeditions/*.

UNIT 1

Introduction and Overview of Administration

Unit Selections

1. **Time of Turbulence**, Astrid E. Merget
2. **In Memoriam: David O. "Doc" Cooke**, Warren Master
3. **Doc Cooke's Reflections on Effective Public Management**, *The Public Manager*
4. **The Odyssey of Senior Public Service: What Memoirs Can Teach Us**, J. Patrick Dobel

Key Points to Consider

- Identify and discuss what you think are the three most important challenges facing public administrators that are identified in Astrid Merget's Donald Stone lecture. Identify and discuss at least one public administration challenge that is not identified in her lecture. Why do you think your challenge is important for public administrators?
- Who was "Doc" Cooke? What do you think about his management advice for the secretary of defense? In your opinion, how does the current secretary of defense, Donald Rumsfeld, measure up to Doc Cooke's analysis?
- Identify and discuss some of the things that public administrators can learn from reviewing the memoirs of senior public officials.

Links: www.dushkin.com/online/
These sites are annotated in the World Wide Web pages.

American Society for Public Administration (ASPA)
http://www.aspanet.org

***Public Administration Review* (PAR)**
http://www.aspanet.org/publications/par/index.html

The articles in this first unit are provided as an introduction and overview to the field of public administration. They are designed to give the reader a review of the historical background of public administration and an identification of the questions and challenges that public administrators will face in the twenty-first century.

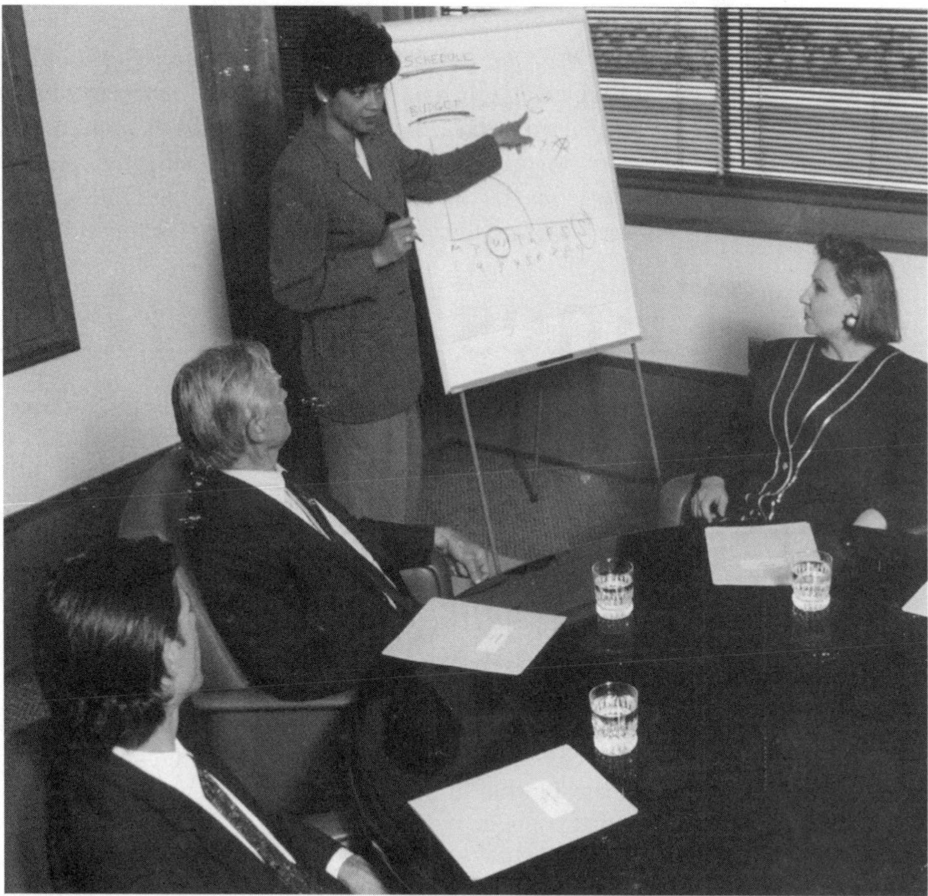

Many of the challenges are identified and discussed in Astrid Merget's Donald Stone Lecture, "Time of Turbulence," which was delivered at the 2002 National Conference of the American Society for Public Administration (ASPA). Dr. Merget's lecture described how events like 9/11 and ongoing trends such as globalization and rapid technological advancement have influenced the public administration profession in the United States and around the world. The big question for public administration according to Merget is how the public administration profession will react to these changes.

The public administration profession lost a giant recently. His name was David O. "Doc" Cooke, a senior Pentagon civil servant. Doc was an effective leader, manager, and mentor for more than five decades at the Pentagon. His advice on what makes an effective public servant and an effective secretary of defense seems especially timely in today's world where the actions of the secretary of defense are being so closely scrutinized by the media and the public.

We can view some of the major challenges to the public service by reviewing the memoirs of senior public officials. These memoirs are analyzed in Patrick Dobel's article, "The Odyssey of Senior Public Service: What Memoirs Can Teach Us." Dobel's article reveals how senior public officials view the impact of public service on their lives and discusses how such senior officials handle the tension of being caught between the ideals and reality of life in the public service. Managers in the not-for-profit sectors are also reviewing some of the big questions of public administration.

Donald C. Stone Lecture

In July 1995, the American Society for Public Administration's Endowment Board established the Donald C. Stone Fund to honor the memory of this public administration legend. Income from this fund is used to sponsor a lecture or symposium at ASPA's national conference, which reflects Stone's varied interests and contributions to the field. This year marked the eighth Donald C. Stone Lecture. On March 18, Astrid E. Merget was ASPA's Stone Lecturer and gave the following speech.

Times of Turbulence

This is indeed an astonishing and poignant honor for me to be able to deliver the lecture in honor of Donald Stone. Without a doubt, he was, during his long life, an exemplar in public service and an inspiration for all of us in the profession of public administration. More personally, Don Stone and I shared two academic institutions—although at different times. We both treasured our graduate education at the Maxwell School of Citizenship and Public Affairs at Syracuse University that endowed us with a lifelong pursuit of the Athenian Oath. What Maxwell gave us was an ideology in the spirit and words of that oath and a set of icons in the statues of George Washington in the school's foyer and of Abraham Lincoln in the courtyard. And we both cheered the much younger, but equally spirited School of Public and Environmental Affairs at Indiana University. He would have affirmed that school's motto to "make a world of difference." There his legacy endures.

What always amazed me was that Don Stone was a visionary: he was not an elder who devoted mind and time to reminiscing about the halcyon days of the New Deal or World War II; instead he was always contemporary in charting where the field of public administration was going and should go. He galvanized others in confabs and colloquy to exchange views, to debate and deliberate over issues rather than just affirm his own priorities and preferences—although opinions he did have with tenacity.

Hence, it is a daunting task to aspire to live up to this lecture—even a little bit—entitled after Don Stone's legacy and legend. But in partaking of that spirit of contemplating the future, several themes have crystallized for me—whether as an educator in critical reflection about my own school and others in the leagues of NASPAA (National Association of Schools of Public Affairs and Administration) and APPAM (Association for Public Policy Analysis and Management), or whether as a sometimes administrator in government, or whether as a citizen of this great, albeit complex, nation. Some three decades ago, another icon of mine, Dwight Waldo, penned a book entitled *Public Administration in a Time of Turbulence.* It does seem to me that public administration is always in a time of turbulence. It is a dynamic field that partakes of all currents of change coursing through our increasingly global nation-state. Unlike many academic disciplines—even those in the social sciences—ours is a porous field imbibing as much in, as detaching from, the field of practice. (As such, I exercise some license of authorship and deviate from the published title of this address, I trust I honor the spirit of the conference's banner, The Power of Public Service.)

Let me share with you a half dozen of my sampler of changes and describe how our field has some special assets to embrace those changes even though there are deficits to remedy. My order does not confer any priority on these; they are all important and interrelated.

First, there is the globalization of our political economy, as is so popularly depicted these days and heralded years ago by the Stone lecturer of the year 2000, Harlan Cleveland. The interdependency of our political, economic, and social systems with nations around the world prompts me to rethink what had been an American centric model of public administration and to reconstruct what we once called international relations. If there was a jolting message in Osborne and Gaebler's celebrated, albeit controversial, work on reinvesting government over a decade ago, it was that some powerful reforms in state and local government did not always originate here. For inspiration on new models of conducting the government's affairs, other nations—in that case New Zealand and Australia—offered potent, penetrating lessons.

Similarly, issues of public policy transcend national boundaries and cultures as in the case, historically, of national security and more recently of trade, of environmental pollution and protection, of immigration, and of virtually every other policy domain. Indeed our State Department's ambassadors abroad do not just serve that agency and its role in foreign affairs; they serve all the departments of our federal government. Moreover, every agency—whether once considered domestic or not—has some kind of office of international affairs to infuse a more global perspective into its policy formulation, implementation, and operations. The world of practice has gone global. So have our academic programs. More students from abroad—despite recent constraints with the former INS and now Department of Homeland Security—seek out American higher education including public administration, in their zeal to learn about American democracy and capitalism. More of our own students reach out to understand their colleagues from around the world. Dealing with diversity is a corollary. Enduring concerns about equity, fairness, and justice assume new meaning and proportion in a multicultural context.

Fortunately an asset of our once domestic-centric field in public administration is our multidisciplinary nature. Understanding the phenomenon of globalization and its implications for policy and administration requires the critical scrutiny of a myriad of disciplines—political science, economics, sociology, history, anthropology, geography, and law—to mention a few obvious candidates. Similarly, our intellectual gestalt has liberated itself in recent decades from the vacuous quest to formulate what would be fragile frameworks or to search for an elusive, single paradigm. Now scholars and practitioners like to assert a more pragmatic and, hence flexible, approach to ferreting out what works, what doesn't, and why—with a healthy tolerance for experimentation in how we conduct the public's affairs. More and more academicians and public officials in public administration engage with counterparts abroad that were once the exclusive domain of international relations or foreign affairs.

Another asset is the normative stance of our field. As a field once so enmeshed in the American experience, we celebrated the fundamental tenets of democracy as perhaps the ethos—or if you will, the ideology—of the field. Values like equality, liberty, and justice animated our doing and thinking about public administration and lent purpose to our endeavors. Despite the tension and strains of September 11 and our precarious stance vis-à-vis Iraq, these values help extend tolerance for and appreciation of diverse cultures in this global village. Revived appreciation for equity as a leitmotif also creates the proclivity to advance rather than recoil from globalizing dynamics in our political economy and its political culture.

As receptive as the field of public administration may be to globalization, there are some deficits. I, for one, question in my own school and those of other institutions just how well we are preparing the next generation of public servants for the global setting of their profession. To be sure, many MPA programs have fields or minors in comparative or development administration that are typically elective. These tend to be compartmentalized in a curriculum. And most faculty tend to segregate the curriculum along their own expertise, which is largely domestic, although more and more of them conduct research and consultation outside the United States. More often than not, the core curriculum—whether disguised as generic—remains domestic in content. To be sure, there is a subset to our schools who member APSIA (Association of Professional Schools of International Affairs) and showcase an international and comparative focus.

What concerns me is the young city manager in a smaller municipality who may have to broker trade deals, manage immigration, or deal with such unsavory problems as drug trafficking across borders or pollution spilling in from a neighboring country on the border. The challenge for us as academics educating that next generation is to enrich our curriculum and our research with global perspectives. Similarly for professionals in the field, conferences or sabbaticals and leaves in other countries would help amplify our ability to learn from others while imparting our own experiences—not necessarily as models to imprint on other cultures, but as lessons learned and insights gained with cultural sensitivity and with humility.

A second current of change is technology. The breakthroughs of an information and computer age are not only advancing globalization but are also recasting public policy and management. The impact is rapid and continually changing. On the educational side of public administration, most MPA programs have altered many facets of the educational enterprise accordingly. Not only are there courses exclusively devoted to inculcating expertise; but also many courses, in say finance or budgeting, rely on computers and information systems in their pedagogy.

The assets of the field that usher in the information age are substantial. Computers and statistics have been mainstays of the curriculum for most MPA programs for several decades and have supported the research of many scholars who rely on large databases like the U.S. Census and undertake rigorous quantitative analyses. Similarly advances are apparent in government, particularly at the federal level, whose own investments in the computer propelled this whole field, especially in the Department of Defense and the military services.

The normative basis of the field also defines a receptive venue. The field's historic preoccupation with rational, objective decision making revered information and analyses as essential tools of policy making. Offices of evaluation punctuate the federal landscape of agencies and legitimate the importance of basing policy in its formulation and implementation on exacting analysis. Technology not only facilitates that premise but also accelerates and disseminates it. Cost-benefit analyses, queuing theories, operations research, TQM (total quality management) and best practices—these and other modern techniques have especially refined policy in finance and in the delivery of many services like transportation, the deployment of the military, the location and scale of major investments in the infrastructure, and the like.

But where technology portends some very fundamental shifts in how we conduct the public's businesses, change is slow. For example, agencies still conform in structure and, to some degree, in behavior to the hierarchical, command-and-control models of the past; these tend to insure stability but they also engender rigidity, incrementalism, rule-bound decisions, and other dysfunctions. What technology with its capacity to span time and space and with its rapidity of transmitting information promises, is the advent of new modes of organizing, decision making, and implementing, with evaluation as its handmaiden. Greater reliance on teams; greater flexibility in organizing for work; greater capacity to coordinate across units and geography—these manifestations of change are slow to materialize against the ponderance of past practice. As an example, during my tenure at the U.S. Department of Health and Human Services, I was dazzled by new software that permits service providers at the local level to treat people in need as whole people rather than categories of service, as dictated by the way statutes and implementing regulations label them. The new technology would have facilitated "one stop" shopping for a person in need with greater coordination across the many caseworkers segregated in the silos of their respective agencies. In part because of costs and privacy issues, this new technology is slow to revolutionize how government deals with people. That failure finds its costs in time-consuming, and often redundant, procedures; in the indignities sustained by clients; and in the inconsistencies across policies with respect to eligibility, certification, and service. This is but one example of just how hard change is, even with the prospect of a path-breaking technology.

As educators, our tendency is to compartmentalize courses in computers, information, and their collateral techniques into toolboxes. Our challenge is to integrate such knowledge and skill into the substance of the field in an attempt to hone creativity in problem solving and to dispel myths of one best solution for public problems. Integration would enliven the meaningfulness of technology and overcome its marginal status in many curricula.

A third current of change is the imperative for public, private, and nonprofit partnerships. Tackling problems in the public domain requires more than channeling resources through bureaucratic agencies of government. Cleaning the air, water, and earth; revitalizing communities; stimulating economies; making the nation and its communities healthy, safe, and secure—these, and virtually all matters in the public domain, cannot be secured by government alone. The private and nonprofit sectors are essential in that collaboration.

Although the field of public administration has historically riveted its academic and professional sights on government, there is a long history of reliance on the private sector. Contracting out, especially for major defense and public works investments, dates way back. In recent decades the theme of privatization—problematic, as it may be—has enlarged the realm of potential interaction with both the private and nonprofit sectors. As fiscal constraints dampened the growth in the public workforce, nonprofit agencies became the frequent vehicles for direct service provision with public dollars—enriched by philanthropic support—in many communities for addressing social and cultural needs. The recognition of "third-party" governments is by now universal in this country.

The academic community in its research and teaching missions has extended its concept of the nonprofit sector not only as a vital partner in supplying services and goods but also as an enabling advocate in championing democracy throughout a pluralistic society. Many MPA programs feature courses in the nonprofit sector often assembled as a major field of concentration. Paul Light's chronicle of graduates from major programs documents that graduates have been increasingly gravitating to both the private and nonprofit sectors in pursuit of public service. In a sense, the field of public administration has come to subscribe to the notion that there are many ways to serve the public. Some in our field, of course, lament this development because government needs to replenish its ranks with the very best talent for the future. Others applaud the professionalization of the nonprofit sector with skilled managers and analysts, while others welcome the infusion of a public understanding into many private ventures, especially in the for-profit consulting firms with governments often their regular clients. As the pursuit of public service finds more dispersed outlets, a number of academic programs have adjusted their curricula—at least incrementally. This further validates that our field is permeable across its academic and professional domains.

There is, however, an imbalance here. Many MPA programs readily embraced the nonprofit sector—perhaps because of the congruence of their normative foundations. The philanthropic community prides itself on "good works" not unlike the public service mission of government. Many students of the nonprofit sector see its advocacy role as reinforcement for a robust political culture and as an outlet for citizenship. The business schools, for the most part, do not share such a normative alliance, although many of their technical courses are especially germane to the nonprofit sector. Hence, the linkage between public administration and the nonprofit sector is not surprising: there is the noble nexus of values and the practical need for professional training. Where not long ago there was a void in higher education for philanthropy, there is now a locus in public administration among other collateral fields.

In contrast, despite the inclusive nature of our field—a real asset to a dynamic public sector—there remains a deficit of sorts. A focus on the business world is limited to contracting out or privatization and to regulation. Often where the private sector creeps into an MPA curriculum, it is under the rubric of regulation to correct for systematic market failures or the irregularities of its individual firms or to orchestrate the macroeconomy through fiscal and monetary, policy—however haphazardly. Rarely are the powerful partnerships celebrated, as in rejuvenating local communities as has happened in Cleveland or Pittsburgh or Indianapolis—to name a few. There, corporate leaders, philanthropists, and public officials came together to marshal plans for energizing communities and their economies. Indeed, seldom would an MPA student be exposed to the legitimate logic of decision making that characterizes a for-profit enterprise. Most faculty do not have a clue either. This is a tremendous disservice to the next generation of public leaders. To resolve major issues in a community or in the nation or around the globe, the interaction of business and government needs to blueprint collaborative enterprises rather than espouse adversarial postures.

The city manager or top local administrator needs not only to feel comfortable with business leaders in the board rooms but also must understand the logic and motives they bring to decisions at the table. Of course, in obvious federal agencies like Treasury and Commerce, that understanding needs to permeate their ranks. For too long the nexus between government and business has been contentious and regulatory in nature; both sectors are at fault.

More interaction across business schools and public affairs schools might help, even though anecdotally my students over the years have preferred the more consensual, collegial setting of public affairs rather than what they see as the competitive, profit-motivated culture of the former. To be sure, more business schools have become insular with the surge in demand for a bachelor's and/or master's degree in business administration. Still, means of mutual understanding can be found with executives-in-residence, with sabbaticals in corporate settings, and with professional exchanges across the sectors.

A fourth current of change entails a renewed and amplified view of institution building. As the world transforms with many countries opting for market-based economies and tilting toward democracy in all their mutations, our expertise in public administration is in demand around the globe. How to develop a tax code and revenue systems; how to budget with public dollars; how to design and develop freely-elected legislative and executive branches; how to codify laws and honor the rule of law; how to frame regulations and incentives to protect natural resources; how to discharge agencies to implement public policy with efficiency and effect; how to achieve justice in a civil society—these and other competencies ingrained in public administration are pivotal to many transforming nations.

The field is replete with expertise in such foundations that are the cornerstones in building the institutions that govern a civil society. That expertise has evolved with this country's rule of law and Constitution that are distinctively American and captured so well in the voices of the *Federalist Papers.* Do our institutional prescriptions fit other cultures with their own distinct values and history? Probably not. Our years of experience with development administration disclose that we cannot simply transpose our institutional frameworks on other cultures.

Notwithstanding unfolding events, we have been humbled by those efforts and have become respectful and appreciative of other nation-states. The assets that we do have are a transparent chronicle of what has worked for us, and what has not, and what has had to be adapted as times change. Those are the prerequisites for an honest discourse or dialectic with other countries, as they embark on transforming their own political and economic systems. Our 200-plus years of a turbulent history should lend a wisdom that disavows didactic prescriptions for our global partners.

Probably a deficit (that is paradoxically an asset) is that we are all pioneers in this global village. What is transforming in the former Soviet block and in China and elsewhere is indeed just as experimental as what the founding fathers attempted with the Constitutional Convention and the new republic. The current times require a different frame of mind than the one public administrators conventionally assume and revere. Instead of rational bromides, trial and error strategies are appropriate. Instead of a nationalistic-centric platform, sensitivity to diversity is imperative. Instead of an imperialistic imprimatur, a sense of integrity, legitimacy, and authenticity should honor the pluralism of cultures.

Educators similarly need to eschew simple textbook answers and tolerate experimentation. Our students with exposure to case studies and with a self awareness of our distinctive cultural heritage relative to others, need their instructors to convey the uncertainties and unpredictabilities of our world, whether grounded at the grassroots or at the globe.

A fifth current of change is the challenge to manage complexity and change. With an accelerated pace of change and with boundaries blurring across sectors and countries, leaders in the public domain can no longer rely on the neat command-and-control template of bureaucracy. Flexibility and adaptability are requisite attributes for the next generation of public leaders to not only organize and manage but also—and more importantly—to lead. Sometimes, I, as an academic, think we do our students a disservice in our efforts to proffer simple theories and logic as we attempt to make sense of a chaotic world. To be sure there is some intellectual and practical necessity to search for patterns, trends, as well as anomalies. But the construct of the rational person is just that—a construct. The situations, which will confront our students as leaders in the public arena, will often be unpredictable and vexing. Hence honing their skills in problem solving is the sine qua non of their professional education.

In this regard, we have a treasury of experience documented in a more robust research record and a renewed appreciation for case studies. Most schools have reinvented their pedagogy to rely on teams and clients that lend more reality to learning, as do internships. Many have complemented our academic ranks with executives-in-residence or professors of practice—drawing on the insights that practitioners can thoughtfully and critically impart. These enlivening elements can help our students grasp the importance of judgment.

What has concerned me for years, when the quantitative revolution took root in the sixties, was that for a long time we conveyed rational choice and objectivity in decision making as the preferred model or end state, rather than as a tool to help reduce uncertainty in making what are judgments. Alice Rivlin spoke so thoughtfully and lucidly about this in her seminal book, *Systematic Thinking for Social Action*. Then, in the era of policy analysis as preeminent in its promise, when our graduates did enter government and savored the realpolitik of decision making, many became cynical and felt mismatched in the messy, turbulent, and uncertain world of politics and administration. As educators of the next generation or as mentors to professional public administrators, we have an obligation to help heighten the skills of judgment, when values and evidence collide, as the quintessential talents for managing complexity and change.

A sixth current of change, which may put me at the risk of contradicting myself, is the importance of policy predicated on research, while asserting a healthy respect for its political milieu. With the advance of knowledge and with the maturation of scholarship in our field, diagnosing—let alone solving—problems in the public domain depends on rigorous research. To be sure, policies do ultimately turn on political judgment. But as the body of research accumulates on physical, social, and economic problems, policy makers are exacting higher standards for the predicates of policy.

The assets of the field are enormous. Not only is our wealth in our multidisciplinary talent but it also inheres in our distinctive style of research. Some decades ago, we often drew invidious comparisons of our field to other disciplines that had all the hallmarks of scholarly prowess—theory or theories to order phenomena, categories for framing problems, accumulated findings to test hypotheses, continual refinements to concepts, and the like. Indeed our tools of analysis and measurement have invested cardinal notions like accountability with concrete meaning, as we are better able to calibrate performance, outcomes, and impacts of policy—as implemented, then evaluated, and eventually informing formulation.

As we have matured, our research has come to matter not only to other scholars but also to policy makers. In this permeable field across the academy and the professional sectors, dialogues help us discover what are the truly worthwhile issues and problems to study. Instead of the proverbial identity crisis of discipline versus profession that plagued our field for so long, my sense is that our scholars have coined their distinctive currency, as mounting purposeful research. By now, as we have educated many generations of professionals and conveyed to them the salience of research as a predicate of policy—not necessarily a determinant—the debates become, hopefully, more informed and less confused. They will always be messy at some level, as well they should be as our officials and citizens struggle to forge consensus out of conflict. Too often, we as educators, and often as administrators, denigrate the untidy state of politics in our predilection for rational decision making. Simply put: Politics is the lifeblood of democracy. Debate, discourse, deliberation—as antecedents to choice—are talents that we as educators need to foster in our students, that we as professionals need to respect, and that we as citizens need to cherish. Politics is not neat. It is confrontational, emotional, belligerent, and self-centered at its worst; politics is reasonable, detached, civil, and public-spirited, at its best.

I trust we have heeded the admonition of some 30 years ago, intoned by Alice Rivlin, the Elliot Richardson speaker of this conference. Research and analysis will not displace politics, rather research and analysis can and should reduce the range of uncertainty that invades decision making.

Finally, why all these exhortations? In the field of public administration what Don Stone implicitly taught us was that public administration has an ethos—or, more precisely, an ideology—that invests our efforts as academics, as professionals, and as citizens with an ennobling purpose. Very simply: that is, to nurture democratic governance and civic engagement. Political disruptions here and abroad are passionate reminders of how precious yet fragile, often ephemeral, democracy is in our singular paradox—the constancy of turbulent times. Why bother to confront globalization; or why bother to embrace and harness technology; or why bother to forge partnerships across the sectors; or why bother to invest in institution building; or why struggle with complexity and change; or why bother to ground policy on research with a respect for politics? WHY? The simple answer is that we as public administrators do have a purpose: To preserve democracy and our citizenship as the nation and the world reverberate to turbulent times. Our purpose is "not to leave the city less beautiful," but rather to let our legacy be a city more beautiful—just as the Athenian Oath entreated our field of public administration and as it became the covenant that Don Stone and I shared with many of you and others in the pursuit of public service.

Thank you for this honor today. Godspeed to our men and women in the armed services. And thank Don Stone for his legacy.

Astrid E. Merget** is the dean of the Indiana University School of Public and Environmental Affairs. A fellow of the National Academy of Public Administration, she is also a member of the board of trustees of Mount Holyoke College, the regional screening committee for the Harry S. Truman Foundation, and the U.S. Comptroller General's Research and Education Advisory Panel. She cochaired the Task Force on Outcomes for the United Way of America. **Email: merget@indiana.edu.

From *Public Administration Review*, July/August 2003, pp. 390-395.

In Memoriam: David O. "Doc" Cooke

This summer, those of us in public management—particularly in the career federal civil service—lost one of our giants. David O. "Doc" Cooke, director of administration and management for the Office of the Secretary of Defense and long-time contributor to this journal and supporter of a positive image for public service, died June 22 of injuries received in a car accident just outside Charlottesville, VA earlier in the month.

In addition to his leadership position as "mayor of the Pentagon" and through so many other roles that cut across departmental lines, Doc was an influential mentor to literally hundreds if not thousands of career and noncareer public managers during the more than five decades in which he served.

It is with special fondness that I express a personal appreciation for Doc's impact on my own view of the public service beginning with a one-on-one job interview in his storied Pentagon office 15 years ago. It was with Doc's encouragement that I moved on from 20 years in human services and social justice programs—most with the Department of Health and Human Services—to a one-year loaned executive assignment with the relatively new President's Council on Management Improvement. For the next 10 years, including time spent with subsequent initiatives of the President's Management Council, the National Performance Review and the General Services Administration, I simply applied the passion that had brought me into public service to more generic issues of government management reform.

Similarly, and ironically, although he was anchored in Pentagon "staff" operations, Doc was at his best as a field general among the ranks of line managers from all corners of the federal bureaucracy. He was a public manager for all seasons. He cut through red tape and other extraneous matters and focused his energies (and those of countless interagency organizations in which he participated) on core issues and actions needed to move business forward. And while he was an indefatigable devil's advocate, Doc also was the ultimate optimist. With great efficiency—and a few well-placed words—the mayor of the Pentagon was the oil that made the monumental bureaucracy hum.

Now, this man of great stature will be greatly missed. What remains is for us to follow his example.

—***Warren Master***

From *The Public Manager*, Vol. 31, No. 2, Summer 2002, p. 33.

Doc Cooke's Reflections on Effective Public Management

Five decades in the federal service have offered me an opportunity to observe how different managerial approaches work. Obviously, some methods do work better than others. ...[speaking of successive management fads] Nothing is inherently wrong with these schools of thinking—we just tend to expect too much from them. They are only techniques... proponents... implicitly suggested that if we just learned their buzzwords (they always came with new terminology), accepted a different way of doing things, and "got on with it," productivity would soar and human problems would disappear. Management is not that easy... This suggests that there is a great deal more to effective management than technique.

... [Successful secretaries of Defense] had an ability to create shared purpose. They could communicate a sensible vision of what the department must do to fulfill its mission. For this reason, they also could afford to permit large numbers of people to exercise discretion.

... consensus evolved because the secretaries were able to articulate the nexus between what was generally reasonable, the nation's interests, and what they viewed as the department's proper role in creating a posture consistent with these "reasonable interests." Ingenuity following in the wake of such consensus. Government/industry partnerships flourished as the fruits of this ingenuity.

In addition to "finding and explaining the nexus," the department's best leaders usually have a simple management approach. They keep sight of the basic mission; assure organizational arrangements are simple; work closely with key people; and delegate. In spite of the importance of a well-expressed vision and simplicity of operation, my experience has been that these alone cannot animate the workforce. Another element is requried...

This last factor is character, or maybe it would be better put as the ability to project and "sell" emotional convictions about what is right and wrong. Effective managers do this well. They can, among large numbers of people, create the feeling that "we trust each other in an unquestioning way." For many people this shared perception settles the intellectual risk of interaction. The very best secretaries have deserved the loyalty and absorbed the energy of the department's people because they recognized the importance of their own credibility...

The best managers with whom I have been associated, "informed their subordinates discretion" through a well-articulated vision while demonstrating character and personal courage.

This outlook, distilled to its simplest essence, can be expressed as, "take your job seriously, but not yourself." Practiced widely, this perspective would assure spirited intellectual participation in the major controversies of corporate life. What is even more important, leaving our egos behind would assure a gentler and more effective commerce with one another.

(Excerpted from The Public Manager, *Summer 2000)*

From *The Public Manager,* Vol. 31, No. 2, Summer 2002, p. 64.

The Odyssey of Senior Public Service: What Memoirs Can Teach Us

This article examines the political, psychological, and moral challenges of senior public service in the executive office. The study uses memoirs published by members of the Clinton administration. The memoirs discuss the consistent background conditions of senior public service as the personality of the chief executive, the vagaries of election cycles, the tension between staff and agency executives, and the role of the media. Senior executives adopt a number of stances to address the tension between the realities of public service and the ideals they bring. The memoirs suggest several stances, such as politics as original sin, seduction, hard work and compromise, and game. The memoirs demonstrate the high cumulative cost that public service exacts on the health and personal lives of senior officials. Finally, the study reveals a number of consistent themes about how senior appointed public officials can navigate the dilemmas and challenges of senior public service at all levels of government.

J. Patrick Dobel
University of Washington

Serving at the senior executive levels of government, whether at the local, state, or national level, offers the most complex and interesting moral and political challenges of modern public life. Senior executives and staff embark on a journey that is replete with monsters to slay, loyal allies, intrepid crews, and skilled and tenacious adversaries. Complicated loyalties create cross-currents that tug individuals in different directions as they navigate the winds of integrity and achievement, swirling with power and opposition. The journey requires skill, character, and tenacity, with no safe havens. Although modern case studies provide intense and schematic insights into executive and managerial practice, they seldom illuminate the full texture of life as it is experienced by political actors. Memoirs of senior officials provide important evidence about the nature of such service.

The Clinton administration was one of the most self-conscious of presidential administrations and spawned a spate of memoirs, 10 of which have already been published. While administrations leave a variety of artifacts such as memos, laws, scandals, and policy successes and failures, historically some of the most intriguing artifacts are officials' political memoirs: They can reveal the depth, honor, and gravity of daily political life and strife as well as its absurdity, conflict, and heartlessness.

Twenty years ago, publishing memoirs before the end of an administration would have been unseemly and even disloyal. Memoirs possessed a degree of intellectual and moral weight. They served as tomes to sum up, reflect, make sense of, contribute to, or set the record straight. They often aspired to serve as part of the official record or to dominate the telling of the story. This means that all memoirs are political as well as personal documents. Usually, they were reserved for very senior officials.

The flood of Clinton memoirs—some published even before the administration left office—reveals as much about modern American culture as it does the administration it chronicles. The unseemly haste of many memoirs is abetted by the pressure to make money quickly and pressure from publishers to add titillating "kiss-and-tell" aspects. This may subvert the integrity of the memoirs and their documentary worth. Memoirs, however, always have complex genealogies, sometimes written to justify actions, defend policies, or settle old scores. These covert and not-so-hidden agendas mean that memoirs seldom can be taken as stand-alone documents for historical purposes. On the other hand, collectively, they often reveal patterns and tendencies and even cross-check each other. This essay examines 10 Clinton administration memoirs and their insight into the moral and psychological world of the individuals serving at senior levels of government.

This article will not assay the truth of the reflections; rather, it will discuss the surprising consistency in narra-

The Value of Memoirs

J. Patrick Dobel is one the field's most thoughtful and creative scholars. His book, *Public Integrity* (Johns Hopkins University Press, 1999), is widely recognized as a groundbreaking work that provides important insights into the trials and tribulations of those who hold public office. In the article below, Dobel continues the journey begun in *Public Integrity*. Drawing on the memoirs of senior executives in the Clinton administration, he exposes *PAR* readers to the responsibilities, pressures, and dilemmas faced by these public servants. Dobel makes an important contribution to the field by skillfully demonstrating that memoirs are a valuable source of information for understanding the moral and political challenges of senior executives. For these reasons and more, the editors thought that this work would be of interest to *PAR*'s broad, diverse audience.

—*LDT*

tive structures and positions that emerge from the memoirs. The first part discusses the background conditions that affect senior political actors and how these shape their concerns. The second discusses four approaches toward political action that the memoirs reveal. These reflect an obsessive concern with how individuals match their high ideals with the realities of political responsibility. The third analyzes the costs of modern senior public service as it is perceived by the actors. Finally, the essay discusses the lessons that the cumulative insights of the memoirs suggest about how to act with integrity and effectiveness at the level of senior public service.

The Odyssey of Ideals

Most people enter public life to achieve good. Their motives entwine with self-interest and enjoyment of power and achievement, but most seek out the underpaid and difficult world of political activism to make a difference. This purpose anchors their identity and fuels their energy and personal sacrifice. It also armors them against the travails and tensions of office. This batch of memoirs heightens the importance of the commitment to make a difference: Four of them chronicle neophytes to the executive service (Alexander 2000; Hubbell 1997; Hundt 2000; R. Reich 1997), while one reflects great youth and passion (Stephanopoulos 1999). Only two writers, Christopher (1997) and Gergen (2000) had worked at senior levels of national government before. The paradox of doing good in public office hinges on the need to gain and keep office and power in order to achieve durable political success.

Vince Foster, the president's old friend from Arkansas and senior advisor, committed suicide in the first year of the Clinton administration. The event scarred the administration and epitomized the most consistent threat that runs through the memoirs—how do individuals cope with the tension between their ideals and the moral attrition of political life? Webb Hubbell, one of Hillary Clinton's best friends and law partners, writes a rueful and chastened memoir that captures the all-too-real experience of idealists entering the world of high-stake political leadership. He tells of Foster speaking to the graduating class at the University of Arkansas law school. Foster describes seeing the lines of people who stand around the White House, "When I look into their faces, I can tell that each has hope for something from their government. It is a wonderful reminder of why we are here." Hubbell came to Washington with the Clintons. He served well as the deputy attorney general for civil rights and says, "We told ourselves we had to remember that… he was trying to remember that we had come to Washington together, all good friends, all of us playing out parts in something grand and historic, something important, something bigger than we were" (Hubbell 1997, 9).

Senior political and managerial leadership requires dealing with opponents and allies, managing staff and organizations, acquiring scarce funds, and balancing competing priorities and obligations to protect institutions as well as one's administration. The daily balancing act challenges a form of idealism that postulates morality as the pursuit of pure ideals. In her literate and spirited memoirs, Jane Alexander, chair of the National Endowment for the Arts for four years, talks about how she reluctantly mastered the art of building coalitions to protect her beleaguered agency. She reflects, "The gilded idealism with which I'd been suffused on taking office was tarnishing fast" (Alexander 2000, 230). The notion of tarnished, corrupted, or seduced ideals permeates many of the memoirs and becomes a leitmotif for some of them. How one engages this problem morally and psychologically is a central challenge of senior government.

The combined accounts of the memoirs expose themes that affect all executive administrations and illuminate the enduring moral challenges that individuals face at the senior levels of government service. Consistent themes in the memoirs identify enduring institutional challenges that senior officials face, as well as the moral stances that individuals choose toward the moral and institutional challenges. The positions present durable and consistent approaches that others will find useful.

The World of Senior Public Service

The political realities of senior executive positions shape the decisions of senior political actors, whether they are elected, appointed, or career. Four aspects profoundly influence the environment. First, all of the individuals serve in an administration dominated by the central character of the chief executive and his agenda, as well as a network of power and principals. This enmeshes each actor in responsibilities to the chief executive, administration, agenda, and a network of principles. Second, the ebb and flow of power and elections heavily influences the range of options. Third, this network of obligation and power exposes a critical institutional distinction—those who serve at will and in proximity to the principal and those who hold institutional positions within the formal bureaucracies. The agency heads possess obligations to the organization, its mission, and constituencies as well as to the executive and his agenda. Finally, the modern media and its appetites dominate the horizons of governance.

The Chief Executive

Senior executive officials serve in administrations built around the elected executive. The nature of the principal, his style, interests, and agendas affect the actions and obligations of those who work on his behalf. All of the memoirs pay attention to President Clinton, and perceptions of him shape individuals' actions and decisions. Most of the memoirs were published before the Lewinsky affair, in which Congress impeached President Clinton for his behavior toward an intern and subsequent coverups. Even those published after the affair have little to say about it. Several features of Clinton's difficult and ambiguous style and character, however, affect how individuals comport themselves: (1) His style of information gathering and decision influenced the world around him. Clinton culled ideas from all over and widely consumed information. This included using many different advisors in informal and unstructured situations (Stephanopoulos 1999, 329ff, 389; Morris 1999, XXXIII, 101–2; Hubbell 1997, 92–93; Gergen 2000, 276–78). (2) This approach encouraged constant infighting and jockeying to get his ear as well as engendering nagging uncertainty about the agenda and decisions. Decisions came hard and obliquely and often got reversed, creating a dynamic that could paralyze action. (3) Clinton excelled at tactical decision making but missed strategic vision in both decision and processing the information. He seldom prioritized time, information, or decisions (Morris 1999, 101–2, 164; Hubbell 1997, 92–93; Gergen 2000, 270–75). (94) Early on, Clinton shied away from a clear hierarchy or filtering system and permitted remarkable access and power to the first lady and to the vice president. This generated multiple rings of decision making with overlapping domains of power that exacerbated conflict and hesitant decision making (Gergen 2000, 256–60, 276–77, 290–93; Stephanopoulos 1999, 171ff, 190ff; Morris 1999, 39–41, 110–113, 137ff). (5) Hillary Clinton exercised immense influence and served as his closest advisor, making access issues and final decisions perilous and difficult to attain. Her presence created a back door for fighting policies. This divided loyalties among those closest to the president and undercut the clarity of service to him (Stephanopoulos 1999, 171, 190, 388–89; Gergen 2000, 288–93; Morris 1999, 39–44, 136–38). (6) The memoirs highlight the seldom-broached point that Clinton overworked himself and often appeared tired and exhausted, falling asleep at meetings, snapping at staff, and sometimes this affected his judgment (Morris 1999, 101–102, 124–26, 150–52; Matalin and Carville 1994, 249ff; R. Reich 1997, 63–64; Gergen 2000, 261–62).

The Influence of Elections

The memoirs reveal the overwhelming shadow cast by the failure of Clinton's health care initiative in 1993 and the congressional elections of 1994. These elections vaulted Speaker of the House Newt Gingrich to power and handed Republicans control of the House and Senate. This event permeated the presidency and changed the lives of all who served. It enshrined budget politics at the center of everything and shifted the agenda of the country and presidency (Morris 1999, 162–65).[1] From that point on, most agencies experienced a constant Republican effort to limit their scope of action. The administration pressed agencies to restrain policy and cut budgets. Jane Alexander at the National Endowment of the Arts curtailed programs and budgets and fought for survival against powerful conservative Republican legislators who sought to eliminate the agency (Alexander 2000, 135, 208, 213–15, 271). Most policy initiatives had been deferred while Clinton amassed political capital for the health care initiative. When it failed, not only had other initiatives lost momentum, but the imperatives of lost power and reelection forced wrenching change in priorities. Robert Reich, secretary of labor in the first term, rails against Clinton's senior advisors for focusing on balancing the budget in ways that undercut his major policy initiatives for human capital investment (R. Reich 1997, 63–64, 120–22, 260–61). Warren Christopher, secretary of state in the first term, argued against ongoing cuts of essential operations and Congress's refusal to update telecommunications and security functions. (Christopher 1998, 315–28, 524–38). Reed Hundt, chair of the Federal Communications Commission, found the political strength of the major telecommunications companies arrayed against his policy initiatives after the election even as he had to cut field offices (Hundt 2000, 66–77, 81, 85–87, 97–98, 129).

The health care failure and midterm elections threw the administration on the defense, entrenching a balanced budget at the center of the policy agenda. The budget obsessions grew from Clinton's desire to get reelected and take back control of the agenda. James Carville, Clinton's campaign manager and advisor, stated, "We wanted to win because we wanted to win, and it was good for us, but we also believed it was good for the country.... There's a great myth that people in politics don't believe in anything except getting elected. We do believe in getting elected; it would be goofy to deny that winning elections is important to us. But it's just as goofy to assert that you can't believe in what you're doing and believe in winning at the same time. I've never had much trouble reconciling the two" (Matalin and Carville 1994,

446). The debacle left the administration shattered and sinking. Clinton turned to Dick Morris, his old campaign advisor from his Arkansas days, to regain political ballast. Morris's unctuous but compelling memoir discusses the internal battles that he and others fought to reconfigure Clinton's campaign themes and realign Clinton's staff where an ongoing battle occurred between the moderates and liberals. Under Morris's tutelage, Clinton came to believe the only way he could regain control was to co-opt the issues, tighten his own initiatives, and limit expenditures. At the same time, the Republicans in Congress sought to control not only spending but also the agenda in a manner closer to parliamentary democracy than classic American separation of power (Gingrich 1998). Clinton entered a continuous campaign mode that limited his ability to create stable bipartisan alliances because it required him to dominate or demonize the Republicans rhetorically (Gergen 2000, 330–40). Stephanopoulos, who regarded himself as a liberal standard bearer, ruefully concluded he had to "deal with it" (Stephanopoulos 1999, 329–30, 348). Morris urged Clinton to undertake incessant and very expensive polling and advertising. This moved Clinton to the center, focused on smaller concrete and telegenic initiatives, but this change also meant Clinton had to invest exhausting effort to raise the money (Morris 1999, 124–25, 150–51; Stephanopoulos 1999, 334–36).

Core and Periphery

Senior public officials inherit predictable institutional positions that shape their agenda. The core–periphery and court politics problems exist at all levels of government. The group closest to the elected executive possesses substantial influence and access. They worry about the executive's electability and consistency of policy and influence the particulars of where executive capital will be expended. Individuals serving in agencies feel the costs of their lack of proximity and the centrifugal pull of their agencies' agendas and constituencies. The politics of access to the executive and ongoing battles between moderates and liberals or pragmatists and ideologues pervade every administration. Clinton's own haphazard style of decision making aggravated this conflict.

Court Politics. Access as a guarantor of influence and effectiveness obsesses all of the memoirs. Past memoirs emphasize this point, and the latest group simply reinforces a fundamental truth of public life and power. David Gergen, in his thoughtful reminiscences of four presidents remarks, "nothing propinqs like propinquity" (Gergen 2000, 295). The battles over access present a leitmotif for survival and effectiveness in the elliptical and overlapping circles around centers of power. Any aide or deputy knows the challenges. To gain and keep access becomes a never-ending preoccupation, and the process of earning trust and proving one's ability dominates life. George Stephanopoulos summarizes it well: "I wanted to be able to tell him things he didn't already know. To make myself indispensable" (Stephanopoulos 1999, 89). He describes his reluctance to leave Clinton's side during the campaign, "to relinquish the power that accompanies proximity. Out of sight, I feared, out of mind" (87). Stephanopoulos captures the angst and confusion when he loses trust after improvidently giving privileged access to Bob Woodward for *The Agenda*, which embarrassed Clinton. This soured his relations with the Clintons, leaving him at sea because "I no longer knew where I fit in" (Stephanopoulos 199, 317–19; Woodward 1994). He describes the frantic maneuvering involved when Clinton brought in Dick Morris as an outside advisor to craft a campaign and policy response to recover from the midterm debacle. Most participants experience policy making and access as a zero-sum game, especially with someone like Clinton, who used many advisors and often played them against each other. "As Dick's power grew, mine receded" (330). Many senior aides feel the battle as one not only for personal influence, but also for the post-glacial soul of the administration. Stephanopoulos argues, "I wanted to fight my way back, certain there was too much at stake, both personally and politically" (330). Stephanopoulos saw himself as the protector of Clinton's liberal ideals, while Morris represented Clinton's need to trim his sails. Morris points out, "Bill only wants me when his dark political side is coming out" (333).

Morris experienced the world of court politics and access the same way. His reentry into Clinton's inner circle coincided with the midterm repudiation and Hillary Clinton's desire to resurrect a viable political and policy agenda (Stephanopoulos 1999, 333–35; Morris 1999, 106–38). He is more blunt about the nature of power in executive offices: "The White House staff is like the moon. It cannot shine without the rays of the sun, the President. If those rays don't illuminate it, nobody knows that the staff is even there" (200). Morris also sees it as a battle for the soul, with most of the staff confirmed liberals whose politics have gotten Clinton into the mess and cannot hope to win an election. Morris believed his job was to offset the baleful influence of people such as Harold Ickes and even Leon Panetta, who became Clinton's chief of staff (126–32). David Gergen also acknowledges the infighting in the administration, but he suggests this is endemic because he experienced the same conflicts between ideologues and moderates in the Gerald Ford, George Bush, and Ronald Reagan administrations (Gergen 2000).

All of the stories emphasize the moral stakes that motivate keeping access and realize how fragile access can be. Hubbell pointedly remarks, "in a town in which proximity to power is power, then proximity to disgrace becomes too dangerous to chance" (Hubbell 1997, 283). A tabloid exposes Morris's relationship with a prostitute the night of Clinton's renomination. The next day, Stephanopoulos attends a meeting and rues "I didn't like Dick—hell, I hated him. I wanted him gone. But to face such a public disgrace on a day of such personal triumph.… No one should have to endure such a mythic turn of fate." Soon after, "Panetta took Dick's chair and gave a perfunctory thirty-second, "'Now that Dick is gone...'" speech. That was that. I was there. Dick wasn't. I had won. But *Man,* I thought, *this is one cold-blooded business we're in"* (Stephanopoulos 1999, 423–24). The world of senior public service isolates three different and competing obligations—commitment to one's own policy goals, keeping access and power while protecting the interests of the principal and the administration, and serving the legal mandates of the position and agency (Dobel 1999). The White House experience only lends greater clarity to the experience of all levels of senior public service.

The Periphery. Leaders in agencies experience the frustration of being far from the sources of power and decision or being left on their own. When Jane Alexander received the appointment to head the National Endowment of the Arts, a mentor told her, "Always talk to the President" (Alexander 2000, 31). Like many agency heads, beyond a few brief meetings, always polite but noncommittal, she found herself on her own. When she asked Bruce Lindsey, Clinton's senior domestic policy advisor, "what the administration expected of me. 'Stay out of the headlines,' Bruce replied. I took that to mean no negative press, as it would reflect badly on the President" (Alexander 2000, 65). The rule to stay out of trouble is the first rule for agency heads (Heymann 1987). Robert Reich, a prior "Friend of Bill," one of the wide networks of individuals Clinton had cultivated in his years in public service, found a similar experience. He believed that most of his memos did not make it to the president. Clinton sometimes fell asleep at meetings Reich attended, and Reich found that getting time alone to plead his case was rare. He chafed under the arrogance of White House staff and demands to schedule events to support the reelection campaign (R. Reich 1997, 63–65, 109–10). The problem of periphery, coupled with constant competition with the turf-conscious chief executive's staff, places special burdens and challenges for senior institutional leaders.

The Influence of the Media

The media fundamentally influences the life of senior public officials. All executives function in a glass house, and the weight of the media bears on every memoir. Every action reflects on the administration's political status and capital. Any successful initiatives require wooing and influencing the press. The modern American press is hypervigilant about government abuse and mistakes, and it uses scandal as its stock and trade. Its proneness to media frenzies makes every mistake a potential disaster (Sabato 1991). At the same time, the boundaries between private and public life have become so porous that senior officials lose almost all privacy and find themselves subject to intense and embittering media scrutiny and attack (Dobel 1999).

The media amplifies missteps, and mistakes will be used by opponents. Likewise, any successful policy initiatives and most managerial initiatives require support by strong media strategies. The advice Lindsey gave to Alexander meant something: Every single memoir recounts mistakes that hurt or crippled policy and status. Media misfires also hurt the administration and the president and violate the obligations to protect the interests of both. Reed Hundt recounts how his initial mistakes led to constant media bombardments that used him to attack his friend and ally, Vice President Gore (Hundt 2000, 29–34, 49–51). Hundt contends that one of the basic skills he had to learn was how to develop media campaigns to support policy initiatives and develop the discipline necessary to control what he said in public. He maintains that "publicity precedes persuasion" and hired a media coach to help him (Hundt 2000, 70–71, 176–78, 182–85). Alexander points out that leaders must watch and engage the media constantly because "rumors become truth, and lies become ingrained in the memory of readers, despite retractions" (Alexander 2000, 112–13). Reich, on the other hand, demonstrates an almost truculent unwillingness to discipline his words or public attitudes and brought a barrage of problems on himself (R. Reich 1997, 109–18, 143–46, 164–66). Alexander at the National Endowment for the Arts discovered she could use her demeanor as an actor to think of politics as a drama in which she played a role. Like Hundt, after early stumbles, she worked carefully with aides to deploy media strategies, especially ones linked to local news outlets, to build support. She points out, it's not whether a review of a production is good or bad, "it's the name they remember," so she works to keep the Endowment in the news with strong support (Alexander 2000, 218–25, 234–35).

The Dirty-Hands Problem

This complex and treacherous world beckons individuals of ideals, commitment, and ambition who seek to make a difference. Every memoir emphasizes how the individuals are driven to help make the world a better place. Despite popular cynicism, no shortage of idealism exists in the senior public service. Many individuals leave higher-paying and successful positions to enter government service. Because idealism and commitment motivate senior leaders so strongly, yet coexist with their ambition and the imperatives of gaining and exercising power, most of the memoirs grapple with how to integrate ethical ideals with the realities of political service. I will focus on one of the most fascinating attributes of the memoirs—how they characterize the moral world of politics and how individuals adapt their ethical commitments to public life. In this they are not alone, as most political memoirs address the conflict aptly summarized by Clark Clifford's memoirs of his service in four administrations: "This decision reflected the perennial struggle in government between the ideal and the possible, the perfect and the practical. There is no simple answer in this conflict" (Clifford 1991, 85). The memoirs depict four ways of understanding the engagement of individuals with politics—politics as original sin, as seduction, as compromise, and as game. How an individual conceives of politics influences their moral stance as well as the possibility of success.

Politics as Original Sin

Thinking of morality as a purity of intention and means dominates the thoughts of several of the memoir writers. This is a position that is usually deeply held by advocates who enter government or by newcomers. Because the writers view their morality as a form of sanitized integrity, the modalities of politics appear dangerous and destructive to morality. Politics represents the fallen world that individuals enter at peril to their soul. George Stephanopoulos served as President Clinton's chief policy advisor for four years, and his dark, self-referential, and pungent memoir constantly obsesses about this ideal of integrity as moral purity. "We saw ourselves as smart, and tough, and good.... Now we had work to do, lots of it... but we'd waited a long time—the country had waited a long time—for our chance to change America, and we were going to do it" (Stephanopoulos 1999, 122). He quotes Vince Foster's haunting line, "Before we came here, we thought of ourselves as good people" (187). Early on, working for a member of Congress, Stephanopoulos advised the member to speak against President Reagan's invasion of Grenada. It cost the member dearly, and Stephanopoulos discovers a basic lesson of political and organizational life: "I had made a tactical error in allowing my personal views to cloud my political judgment. Even if I believed I was right on the merits, I was wrong on the politics." The advice put his boss at risk, and Stephanopoulos isolates the unique moral torque in senior public service. "I learned that day to separate what I thought was right from what I thought would work, a skill that would serve me well—at a price.... If you can't predict what will work, you can't survive in office. If you don't keep your job, you can't achieve what you think is right." He touches on the abiding dilemma that can erode integrity over time: "The danger is when you stop caring about the difference between being right and being employed, or fail to notice that you don't know what the difference is anymore" (18–19). He discusses the drive to win as the most telling danger to moral purpose: "I wasn't always proud of the way I handled myself during the campaign. I had learned to calculate, scheme, and maneuver—to say things I didn't fully believe and do things I might later regret while telling myself that, maybe, it would do some good.... I believed that our compromises and our trials were our contributions to the common good—and that anything was possible.... If only we could win" (Stephanopoulos 1999, 86).

Reich's memoir evinces the same spirit of politics as an inherent corruption of the pure soul. Prior to leaving his teaching post at Harvard, he confesses that he distrusts public office not only because of his own lack of experience, but he fears contamination of working for a real life politician. "He's (Clinton) had to compromise, get what could be got, keep an eye on the next election and the one after that. Politicians cannot be pure, by definition. Their motives are always mixed. Ambition, power, public adulation, always figure in somehow. Means get confused with the ends" (R. Reich 1997, 9). Reich's arrogant, petulant, and sometimes unreliable memoirs acknowledge that "governing involves tough compromises and gritty reality" (13), and they reluctantly and self-pityingly conclude, "Maybe I've been too much of an idealist. Maybe that awful cliché—politics is the art of the possible—is true after all" (330).[2] Reich's lament, "Will I find myself compromised simply by virtue of being connected to his compromises?" (9) reveals a moral fastidiousness often displayed by advocates and outsiders toward politics. Reich complains about how his students at Harvard dichotomized—"Policy was clean—it could be done on a computer. Politics was dirty—unpredictable, passionate, sometimes mean-spirited or corrupt. Policy was good; politics, a necessary evil" (106). Ironically, Reich's actions betray his own belief in the moral dichotomy. As Hubbell ruefully concludes, "It didn't turn out quite the way we hoped. Instead of achieving great things, we lost who we were. At least Vince (Foster) and I did. Vince lost his life, and I lost my way" (Hubbell 1997, 329). This desire for purity of outcome and means leaves individuals ill prepared to steer the messy, imperfect, but not necessarily immoral means of public life in a liberal democracy.

Politics as Seduction

Another position postulates the satisfactions and adrenaline high of senior public service seduce people to value holding power more than purposes. Ever casting shadows on his motives, Stephanopoulos agrees to work with Dick Morris even though he despised Morris and his tactics. "I needed to be in those strategy sessions. Exclusion made me feel like a poster boy for downward mobility.... I rationalized, telling myself that I was getting my hands dirty for the sake of Clinton and our cause, that somebody like me had to hug Morris to stop his crazy ideas before they went too far" (Stephanopoulos 1999, 378). Even in victory, Stephanopoulos keeps a T. S. Eliot quote on his desk: "The last temptation is the greatest treason: To do the right deed for the wrong reason," in this case the hunger to keep office (382–83). Morris's insightful, if self-justifying, memoir captures the dynamic, "Ego is the occupational disease of politics. It infects idealism and turns it into self-righteousness. It distorts a desire to make positive change into a search for power" (Morris 1999, 88). As his own influence in the White House grew, "I became more and more arrogant. As my predictions came true, I began to believe in my perspicacity as it was reported in the press." He describes his own brusqueness and unkindness and even his dalliance with a prostitute that led to his downfall (170–73). "I could get away with anything. I felt. I wanted Clinton to win. To do that, I had to help change his course, as he had directed me to do. To do that, I needed power. But power corrupted me and became an addiction. I came to feel I could change all the rules" (171). Even Reich, normally protected by his petulant disdain, confesses to a moral and psychological high after one successful speech, "This is the closest I've come to the narcotic of demagoguery. The combination of adrenaline and adoration has a sweet intensity that's almost sexual. I understand how human beings can succumb to this dangerous addiction" (R. Reich 1997, 279). Senior public life is relentless and draining, but as Secretary of State Dean Acheson mentions in his honored memoir, public life permits "the exercise of vital powers along lines of excellence in a life affording them scope." For him, "public life is not only a powerful stimulant but a habit forming drug." Like many others, he describes how, after leaving government service, people experience the "flatness of life" (Acheson, 1969, 238–39). Senior public service provides an abiding sense of being at the center of the action, making a difference, and being needed and sought after by people. It is hard to relinquish once a person develops a taste for it.

Politics as Hard Work and Compromise

In another stance, individuals accept the discrepancy between aspiration and reality as part of the human condition. All of life—family, religion, work—shares the common disjunction between aspiration and imperfect reality. People balance compromises in personal and professional life daily to accommodate the complexity of moral and social reality (Dobel 1990). This means viewing public service as its own work, with its own work codes, honor, and pitfalls. James Carville acknowledges the problems but enjoys the world. In his witty memoir/love story of the campaign, in which he alternates stories and reactions with his now-wife and then–Bush communications director Mary Matalin, he conveys the joy, angst, and craziness of a full-tilt boogie political campaign. What Reich fears and resents, he embraces and expects as part of the human comedy: "Deep down inside, I and most of the people on the campaign were really good Democrats. We wanted to win because we wanted to win, and it was good for us, but we also believed it was good for the country. I'm sure the Republicans believed no less in their candidate (Matalin and Carville 1994, 446)." He and Stephanopoulos argue about the morality of employing "a less than righteous means to achieve a righteous goal" (341). Campaigns bond people with a closeness that supports them in the chaotic decisions. Mary Matalin could be speaking for Carville or others when she says, "I loved the people in the campaign—they were my family" (335). Many campaigners are not suited to govern, which simmers with complexity and hands up few clear-cut victories while never ending.

Webb Hubbell, who served as Janet Reno's deputy at the Department of Justice, depicts how individuals engage senior management and politics with moral balance and effectiveness. He works on shaping the new crime bill by "trying to shape its direction so that it was consistent with the President's agenda, Janet's agenda, and the political realities of the time." Hubbell enjoyed the tensions as well as the ability to connect the different sides. When Deputy Attorney General Phil Heymann resigns over differences in style and policy, he tries to be a "matchmaker between Reno and Heymann." Living at the intersection of differing agendas and political constraints posed challenges and opportunities that he relished. His tragedy lay in earlier decisions to embezzle from his law firm. Shortly after his work on the crime bill, he had to resign (Hubbell 1997, 260, 263, 268–74, 279–82). Jane Alexander speaks of how "gilded idealism" was tarnished as she worked hard to build coalitions and stop the conservative Republicans from eviscerating the agency (Alexander 2000, 230–32). She points out the similarity of politics to theater, with its lines and performance, "It wasn't possible to be in politics and not compromise to within an inch of your life. Perhaps that was the meaning of politics: compromise, finding the middle ground" (241). Her tone, like Hubbell's suggests that compromising, planning media campaigns, and building support takes hard work, discipline, effort, and judgment, rather like the rest of life. She knew "in the eye of a beholder I was certainly walking a fine line, but I hoped I was still dancing rather than bowing" (220).

Warren Christopher, in his partial memoir and book of speeches, imparts the tone that an experienced professional adapts toward the incessant battles in policy making. To discuss what could have been a breathless account of infighting prior to a speech, Christopher dryly remarks, "after the usual last minute negotiations with the White House and other interested agencies" (Christopher 1998, 454). His book exhibits a tone that accepts the inevitability of difficult moral encounters and costs. He deals with them and then carries on for the public purpose. Mentioning how he was passed over to succeed Cyrus Vance as secretary of state, he offers no complaints, no tell-alls, just "swallowing my disappointment, I continued to serve" (7). When his State Department people die on the ground seeking settlement in Bosnia, he experiences a "tremendous emotional blow," but he and his staff must "push forward" (349–50). Carville points out that at the senior level of public service, the payoff for achievement and power is loyalty to the principal. This person's interests always matter and limit what people can accomplish: "I doubt that there's anybody that's served a king that hasn't felt compromised from time to time. I think the message is: If you don't want to be compromised, be the king" (Carville 2000, 188). This approach does not express an anguished cry for lost purity, but holds out a realistic assessment of the costs of being a successful leader. It also recognizes there are limits. Reed Hundt describes the daily friction of doing business at the Federal Communications Commission with a strongly conservative Congress: "The Gingrich revolution would prove to define the nature of my public service: whether I could learn to fight and what to fight for, whether I could be loyal in deed as well as thought. The Speaker taught my team and me the line between necessary and gratuitous compromises. Some compromises are necessary to accomplish any practical goal. But other acquiescence to the wishes of the new majority would in truth serve no purpose other than easing the daily difficulties of my job of making me a serviceable deliverer of professional advice in some post-government career" (Hundt 2000, 97–98).

Politics as a Game

Senior level policy and management involve high stakes, excitement, intense satisfaction as well as sophisticated political maneuvering. Some see it as a game with its rules, and they focus upon winning and losing. Campaigns bring this out most intensely since they resemble great games with one winner and one loser. James Carville speaks of the fun and excitement of the elections. Elections consume one's life and create a sense of purpose, being needed and intense loving camaraderie that few other experiences duplicate. He concludes, "I think the reason most people get professionally involved in campaigns is that they like the intensity. I do. I like the short duration of a political campaign. I like the fact that it has a definitive result. They do keep score" (Matalin and Carville 1994, 471–72). Morris, another campaign specialist, confesses that "politics has been my whole life.... I do have political convictions.... I am happiest when I can put my technical skills at the service of someone I admire.... I am a specialist in figuring out how politicians can advance issues that move voters and win elections" (Morris 1999, 6–7). The morality of ends—getting elected, keeping power—tends to crowd out other considerations. Morris tells Clinton, "stop trying to get elected for the right reasons. Just try to get elected" (12–13). Stephanopoulos, a superior campaigner, complains that Clinton and Morris "believed in the power of politics to help people but loved the sport of it even more" (332–33). Morris loves the sport and guards Clinton not to let his ideals get the better of him (Morris, 1999, 12–14). Mary Matalin explains, "For some people, campaigning is a profession. People like Carville and me do it as a career and love the ups and downs. Others... these guys hate campaigns, it's like taking medicine, and they get through the jobs with their noses held and lumps in their throats because the only way you get to govern is to get elected. Campaigning is the ugly price they pay for the opportunity to practice statecraft" (Matalin and Carville 1994, 300). A game or sport has rules and involves a professional combination of commitment and detachment. It resembles politics as a profession with its own logic, limits, and satisfactions.

The Costs of Service

Public officials constantly talk about the cost exacted by modern public service. Leaving aside the ruminations about the penalty to moral purity, the costs group in several areas and correlate to the relentless pace of senior public service as well as the nature of a polarized and media-driven politics.

Senior public service exacts high costs on the physical and mental health of participants. With the exception of David Gergen, every memoir emphasizes at some point the exhaustion and physical debilities that catch up with people. Jane Alexander hurts her knee early on and never recovers. The effects of interminable tension and flights catch up, and her back goes out. She spends five days immobilized and ruefully acknowledges, "politics was ruining my health" (Alexander 2000, 149–50, 222–23). The normally phlegmatic Warren Christopher talks about how Clinton worried about him because "I was pushing myself beyond reasonable limits" because the stakes are so high (Christopher 1998, 546). Carville and Matalin discuss the physical breakdowns on staff during the pace of campaigns (Matalin and Carville 1994, 454–56). This may be the first set of political memoirs in which several writers admit to working with psychiatrists or taking antidepressants to keep balance (Morris 1999, 60–62; Stephanopoulos 1999, 409–11; Hubbell 1997, 293–94). Stephanopoulos confesses his own despair over losing battles that drives him to contemplate suicide and seek help from a psychiatrist (378–79). Vince Foster's suicide haunts the entire Clinton staff.

The never-ending scrutiny and partisan attacks take a heavy toll. Hundt talks of the pain and bemusement of seeing cartoons and hearing attacks on him and not even recognizing the person attacked: "I hated the person who was depicted in the press" (Hundt 2000, 46, 33–50). The prying into personal lives and the demands for personal revelations in public appearances appall the writers. Hundt realizes that "public life requires not just thick skin but no skin at all" (Hundt 2000, 62; Alexander 2000, 23). Stephanopoulos enjoys the limelight but suffers public humiliation when his untimely interviews with Bob Woodward cause a scandal for the administration. As he puts it, "Live by celebrity, die by celebrity" (Stephanopoulos 1999, 151). In modern public life, no one has any secrets.

The demands of senior public service isolate people from the shelter and support of home and friends. Stephanopoulos talks about not only losing his girlfriend, but the isolation of not having time for any social life (Stephanopoulos 1999, 135–38). Alexander never unpacks or sets up an apartment until half a year later, when her goddaughter does. She complains how disorienting and how hard it can be to live in Washington without family support (Alexander 2000, 78–79). The whining tone of Reich's book is accentuated by his constant grumbling about how his wife and family resent his public service and move back to Boston, leaving him bereft (Reich 1997, 5–10, 68, 223, 335). Family and friends can become subject to partisan attacks or media scrutiny. During the campaigns, President Bush's children were scrutinized for their economic dealings (Matalin and Carville 1994, 290). Morris's affair with a prostitute is revealed in the press to his wife and friends (Morris 1999, 333–39). Hubbell speaks of how "the life we found ourselves living puts a great strain on any marriage" (Hubbell 1997, 190–93). Hubbell watches his own friends caught up in the media frenzy and having their own privacy violated, lives prodded, and integrity impugned because of their association with him (286, 327). This isolation erodes the buttresses of personal integrity and endurance and exacts a high personal cost over time. Ultimately, Hubbell and Clinton, who had shared honest and candid advice in their friendship, cannot talk to one another for fear of legal repercussions (288). When Morris resigns in disgrace, Clinton tells him, "We have to fight the disintegration of our personal lives in this business. It's a very lonely business. You sleep in a different hotel every night and if you don't work hard to hold your personal life together, it just disintegrates on you" (Morris 1999, 345–46). Hubbell's own book lends poignant credence to the costs of public life when he describes the ways in which Hillary Clinton—from giving up her last name to tolerating Clinton's infidelities—"gives up pieces of herself" (Hubbell 1997, 48ff., 102–104, 118–19).

The modern state contributes to the petty humiliations of senior public service. The constant scrutiny of the press, coupled with ethics concerns, puts a very high premium on neo-Puritanism. Modern ethics rules have become weapons to destroy careers. Most memoirs mention the aggravation of being forced to travel coach to prove their plebian credentials, to the detriment of their health and effectiveness (Alexander 2000, 149–50). Lynn Martin, the outgoing secretary of labor, warns Reich, "watch your travel" and "don't go home too often" because the media will attack over the flights (R. Reich 1997, 43). Like other officials, Alexander gets caught up in the arcane ethics requirements, which even force her to cancel a series of commercials with AT&T (Alexander 2000, 24). The administration warns Alexander to keep a diary for legal reasons, and several memoirs talk about the huge expenses incurred by the need for lawyers in the age of constant ethics investigations. Reich mentions his first government act as taking a urine test (Stephanopoulos 1999, 250ff; Alexander 2000, 64–65; R. Reich 1997, 46). The impeccable Warren Christopher has to endure an assault from Jesse Helms, who intimates that Christopher's business dealings undermine his independence (Christopher 1998, 21).

Surviving the Odyssey

The memoirs etch the costs with powerful clarity. They also reveal the moral and psychological approaches that persons develop to balance the moral tensions and challenges of high-level office. The memoirs reveal consistent stories about how individuals can cope and thrive with their moral commitments and integrity intact as they engage the realities and costs of senior public service.

Cultivate Strong Relationships with Principals and Staff

The first point emphasizes understanding the importance and obligations of relationships. It directs individuals to cultivate and know where they stand with principals. Senior officials and staff have strong obligations to work for their principal's ends and protect them. They also have strong responsibilities to assess and hire their own staff and agents as well as cultivating their own network. Jane Alexander points out that "in Washington you are only as valuable as the people you know who support you and your cause" (Alexander 2000, 97). Reed Hundt admits to seeking the job and felt special obligations because he relied on friendship with Vice President Gore to attain it. He told Gore, "I won't let you down. Or the President.... My duty, as I saw it, would be to fulfill Al's vision for the information highway" (Hundt 2000, 6–7). Hundt had the inestimable advantage of a personal relationship with the vice president and a salient issue. He headed an agency at the center of Clinton and Gore's technology agendas, so he could actually rely on their attention, unlike most agency heads. The relationship also meant that "I was his agent" and everything Hundt did would reflect upon Gore (Hundt 2000, 23). The shadow side of such a close relationship is that when Hundt ignited political firestorms after stopping a merger between Bell and TCI, within two months he was known as "an old friend of Al's who had let the Vice President down" (33). Hundt comments on a universal but double-edged sword for public service: "It is a fine thing, I thought, to have the favor of your king or your vice-king" (165). He, Alexander, and Reich all emphasize how vital it is to hire good staff, especially members who can keep them organized and focused, understand congressional relations and the byways of Washington power struggles (Alexander 2000, 160–67, 218–19; R. Reich, 53–54; Hundt, 12–13, 23–24). The staff can do everything from schooling individuals on how to approach senior legislators, avoid undisciplined remarks, or stay on a tight, policy-focused schedule. All emphasize the importance of competence, but also the relationships. Hundt aggressively sought out "trusted friends and acquaintances" to staff new bureaus when he refocused the mission (69).

All senior-level executive officials must develop relationships with legislative allies and enemies. Christopher talks about his habit of consulting constantly with Congress as one that pays huge dividends. He consciously seeks out those who oppose him (Christopher 1998, 20–22). Hundt's most painful lessons involve attending to the concerns and needs of members of Congress. After early missteps, he works very closely with Senators Jay Rockefeller and Olympia Snow to gain support for the administration's major initiative to wire public schools (Hundt 2000, 109–110). Alexander spends immense amounts of time dealing with her bête noire, arch-conservative senator Jesse Helms, and cultivates close relationships with Republicans Orin Hatch and Allen Simpson while acquiring Congress member Sid Yates as a mentor. Although she cannot get the president's attention or public support, her congressional base becomes crucial to protecting the agency (Alexander 2000, 51, 116–17, 190–94, 240–42, 263). In his understated way, Warren Christopher speaks of the vital importance of keeping up formal—if cool—relations with Jesse Helms, who headed the Foreign Affairs Committee. Using very careful words such as "frosty," he ascribes the relationship to the "severe limitations" on them because they differ on "positions of substance" (21–22). Reich, on the other hand, illustrates antithesis with this approach. He hired experienced handlers and legislative aides and then regularly ignored them and chaffed about their excessive control. Most of the media fiascoes he precipitated came from ignoring or not consulting with his staff. He refused to work hard to tend vital relationships and alienated Lane Kirkland, head of the AFL-CIO, and the senior union supported Democrats in the House. At the same time, he exhibited boredom and disdain at social engagements where he should have been building relationships (R. Reich 1997, 51–54, 67–69, 82, 91–100, 164–66).

Develop Self-Mastery

The second dimension involves attaining rigorous self-mastery. The polarization of politics, the role of the media, and the willingness of opponents to attack principals through their agents will amplify every action in unanticipated ways. Jane Alexander could have been speaking for everyone who wrote a memoir from this time, "I never doubted that I'm under attack" (Alexander 2000, 190). Warren Christopher points out that in the media driven politics world "credibility is not divisible" (Christopher 1998, 373). Politics begins and ends with words. Christopher's own book records his speeches interspersed with reflections because he believes profoundly in the importance of his words and how others understand them (9–12). Every newcomer learns the lesson that George Stephanopoulos stated to Reich after a Reich speech gets the president in trouble: "[Y]ou're not a private person anymore.... You've got to *watch* what you say" (R. Reich 1997, 212). After a number of incidents precipitated by off-the-cuff remarks, Alexander learns to have staff brief her before telephone calls and agrees to listen more carefully to them, for "an undisciplined remark on my part could have ramifications for months to come" (218).

The self-mastery extends to understanding the importance of embodying the symbolic dimension of office in the public presentation of self. Reich's memoir, if reliable, recounts the point about self-discipline. A young black staffer points out to Reich that he has no respect for the office and holds himself badly. "You a member of the cabinet of the *President of the United States* and you act like an insurance salesman" (Reich 1997, 125–27). He often fails to control his demeanor, and his chief of staff lectures him, "Everyone around here is in a tailspin because you're depressed." Reich typically resents being told to hold himself like a leader. "People watch you for subtle clues about whether our team is winning or losing, and whether *they're* doing what you want them to. Every one of the assistant secretaries and their deputies along with hundreds of senior staff around here, see that hang-dog look in your eyes, the way your shoulders stoop. They listen to the hesitation in your voice, and that pathetic little whine you've been giving off lately. And they get discouraged. People in your position set the *tone*" (R. Reich 1997, 158–59)." The lesson applies to everyone taking senior positions in which their actions reflect upon the stature of the office as well as lead and motivate. This requires a demeanor carried over into the other realms of life where officials negotiate, create networks, and represent the agency. Reich demonstrates how not to engage senior service. At one point, his memoirs gleefully make fun of going to Camp David, where Gore is trying to build team camaraderie among the incoming administration. At an international conference he gets bored, ignores the proceedings, and laughs inappropriately (47–50, 307).

The self-discipline demanded of senior public officials means they subordinate ego in ways that do not compromise integrity, but maximize the chance of political success. Alexander recounts several cases in which she self-consciously dressed in conservative clothes when meeting with Congress members to avoid any extraneous targets and maximize her chances of being listened to. "I was boring myself with my daily dress... my dress was self-inflicted" (Alexander 2000, 127–28). This reinforces the point that Hundt learns: that leaders have to focus on the message and not let other issues, including their personalities, undermine it. This requires the discipline to focus on the heart of issues, keep on message in speeches and meetings while providing consistency across the agency. Like Alexander, he travels to spread the message and develops elaborate media contacts at each location. He courts public controversy because he believes that "publicity precedes persuasion" in the modern media glut (Hundt 2000, 23, 34–35, 176–77, 182–85). Alexander visits all 50 states and celebrates the arts there while expanding partnerships in the corporate and nonprofit sectors, even enlisting Hollywood and the National Basketball Association (Alexander 2000, 50, 83–85, 112–13, 265–70, 136, 245–350, 287–89). Alexander and Hundt face moments when they take public heat and even lose issues to protect the integrity of the organization and gain internal credibility for their leadership (Hundt 2000, 89–90; Alexander 2000, 87). The Republican Congress exerted strong pressure on Hundt to end an investigation into Rupert Murdoch's Fox network. He knew that backing down "would destroy my credibility with the Commission staff and television networks," and he held his ground because "Principle also was a weapon against the new Congress" (Hundt 2000, 90).

Balance Commitment and Patience

The third point underlines the importance of holding passion and patience together in decision and action. The emotional attributes of optimism and tenacity enable one to endure and succeed. At the same time, a person has to learn not to take things personally. The ability to endure with one's emotional and moral resources intact is vital for Hundt, who points out, "No fight ends in politics, it evolves" (Hundt 2000, 225). Stephanopoulos provides an interesting counterpoint given the universal agreement about the "dark" moods that drives him to be so scrupulous about anticipating the downsides of issues and tactics (Matalin and Carville 1994, 340–42). The interesting point for Stephanopoulos is that he needed to satisfy only one constituent, the chief executive. His own demeanor actually helps him to endure Clinton's tantrums, anger, and sometimes abusive behavior while enabling him to complement Clinton's or staffers' congenital optimism. Yet Stephanopoulos personally has a hard time letting go of defeats, and this undermines his relations with others. After losing on Clinton's decision to support a balanced budget, he cannot let go of it. Finally, pressure from Secretary of Treasury Robert Rubin and White House Counsel Erskine Bowles force him to tell himself, "The president has made a decision. Deal with it" (Stephanopoulos 1999, 177–78, 286, 348–49).

Beyond the confines of the inner court of the executive office, most senior officials must mobilize agencies and constituencies, as Reich's chief of staff pointedly reminded him. This requires sustained exercises in patient initiative. The dogged optimism that Christopher calls being able to see the "glimmer" even in darkest moments keeps people going. This supports the persistence necessary to make progress against the inevitable bureaucratic and political forces arrayed against any changes (Christopher 1998, 525, 541–50). Alexander talks about how going on the road restored her as she experienced firsthand the impact of National Endowment for the Arts funding on local artists and how she grew to like it even as she "played politics" (Alexander 2000, 136, 236–38). Alexander's enjoyment reflects another vital point—senior officials need to remember and celebrate accomplishments, because the failures will always outnumber them and weigh a person down. Reich's wise chief of staff enumerates for him in detail what the agency has accomplished (R. Reich 1997, 157–58). Gore emphasizes to his staff and allies that politics is a chance to do good, and they should have "fun" (Hundt 2000, 4). Hubbell, before his fall, loves working for Reno and emphasizes the intrinsic joys and satisfactions of working for major policy change and managing in a team of committed and talented leaders (Hubbell 1997, 210–20). Morris, although deeply resented for this approach by many Clinton advisors, stressed the small, cumulative victories as a way to frame policy and accomplishment in order to connect with people (Morris 1999, 6–9, 12–13, 585–90). In all of the memoirs, individuals recount their own deep satisfaction at knowing they have made a difference. While enumerating and celebrating accomplishments may seem self-aggrandizing, remembering success provides material to replenish the emotional wells needed to sustain the passion and patience of leadership.

Balance Public and Personal Life

The fourth point urges keeping a balance in life among friends, family, and office. The memoirs all emphasize, however, that this may be impossible in modern executive politics, but it is vital. Hundt tells the vice president he must resign because "I haven't been fully part of my family for four years.... The job consumes me." Gore somewhat sheepishly tells Hundt, "'I put up limits.... I block off time.' I knew he was referring to the fact that he scarcely ever missed watching his big son play football or one daughter play all star soccer or the other daughter lead her field hockey team" (Hundt 2000, 214). One of the most depressing messages the memoirs confirm is how it is almost impossible to enter senior public service in modern public life and do justice to friends and family.

Reich addresses an interesting dilemma when he posits the choice between hiring friends or professional staff to work with him. He hires seasoned professionals to complement him, rather than those like him (R. Reich 1997, 53–55). The constant carping of Reich's family undermine personal support and sap his energy and satisfaction in the job and become a major reason to leave (21–22, 68, 223–25, 335–36). Hundt melds personal and public life by hiring good friends for senior advisors who serve as much as a support group as allies in the major policy battles. The team becomes so close that he and his top aides leave at the same time (Hundt 2000, 69–72, 209–10). Alexander develops close relationships with Sid Yates and Allen Simpson, who become mentors and friends. At the same time, she militantly sets aside time for good vacations with her family (Alexander 2000, 51, 116–19, 291–95, 297–99). Stephanopoulos cannot bring himself to take time off and slowly burns out.

Keeping the balance also means not making it personal. When Hundt first meets John Dingell, a powerful house member from Michigan, Dingell admonishes him, "Son, you're going into politics. Here's my advice: Grow thick skin" (Hundt 2000, 29). Morris reiterates the claim about the need to grow some protection against the flaying administered by the media and opponents (Morris 1999, 33–50, 65). Without some perspective or grim humor about the attacks, persons will eat themselves alive. Morris speaks of the need to wear a mask in public and the terror when "the mask had now become my skin" (107). This mask includes the self-discipline that Christopher and Alexander demonstrate in dealing with arch-conservative senator Jesse Helms to not let the anger or hatred of "enemies" infect their ability to maintain civil relations because "you cross another person at your peril. You never know who might be on top in the future and whose help you might need" (Alexander 2000, 97, 53–64, 108–109, 182–187; Christopher 1998, 20–22). Growing thick skin can have its own dangers. The outer skin can become a shell, making a person impervious to learning.

The hardness impedes relationships and subverts an inner life or the intimacy and creativity needed to support integrity and energy over the long haul of senior management and policy making.

Know When to Leave

The fifth point requires knowing limits and when a person must draw their line in the sand. In his magisterial memoirs, George Shultz points out that "I could not want the job too much" (Shultz 1993, 792). Stephanopoulos, in his realist vein, points out that "timing is everything" in politics, and nowhere is that more true than for senior public officials and their decisions to stay or leave, to go along or get out (Stephanopoulos 1999, 398). In the end, the decisions originate either with the individual or with the administration. Erskine Bowles, presidential counsel, tells Stephanopoulos in the throes of one of his anxiety attacks over his status, "If the President wants you to leave, you'll be gone. Until then, do your job" (354). The memoirs are littered with the discarded bodies of individuals such as Robert Altman, Bernard Nussbaum, Webb Hubbell, Mac McLarty, Dee Dee Meyers, Henry Cisneros, Mike Espy, and Dick Morris, who resign in disgrace or are forced out for their performance. High-stakes politics in Washington makes it—or any capital—a "cruel town" (Stephanopoulos 1999, 151).

Understanding one's own limits keys the understanding the multiple obligations to the office, principal, effectiveness, and oneself. The memoirs reveal how fundamental the decision to stay or leave becomes in defining a person's service and response. Interestingly, enough, the Lewinsky affair does not figure in anyone's calculations, although many had left by the time it occurred. Morris reveals the importance of Shultz's point when he expresses shock and surprise that he must resign after being identified as someone who shared presidential secrets with a prostitute! His attitude depicts his point about how persons come to misunderstand their importance (Morris 1999, 333–34).

The ethics of leaving senior service unfold in several ways. After the midterm election debacle, Christopher offers to resign to help Clinton rebuild a team (Christopher 1998, 240–41). Hubbell offers his resignation to Attorney General Janet Reno after the debacle at Waco, where many members of a cult died when the FBI stormed their compound (Hubbell 1997, 218–29). Their offers reflect the primary concern that their status has become an impediment to the principal's policy and power. Morris angrily offers to resign after what he regards as abusive behavior and Clinton's waffling on Morris's authority (Morris 1999, 191–93). Clinton's refusal to accept, as with Christopher, gives both Morris and Christopher new lease to pursue their initiatives with principal support.

Reich, Hundt, Christopher, and Alexander all offer very similar portraits of when they finally resign. Judy Harris, Hundt's good friend and prior aide, tells him, "It's time to go. You're finished. You have done what you wanted. You are exhausted. Your family does not know you. You're probably broke. There's time for everything, and it's time to go." When he balks she responds "Everyone thinks they are irreplaceable.... You're not" (Hundt 2000, 209). Alexander states, "I was starting to lose faith in the process.... I was afraid I would not be able to hold my tongue much longer, and I did not want to embarrass the president." When her stepson dies, and she knows she cannot hold the self-control needed: "I needed to be home with my husband at this time" (265, 309).

Individuals also speak of losing vital staff or allies who provided emotional support and guidance. All emphasize they could not muster the emotional and moral energy to carry out the duties of office with verve and commitment, and it was time to move on and let someone else with energy and commitment serve. Individuals hint they could not rally the emotional strength to maintain the self-discipline necessary to deal with opponents, handle abuse, and control one's words in ways that further their positions and protect their institutions and principals. The memoirs expose how profound the emotions and psychological vigor are to keep up the moral and political discipline needed to lead at the senior level. Alexander regrets that it is "no fun anymore" (Alexander 2000, 295). While the statement sounds almost self-indulgent, she is right to identify that when senior officials can no longer experience the zest and enjoyment of their vocation, they risk losing the depth of commitment and energy to perform at a high level and inspire others who work with them.

Clinton's signing of the welfare reform bill precipitates the most soul searching in the administration. In his defense of loyalty to Clinton written after the Lewinsky affair, James Carville argues that having an affair with a young intern violates marriage and family, but it does not prove moral turpitude and does not warrant resigning. But he sees differences over policy as fundamental when one discovers "a principle big enough to draw the line and resign." Carville felt "sickened by the president when he signed the bill. I think it was a chickenshit thing to do." He decides not to jump but believes, like Stephanopoulos and Reich, that Clinton signs the bill that set limits on welfare payments to get reelected (Carville 2000, 135–36; R. Reich 1997, 320–21; Stephanopoulos 1999, 421–26). Carville admires Peter Edelman, who resigns as assistant secretary at the Department of Health and Human Services because "I disagreed profoundly with that legislation" (Carville 2000, 136–37; Edelman 2001). As Reich fulminates, "There's no point in winning reelection if it has to be done this way" (R. Reich 1997, 321). They all choose to stay, but the policy that affected the most vulnerable in society forced each to wrestle with real policy issues and whether they could collaborate with a regime that had violated deep moral commitments. Morris, however, sees it as a pure decision to win the election, believing that if Clinton did not deliver on welfare reform and steal the issue from the Republicans, the entire administration would have been thrown out with all its other good policies. He believed that Clinton could recoup many of the issues slowly in the second term (Morris 1999, 298–304). For all of them, it etched with acid clarity the tension between the means needed to gain power and govern and the often compromised ends pursued.

The moral odysseys portrayed in the memoirs provide insights into the journey of senior public service. These Clinton administration memoirs reflect a range of youth and experience, private citizens and experienced politicians, those discredited by scandal and those who served with honor. Yet across the range of stories, a remarkably consistent picture arises of the pressures and dilemmas of modern senior public service. All of the forces bear down on the ability to translate one's ideals and moral commitments into political and institutional reality. For many who enter politics—not as a game or pure self-interested ambition—this disjunction between the means and ends and the ends and the ideals generate constant moral pressures to address the gap.

The memoirs' depiction of how actors view the political world and how deeply this affects how they both hold their beliefs and pursue the means with energy and commitment reflects very common and widely held perspectives. The memoirs also remind people of the terrible costs of senior public service in modern public life. These costs, combined with the constraints, really do make the metaphor of moral odyssey correct for the voyage senior political actors undertake. The memoirs also offer understanding as to how individuals work to hold the compromises and conflicts of public life in tension with the satisfactions, joys, and pure fun of high-level public leadership.

Notes

1. Drew (1996) and Gingrich (1999) emphasize how far reaching the aspirations of the Republican Party were and how their power and concerns dominated Clinton's agenda and political tactics.
2. Reich's memoir generated very serious discussion about its inaccuracies and invented conversations. See Wines (1997), Kurtz (1997), and J. Reich (1997).

References

Acheson, Dean. 1969. *Present at Creation: My Life in the State Department.* New York: W. W. Norton.

Alexander, Jane. 2000. *Command Performance: An Actress in the Theater of Politics.* New York: Public Affairs.

Carville, James. 2000. *Sticken': The Case for Loyalty.* New York: Simon and Schuster.

Christopher, Warren. 1998. *In the Stream of History: Shaping Foreign Policy for a New Era.* Stanford, CA: Stanford University Press.

Clifford, Clark, with Richard Holbrooke. 1991. *Counsel to the President: A Memoir.* New York: Random House.

Dobel, J. Patrick. 1990. *Compromise and Political Action: Political Morality in Liberal and Democratic Life.* Baltimore, MD: Rowman and Littlefield.

_____. 1999. *Public Integrity.* Baltimore, MD: Johns Hopkins University Press.

Drew, Elizabeth. 1996. *Showdown: The Struggle between the Gingrich Congress and the Clinton White House.* New York: Simon and Schuster.

Edelman, Peter B. 2001. *Searching for the American Heart: RFK and the Renewal of Hope.* Boston, MA: Houghton Mifflin.

Gergen, David. 2000. *Eyewitness to Power: The Essence of Leadership: Nixon to Clinton.* New York: Simon and Schuster.

Gingrich, Newt. 1998. *Lessons Learned the Hard Way: A Personal Report.* New York: Harper and Row.

Heymann, Phillip B. 1987. *The Politics of Public Management.* New Haven, CT: Yale University Press.

Hubbell, Webb. 1997. *Friends in High Places: Our Journey from Little Rock to Washington, D.C.* New York: William Morrow.

Hundt, Reed E. 2000. *You Say You Want a Revolution: A Story of Information Age Politics.* New Haven, CT: Yale University Press.

Kurtz, Howard. 1997. Locked in the Cabinet: Was the Truth Shelved? *Washington Post,* May 29, B-1.

Matalin, Mary, and James Carville (with Peter Knobler). 1994. *All's Fair: Love, War, and Running for President.* New York: Random House.

Morris, Dick. 1999. *Behind the Oval Office: Getting Reelected Against All Odds.* Los Angeles: Renaissance Books.

Reich, Jonathan. 1997. Robert Reich: Quote Doctor. *Slate Magazine,* May 29.

Reich, Robert B. 1997. *Locked in the Cabinet.* New York: Alfred A. Knopf.

Sabato, Larry J. 1991. *Feeding Frenzy: How Attack Journalism Has Transformed American Politics.* New York: Free Press.

Schultz, George P. 1993. *Turmoil and Triumph: My Years as Secretary of State.* New York: Scribner's.

Stephanopoulos, George. 1999. *All Too Human: A Political Education.* New York: Little, Brown.

Wines, Michael. 1997. Ex-Labor Chief's Memoirs Finds Humans in Masks of Power. *New York Times,* March 30.

Woodward, Bob. 1994. *The Agenda, Inside the Clinton White House.* New York: Simon and Schuster.

__J. Patrick Dobel__ is a professor at the Evans School of Public Affairs at the University of Washington and an adjunct professor of political science. He teaches ethics, public management, and leadership. He has written numerous articles on public ethics, as well as the books Compromise and Political Action: Political Morality in Liberal and Democratic Life *(Rowman Littlefield) and* Public Integrity *(Johns Hopkins). He presently sits on the Seattle Ethics and Election Commission.* ***Email: pdobel@u.washington.edu.***

UNIT 2

Governmental and Organizational Behavior

Unit Selections

5. **Predictable Surprises: The Disasters You Should Have Seen Coming**, Michael D. Watkins and Max H. Bazerman
6. **Is Silence Killing Your Company?** Leslie Perlow and Stephanie Williams
7. **Wireless Interoperability: A Key Element of Public Safety**, Edwin Daley
8. **Does Government Need a Sarbanes-Oxley Type Reform Act?** Kevin M. Bronner
9. **Underestimating Costs in Public Works Projects: Error or Lie?** Bent Flyvbjerg, Mette Skamris Holm, and Soren Buhl
10. **Roadblocks in Reforming Corrupt Agencies: The Case of the New York City School Custodians**, Lydia Segal

Key Points to Consider

- What are some of the things that you can do in your organization that will help you in the event of a disaster? What disaster planning actions can you take prior to an event taking place?
- What did you think about Florida's overhaul of its personnel system? Do you agree with the elected officials that it will lead to a more efficient and effective civil service? Why or why not?
- What are the major problems associated with silence in the organization? What are some of the actions that a manager can take to promote communication in the workplace after a disaster or crisis has taken place?
- Why is it important for public sector organizations to have "interoperability" of communications? What are some of the problems that can occur in its absence?
- What are some of the reasons that contractors consistently underestimate cost estimates for public works projects? What, if anything, can be done about it?
- Why are financial and auditing controls by themselves not going to solve the problems of ethical violations and corruption? What are your recommendations for solving these problems?

Links: www.dushkin.com/online/
These sites are annotated in the World Wide Web pages.

Government Accounting Standards Board (GASB)
http://www.gasb.org

National Academy of Public Administration (NAPA)
http://www.napawash.org

National Center for Public Productivity
http:/newark.rutgers.edu/~ncpp/

Partnership for Public Service (PPS)
http://www.ourpublicservice.org

Public Sector Continuous Improvement Site
http://curiouscat.com/psci/index.html

Stateline.org
http://www.stateline.org

The articles in this unit focus on governmental and organizational behavior including productivity, performance, organizational communication, and ethics in public and private sector organizations.

Because of events such as Enron's collapse, the 9/11 attack, and the August 2003 power blackout, the role of government as a regulator has been called into question. In today's world, the public administrator must now pay special attention to disaster prevention and mitigation.

In the first subsection, articles center on the topic areas of leadership and management behavior in the face of stress, disaster, and catastrophe. The articles try to answer the question of how to achieve higher productivity in the public sector in the face of these problems.

The articles in the second subsection are centered on improving organizational communication. They focus on new organizational communications skills such as collaboration and negotiation that public managers must have in order to be successful in a modern world. Key elements in this strategy are how to keep silence from killing the organization and how to link communication systems for emergency personnel.

The third subsection concentrates on the area of ethics and values, which are essential elements for a democratic government. Ethical behavior and ethical decisions maintain citizen trust and ensure effective and efficient use of resources.

Productivity and Performance

In today's world we are dealing with improving productivity and performance of public organizations during normal times, and also focusing on keeping the public sector going in the face of chaos and disaster.

Michael Watkins and Max Bazerman in their article, "Predictable Suprises: The Disasters You Should Have Seen Coming," identify and discuss the ways in which managers can do disaster planning by taking a series of steps from recognizing the threat to mobilizing the resources to stop it.

Organizational Communication

"Is Silence Killing Your Company?" by Leslie Perlow and Stephanie Williams, illustrates how silence can lead to disaster and/or situations such as the Enron mess. According to the authors, silence can generate feelings of humiliation, anger, and resentment, which can shut down creativity and undermine organizational communication and productivity.

Communication can be used in the face of tragedy or disaster to promote healing and to keep people moving forward. Martha Craumer in her article, "Leading the Way Back," discusses concrete actions that managers can take to recapture productivity.

In an environment of shrinking resources, managers need to keep the channels of communication open between managers and employees. Dennis Branson's article, "Shared Neutrals Mediation Brings Harmony and Saves Resources," discusses how the techniques of alternative dispute resolution in general and mediation in particular can improve organizational communication.

"Wireless Interoperability: A Key Element of Public Safety," by Edwin Daley, discusses how disasters such as 9/11 and the "sniper" shootings in the Washington, D.C., area require public safety officials to enhance emergency communications and interoperability, which is the emergency incident responders' ability to communicate directly with and transmit data to other emergency service personnel through mobile radios.

Ethics and Values

The scandal of Enron has focused on the need for government to control corruption and to review the regulations that govern the accounting industry. The articles in this section point out that although new regulations are necessary, regulations by themselves will not do the job that is needed to control fraud, waste, and the abuse of public trust.

"Does Government Need a Sarbanes-Oxley Type Reform Act?" by Kevin Bronner, reviews the need for upgraded accounting standards and regulations through the establishment of reform legislation such as the Sarbanes-Oxley Act that regulates private companies through the Securities and Exchange Commission (SEC).

"Underestimating Costs in Public Works Projects: Error or Lie?" by Bent Flyvbjerg, Mette Skamris Holm, and Soren Buhl, states that cost estimates for public works projects are consistently underestimated and highly and systematically misleading. The authors feel those legislators, administrators, investors, and others who value honest numbers should not trust cost estimates and cost-benefit analysis produced by project promoters and their analysts.

"Roadblocks in Reforming Corrupt Agencies: The Case of the New York City School Custodians," by Lydia Segal, points out that reformers have traditionally assumed that agencies can combat corruption through tighter financial and auditing controls. This case study shows how a corrupt agency can derail these devices. According to the author, true reform requires strategies like overhauling management, eradicating special interests, and aggressively punishing misconduct.

Predictable Surprises: The **Disasters** You Should Have Seen Coming

The **signs of an impending crisis** often lie all around us, yet we still don't see them. Fortunately, there are ways to **spot danger** before it's too late.

by Michael D. Watkins and Max H. Bazerman

APRIL 29, 1995, WAS NOT A GOOD DAY FOR ROYAL DUTCH/ Shell. That morning a small group of Greenpeace activists boarded and occupied the Brent Spar, an obsolete oil-storage platform in the North Sea that Shell's UK arm was planning to sink. The activists brought with them members of the European media fully equipped to publicize the drama, and announced that they were intent on blocking Shell's decision to junk the Spar, arguing that the small amounts of low-level radioactive residues in its storage tanks would damage the environment. Greenpeace timed the operation for maximum effect—just one month before European Union environmental ministers were scheduled to meet and discuss North Sea pollution issues.

Shell rushed to court, successfully suing Greenpeace for trespassing. In the full glare of the media spotlight, the activists were forcibly removed from the platform. For weeks afterward, as the cameras continued to roll, Shell blasted Greenpeace boats with water cannons to prevent the group from reoccupying the Spar. It was a public relations nightmare, and it only got worse. Opposition to Shell's plans—and to Shell itself—mounted throughout Europe. In Germany, a boycott of Shell gas stations was organized, and many of them were firebombed or otherwise vandalized. Pilloried in the press and criticized by governments, Shell finally retreated. It announced on June 20 that it was abandoning its plan to sink the Spar.

Shell's uncoordinated, reactionary, and ultimately futile response to the Greenpeace protest revealed a lack of foresight and planning. The attack on the Spar had clearly come as a surprise to the company. But should it have? Shell actually had all the information it needed to predict what would transpire. The company's own security advisers entertained the possibility that environmental activists might try to block the dumping. Other oil companies, fearing a backlash, had protested Shell's plans when they were originally announced. Greenpeace had a history of occupying environmentally sensitive structures. And the Spar was nothing if not an obvious target: Weighing 14,500 tons, it was one of the largest offshore structures in the wold and only one of a few North Sea platforms containing big storage tanks with toxic residues.

But, even with all the warning signs, Shell never saw the calamity coming. Unfortunately, its experience is all too common in the business world. Despite thoughtful managers and robust planning processes, even the best run companies are frequently caught unaware by disastrous events—events that should have been anticipated and prepared for. Such predictable surprises, as we call them, take many forms, from financial scandals to disruptions in operations, from organizational upheavals to product failures. Some result in short-term losses or distractions. Some cause damage that takes years to repair.

Are You to Blame?

Predictable surprises arise out of failures of recognition, prioritization, or mobilization. The best way to figure out whether a disaster could have been avoided, as the diagram at right illustrates, is to ask the following:

Did the leader recognize the threat? Some disasters can't be foreseen. No one, for instance, could have predicted that the HIV virus would jump the species barrier to infect humans on such a vast scale. But in examining the unforeseen disasters that strike companies, we've found that the vast majority should have been predicted. The way to determine whether a failure of recognition occurred is to assess whether the organization's leader marshaled resources to scan the environment for emerging threats. That includes ascertaining whether he did a reasonable job of analyzing and interpreting the data. If not, then the leader should be held accountable.

Did the leader prioritize appropriately? Predictable surprises also occur when a threat is recognized but not given priority. Failures of prioritization are particularly common, as business leaders are typically beset by many competing demands on their attention. How can they possibly distinguish the surprise that will happen from the myriad potential surprises that won't happen? The answer is that they can't make such distinctions with 100% accuracy. Uncertainty exists—high-probability disasters sometimes do not occur, and low-probability ones sometimes do. If, therefore, a leader performs careful cost-benefit analyses and gives priority to those threats that represent the highest costs, he should not be held accountable for a failure of prioritization.

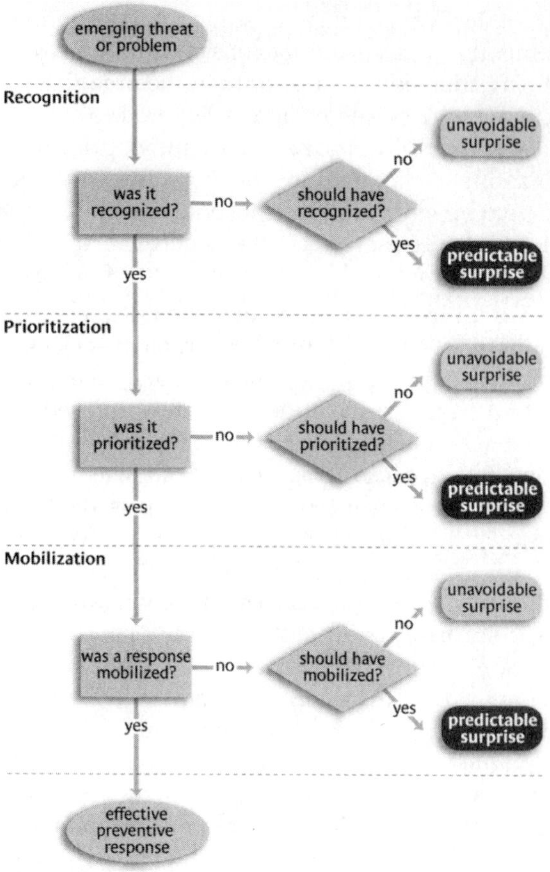

emerging threat or problem
Recognition
was it recognized? — no → should have recognized? — no → unavoidable surprise; yes → predictable surprise
yes
Prioritization
was it prioritized? — no → should have prioritized? — no → unavoidable surprise; yes → predictable surprise
yes
Mobilization
was a response mobilized? — no → should have mobilized? — no → unavoidable surprise; yes → predictable surprise
yes
effective preventive response

Did the leader mobilize effectively? When a threat has been deemed serious, the leader is obligated to mobilize to try to prevent it. If he takes precautionary measures commensurate with the risks involved, he should not be held accountable. Nor should he be blamed if he lacked the resources needed to mount an effective response.

And some are truly catastrophic—the events of September 11, 2001, are a tragic example of a predictable surprise.

The bad news is that all companies—including your own—are vulnerable to predictable surprises. In fact, if you're like most executives, you could probably point to at least one potential crisis or disaster that hasn't been given enough attention—a major customer that's in financial trouble, for instance, or an overseas plant that could be a terrorist target. But there's good news as well. In studying predictable surprises that have taken place in business and government, we have found that organizations' inability to prepare for them can be traced to three kinds of barriers: psychological, organizational, and political. Executives might not be able to eliminate those barriers entirely, but they can take practical steps to lower them substantially. And given the extraordinarily high stakes involved, taking those steps should be recognized as a core responsibility of every business leader.

Three Ways to Fail

It's all too easy, of course, to play Monday-morning quarterback when things go terribly wrong. That's not our intent here. We readily admit that many surprises are unpredictable—that some bolts out of the blue really do come out of the blue—and in those case leaders shouldn't be blamed for a lack of foresight. Nor should they be blamed if they've taken all reasonable preventive measures against a looming crisis. But if a damaging event happens that was foreseeable and preventable, no excuses should be brooked. The leaders' feet need to be held to the fire.

So how can you tell the difference between a true surprise and one that should have been predicted? Anticipating and avoiding business disasters isn't just a matter of doing better environmental scanning or contingency planning. It requires a number of steps, from recognizing the threat, to making it a priority in the organization, to actually mobilizing the resources required to stop it. We term this the "RPM process": recognition, prioritization, mobilization. Failure at any of these three stages will leave a company vulnerable to potentially devastating predictable surprises. (See the sidebar "Are You to Blame?" for a further discussion of the RPM process.)

Lapses in recognition occur when leaders remain oblivious to an emerging threat or problem—a lack of attention that can plague even the most skilled executives. After European Commission regulators refused to approve General Electric's $42 billion acquisition of Honeywell in 2001, for example, Jack Welch was quoted as saying, "You are never too old to be surprised." Welch is a famously hard-nosed executive, and if anyone could have been expected to do his homework, it would have been him. But was Welch correct in viewing the decision as a true surprise, an event that couldn't have been foreseen? The evidence suggests he was not. The *Economist* reported at the time that there were many warning flags of the EC's intent to scuttle the deal. For some time, the magazine pointed out, a philosophical gap had been widening between Europe and America over the regulation of mergers. And Mario Monti, the recently appointed head of the European Commission's competition authority, was widely believed to be looking for an opportunity to assert Continental independence.

Anticipating and avoiding **business disasters** requires a number of steps, from recognizing the threat, to making it a priority in the organization, to actually **mobilizing the resources** required to stop it.

It seems the real reason Welch was surprised is that he just didn't pay enough attention. According to the Associated Press, when GE's CEO and his counterpart at Honeywell, Michael Bonsignore, were rushing to close the deal (United Technologies was also eager to acquire Honeywell), they "reportedly never held initial consultations with their Brussels lawyers who specialize in European competition concerns." Welch appeared to assume that the merger would sail through the antitrust review. But while it did pass easily through the U.S. review—no doubt further reinforcing his confidence—it smashed on the rocks in Europe. Had Welch recognized the potential for a negative decision ahead of time, he almost certainly would have managed the merger negotiations and antitrust consultations differently—and Honeywell might well be a part of GE today.

Failures of prioritization arise when potential threats are recognized by leaders but not deemed sufficiently serious to warrant immediate attention. Monsanto fell into this trap in late 1999 when CEO Robert Shapiro and his advisers failed to concentrate on winning public acceptance of genetically modified foods in Europe. Betting the company on a "life sciences" vision, Shapiro has sold or spun off Monsanto's traditional chemical businesses and moved aggressively to acquire seed companies. Dazzled by the seemingly modified plants, the company pressed forward with launches of GMO food products in Europe, giving far too little weight to the fact that Europeans were still reeling from the mad cow disease crisis, reports of dioxin-contaminated chicken, and numerous other food-related concerns. By focusing on technical and strategic challenges, not on the hard work of winning hearts and minds, Shapiro ultimately lost his company. He was forced to sell Monsanto to Pharmacia-Upjohn, which bought it for its pharmaceutical division, valuing the agricultural biotechnology operations at essentially zero.

Breaks in the third link in the chain—failures of mobilization—occur when leaders recognize and give adequate priority to a looming problem but fail to respond effectively. When the Securities and Exchange Commission tried to reform the U.S. accounting system—well before the collapses of Enron and WorldCom—the Big Five accounting firms fiercely lobbied Congress to block new regulations that would have limited auditors' ability to provide consulting services. Appearing at congressional hearings in 2000, accounting firm CEOs assured legislators that no real problem existed. Joseph Berardino, then the managing partner of Arthur Anderson, stated in a written testimony that "the future of the [accounting] profession is bright and will remain bright—as long as the commission does not force us into an outdated role trapped in the old economy. Unfortunately, the proposed rule [on auditor independence] threatens to do exactly that." The Big Five also spent millions of dollars urging members of Congress to threaten the SEC leadership with budget cuts if it imposed limits on auditor services. The lobbying worked. The SEC backed off, and the all-too-predictable accounting scandals soon began to unfold.

It's important to note that the leadership failure here lies not just with the SEC but also with the accounting firms, which were well aware that their addiction to consulting fees was compromising their independence as auditors. Also culpable were political leaders—Republicans and Democrats, in the executive branch and in Congress—who lacked the courage to risk political damage and take a stand on the issue.

Sometimes leaders actually set themselves up for predictable surprises. A classic example is the 1998 decision by a coalition of 39 pharmaceutical companies to sue the government of South Africa over its attempt to reduce the cost of HIV drugs through parallel importation (buying pharmaceuticals in countries with lower prices and then importing them) and compulsory licensing (requiring patent holders to allow others to manufacture and sell their drugs at far lower cost). The companies feared that the precedent set by the South African move would undermine their control over valuable intellectual property in the developing world. But the suit sparked international outrage against the industry, prompting a very public and unflattering look at drug firms' profit margins and industry practices, which the press juxtaposed against the grim realities of AIDS in southern Africa. In response, governmental and nongovernmental organizations formed a coalition that ultimately won big public health exemptions on international intellectual property protection in developing countries. By mobilizing to win the narrow legal battle in South Africa, and not focusing on the broader context, the industry suffered a severe setback.

Why We're Vulnerable

When we studied examples of predictable surprises occurring at every stage of the RPM process, we found that they share similar causes. Some of those causes are psychological—cognitive defects that leave individuals blind to approaching threats. Others are organizational—barriers within companies that impede communication and dilute accountability. Still others are political—flaws in decision making that result from granting too much influence from special interests. Alone or in combination, these three kinds of vulnerabilities can sabotage any company at any time. All of them, as you'll see, were apparent in Shell's failure to anticipate the Brent Spar controversy.

Psychological Vulnerabilities. The human mind is a notoriously imperfect instrument. Extensive research has shown that the way we process information is subject to a slew of flaws—scholars call them cognitive biases—that can lead us to ignore or underestimate approaching disasters. Here are a few of the most common:

- We tend to harbor illusions that things are better than they really are. We assume that potential problems won't actually materialize or that their consequences won't be severe enough to merit preventive measures. "We'll get by," we tell ourselves.
- We give great weight to evidence that supports our preconceptions and discount evidence that calls those preconceptions into question.
- We pay too little heed to what other people are doing. As a result, we overlook our vulnerability to predictable surprises resulting from others' decisions and actions.
- We are creatures of the present. We try to maintain the status quo while downplaying the importance of the future, which undermines our motivation and courage to act now to prevent some distant disaster. We'd rather avoid a little pain today than a lot of pain tomorrow.
- Most of us don't feel compelled to prevent a problem that we have not personally experienced or that has not been made real to us through pictures or other vivid information. We act only after we're experienced significant harm or are able to graphically imagine ourselves, or those close to us, in peril.

All of these biases share something in common: They are self-serving. We tend to see the world as we'd like it to be rather than as it truly is. Much of Shell's failure to anticipate the disastrous response to its decision to dump the Brent Spar can be traced to the self-serving biases of its people—to their unshakable belief that they were right. Shell was an engineering company run by executives trained to make decisions through rigorous technical and economic analysis. Having reviewed more than 30 independent studies and arrived at "the correct answer" about the Spar, and having received approval from the British government to sink it, executives at Shell UK were utterly confident that their decision made the most sense, and they assumed that every reasonable person would see the issue their way. They were unprepared to deal with a group of true believers who opposed any dumping on principle and who were skilled at making emotional arguments that resonated with the public. In the context for people's hearts and minds, emotion easily defeated analysis—much to the consternation of Shell executives. Even well after it was obvious that they were losing the battle, the leaders of Shell UK still couldn't back away from a failing course of action.

Self-serving bias can be particularly destructive when there are conflicts of interest. Think of the many business scandals that arose after the Internet bubble burst. Although corruption certainly played a role in these disasters, the more fundamental cause was a series of biased judgments. Professional auditors distorted their accounting in ways that served the interests of their clients. Analysts on Wall Street gave overly positive assessments of companies that were clients of their firms' investment-banking arms. Corporate directors failed to pay enough attention to the actions of the CEOs who appointed and paid them. Many of these auditors, analysts, and board members knew that the bubble would burst, but their unconscious biases prevented them from fully acknowledging the consequences or taking preventive action. (For an in-depth discussion of how biases distort accounting results, see "Why Good Accountants Do Bad Audits," by Max H. Bazerman, George Loewenstein, and Don A. Moore, in the November 2002 issue of HBR.)

Organizational Vulnerabilities. The very structure of business organizations, particularly those that are large and complex, makes it difficult to anticipate predictable surprises. Because companies are usually divided into organizational silos, the information leaders need to see and

9/11 The Surprise
That Shouldn't Have Been

When fanatics commandeered jetliners on September 11, 2001, and steered them into buildings full of people, it came as a horrifying shock to most of the world. But however difficult it might have been to imagine individuals carrying out such an act, it shouldn't have been a surprise. Portents had been building up for years. It was well known that Islamic militants were willing to become martyrs for their cause and that their hatred and aggression toward the United States had been mounting throughout the 1990s. In 1993, terrorists set off a car bomb under the World Trade Center in an attempt to destroy the building. In 1995, other terrorists hijacked an Air France plane and made an aborted attempt to fly it into the Eiffel Tower. Also in 1995, the U.S. government learned of a failed Islamic terrorist plot to simultaneously hijack 11 U.S. commercial airplanes over the Pacific Ocean and then crash a lightplane filled with explosives into the CIA's headquarters near Washington, DC. Meanwhile, dozens of federal reports, including one issued by then Vice President Al Gore's special commission on aviation security, provided comprehensive evidence that the U.S. aviation security system was full of holes. Anyone who flew on a regular basis knew how simple it was to board an airplane with items, such as small knives, that could be used as weapons.

But despite the signals, no precautionary measures were taken. The failure can be traced to lapses in recognition, prioritization, and mobilization. Information that might have been pieced together to highlight the precise contours of the threat remained fragmented among the FBI, the CIA, and other governmental agencies. No one gave priority to plugging the security holes in the aviation system because, psychologically, the substantial and certain short-term costs of fixing the problems loomed far larger than the uncertain long-term costs of inaction. And the organizations responsible for airline security, the airlines, had the wrong incentives, desiring faster, lower-cost screening to boost profitability. Inevitably, plans to fix the system fell afoul of concerted political lobbying by the airline industry.

assess an approaching threat is often fragmented. Various people have various pieces of the puzzle, but no one has them all. In theory, corporate management should play the role of synthesizer, bringing together the fragmented information in order to see the big picture. But the barriers to this happening are great. Information is filtered as it moves up through hierarchies—sensitive or embarrassing information is withheld or glossed over. And those at the top inevitably receive incomplete and distorted data. That's exactly what happened in the months and years leading up to September 11. Various government agencies had pieces of information on terrorists' methods and plans that, had they been combined, would have pointed to the type of attack that was carried out against the World Trade Center and the Pentagon. Tragically, the information remained fragmented. (For more on September 11, see the sidebar: "9/11: The Surprise That Shouldn't Have Been.")

Organizational silos not only disperse information; they also disperse responsibility. In some cases, everyone assumes that someone else is taking responsibility, and so no one ever acts. In other cases, one part of an organization is vested with too much responsibility for a particular issue. Other parts of the organization, including those with important information or perspectives, aren't consulted or are even actively pushed out of the decision-making process. The result? Too narrow a perspective is brought to bear on the issue, and potential problems go unrecognized or are given too little priority.

Put another way, decision makers focus on an "impact horizon" that is too narrow, neglecting the implications for key constituencies. This sort of organizational parochialism was clearly evident within Shell. The company failed to see that sinking the Spar would set a precedent for dealing with other obsolete structures in the North Sea and that it was probably the worst structure to start with given its size and toxic residues. The company's decentralized management structure, made up of autonomous national business units, worked well when dealing with routine problems such as customizing marketing efforts to local customers. But it worked very badly when dealing with crises that crossed national lines. The Brent Spar was located in the British part of the North Sea, so responsibility for disposing of it was naturally vested with Shell UK. Shell UK, in turn, dealt with the British government to get the necessary permissions and consulted with British environmental groups. But Greenpeace changed the game by focusing its public relations attack not in Britain but in Germany. The German Shell operating company had not been involved in the process and had no part in the decision to dump the Spar. But it became the target of most of the pressure—financial and political—from

Greenpeace. Indeed, the chairman of Shell Germany, Peter Duncan, remarked publicly that he first heard about the planned sinking of the Spar "more or less from the television." Once the crisis broke, Shell's decentralized structure inhibited the company from coordinating crisis response activities and notifying employees of decisions and events. Senior Shell management outside the UK publicly criticized both the disposal plans and each other through the press.

Political Vulnerabilities. Finally, predictable surprises can emerge out of systemic flaws in decision-making processes.Imbalances of power, for example, may lead executives to overvalue the interests of one group while slighting those of other equally important groups. Such imbalances tend to be particularly damaging during the mobilization phase, when vested interests can slow or block action intended to resolve a growing problem. A case in point is the U.S. Congress, where single-interest groups, such as the National Rifle Association or the AARP, wield disproportionate influence. Through a combination of focused contributions to reelection campaigns, well-connected lobbyists, nurtured relationships with committee chairpeople and staff members, and intimate knowledge of leverage points by key processes, special-interest groups routinely stall or torpedo policy changes, even when there is a broad consensus that action is needed.

We saw this dynamic play out after Enron collapsed and WorldCom and other companies restated their financial results. Following an early burst of enthusiasm for seriously tightening corporate governance rules, Congress retreated in the face of intense lobbying by an array of business groups. In the critical area of auditing, for example, accounting industry lobbyists succeeded in watering down the Sarbanes-Oxley Act on corporate responsibility, enabling "independent" auditors to continue to provide consulting and other lucrative services to audit clients and to be rehired indefinitely by the clients, as well as allowing audit-firm staffers to take jobs with their clients. Efforts to reform pension laws to help protect workers from future Enron-like debacles were also beaten back by lobbyists representing employers. As a result, companies and investors remain vulnerable to damaging new "surprises."

Companies are all too often oblivious to the dynamics of government systems. Shell, for example, failed to anticipate and shape European political responses to its Brent Spar plan. Company officials had finalized the disposal plan after four years of study and quiet negotiations with the British government, which approved the dumping. After signing on to the Shell plan, the British government notified the other European governments with oil development and other interests in the North Sea. These governments raised no objections at that time, but the absence of objections is by no means the same as active support. As Greenpeace applied more pressure on the Continent, the German government responded by openly undercutting the UK's decision to allow Shell to sink the Spar. Through public criticism and direct requests, Germany pressured the UK to reverse its decision. Not building a broad consensus—with governments and with other oil companies—on how to deal with aging North Sea oil rigs cost Shell dearly.

Political vulnerabilities can also crop up within companies. Sanford Weill, the chairman of Citigroup, recently came under fire for apparently using corporate resources to provide personal assistance to Jack Grubman, a star analyst at Citi's Salomon Smith Barney. Weill allegedly helped get Grubman's children into a prestigious day care center in return for issuing a more favorable report on AT&T, a very important client of Salomon's investment-banking unit. But broader organizational politics also appear to have played a role in Weill's actions. As the *Economist* reported, "There is much speculation, and some e-mail evidence, that the recommendation helped to win support for Mr. Weill's successful ousting of [Citigroup's co-CEO, John] Reed from Michael Armstrong, AT&T's chief executive, who also happened to sit on Citi's board." The resulting damage to the reputations of Weill and his company was entirely predictable.

What You Can Do

"Prediction is very difficult," physicist Niels Bohr once said, "especially about the future." Difficult, yes. Impossible, no. Even though many organizations are caught unprepared for disasters they should have seen coming, many have successfully recognized approaching crises and taken evasive action. In the public sector, for example, governments, corporations, and charitable organizations banded together to curtail the use of CFC refrigerants once it became clear they were damaging the ozone layer. In the business arena, leaders are today sponsoring what we call "surprise-avoidance initiatives" on topics ranging from genomics research and stem cell biology to Internet security to the reform of corporate governance.

By actively encouraging people to **speak up**, executives can bring to the surface many problems that might otherwise go unmentioned.

Individual companies can learn a lot from such efforts. We have distilled from our own research a set of practical steps that managers can take to better recognize emerging problems, set appropriate priorities, and mobilize an effective preventive response. The first step is the simplest: Ask yourself and your colleagues, "What predictable surprises are currently brewing in our organization?" This may seem like an obvious question, but the fact is, it's rarely asked. People at various levels in organizations, from the top to the bottom, are often aware of approaching storms but choose to keep silent, often out of a fear of rocking the boat or being seen as troublemakers. By actively encouraging people to speak up, executives can bring to the surface many problems that might otherwise go unmentioned.

Some threats, of course, are invisible to insiders. To ferret out these potential dangers, companies should use two proven techniques—scenario planning and risk assessment. In scenario planning, a knowledgeable and creative group of people from inside and outside the organization is convened to review company strategies, digest available information on external trends, and identify critical business drivers and potential flash points. (It's essential to include outsiders in this group as a counterweight to the self-serving biases of employees). Based on this analysis, the group constructs a plausible set of scenarios for potential surprises that could emerge over, say, the coming two years. These scenarios form the basis for the design of preventive and preparatory measures. This exercise should include scenarios that, while unlikely, would have a very large impact on the organization if they occurred. A full scenario-planning exercise should be conducted annually, and formal updates of changes in the organization and its environment should be scheduled every quarter.

Rigorous risk analysis—combining a systematic assessment of the probabilities of future events and an estimation of the costs and benefits of particular outcomes—can be invaluable in overcoming the biases that afflict organizations in estimating the likelihood of unpleasant events.

Michael D. Watkins is an associate professor of business administration at Harvard Business School in Boston. **Max H. Bazerman** is the Jesse Isidor Straus Professor of Business Administration at Harvard Business School.

Is Silence Killing Your Company?

Faced with organizational or interpersonal problems at work, people often decide not to speak up. "It's not worth it," they say, and soldier on. But disturbing new research shows that the price of silence is much greater than we realize.

by Leslie Perlow and Stephanie Williams

SILENCE IS ASSOCIATED with many virtues: modesty, respect for others, prudence, decorum. Thanks to deeply ingrained rules of etiquette, people silence themselves to avoid embarrassment, confrontation, and other perceived dangers. There's an old saying that sums up the virtues of silence: "Better to be quiet and thought a fool than to talk and be known as one."

The social virtues of silence are reinforced by our survival instincts. Many organizations send the message—verbally or nonverbally—that falling into line is the safest way to hold on to our jobs and further our careers. The need for quiet submission is exaggerated by today's difficult economy, where millions of people have lost their jobs and many more worry that they might. A Dilbert cartoon poignantly expresses how pointless—and perilous—many people feel it is to speak out. Dilbert, the everyman underling, recognizes that a senior executive is making a poor decision. "Shouldn't we tell her?" he asks his boss, who laughs cynically. "Yes," the boss replies. "Let's end our careers by challenging a decision that won't change. That's a great idea."

To be sure, people who speak out sometimes get their day in the sun: Sherron Watkins of Enron, Cynthia Cooper of WorldCom, and Coleen Rowley at the FBI all ended up on the cover of *Time* as "Persons of the Year." But public recognition of a few people does not mean that speaking out is necessarily viewed as courageous or praiseworthy. Most individuals who go against their organizations or express their concerns publicly are severely punished. If they're not fired outright, they're usually marginalized and made to feel irrelevant.

But it is time to take the gilt off silence. Our research shows that silence is not only ubiquitous and expected in organizations but extremely costly to both the firm and the individual. Our interviews with senior executives and employees in organizations ranging from small businesses to *Fortune* 500 corporations to government bureaucracies reveal that silence can exact a high psychological price on individuals, generating feelings of humiliation, pernicious anger, resentment, and the like that, if unexpressed, contaminate every interaction, shut down creativity, and undermine productivity.

Take the case of Jeff, a team leader at a *Fortune* 100 company who was working on a large, long-term, high-pressure project. Each Tuesday, Jeff and his peers had a project management meeting (PMM) with Matt, their boss. Jeff would start writing his weekly update reports on Wednesday, continuing to work on them when he had time on Thursday and Friday, working even into the weekend. On Monday morning, he would hand in his document to Matt. Jeff figured that a weekly update was probably useful for Matt; all the same, he felt deeply frustrated at the time he was wasting writing the elaborate reports. Yet despite complaining endlessly to his peers, week after week Jeff said nothing to Matt. With each act of silence, Jeff's resentment grew and his respect for Matt disintegrated, even as Jeff became more and more uncomfortable with the idea of questioning Matt. And so the process continued, as the project fell further behind schedule. For his part, when Matt was asked about the value of the PMM, he was mystified: "Not to insult my team leaders, but in my mind, every Tuesday morning I have a Painfully Meaningless Meeting."

The fact that no one suggested an alternative to the PMM was fairly typical of our findings. Individuals are frequently convinced that keeping quiet is the best way to preserve relation-

When to Zip It

Although most people tend to speak up too little rather than too much, there are times when it's better to stay quiet. Some issues are simply not worth raising, and you don't want to unnecessarily turn small differences of opinion into broad conflicts. There's no sense in spending time and effort getting bogged down dealing with every little difference, especially ones that are not likely to affect the quality of people's work or those you're not likely to remember in a week or a month. And if the conflict is in an unimportant relationship or one that won't continue much longer, speaking up may not be crucial. You will still lose out on the creativity and learning that stem from expressing differences, but you don't need to worry about the additional costs of unresolved differences lurking beneath the surface and destroying the relationship.

Even when a difference should be addressed, there is the question of timing. It may be fruitless, for example, to raise a tough issue with your boss when you face an impending deadline—unless speaking up is important for the task at hand and there really is enough time to work through the issue. Waiting until the deadline has passed and people can focus on what you have to say may be the best option. Moreover, initially keeping a lid on differences when your own or the other person's emotions are highly charged can be beneficial in the longer run. If you've just had a row with a colleague and either of you is very upset, arrange a time to talk in the future when both of you have had a chance to cool down and can discuss differences without venting or blaming. But if you defer a difficult conversation, make sure you do not postpone it indefinitely. Otherwise, the unresolved differences will come back to haunt you.

There are no hard-and-fast rules about what needs to be discussed or when it's best to do so. You must rely on your best judgment. What's important is that you shift your mind-set from asking whether this is one of those rare times when you should speak to asking instead whether this is one of those rare times when you should remain quiet.

ships and get work done. In the following pages, we will examine what makes this sort of silence so prevalent in organizations. From there, we will discuss the personal and organizational costs of silence, which often remain hidden for long periods of time even as they grow exponentially with each additional act of silence. Finally, we will investigate several ways to break free from the insidious silent sink.

The Reign of Silence

Silence often starts when we choose not to confront a difference. Given the dissimilarities in our temperaments, backgrounds, and experiences, it's inevitable that we will have different opinions, beliefs, and tastes. Most of us recognize the value of such variety: Who really wants to go into a brainstorming session with people who all have the same views and ideas? But we're also aware of how terribly painful it can be to raise and work through differences. The French word *différend*, tellingly, means "quarrel." Not surprisingly, most people decide it's easier to cover up their differences than to try to discuss them.

Our research shows that this tendency to remain silent rather than express a difference exists both in individual relationships and in groups, where we fear a loss of status or even expulsion if we differ from the rest. Most of us can remember from our adolescence how compelling the desire was to conform. Even as adults, many people in organizations are willing to go to enormous lengths to get along with members of their work groups—at least superficially. We do what we believe other group members want us to do. We say what we think other people want us to say.

Consider what happened at one off-site meeting of top management at a Web-based education company. Concerned about the company's vision, the managers met to share and discuss different perspectives. But one speaker after another just echoed what the previous speaker had said. When any manager did dare to dissent, a colleague would quickly dismiss his idea. Having effectively tabled every discussion in which disagreement surfaced, the management team crowed about the level of "consensus" they had achieved. One by one, team members celebrated their achievement. The head of marketing went first. "We made some great progress today," he said, "I'm excited—passionate—committed to the future." The CFO continued, "I thought today was going to be a lot uglier. I expected battles. Yet things were remarkably consistent." Yet despite the outward expression of consensus, at the end of the day, many of the attendees privately despaired that the off-site had been a waste of time. By silencing themselves and one another, they failed to create a compelling vision, and the company continued with no clear direction.

This meeting shows how the pressure for unanimity can prevent employees of roughly equal grade and status—even top managers—from exploring their differences. More familiar to many is the pressure to keep silent that's created by differences in rank. How easy it is for a boss to send a powerful signal that a worker should be quiet. Take the case of Robert and Linda. Robert was an attorney in charge of his law firm's support staff. Linda, who was head of the library, came to Robert one day to complain about the performance evaluation process. She felt that many of the lawyers weren't being fair in their evaluations

Speed Trap

There's no doubt that pressure to go fast can have its benefits. It can, for example, push us to find more efficient, less bureaucratic ways of working. But it also makes us even more likely to keep silent. How many times has a looming deadline caused you to bite your tongue and think to yourself, "We don't have time to worry about this now; we just need to get it done."

When we perpetually silence ourselves in the short-sighted belief that we are getting our tasks done as expeditiously as possible, we may interfere with creativity, learning, and decision making. If our work depends on divergent thinking, these less-effective processes may in turn result in problems that take time and attention to resolve. Then, in addition to all the work we are rushing to complete, we will also have to address these new problems. That can lead to a vicious cycle that makes us feel the need to go even faster. A little fable about a farmer with a wagon full of apples helps illustrate the point. The farmer stopped a man on the side of the road and asked how far it was to market. The man responded, "It is an hour away, if you go slow." He continued, "If you go fast, it will take you all day." There was a bump in the road, andif the farmer went too fast he would hit it, all his apples would fall out, and he's have to spend the day picking up the fruit. The farmer would then be in all the greater hurry to get to market.

The pressure to go fast ends up feeding on itself, perpetuating an internally generated and self-destructive, ever-increasing need for speed. Overstretched workers become more overstretched; managers already focused on crises become all the more so. In our daily lives, many of us face pressure to go fast, and we end up silencing our differences in response. We need to be careful, though, or we may end up in a self-made "speed trap."

In the end, whether our primary concern is to preserve our relationships or to get our tasks done as expeditiously as possible, we must speak up rather than withhold our differences. Otherwise, we risk undermining both our relationships and our ability to complete our work.[1]

1. For a more detailed discussion of how speed relates to silencing, see Leslie A. Perlow, Gerardo A. Okhuysen, and Nelson P. Repenning, "The Speed Trap: Exploring the Relationship Between Decision Making and the Temporal Context," *Academy of Management Journal* (October 2002).

of the library staff and that they shouldn't have the automatic right to determine the librarians' raises and promotions. Robert disagreed. "If you think of the lawyers as your clients," he advised, "you can see why they have every expectation to be able to critique the quality of service." When Linda pressed again, Robert got irritated and said, "This is the way we do it around here, and this is the way it's going to continue!" Linda said nothing more and quietly left his office.

At least Linda tried to speak up. Many members of organizations silence themselves before the boss has the slightest inkling of what they're thinking. Often in these instances, employees use silence as a strategy to get ahead. Consider Don, a senior analyst at an investment bank who carefully keeps his opinions to himself when he's around his superiors. "It comes down to the hierarchical nature of the bank," he says. "Basically you're just trying to make the person above you love you so you'll get a big bonus. If you start raising uncomfortable questions and being holier-than-thou, you may be absolutely right, but you shoot yourself in the foot. What the managing director says goes."

And it's not just that subordinates feel pressure to keep silent with their bosses. Bosses also may feel uncomfortable expressing their differences with subordinates. It is frequently difficult for managers, for instance, to give negative performance feedback to subordinates—especially in organizations that place a high value on being polite and avoiding confrontation.

The Costs of Suffering in Silence

When we silence ourselves and others—even when we're convinced that it is the best way, the right way, or the only way to preserve the relationships we care about and get on with our work—we may be fooling ourselves. Let's return for a moment to the law firm where Robert and Linda worked. After meeting with Linda, Robert simply forgot about their discussion. As a senior partner, he thought his view was a no-brainer, and he assumed that the issue would just go away. Linda, for her part, was acutely aware that she had been forced into silence, but, given that Robert was the boss, she thought the best course was to say nothing further to him.

Still, she was profoundly angry. In an attempt to release her negative feelings, she complained bitterly to her peers about what Robert had said and how he had shut her down. But gossiping only alleviated Linda's anger temporarily, and news of Robert's insensitivity quickly spread throughout the support staff, which came to view the incident as evidence that "management doesn't listen." Ultimately, Robert's strained relations with the support staff led to high turnover. As he later reflected, "My action that day was probably the single greatest mistake I ever made."

The damage wasn't just to Robert and the organization. Linda, in choosing to respond to Robert with silence, caused herself great damage as well, far more in fact than she may have realized. That's because silencing doesn't resolve anything; rather than erase differences, it merely pushes them beneath the surface. Every time we keep silent about our differences, we swell with negative emotions like anxiety, anger, and resentment. Of course, we can go on for a long time pretending to ourselves and others that nothing is wrong. But as long as the conflict is not resolved, our repressed feelings remain potent and color the way we relate to other people. We begin to feel a sense of disconnection in our relationships, which in turn causes us to become increasingly self-protective.

When we feel defensive in this way, we become all the more fearful that if we speak up we will be embarrassed or rejected. Our sense of insecurity grows. In relationships we care about preserving, more acts of silence follow, which only bring more defensiveness and more distrust. A destructive "spiral of silence" is set in motion.

Caught up in just such a spiral was Maria, a project manager we interviewed at a management consulting firm. At the beginning of her first project, her boss, Max, suggested to Maria ways her team should make its initial presentation to the client. Maria wasn't convinced that Max's approach was the best. But Max was the partner, so Maria kept her concerns to herself. Later, when Max discovered that the team had failed to collect some of the data he wanted, he lost his temper and ordered Maria to push the team harder. Maria thought that the data were irrelevant and that searching for them would just waste the team's time. But, inwardly clenching her fists and gritting her teeth, she deferred to her superior.

A few days later, Maria and her team received a lukewarm response when they presented their finding to the client. Maria later met with Max to discuss the next steps. Convinced that she understood the client's needs better than he did, she was intent on laying out her own point of view and explaining to him the error in his approach. But Maria had become very uncomfortable around Max, so when he launched into a critique of her team's performance, she lost her nerve. Again she stifled her resistance and opted to do as Max said. Maria's discomfort grew each time she chose to remain silent, and she descended down the spiral of silence. Ultimately, her desire and ability to work with Max were destroyed.

There's a cruel and all too common irony here, for the reason Maria had silenced herself in the first place was to preserve her relationship with Max. We don't speak up for fear of destroying our relationships, but in the end our silence creates an emotional distance that becomes an unbridgeable rift.

That's what happened to Shoney, a research fellow in pulmonary and critical-care medicine. When we interviewed him, he had already discovered where the spiral leads. Praveen, a research associate one level higher, was supposed to oversee Shoney's work. In exchange, Praveen's name would appear on everything Shoney published. Eager to maximize Shoney's productivity, Praveen constantly issued him instructions. Shoney resented being bossed around but always did as he was told, never pushing back. Over time, however, Shoney's resentment grew as Praveen continued to treat him more like an unknowing assistant than a highly qualified peer. One day, when Praveen started to question Shoney about how he had spent his time in the lab the previous evening, something inside Shoney snapped. He still said nothing. But from that day forth, Shoney refused to collaborate with Praveen. On their next assignment, they divided the tasks and carried them out independently.

That just made things worse. By shutting himself off, Shoney lost the opportunity to brainstorm with an informed colleague. He also precluded the possibility of sharing anything he may have learned that could have helped Praveen. And he foreclosed on any potential for eliminating redundancy in the two researchers' work. Silencing was not only costly to Shoney, but it was a cost doubly borne, for the organization paid it as well. Each time workers remain silent in the face of conflict, they keep new ideas to themselves and leave alternative courses of action unexplored. And they withhold important information from colleagues that could enhance the quality of both their own and the organization's work.

Breaking the Spiral of Silence

How do we get ourselves and other to speak up? Can the vicious spirals of silence be replaced with virtuous spirals of communication? The answer is yes, but doing so requires that we find the courage to act differently and that we create the context in which people will value the expression of such difference. Managers with a lot of authority need to be especially careful not to punish people, explicitly or implicitly, for speaking out, particularly on issues that may be difficult for the organization to deal with. Harry's case illustrates how a leader can create such a context.

Harry was a battalion commander, whose unit of more than 500 soldiers had just been miserably defeated in a mock battle against another unit. "If this had been a real battle, two-thirds of us would be dead," Harry said to the unit in the debriefing that followed. But he continued, "I was at fault. I failed you." And he went on to explain exactly how, taking full responsibility for the failure.

At first, no one said a word. Then Nick, a very junior scout who was responsible for detecting and alerting the battalion to the enemy's movements, said, "No sir, it wasn't your fault. I fell asleep on duty."

Harry was shocked. But rather than focus on Nick's failure, great as it was, Harry immediately redirected the unit's attention to uncovering the underlying problem—the exhaustion his men were suffering. How many had also slept though the opening rounds of the attack, he asked his soldiers to think to themselves. "Nick is a good soldier," he said. "All of you are good soldiers. We need to focus on the bigger issue: How can we sustain our capabilities during continuous operations in such high-intensity situations?"

Harry set the tone for this discussion. Had he not started by exhibiting his own failures, it's highly unlikely that Nick would have had the courage to speak up. Moreover, Harry carefully framed the ensuing discussion to avoid blame and instead focus on the larger problem they all faced. In the end, this unit gained a rich appreciation for the importance of speaking up and admitting mistakes.

Keeping quiet is too big a problem to be left just to leaders, however. If an organization wants to escape the spiral of silence, everyone has to fight the urge to withdraw and has to work hard to speak up. That's a tough challenge, for all the reasons we've explored, but the following practices can help.

Recognize your power. We all have the power to express ourselves and to encourage other to speak freely, whether they're subordinates, peers, or even bosses. Of course, nobody likes to be the one to break the ice; in the face of personal conflict, passivity always feels safer than action. Who would not prefer to sit back, blame the other person, and wait for him to make the first move? Yet it's almost never the case that something is entirely another person's fault. Instead of waiting for the other person to apologize or to broach the subject, we need to be willing to take the first step ourselves—to bring differences out into the open so that they can be explored.

This can even be a good strategy for dealing with a boss who has overtly silenced a subordinate, like Robert, from the law firm. In that situation, Linda could have chosen to go back to Robert to try to turn the situation around. She could have met with him again and said something like, "I know that you don't think the issue with the performance evaluation process is important. But it is very important to the library staff, and we would like you to understand our point of view. I don't feel comfortable dropping the issue, as you suggested. I would like a chance to better explain my perspective."

When one person finds the courage to take a step like this and presents new information in a way that the other person can absorb, the two are likely to join in a process of mutual exploration of the differences that separate them. Indeed, we all have much more power than we think. Our superiors certainly have formal power over us, but it's also true that their performance depends on how well we are doing. Don't forget: your boss needs you, too. And knowing that should empower you to speak up and help him appreciate your point of view.

Act deviantly. To break the walls of silence, sometimes we have to behave in ways that are not considered appropriate for our particular organization. Put differently, we must act deviantly—for example, by choosing to ask tough questions at a company meeting where employees normally just accept the decisions of top management. Although deviance often carries negative connotations, it is not synonymous with dysfunctionality. Deviance is, at heart, a creative act—a way of searching out and inventing new approaches to doing things. Acts of deviance can point to areas where organizations need to change and can result in fruitful alternatives. The chief thing to keep in mind here is that norms can have exceptions. By challenging a particular norm, we can play a role in changing it.

Build a coalition. Reaching out to others can give us the strength to break the hold of silence. Not only is it easier to speak up when we know we're not alone, but a coalition also carries more legitimacy and resources. Even though it may feel threatening to approach people to join forces with you, it is surprising how often you may find that many people feel the same way you do That's what happened to Nancy Hopkins, a scientist at MIT.[1] Hopkins repeatedly found herself having to fight harder than her male colleagues for resources like lab space. After dealing with the same issues for years, she drafted a letter to the MIT administration. Before sending it, however, she showed it to a female colleague whom she regarded as politically savvy. To Hopkins's surprise, the other woman wanted to add her signature to the letter; the same type of things had happened to her, too. In the end, 14 of the 15 women Hopkins approached decided to sign as well. As a result, a committee was formed, and a pattern of discrimination was uncovered and addressed.

We've recently seen in the scandals at Enron, Tyco, and WorldCom, to name but a few, just how catastrophic situations can become when silence prevails. Yet silence does not have to be about fraud and malfeasance to do grave damage to a company. All too often, behind failed products, broken processes, and mistaken decisions are people who chose to hold their tongues rather than to speak up. Breaking the silence can bring an outpouring of fresh ideas from all levels of an organization—ideas that might just raise the organization's performance to a whole new level.

Note

1. The account here is taken from material in both Nancy H. Hopkins, "Experience of Women at the Massachusetts Institute of Technology," *Women in the Chemical Workforce: A Workshop Report to the Chemical Sciences Roundtable* (CPSMA, 2000) and Lotte Bailyn, "Academic Careers and Gender Equity: Lessons Learned from MIT," *Gender, Work, and Organizations* (March, 2003).

***Leslie Perlow** is an associate professor of organizational behavior at Harvard Business School in Boston. Her book* When You Say Yes but Mean No *will be published this month by Crown Business/Random House.* ***Stephanie Williams** is a research associate at Harvard Business School and a lecturer in the management department of the Leeds School of Business at the University of Colorado at Boulder.*

Wireless Interoperability: A Key Element of Public Safety

Edwin Daley

Popular television shows and movies portray public safety officials as seamlessly coordinated in their communication and response efforts. The reality is different. When public safety agencies *do* communicate with each other, the information generally is shared through communications centers and involves radio operators shuffling messages back and forth between agencies, using commercial cellular services, or even sending runners. Measures such as these demonstrate the urgent need for public safety officials to enhance interoperability, or emergency incident responders' ability to communicate directly with and transmit data to other emergency service personnel through mobile radios. Perhaps, not all local government administrators are familiar with wireless interoperability, but it represents a concept we all need to understand.

In the past, local and state public safety agencies functioned independently of each other, with little need for coordination. When a field officer found it necessary to communicate with personnel from other agencies, it could be done through a dispatcher, who would relay information between them.

Today, however, coordination between agencies is critical. The era of agencies' being able to handle incidents independently of neighboring jurisdictions is over. Agencies must coordinate their responses, and their field officers must be able to communicate directly. This wireless interoperability is necessary during routine responses that take place every day as well as when mission-critical emergencies occur.

During such local catastrophes as a terrorist attack or a major traffic accident, multiple agencies—including state and local police, firefighters, and emergency medical personal—respond. Unfortunately, few if any of these agencies have the capability to quickly share information directly with one another when lives and property are at risk.

This wave of shootings demonstrated that emergency incidents often require a response from a number of local government departments and frequently involve more than one jurisdiction.

Last fall, during the sniper incidents in Virginia, Maryland, and Washington, D.C., a morning shooting took place in Virginia. Personnel at the command center in Montgomery County, Maryland, had reason to believe that the sniper intended to strike again that same evening, in which jurisdiction was uncertain. Citizens throughout and beyond the Washington metropolitan area were nervous, and all were looking for a vehicle of the same specific description.

Communities quickly reviewed their response plans and considered how public safety agencies could coordinate road closures and a search for the vehicle. The highest-priority issue revolved around notifying all personnel from a number of agencies of any incident and of the incident's location. Law enforcement supervisors wanted to be able to seal off an incident area if a sniper shooting occurred in their jurisdiction. They suggested that officers be assigned to respond to various designated highways, instead of having all personnel respond to the incident scene. The key to this proposal would be instant notification of all personnel that a shooting had occurred and at what location.

A police department leader in Frederick County, Virginia, identified the problem. His officers could use mobile radios to communicate with each other and with the jurisdiction's emergency communications center (ECC). They could not, however, communicate directly with the other agencies involved in the field. Personnel were faced with the prospect of having to contact their ECC to relay messages to other ECCs, which would in turn have to notify field personnel from the second agency.

This wave of shootings demonstrated that emergency incidents often require a response from a number of local government departments and frequently involve more than one jurisdiction. Too often, field personnel from these state, local, and volunteer agencies cannot communicate with each other directly through mobile radios. Radio equipment can be incompatible, limiting the ability of emergency service personnel to make a coordinated response to a critical incident.

When federal agencies are involved, the need to communicate directly is magnified because of added types of equipment brought into play. Critical time is lost when field personnel are forced to relay messages through one or more ECCs to speak with other field personnel in an effort to coordinate responses.

National Public Safety Wireless Interoperability Forum

In October 2001, the National Institute of Justice cosponsored a National Public Safety Wireless Interoperability Forum, which was attended by some 150 elected and appointed officials and public safety representatives from all levels of government. ICMA and other national organizations composed of state and local government leaders and public safety officials participated and learned about wireless interoperability problems.

Held in Washington, D.C., one month after the September 11, 2001, terrorist attacks, the forum generated great concern for the inability of field personnel from public safety departments and emergency first responders to communicate with each other directly by mobile radio at critical times.

The incidents discussed ranged from local accidents to such larger events as the Oklahoma City bombing and the Columbine shootings. Participants learned—from recent surveys of existing equipment used by public safety agencies, and the equipment's capacities—that the cost to achieve wireless interoperability on a national basis would exceed $18 billion.

Task Force and Its Mission

It was clear to forum participants that the existing lack of wireless interoperability was unacceptable in this era of rapid communications, multiagency response, and terrorist activities.

Communication gaps identified at the World Trade Center by emergency first responders needed to be addressed. Recognizing that all levels of government must cooperate to address this challenge, 18 national associations representing state and local elected, appointed, and public safety officials formed the National Task Force on Interoperability (NTFI), consisting of 56 members.

The National Institute of Justice offered support through meeting facilitation, outreach, and logistics. An executive committee was formed to provide leadership and organization before the first task force meeting in April 2002. The missions of the task force were to inform state and local government leaders of the benefits of interoperability and of the policy issues that had to be overcome, and to encourage partnerships among public policymakers to address interoperability issues in a more comprehensive way.

Why Can't We Communicate?

NTFI developed an outreach/education program that can be used by national associations and task force members to bring these critical issues to the attention of state and local government leaders and the public.

First, it formed three work groups, to deal with issues involving: 1) spectrum, 2) resources, and 3) governance.

Spectrum is a term for the usable radio frequencies allocated to the land mobile-radio systems of public safety communications. Functioning like an interstate highway, spectrum transmits electronic signals. Almost all public safety agencies use wireless radios as their primary communications mechanism; without spectrum, these radios would be useless.

Public safety agencies were all initially assigned radio frequencies at the low end of the range. But because the growing number of agencies were assigned frequencies on an individual basis without regard for a comprehensive plan, these channels now are found on a variety of bands: high, low, very high, ultra-high, television-sharing, 700 megahertz, and 800 megahertz.

The spectrum work group of NTFI examined the availability of spectrum for public safety agencies and the way in which it is allocated. It also reviewed spectrum regulations, commercial services spectrum, and other issues.

Over a period of several decades, the Federal Communications Commission has assigned public safety agencies radio frequencies in 10 separate bands. This has

Task Force Participants

The National Task Force on Interoperability (NTFI) included representatives of the following 18 national associations:

- Association of Public Safety Communications Officials (APCO)
- International Association of Chiefs of Police (IACP)
- International Association of Fire Chiefs (IAFC)
- International City/County Management Association (ICMA)
- Major Cities Chiefs (MCC)
- Major County Sheriffs' Association (MCSA)
- United States Conference of Mayors (USCM)
- National Association of Counties (NACo)
- National League of Cities (NLC)
- National Association of State Chief Information Officers (NASCIO)
- National Association of State Telecommunications Directors (NASTD)
- National Conference of State Legislatures (NCSL)
- National Criminal Justice Association (NCJA)
- National Emergency Management Association (NEMA)
- National Governors Association (NGA)
- National Public Safety Telecommunications Council (NPSTC)
- National Sheriffs' Association (NSA)
- Council of State Governments (CSG)

Ed Daley, city manager of Winchester, Virginia, and Roberta Lesh, director of police programs at the International City/County Management Association, Washington, D.C., represented IGMA on the task force.

enabled more agencies to obtain a radio frequency; but it also has created the fragmentation that exists today. The spectrum bands allocated to public safety units within a region or state can affect public safety interoperability, as can the funding and deployment decisions made by public policy decision-makers.

The public's need for effective and timely emergency response communications must take precedence over the turf issues and political interests of individual agencies.

Local agencies had tended to favor the purchase and maintenance of communications equipment with independent frequencies because this practice grants them greater autonomy and because the cost of upgrading equipment to make it compatible with other local and state agencies is significantly higher than that of using an independent frequency. This situation, too, can hamper interoperability.

The **resources** work group reviewed funding alternatives and sources. It investigated how the use of existing funds can be made more efficient through collaborative procurement. Savings can be achieved through local agencies' working together or through state purchasing contracts. Emergency communications systems can be shared by two or more agencies, instead of each insisting upon remaining autonomous and not interoperable.

Local agencies must develop a joint, comprehensive financing strategy instead of continuing to make piecemeal purchases that worsen the problem. A number of such long-term financing alternatives as lease/purchase, municipal bonds, and special taxes are available to communities that recognize the necessity of wireless interoperability. The federal government and the states can encourage interoperability by providing incentive funding through grants and low-interest financing.

The **governance** work group of NTFI looked at the governance structures then in effect for public safety and communications organizations to evaluate how successful agencies had been in achieving communications interoperability. Clearly, an effective governance structure is the foundation of a successful interoperability strategy. State and local governments need to create areawide, multiagency bodies and grant them adequate powers to ensure that decisions concerning emergency communications are made in the best interest of wireless interoperability.

The public's need for effective and timely emergency response communications must take precedence over the turf issues and political interests of individual agencies. Multiagency boards can be formed by state directive or by local agreement. But they must have the authority to develop and implement an effective interoperability strategy. Regional agencies, which coordinate the purchases of compatible communications equipment and the resources to make these purchases, are key factors in a successful interoperability program.

Overall, the NTFI work groups met four times in Washington and held numerous conference calls and chat-room exchanges. A final task-force report entitled *Why Can't We Talk? Interoperability—Working Together to Bridge the Communications Gap to Save Lives: A Guide for Public Officials*, accompanied by a brochure and supplemental resources, was released at a press conference on February 6, 2003.

This report includes recommendations for all levels of government to enhance interoperability and to help ensure that emergency service personnel can properly communicate with one another in order to coordinate their responses. Members of NTFI also called on Congress to use the proceeds from the auction of public airway spectrum licenses to set up a permanent public-interest trust

Look to ICMA

Here are publications that can be useful to managers as they consider enhancing interoperabiity in their public safety operations:

ICMA's MIS Report *Siting Wireless Telecommunications: Planning and the Law* (1997, 19 pages, Item no. 42187, $14.95) describes policy and management options available to local governments in developing a siting ordinance and working with citizens, service providers, and other local governments.

IQ Report *Information and Communications Technology for Public Safety* (2000, 19 pages, Hard copy, Item no. 42560, Downloadable e-document E43009, $14.95) describes information and telecommunications technologies that have applications for public safety. It discusses implementation issues for integrated justice systems, trunked radio systems, global positioning satellite systems, wireless communications, and more. Case studies included.

ICMA's Clearinghouse Report *Communications Planning Report* (2001, 122 pages, Item no. 42654, $18.00) concentrates on three areas in upgrading local government communications: voice systems (phones, pagers, fax); audio visual and multimedia systems (public access channel, video conferencing, and police and fire training); and wide/metropolitan area networks (fiber-optic cable infrastructure, leased high-speed telecom services, wireless technology, and Internet access). It provides an analysis of current systems and recommendations, including appendixes.

Special Report *Information and Communication Technology in Local Government: A Practical Guide for Managers* (2001, 218 pages, Item no. 42673, $40.00) shows how to manage information technology in local government—planning, organizing, contracting, purchasing, networking, servicing—and discusses applications for specific functions.

More information on these publications can be viewed at ICMA's Bookstore&More Web site at: bookstore.icma.org. Secure ordering is available online or call ICMA's distribution center at 800/745-8780.

fund that would award grants promoting interoperability efforts.

Why Can't We Talk makes recommendations on spectrum needs, funding, and cooperation among all levels of government. Here are some of the major findings:

- Five key reasons why public safety agencies can't communicate are that 1) a great deal of wireless equipment is aging and incompatible; 2) funding for new equipment has been limited and fragmented; 3) planning for emergency communications systems has been done from a short-term, fragmented, and limited-funding perspective; 4) state and local public agencies and governing bodies have failed to develop service programs on a cooperative and coordinated basis; and 5) overview of the assignment of radio spectrum to public safety agencies has been limited and uncoordinated.
- To achieve interoperability in your community, determine the types of emergencies, such as traffic accidents, that occur and who responds; which agencies need to talk to one another daily; who should be in communication in the first eight hours of an emergency; and who will need to be added to this initial group if the emergency surpasses the eight-hour period.
- Developing tips on how to communicate can help achieve interoperability: devise a plan for improving interoperability that includes goals and objectives; outline the problems or needs to be addressed; identify potential partners; propose a detailed budget; outline a marketing strategy; and include an operational plan that addresses how the project will be funded.
- As funding strategies, use shared systems that will automatically reduce the shared costs for agencies; exploit existing infrastructures; and obtain pricing information from other governmental units that have already contracted with prospective vendors.

The recent loss of the space shuttle Columbia required emergency responders from a number of federal, state, and local agencies to coordinate their recovery efforts. Again, some personnel could not communicate with others in the field. Information and decisions had to be relayed through a large number of communications centers, and field operatives couldn't just talk to each other directly. This incident has reminded us once again that emergency response is a multifaceted local issue involving multiple agencies that are severely hamstrung when they lack wireless interoperability.

So What's It to You?

Why should local government officials concern themselves with the challenges presented by the interoperability issue? The answer is quite simple: these problems affect the safety of all citizens and government officials. Many separate communications systems, owned by different government and volunteer emergency-response agencies continue to procure whatever communications systems work well with their own equipment and procedures, regardless of their ability (or inability) to communicate with other agencies.

There are many different ways for public safety entities to fund their communications needs without having to coordinate their purchases with the other agencies they work with during emergencies. Some of the funding options require wireless interoperability with other agencies. Others do not.

Ideas in Action PM

Electronic Council-Packet Program

Members of the Greenwood Village, Colorado (population 11,035), City Council now receive their meeting agendas and associated documents on compact discs. Instead of bringing three-ring binders to council meetings, members bring laptop computers. During the meetings, the city's mayor and nine councilmembers can search for information with the click of a mouse or use special software to make notes on any of the material. Hyperlinks connect agenda items with relevant documents and references to the municipal code, and several documents can be viewed on the screen simultaneously. Councilmembers love the ease of the new system.

The city spent $50,000 for laptops for the mayor; the council, and the executive management team. The amount of labor to produce and distribute the documents is about the same as for paper documents; it takes approximately an hour to burn all the CDs that are distributed.

Source: Ideas in Action: A Guide to Local Government Innovation, *copyright 2003, published by ICMA, Washington, D.C.*

In numerous cases, even subunits of the same state or local government cannot communicate or transmit data directly, thanks to a lack of wireless interoperability. Local government managers and administrators need to conduct an audit of their agencies' wireless communications equipment to ensure interoperabiity. They must then determine the ability of their field personnel to communicate and transmit data to other agencies that are likely to participate with them, and the need to communicate with these entities during emergency incidents.

The NTFI report recommends that local officials convene a meeting of all stakeholders to assess the current interoperability status of their wireless communications equipment and to develop a plan for upgrading that equipment to achieve complete interoperability. Lives may be lost otherwise.

The bottom line is that law enforcement professionals and their counterpart first responders may find their emergency efforts at cross-purposes. And this kind of failure can actually deepen tragedies.

For More Information

Copies of the National Task Force on Interoperability materials can be found on the Web site at http://www.agileprogram.org/ntfi. For additional information, contact David Hess, DOJ, Office of Justice Programs, at 202/305-0779 or 202/305-0703; e-mail, hessd@ojp.usdoj.gov. Or contact Roberta Lesh at ICMA, 202/962-3575; e-mail, rlesh@icma.org.

Ed Daley is city manager of Winchester, Virginia (ecd@ci.winchester.va.us).

Does Government Need a Sarbanes-Oxley Type Reform Act?

Kevin M. Bronner

There have been many widely publicized corporate scandals over the past two years involving companies such as Enron and WorldCom. The federal government has taken steps to address many of the issues that arose through the passage of the Sarbanes-Oxley Act of 2002. The Sarbanes-Oxley act enhances the manner in which the Securities and Exchange Commission (SEC) regulates private business. There are many excellent reform mechanisms in the Sarbanes-Oxley act that relate to private businesses. In the public sector, many larger and high profile governments have multiple mechanisms to ensure that adequate financial controls exist. For instance, the State of New York has several groups participating in its financial affairs including the governor, a state comptroller, an attorney general with powers to search for irregularities, a state legislature with highly trained fiscal policy staffs and a number of public interest groups that examine fiscal issues. It is questionable, however, whether many smaller governmental units have an intense structure of financial controls. There are over 80,000 governmental units in the United States and, given the complexity of their financial affairs, it is most likely that some of them will run into some financial difficulties in the future.

A number of local governments in New York State have run into financial problems in the past 25 years, which has led to financial oversight control boards being implemented by New York State to oversee their operations. Examples include New York City, Nassau County on Long Island and the City of Troy in upstate New York. Financial specialists should examine the problems with the corporate scandals and the solutions developed by the federal government in the Sarbanes-Oxley Act to see if there are lessons learned that can be applied to the public sector.

I believe that there are at least four important issues that are being solved by the Sarbanes-Oxley Act that can be applied to all levels of government. These issues include the following four items:

1. Ensure that there is no conflict of interest between the local government and its public accounting firm.
2. Require that the chief executive and chief financial officer of each government be required to personally sign off on the financial statements.
3. Use of derivatives and all off balance sheet transactions should be clearly outlined in the financial statements and the notes to the statements.
4. The legislative branch of government, such as a city council, town board or county legislature should have at least one designated financial expert to help oversee the financial status of the governmental entity.

Background on the Sarbanes-Oxley Act

The Sarbanes-Oxley Act attempts to change a number of structures and processes that relate to private businesses. The recent corporate scandals involved a large and complex network of organizations that have a role in regulating business in the United States. While the SEC is one of the key governmental organizations, other entities such as the management of private corporations, public accounting firms, internal auditors, the Board of Directors of the companies and the Audit Committee of the Board of Directors all play an important role. The Wall Street investment banking firms and stock research firms are also important. Bond rating firms such as Moody's Investors Service and Standard & Poor's Corporation are also involved.

It appears that many of these organizations contributed in some manner to the corporate scandals. Some firms have been indicted for criminal behavior and others simply mislead investors. Others failed to detect the financial problems on a timely basis. Governments deal with many of the same public accounting firms and bond rating firms and accounting oversight issues are important to governments.

Government accountability can be enhanced by studying the history of the events that led up to the passage of the Sarbanes-Oxley bill and applying the lessons learned to governments. It became obvious in 2001 and 2002 that reform in corporate America was imperative. The new Sarbanes-Oxley Act proposes reform in six areas. First, there will be additional oversight of public accounting firms through the creation of the Public Company Accounting Oversight Board. Second, the act implements procedures at the SEC to ensure that public accounting firms remain independent from the firms they audit. In the past it became clear that many of the public accounting firms designed managerial processes for various corporations and then audited the same processes they designed. It became evident that the use of consulting processes by public accounting firms was problematic. Third, the Sarbanes-Oxley Act requires that corporations become more responsible by requiring that the chief executive officer (CEO) and the chief financial officer (CFO) sign a certification that their financial statements are correct and are not hiding significant negative financial events. The fourth part of the act requires corporations to disclose items such as special purpose entities (SPEs) that are designed to hide off-balance sheet financings. Fifth, the legislation requires securities analysts to separate their stock advisement business from their securities underwriting function. Lastly, the act prescribes a series of civil and criminal penalties for offenders.

Applying the Features of the Sarbanes-Oxley Act to Governments

Many of the problems that the Sarbanes-Oxley Act is trying to correct could apply to governments also. There are at least four areas where governments could benefit by replicating some of the structures and processes implemented for the private sector. Four recommendations are offered below:

1. Governments should use different accounting firms to design managerial control systems and to audit their books.
2. The chief executive and chief financial officer of each government should be required to personally sign off on the financial statements.
3. The use of derivatives and all off-balance sheet transactions should be clearly outlined in the financial statements and the notes to the statements.
4. The legislative branch of government, such as a city council, town board, or county legislature should have at least one designated financial expert to help oversee the financial status of the governmental entity.

Each of the four recommendations is discussed below. The first issue concerns the problem of when a governmental body hires its regular public accounting firm to design a managerial process such as a cash management system. There is a potential issue in that the public accounting firm may have a conflict of interest in auditing a process it designed. The accounting firm may have an interest in overlooking internal control problems if it helped to design the system. This issue was clearly a problem in the corporate scandals and it can be easily avoided in the public sector if governments use different accounting firms to design managerial systems and to conduct year-end audit services.

The second recommendation concerns the requirement that the chief executive officer of any government, as well as the chief financial officer, sign off on all financial statements. In some jurisdictions signatures accompany the financial statements, but the sign-offs should be given greater importance in the governmental model in the same way as now occurs in the private sector model. The financial statements are important since they are used by bond rating firms, investors and others to access the credit quality of individual jurisdictions. While there are not a lot of public scandals now concerning governmental accounting, there were in the past. For instance, after the New York City financial crisis in the 1970s, there was much discussion about the lack of good financial information that was available for governments. Also, the Orange County California derivatives problems in the 1990s indicated that not enough financial information was available. Today, governmental finance is complex. For instance, there are many complex structured financings, such as tobacco related long-term bonds, industrial development authority bonds involving numerous parties and other transactions that can lead to financial problems. To ensure that all governments are held accountable, the chief executives and chief financial officers should be required to sign off on their financial statements by certifying that they are correct in terms of generally accepted accounting principles. This is similar to the process at the SEC in Washington where major corporations must submit such filings. For governments, the filings could be mandated by the chief financial officer in each state.

The third recommendation is that governments should be required to disclose any use of derivatives such as interest rate swaps or other transactions that they may be using. Also, any type of off-balance sheet financial structures should be presented in the notes to the financial statements. These types of transactions should be clearly presented in the footnotes of the Consolidated Annual Financial Report (CAFR). This will enable bond rating firms, investors and others to have a transparent statement of the risk associated with such transactions. The recent history of the corporate scandals in the United States illustrates that many of the problems started off as routine derivative transactions. If the transactions go wrong, they can trigger covenants in bond indentures and other financing agreements that can set off an extreme financial crisis.

The fourth area of government reform concerns oversight by the legislative body of a government. The issue was discussed in the private sector in the Sarbanes-Oxley Act. Private corporations generally have a Board of Directors and a separate Audit Committee of the Board of Directors to oversee various financial matters. Many believe that the corporate scandals would have been avoided or greatly mitigated had the Audit Committee of the Board of Directors performed an adequate job. The Sarbanes-Oxley Act has many reforms that must be implemented for audit committees. Three of the directors on the committee must be independent in that they do not work for the corporation in a role other than being a member of the Board of Directors. The act also requires that at least one member of the audit committee be certified as a "financial expert." This requires that the designated individual have the requisite education and experience as an accountant, senior financial officer or other related position that permit him/her to understand financial and accounting issues.

The aspects of using an audit committee represent a special problem for governments since they are generally run by a chief executive and some type of legislative body. The requirement that someone on the legislative body (such as a city council member or a town board member) have a financial background could easily be adapted to a governmental setting. One position on such bodies could be designated as a financial specialist and the public should vote to ensure that a true financial specialist is voted into such a position.

The Sarbanes-Oxley Act of 2002 is designed to protect investors in the private sector by ensuring that transactions and financial statements are presented to investors in a fair and complete manner. The act will change the manner in which key information is reported, and it will change the roles and responsibilities of many of the men and women working in corporate America and in business oversight roles. There are important parallels to government that we should consider implementing to ensure that scandals do not envelop the public sector as they did in the corporate sector over the past few years. We can draw from the knowledge learned in the corporate scandals to improve the financial integrity of all local governments throughout the United States.

ASPA member Kevin M. Bronner is a professor of public service at the University of Albany. E-mail: krbron@nycap.rr.com

Underestimating Costs in Public Works Projects
Error or Lie?

This article presents results from the first statistically significant study of cost escalation in transportation infrastructure projects. Based on a sample of 258 transportation infrastructure projects worth US$90 billion and representing different project types, geographical regions, and historical periods, it is found with overwhelming statistical significance that the cost estimates used to decide whether such projects should be built are highly and systematically misleading. Underestimation cannot be explained by error and is best explained by strategic misrepresentation, that is, lying. The policy implications are clear: legislators, administrators, investors, medical representatives, and members of the public who value honest numbers should not trust cost estimates and cost-benefit analyses produced by project promoters and their analysts.

Bent Flyvbjerg, Mette Skamris Holm, and Søren Buhl

Comparative studies of actual and estimated costs in transportation infrastructure development are few. Where such studies exist, they are typically single-case studies or they cover a sample of projects too small to allow systematic, statistical analyses (Bruzelius et al., 1998; Fouracre et al., 1990; Hall, 1980; Nijkamp & Ubbels, 1999; Pickrell, 1990; Skamris & Flyvbjerg, 1997; Szyliowicz & Goetz, 1995; Walmsley & Pickett, 1992). To our knowledge, only one study exists that, with a sample of 66 transportation projects, approaches a large-sample study and takes a first step toward valid statistical analysis (Merewitz, 1973a, 1973b).[1] Despite their many merits in other respects, these studies have not produced statistically valid answers regarding the question of whether one can trust the cost estimates used by decision makers and investors in deciding whether or not to build new transportation infrastructure. Because of the small and uneven samples used in existing studies, different studies even point in opposite directions, and researchers consequently disagree regarding the credibility of cost estimates. Pickrell (1990), for instance, concludes that cost estimates are highly inaccurate, with actual costs being typically much higher than estimated costs, while Nijkamp and Ubbels (1999) claim that cost estimates are rather correct. Below we will see who is right.

The objective of the study reported here was to answer the following questions in a statistically valid manner: How common and how large are differences between actual and estimated costs in transportation infrastructure projects? Are the differences significant? Are they simply random errors? Or is there a statistical pattern to the differences that suggests other explanations? What are the implications for policy and decision making regarding transportation infrastructure development?

Four Steps to Understanding Deceptive Cost Estimation

We see four steps in the evolution of a body of scholarly research aimed at understanding practices of cost underestimation and deception in decision making for transportation infrastructure. The first step was taken by Pickrell (1990) and Fouracre, Allport, and Thomson (1990), who provided sound evidence for a small number of urban rail projects that substantial cost underestimation is a problem, and who implied that such underestimation may be caused by deception on the part of project promoters and forecasters. The second step was taken by Wachs (1990), who established—again for a small sample of urban rail projects—that lying, understood as intentional deception, is, in fact, an important cause of cost underestimation. Wachs began the difficult task of charting who does the lying, why it occurs, what the ethical implications are, etc.

The problem with the research in the first two steps is that it is based on too few cases to be statistically significant; the pattern found may be due to random properties of the small samples involved. This problem is solved in the third step, taken with the work reported in this article. Based on a large sample of transportation infrastructure projects, we show that (1) the pattern of cost underestimation uncovered by Pickrell and others is of general import and is statistically significant, and (2) the pattern holds for different project types, different geographical regions, and different historical periods. We also show that the large-sample pattern of cost underestimation uncovered by us lends statistical support to the conclusions about lying and cost underestimation arrived at by Wachs for his small sample.

The fourth and final step in understanding cost underestimation and deception would be to do for a large sample of different transportation infrastructure projects what Wachs did for his small sample of urban rail projects: establish whether systematic deception actually takes place, who does the deception, why it occurs, etc. This may be done by having a large number of forecasters and project promoters, representing a large number of projects, directly express, in interviews or surveys, their intentions with and reasons for underestimating costs. This is a key topic for further research.

In sum, then, we do not claim with this article to have provided final proof that lying is the main cause of cost underestimation in transportation infrastructure projects. We claim, however, to have taken one significant step in a cumulative research process for testing whether this is the case by establishing the best and largest set of data about cost underestimation in transportation infrastructure planning so far seen, by carrying out the first statistically significant study of the issues involved, and by establishing that our data support and give statistical significance to theses about lying developed in other research for smaller, statistically nonsignificant samples.

As part of further developing our understanding of cost underestimation, it would also be interesting to study the differences between projects that are approved on a competitive basis, by voters at an election, and those that are funded through formula-based allocations. One may speculate that there is an obvious incentive to make a project look better, and hence to underestimate costs, in the campaign leading up to an election. A good single-case study of this is Kain's (1990) article about a rail transit project in Dallas. Votes are cast more often for large rail, bridge, and tunnel projects than for road projects. For example, most U.S. highway funds are distributed to states based on a formula (i.e., there is no competitive process). A state department of transportation (DOT) is likely to have a fixed annual budget for construction. The DOT leadership would presumably want fairly accurate cost estimates before allocating the budget. One may speculate that large cost underestimation is less likely in this situation. There are exceptions to this scenario. Sometimes DOT officials want to persuade state legislators to increase their budget. And states occasionally submit bond issue proposals to voters. In Europe, the situation is similar on important points, although differences also exist. This may explain the result found below, that cost underestimation is substantially lower for roads than for rail, bridges, and tunnels, and that this is the case both in the U.S. and Europe. Needless to say, more research is necessary to substantiate this observation.

Finally, we want to emphasize that although the project sample used in this study is the largest of its kind, it is still too small to allow more than a few subdivisions, if comparative statistical analyses must still be possible. Therefore, in further work on understanding cost underestimation, the sample should be enlarged to better represent different types of projects and different geographical locations. As to project types, data for more private projects would be particularly useful in allowing statistically valid comparisons between public and private sector projects. Such comparisons do not exist today, and nobody knows whether private projects perform better or worse than public ones regarding cost underestimation. The sample should also be enlarged to contain data for more fixed-link and rail projects. Such data would allow a better (i.e., a statistically corroborated) comparative understanding of cost underestimation for more specific subtypes of projects such as bridges, tunnels, high-speed rail, urban rail, and conventional rail. Such an understanding is nonexistent today. As to geography, immediate rewards would be gained from data for projects outside Europe and North America, especially for fixed links and roads. But even for Europe and North America, data on more projects are needed to allow better comparative analysis.

Measuring Cost Inaccuracy

The methods used in our study are described in the Appendix. All costs are construction costs. We follow international convention and measure the inaccuracy of cost estimates as so-called "cost escalation" (often also called "cost overrun"; i.e., actual costs minus estimated costs in percent of estimated costs). Actual costs are defined as real, accounted construction costs determined at the time of project completion. Estimated costs are defined as budgeted, or forecasted, construction costs at the time of decision to build. Although the project planning process varies with project type, country, and time, it is typically possible for any given project to identify a specific point in the process as the time of decision to build. Usually a cost estimate was available at this point in time for the decision makers. If not, then the closest available estimate was used, typically a later estimate resulting in a conservative bias in our measure for inaccuracy (see the Appendix). All costs are calculated in fixed prices in Euros by using the appropriate historical, sectoral, and geographical indices for discounting and the appropriate exchange rates for conversion between currencies.

Project promoters and their analysts sometimes object to this way of measuring cost inaccuracy (Flyvbjerg et al., in press). Various cost estimates are made at different stages of the process: project planning, decision to build, tendering, contracting, and later renegotiations. Cost estimates at each successive stage typically progress toward a smaller number of options, greater detail of designs, greater accuracy of quantities, and better information about unit price. Thus, cost estimates become more accurate over time, and the cost estimate at the time of making the decision to build is far from final. It is only to be expected, therefore, that such an early estimate would be highly inaccurate. And this estimate would be unfair as the basis for assessing the accuracy of cost forecasting, or so the objection against using the time-of-decision-to-build estimate goes (Simon, 1991). We defend this method, however, because when the focus is on decision making, and hence on the accuracy of the information available to decision makers, then it is *exactly* the cost estimate at the time of making the decision to build that is of primary interest. Otherwise it would be impossible to evaluate whether decisions are informed or not. Estimates made after the decision to build are by definition irrelevant to this decision. Whatever the reasons are for cost increases after decision makers give the go-ahead to build a project, or however large such increases are, legislators and citizens—or private investors in the case of privately funded projects—are entitled to know the uncertainty of budgets. Otherwise transparency and accountability suffer. We furthermore observe that if the inaccuracy of early cost estimates were simply a matter of incomplete information and inherent difficulties in predicting a distant future, as project promoters often say it is, then we would expect inaccuracies to be random or close to random. Inaccuracies, however, have a striking and highly interesting bias, as we will see below.

Another objection to using cost at the time of decision to build as a basis of comparison is that this supposedly would entail the classical error of comparing apples and oranges. Projects change over the planning and implementation process. When, for instance, the physical configuration of the original Los Angeles Blue Line Light Rail project was altered at substantial cost to comprise grade-crossing improvements, upgrading of adjacent streets, better sidewalks, new fences, etc., the project was no longer the same. It was, instead, a new and safer project, and comparing the costs of this project with the costs of the older, less safe one would supposedly entail the apples-and-oranges error. A problem with this argument is that existing research indicates that project promoters routinely ignore, hide, or otherwise leave out important project costs and risks in order to make total costs appear low (Flyvbjerg et al., in press; Wachs, 1989, 1990). For instance, environmental and safety concerns may initially be ignored, even though they will have to be taken into account later in the project cycle if the project lives on, and the project is more likely to live on if environmental and safety concerns are initially ignored. Similarly, ignoring or underplaying geological risks may be helpful in getting projects approved, and no other risk is more likely to boomerang back and haunt projects during construction. "Salami tactics" is the popular name used to describe the practice of introducing project components and risks one slice at a time in order to make costs appear low as long as possible. If such tactics are indeed a main mechanism in cost underestimation, as existing research indicates, then, clearly, comparing actual project costs with estimated costs at the time of decision to build does not entail the error of comparing apples and oranges but is simply a way of tracking how what was said to be a small, inexpensive apple turned out to actually be a big, expensive one.

Finally, we observe that if we were to follow the objections against using the cost estimate at the time of decision to build as the basis of tracking cost escalation, it would be impossible to make meaningful comparisons of costs because no common standard of comparison would be available. We also observe that this method is the international standard for measuring inaccuracy of cost estimates (Fouracre et al., 1990; Leavitt et al., 1993; National Audit Office & Department of Transport, 1992; Nijkamp & Ubbels, 1999; Pickrell, 1990; Walmsley & Pickett, 1992; World Bank, 1994). This standard conveniently allows meaningful and consistent comparisons within individual projects and across projects, project types, and geographical areas. This standard, then, is employed below to measure the inaccuracy of cost estimates in 258 transportation infrastructure projects worth US$90 billion.

Inaccuracy of Cost Estimates

Figure 1 shows a histogram with the distribution of inaccuracies of cost estimates. If errors in estimating costs were small, the histogram would be narrowly concentrated around zero. If errors in overestimating costs were of the same size and frequency as errors in underestimating costs, the histogram would be symmetrically distributed around zero. Neither is the case. We make the following observations regarding the distribution of inaccuracies of construction cost estimates:

- Costs are underestimated in almost 9 out of 10 projects. For a randomly selected project, the likelihood of actual costs being larger than esti-

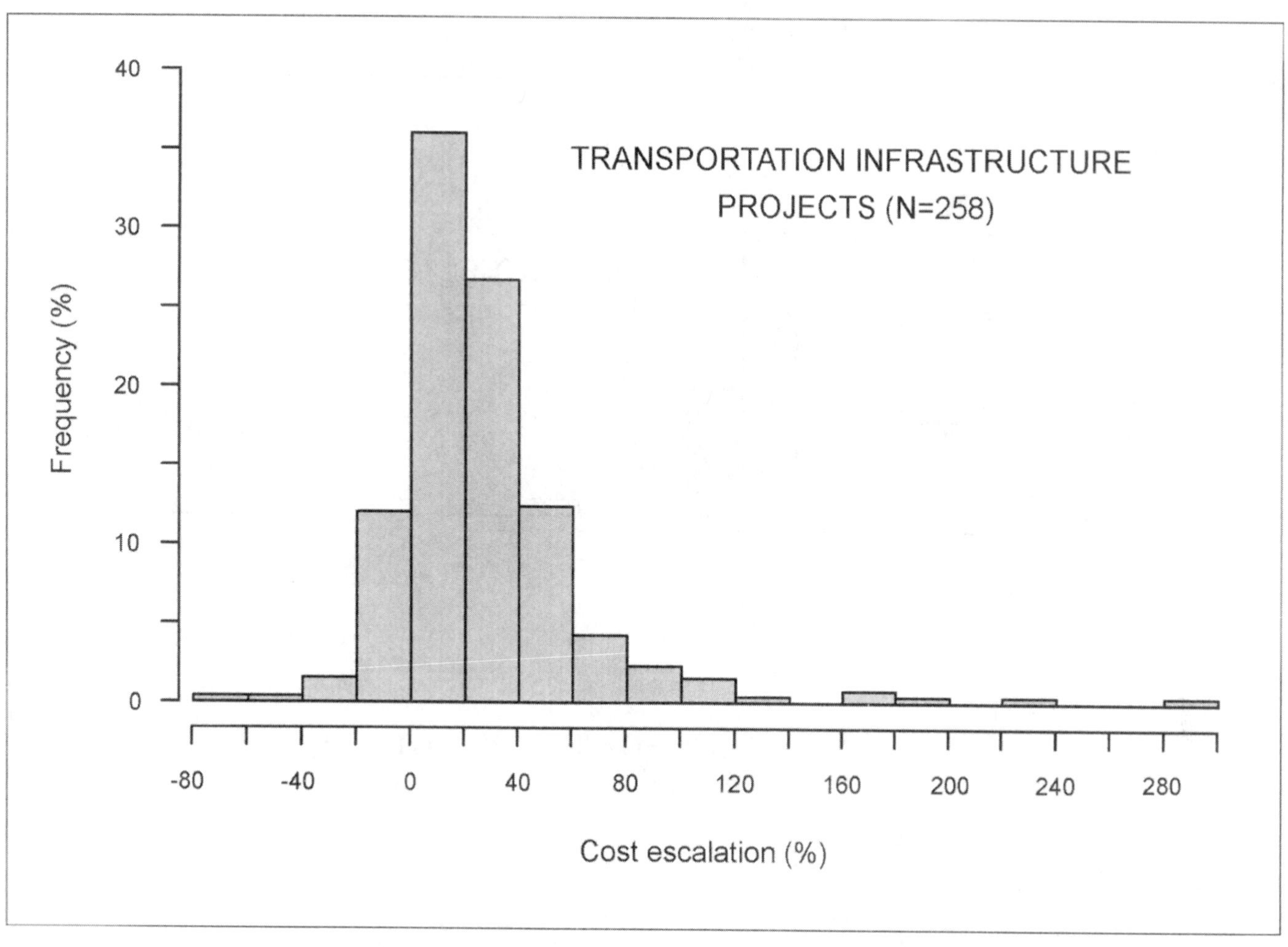

FIGURE 1. Inaccuracy of cost estimates in 258 transportation infrastructure projects (fixed prices).

TABLE 1. Inaccuracy of transportation project cost estimates by type of project (fixed prices).

Project type	Number of cases (N)	Average cost escalation (%)	Standard deviation	Level of significance (p)
Rail	58	44.7	38.4	<0.001
Fixed-link	33	33.8	62.4	0.004
Road	167	20.4	29.9	<0.001
All projects	258	27.6	38.7	<0.001

mated costs is 86%. The likelihood of actual costs being lower than or equal to estimated costs is 14%.

- Actual costs are on average 28% higher than estimated costs (s d = 39).
- We reject with overwhelming significance the thesis that the error of overestimating costs is as common as the error of underestimating costs (p<0.001; two-sided test, using the binomial distribution). Estimated costs are biased, and the bias is caused by systematic underestimation.
- We reject with overwhelming significance the thesis that the numerical size of the error of underestimating costs is the same as the numerical size of the error of overestimating costs (p<0.001; nonparametric Mann-Whitney test). Costs are not only underestimated much more often than they are overestimated or correct, costs that have been underestimated are also wrong by a substantially larger margin than costs that have been overestimated.

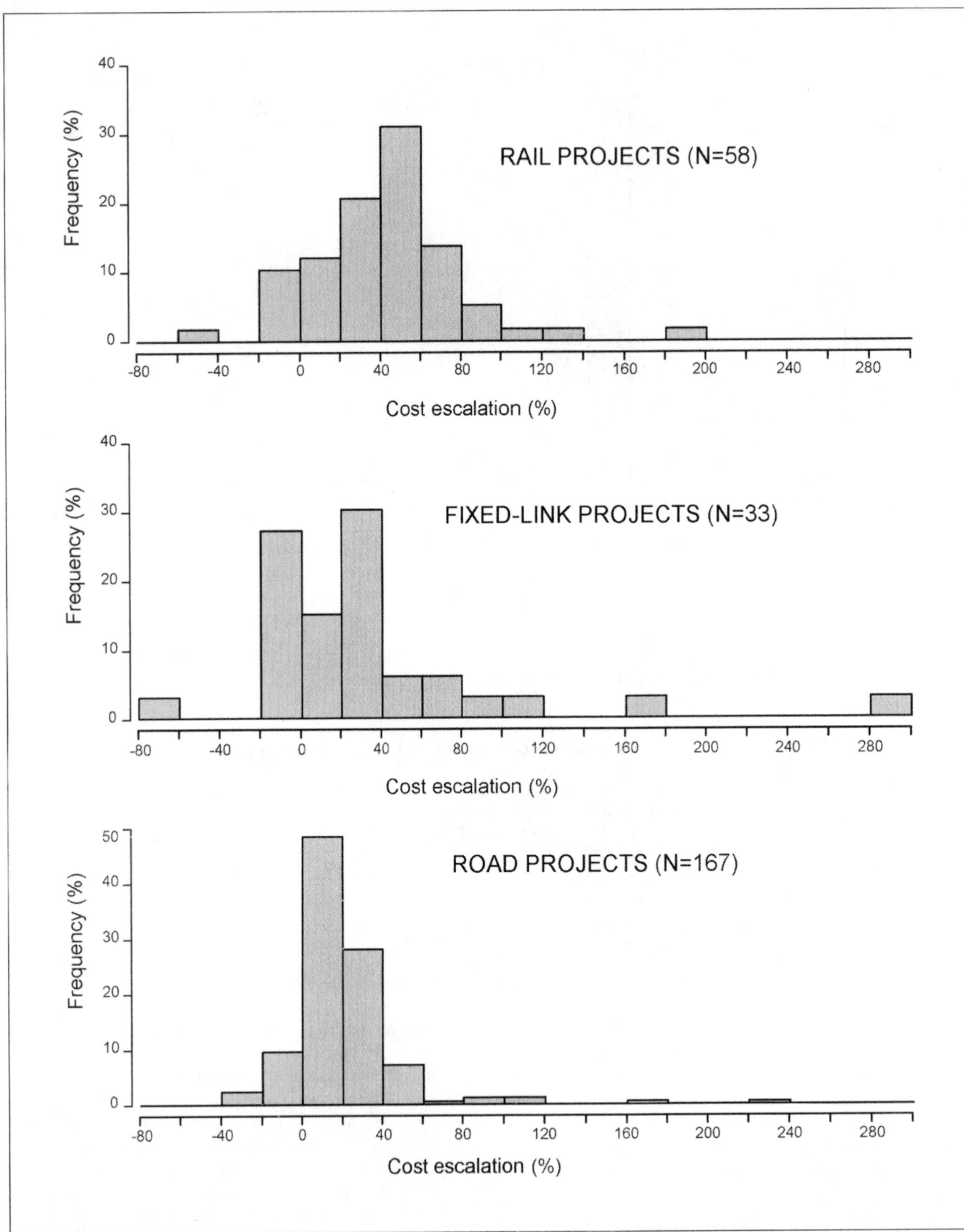

FIGURE 2. Inaccuracy of cost estimates in rail, fixed-link, and road projects (fixed prices).

We conclude that the error of underestimating costs is significantly much more common and much larger than the error of overestimating costs. Underestimation of costs at the time of decision to build is the rule rather than the exception for transportation infrastructure projects. Frequent and substantial cost escalation is the result.

Cost Underestimation by Project Type

In this section, we discuss whether different types of projects perform differently with respect to cost underestimation. (Figure 2 shows histograms with inaccuracies of cost estimates for each of the following project types: (1) rail (high-speed; urban; and conventional, inter-city rail), (2) fixed link (bridges and tunnels), and (3) road (highways and freeways.) Table 1 shows the expected (average) inaccuracy and standard deviation for each type of project.

Statistical analyses of the data in Table 1 show both means and standard deviations to be different with a high level of significance. Rail projects incur the highest difference between actual and estimated costs, with an average of no less than 44.7%, followed by fixed-link projects averaging 33.8% and roads at 20.4%. An F-test falsifies the null hypothesis at a very high level of statistical significance that type of project has no effect on percentage cost escalation ($p<0.001$). Project type matters. The substantial and significant differences among project types indicate that pooling the three types of projects in statistical analyses, as we did above, is strictly not appropriate. Therefore, in the analyses that follow, each type of project will be considered separately.

Based on the available evidence, we conclude that rail promoters appear to be particularly prone to cost underestimation, followed by promoters of fixed-link projects. Promoters of road projects appear to be relatively less inclined to underestimate costs, although actual costs are higher than estimated costs much more often than not for road projects as well.

Further subdivisions of the sample indicate that high-speed rail tops the list of cost underestimation, followed by urban and conventional rail, in that order. Similarly, cost underestimation appears to be larger for tunnels than for bridges. These results suggest that the complexities of technology and geology might have an effect on cost underestimation. These results are not statistically significant, however. Even if the sample is the largest of its kind, it is too small to allow repeated subdivisions and still produce significant results. This problem can be solved only by further data collection from more projects.

We conclude that the question of whether there are significant differences in the practice of cost underestimation among rail, fixed-link, and road projects must be answered in the affirmative. The average difference between actual and estimated costs for rail projects is substantially and significantly higher than that for roads, with fixed-link projects in a statistically nonsignificant middle position. The average inaccuracy for rail projects is more than twice that for roads, resulting in average cost escalations for rail more than double that for roads. For all three project types, the evidence shows that it is sound advice for policy and decision makers as well as investors, bankers, media, and the public to take any estimate of construction costs with a grain of salt, especially for rail and fixed-link projects.

Cost Underestimation by Geographical Location

In addition to testing whether cost underestimation differs for different kinds of projects, we also tested whether it varies with geographical location among Europe, North America, and "other geographical areas" (a group of 10 developing nations plus Japan). Table 2 shows the differences between actual and estimated costs in these three areas for rail, fixed-link, and road projects. There is no indication of statistical interaction between geographical area and type of project. We therefore consider the effects from these variables on cost underestimation separately. For all projects, we find that the difference between geographical areas in terms of underestimation is highly significant ($p<0.001$). Geography matters to cost underestimation.

TABLE 2. Inaccuracy of transportation project cost estimates by geographical location (fixed prices).

	Europe			North America			Other geographical areas		
Project type	Number of projects (N)	Average cost escalation (%)	Standard deviation	Number of projects (N)	Average cost escalation (%)	Standard deviation	Number of projects (N)	Average cost escalation (%)	Standard deviation
Rail	23	34.2	25.1	19	40.8	36.8	16	64.6	49.5
Fixed-link	15	43.4	52.0	18	25.7	70.5	0	--	--
Road	143	22.4	24.9	24	8.4	49.4	0	--	--
All projects	181	25.7	28.7	61	23.6	54.2	16	64.6	49.5

If Europe and North America are compared separately, which is compulsory for fixed links and roads because no observations exist for these projects in other geographical areas, comparisons can be made by t-tests (as the standard deviations are rather different, the Welch version is used). For fixed-link projects, the average difference between actual and estimated costs is 43.4% in Europe versus 25.7% North America, but the difference between the two geographical areas is nonsignificant (p = 0.414). Given the limited number of observations and the large standard deviations for fixed link projects, we would need to enlarge the sample with more fixed-link projects in Europe and North America in order to test whether the differences might be significant for more observations. For rail projects, the average difference between actual and estimated costs is 34.2% in Europe versus 40.8% in North America. For road projects, the similar numbers are 22.4% versus 8.4%. Again, the differences between geographical areas are nonsignificant (p = 0.510 and p = 0.184, respectively).

We conclude, accordingly, that the highly significant differences we found above for geographical location come from projects in the "other geographical areas" category. The average difference between actual and estimated costs in this category is a hefty 64.6%.

Have Estimates Improved Over Time?

In the previous two sections, we saw how cost underestimation varies with project type and geography. In this section, we conclude the statistical analyses by studying how underestimation has varied over time. We ask and answer the question of whether project promoters and forecasters have become more or less inclined over time to underestimate the costs of transportation infrastructure projects. If underestimation were unintentional and related to lack of experience or faulty methods in estimating and forecasting costs, then, a priori, we would expect underestimation to decrease over time as better methods were developed and more experience gained through the planning and implementation of more infrastructure projects.

Figure 3 shows a plot of the differences between actual and estimated costs against year of decision to build for the 111 projects in the sample for which these data are available. The diagram does not seem to indicate an effect from time on cost underestimation. Statistical analyses corroborate this impression. The null hypothesis that year of decision has no effect on the difference between actual and estimated costs cannot be rejected (p = 0.22, F-test). A test using year of completion instead of year of decision (with data for 246 projects) gives a similar result (p = 0.28, F-test).

We therefore conclude that cost underestimation has not decreased over time. Underestimation today is in the same order of magnitude as it was 10, 30, and 70 years ago. If techniques and skills for estimating and forecasting costs of transportation infrastructure projects have improved over time, this does not show in the data. No learning seems to take place in this important and highly costly sector of public and private decision making. This seems strange and invites speculation that the persistent existence over time, location, and project type of significant and widespread cost underestimation is a sign that an equilibrium has been reached: Strong incentives and weak disincentives for underestimation may have taught project promoters what there is to learn, namely, that cost underestimation pays off. If this is the case, underestimation must be expected and it must be expected to be intentional. We examine such speculation below. Before doing so, we compare cost underestimation in transportation projects with that in other projects.

Cost Underestimation in Other Infrastructure Projects

In addition to cost data for transportation infrastructure projects, we have reviewed cost data for several hundred other projects including power plants, dams, water distribution, oil and gas extraction, information technology systems, aerospace systems, and weapons systems (Arditi et al., 1985; Blake et al., 1976; Canaday, 1980; Department of Energy Study Group, 1975; Dlakwa & Culpin, 1990; Fraser, 1990; Hall, 1980; Healey, 1964; Henderson, 1977; Hufschmidt & Gerin, 1970; Merewitz, 1973b; Merrow, 1988; Morris & Hough, 1987; World Bank, 1994, n.d.). The data indicate that other types of projects are at least as, if not more, prone to cost underestimation as are transportation infrastructure projects.

Among the more spectacular examples of cost underestimation are the Sydney Opera House, with actual costs approximately 15 times higher than those projected, and the Concorde supersonic airplane, with a cost 12 times higher than predicted (Hall, n.d., p.3). The data also indicate that cost underestimations for other projects have neither increased nor decreased historically, and that underestimation is common in both First- and Third-World countries. When the Suez canal was completed in 1869, actual constructing costs were 20 times higher than the earliest estimated costs and 3 times higher than the cost estimate for the year before construction began. The Panama Canal, which was completed in 1914, had cost escalations in the range of 70 to 200% (Summers, 1967, p. 148).

In sum, the phenomena of cost underestimation come in four types: technical, economic, psychological, and political. In this section, we examine which explanations best fit our data.

Explanations of Underestimation: Error or Lie?

Explanations of cost underestimation come in four types: technical, economic, psychological, and political.

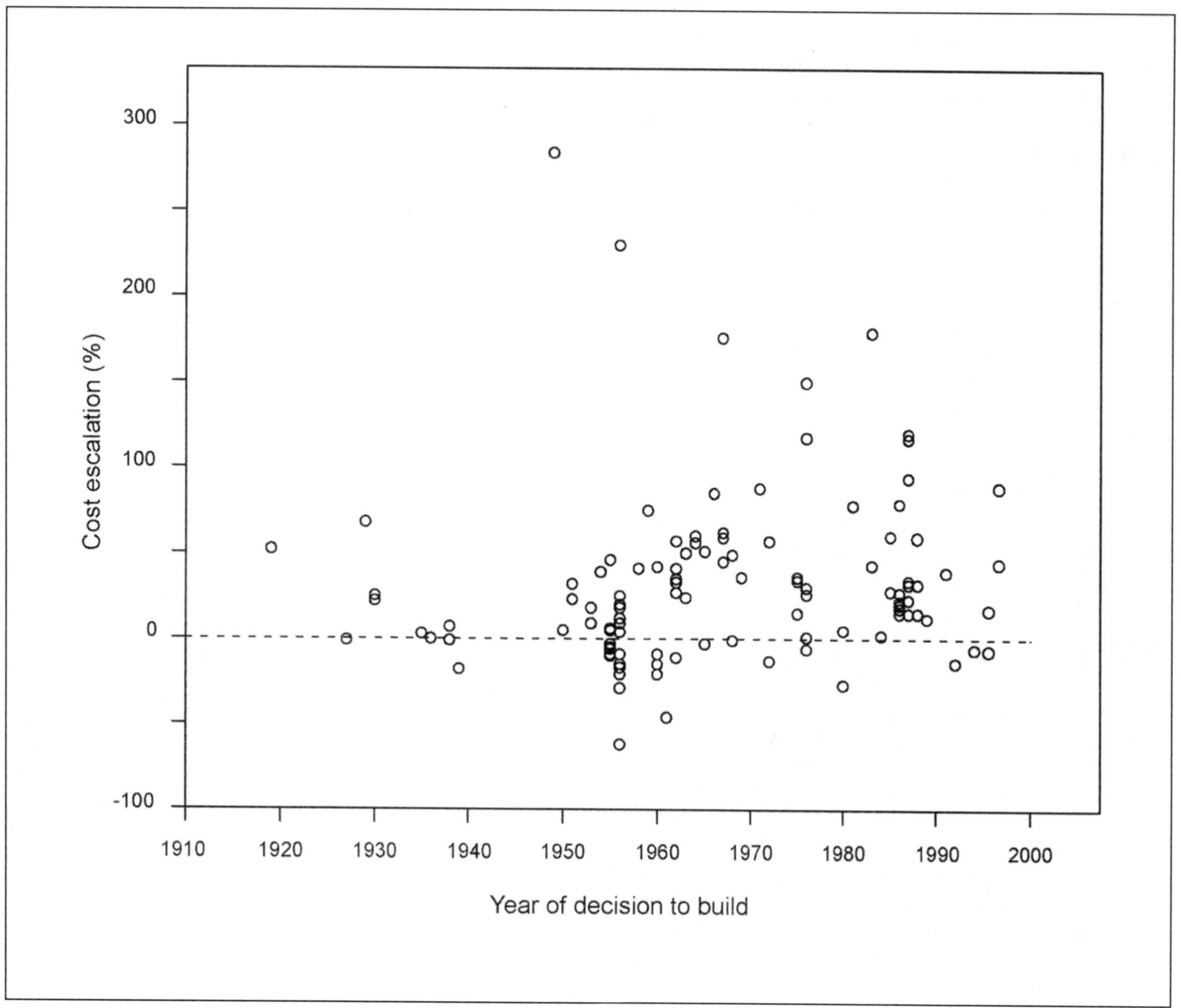

FIGURE 3. Inaccuracy of cost estimates in transportation projects over time, 1910–1998 (fixed prices, 111 projects).

In this section, we examine which explanations best fit our data.

Technical Explanation

Most studies that compare actual and estimated costs of infrastructure projects explain what they call "forecasting errors" in technical terms, such as imperfect techniques, inadequate data, honest mistakes, inherent problems in predicting the future, lack of experience on the part of forecasters, etc. (Ascher, 1978; Flyvbjerg et al., in press; Morris & Hough, 1987; Wachs, 1990). Few would dispute that such factors may be important sources of uncertainty and may result in misleading forecasts. And for small-sample studies, which are typical of this research field, technical explanations have gained credence because samples have been too small to allow tests by statistical methods. However, the data and tests presented above, which come from the first large-sample study in the field, lead us to reject technical explanations of forecasting errors. Such explanations simply do not fit the data.

First, if misleading forecasts were truly caused by technical inadequacies, simple mistakes, and inherent problems with predicting the future, we would expect a less biased distribution of errors in cost estimates around zero. In fact, we have found with overwhelming statistical significance ($p<0.001$) that the distribution of such errors has a nonzero mean. Second, if imperfect techniques, inadequate data, and lack of experience were main explanations of the underestimations, we would expect an improvement in forecasting accuracy over time, since errors and their sources would be recognized and addressed through the refinement of data collection, forecasting methods, etc. Substantial resources have been spent over several decades on improving data and methods. Still our data show that this has had no effect on the accuracy of forecasts. Technical factors, therefore, do not appear to explain the data. It is not so-called forecasting "errors" or cost "escalation" or their causes that need explaining. It is the fact that in 9 out of 10 cases, costs are underestimated.

We may agree with proponents of technical explanations that it is, for example, impossible to predict for the individual project exactly *which* geological, environmental, or safety problems will appear and make costs soar. But we maintain that it is possible to predict the risk, based on experience from other projects, *that* some such problems will haunt a project and how this will affect costs. We also maintain that such risks can and should be accounted for in forecasts of costs, but typically is not. For technical explanations to be valid, they would have to explain why forecasts are so consistent in ignoring cost risks over time, location, and project type.

Economic Explanations

Economic explanations conceive of cost underestimation in terms of economic rationality. Two types of economic explanation exist; one explains in terms of economic self-interest, the other in terms of the public interest. As regards self-interest, when a project goes forward, it creates work for engineers and construction firms, and many stakeholders make money. If these stakeholders are involved in or indirectly influence the forecasting process, then this may influence outcomes in ways that make it more likely that the project will be built. Having costs underestimated and benefits overestimated would be economically rational for such stakeholders because it would increase the likelihood of revenues and profits. Economic self-interest also exists at the level of cities and states. Here, too, it may explain cost underestimation. Pickrell (1990, 1992) pointed out that transit capital investment projects in the U.S. compete for discretionary grants from a limited federal budget each year. This creates an incentive for cities to make their projects look better, or else some other city may get the money.

As regards the public interest, project promoters and forecasters may deliberately underestimate costs in order to provide public officials with an incentive to cut costs and there by to save the public's money. According to this type of explanation, higher cost estimates would be an incentive for wasteful contractors to spend more of the taxpayer's money. Empirical studies have identified promoters and forecasters who say they underestimate costs in this manner and with this purpose (i.e., to save public money; Wachs, 1990). The argument has also been adopted by scholars, for instance Merewitz (1973b), who explicitly concludes that "keeping costs low is more important than estimating costs correctly" (p. 280).

Both types of economic explanation account well for the systematic underestimation of costs found in our data. Both depict such underestimation as deliberate, and as economically rational. If we now define a lie in the conventional fashion as making a statement intended to deceive others (Bok, 1979, p. 14; Cliffe et al., 2000, p. 3), we see that deliberate cost underestimation is lying, and we arrive at one of the most basic explanations of lying, and of cost underestimation, that exists: Lying pays off, or at least economic agents believe it does. Moreover, if such lying is done for the public good (e.g., to save taxpayers' money), political theory would classify it in that special category of lying called the "noble lie," the lie motivated by altruism. According to Bok (1979), this is the "most dangerous body of deceit of all" (p. 175).

In the case of cost underestimation in public works projects, proponents of the noble lie overlook an important fact: Their core argument—that taxpayers' money is saved by cost underestimation—is seriously flawed. Anyone with even the slightest trust in cost-benefit analysis and welfare economics must reject this argument. Underestimating the costs of a given project leads to a falsely high benefit-cost ratio for that project, which in turn leads to two problems. First, the project may be started despite the fact that it is not economically viable. Or, second, it may be started instead of another project that would have yielded higher returns had the actual costs of both projects been known. Both cases result in the inefficient use of resources and therefore in waste of taxpayers' money. Thus, for reasons of economic efficiency alone, the argument that cost underestimation saves money must be rejected; underestimation is more likely to result in waste of taxpayers' money. But the argument must also be rejected for ethical and legal reasons. In most democracies, for project promoters and forecasters to deliberately misinform legislators, administrators, bankers, the public, and the media would not only be considered unethical but in some instances also illegal, for instance where civil servants would misinform cabinet members or cabinet members would misinform the parliament. There is a formal "obligation to truth" built into most democratic constitutions on this point. This obligation would be violated by deliberate underestimation of costs, whatever the reasons may be. Hence, even though economic explanations fit the data and help us understand important aspects of cost underestimation, such explanations cannot be used to justify it.

Psychological Explanations

Psychological explanations attempt to explain biases in forecasts by a bias in the mental makeup of project promoters and forecasters. Politicians may have a "monument complex," engineers like to build things, and local transportation officials sometimes have the mentality of empire builders. The most common psychological explanation is probably "appraisal optimism." According to this explanation, promoters and forecasters are held to be overly optimistic about project outcomes in the appraisal phase, when projects are planned and decided (Fouracre et al., 1990, p. 10; Mackie & Preston, 1998; Walmsley & Pickett, 1992, p. 11; World Bank, 1994, p. 86). An optimistic cost estimate is clearly a low one. The existence of appraisal optimism in promoters and forecasters would result in actual costs being higher than estimated costs. Consequently, the existence of appraisal optimism would be able to account, in whole or in part, for the peculiar bias of cost estimates found in our data, where costs are systematically underestimated. Such optimism, and associated cost underestimation, would not be lying, needless to say, because the deception involved is self-deception and therefore not deliberate. Cost underestimation would be error according to this explanation.

There is a problem with psychological explanations, however. Appraisal optimism would be an important and credible explanation of underestimated costs if estimates were produced by inexperienced promoters and forecasters, i.e., persons who were estimating costs for the first or second time and who were thus unknowing about the realities of infrastructure building and were not drawing on the knowledge and skills of more experienced colleagues. Such situations may exist and may explain individual cases of cost underestimation. But given the fact that the human psyche is distinguished by a significant ability to learn from experience, it seems unlikely that promoters and forecasters would continue to make the same mistakes decade after decade instead of learning from their actions. It seems even more unlikely that a whole profession of forecasters and promoters would collectively be subject to such a bias and would not learn over time. Learning would result in the reduction, if not elimination, of appraisal optimism, which would then result in cost estimates becoming more accurate over time. But our data clearly shows that this has not happened.

The profession of forecasters would indeed have to be an optimistic group to keep their appraisal optimism throughout the 70-year period our study covers and not learn that they were deceiving themselves and others by underestimating costs. This would account for the data, but is not a credible explanation. As observed elsewhere, the incentive to publish and justify optimistic estimates is very strong, and the penalties for having been overoptimistic are generally insignificant (Davidson & Huot, 1989, p. 137; Flyvbjerg et al., in press). This is a better explanation of the pervasive existence of optimistic estimates than an inherent bias for optimism in the psyche of promoters and forecasters. And "optimism" calculated on the basis of incentives is not optimism, of course; it is deliberate deception. Therefore, on the basis of our data, we reject appraisal optimism as a primary cause of cost underestimation.

Political Explanations

Political explanations construe cost underestimation in terms of interests and power (Flyvbjerg, 1998). Surprisingly little work has been done that explains the pattern of misleading forecasts in such terms (Wachs, 1990, p. 145). A key question for political explanations is whether forecasts are intentionally biased to serve the interests of project promoters in getting projects started. This question again raises the difficult issue of lying. Questions of lying are notoriously hard to answer, because in order to establish whether lying has taken place, one must know the intentions of actors. For legal, economic, moral, and other reasons, if promoters and forecasters have intentionally fabricated a deceptive cost estimate for a project to get it started, they are unlikely to tell researchers or others that this is the case (Flyvbjerg, 1996; Wachs, 1989).

When Eurotunnel, the private company that owns the tunnel under the English Channel, went public in 1987 to raise funds for the project, investors were told that building the tunnel would be relatively straightforward. Regarding risks of cost escalation, the prospectus read:

> Whilst the undertaking of a tunneling project of this nature necessarily involves certain construction risks, the techniques to be used are well proven.... The Directors, having consulted the Mâitre d'Oeuvre, believe that 10%... would be a reasonable allowance for the possible impact of unforeseen circumstances on construction costs.[2] ("Under Water," 1989, p. 37)

Two hundred banks communicated these figures for cost and risk to investors, including a large number of small investors. As observed by *The Economist* ("Under Water," 1989,) anyone persuaded in this way to buy shares in Eurotunnel in the belief that the cost estimate was the mean of possible outcomes was, in effect, deceived. The cost estimate of the prospectus was a best possible outcome, and the deception consisted in making investors believe in the highly unlikely assumption—disproved in one major construction project after another—that everything would go according to plan, with no delays; no changes in safety and environmental performance specifications; no management problems; no problems with contractual arrangements, new technologies, or geology; no major conflicts; no political promises not kept; etc. The assumptions were, in other words, those of an ideal world. The real risks of cost escalation for the Channel tunnel were many times higher than those communicated to potential investors, as evidenced by the fact that once built, the real costs of the project were higher by a factor of two compared with forecasts.

Flyvbjerg, Bruzelius, and Rothengatter (in press) document for a large number of projects that the Everything-Goes-According-to-Plan type of deception used for the Channel tunnel is common. Such deception is, in fact, so widespread that in a report on infrastructure and development, the World Bank (1994, pp. ii, 22) found reason to coin a special term for it: the "EGAP-principle." Cost estimation following the EGAP-principle simply disregards the risk of cost escalation resulting from delays, accidents, project changes, etc. This is major problem in project development and appraisal, according to the World Bank.

It is one thing, however, to point out that investors, public or private, were deceived in particular cases. It is quite another to get those involved in the deceptions to talk about this and to possibly admit that deception was intentional, i.e., that it was lying. We are aware of only one study that actually succeeded in getting those involved in underestimating costs to talk about such issues (Wachs, 1986, 1989, 1990). Wachs interviewed public officials, consultants, and planners who had been involved in transit planning cases in the U.S. He found that a pattern of highly misleading forecasts of costs and patronage could not be explained by technical issues and were best explained by lying. In case after case, planners, engineers, and economists told Wachs that they had had to "cook" forecasts in order to produce numbers that would satisfy their superiors and get projects started, whether or not the numbers could be justified on technical grounds (Wachs, 1990, p. 144). One typical planner admitted that he had repeatedly adjusted the cost figures for a certain project downward and the patronage figures upward to satisfy a local elected official who wanted to maximize the chances of getting the project in question started. Wachs' work is unusually penetrating for a work on forecasting. But again, it is small-sample research, and Wachs acknowledges that most of his evidence is circumstantial (Wachs, 1986, p. 28). The evidence does not allow conclusions regarding the project population. Nevertheless, based on the strong pattern of misrepresentation and lying found in his case studies, Wachs goes on to hypothesize that the type of abuse he has uncovered is "nearly universal" (1990, p. 146; 1986, p. 28) and that it takes place not only in transit planning but also in other sectors of the economy where forecasting routinely plays an important role in policy debates.

Our data give support to Wachs' claim. The pattern of highly underestimated costs is found not only in the small sample of projects Wachs studied; the pattern is statistically significant and holds for the project population mean (i.e., for the majority of transportation infrastructure projects). However, on one point, Wachs (1986) seems to draw a conclusion somewhat stronger than is warranted. "[F]orecasted costs always seem to be *lower* than actual costs" (p. 24) he says (emphasis in original). Our data show that although "always" (100%) may cover the small sample of projects Wachs chose to study, when the sample is enlarged by a factor of 20–30 to a more representative one, "only" in 86% of all cases are forecasted costs lower than actual costs. Such trifles—14 percentage points—apart, the pattern identified by Wachs is a general one, and his explanation of cost underestimation in terms of lying to get projects started fit our data particularly well. Of the existing explanations of cost development in transportation infrastructure projects, we therefore opt for political and economic explanations. The use of deception and lying as tactics in power struggles aimed at getting projects started and at making a profit appear to best explain why costs are highly and systematically underestimated in transportation infrastructure projects.

Summary and Conclusions

The main findings from the study reported in this article—all highly significant and most likely conservative—are as follows:

- In 9 out of 10 transportation infrastructure projects, costs are underestimated.
- For rail projects, actual costs are on average 45% higher than estimated costs (sd = 38).
- For fixed-link projects (tunnels and bridges), actual costs are on average 34% higher than estimated costs (sd = 62).
- For road projects, actual costs are on average 20% higher than estimate costs (sd = 30).
- For all project types, actual costs are on average 28% higher than estimated costs (sd = 39).
- Cost underestimation exists across 20 nations and 5 continents; it appears to be a global phenomenon.
- Cost underestimation appears to be more pronounced in developing nations than in North America and Europe (data for rail projects only).
- Cost underestimation has not decreased over the past 70 years. No learning that would improve cost estimate accuracy seems to take place.
- Cost underestimation cannot be explained by error and seems to be best explained by strategic misrepresentation, i.e., lying.
- Transportation infrastructure projects do not appear to be more prone to cost underestimation than other types of large projects.

We conclude that the cost estimates used in public debates, media coverage, and decision making for transportation infrastructure development are highly, systematically, and significantly deceptive. So are the cost-benefit analyses into which cost estimates are routinely fed to calculate the viability and ranking of projects. The misrepresentation of costs is likely to lead to the misallocation of scarce resources, which, in turn, will produce losers among those financing and using infrastructure, be they taxpayers or private investors.

We emphasize that these conclusions should not be interpreted as an attack on public (vs. private) spending on infrastructure, since the data are insufficient to decide whether private projects perform better or worse than public ones regarding cost underestimation. Nor do the conclusions warrant an attack on spending on transportation vs. spending on other projects, since other projects appear to be as liable to cost underestimation and escalation as are transportation projects. With transportation projects as an in-depth case study, the conclusions simply establish that significant cost underestimation is a widespread practice in project development and implementation, and that this practice forms a substantial barrier to the effective allocation of scarce resources for building important infrastructure.

The key policy implication for this consequential and highly expensive field of public policy is that those legislators, administrators, bankers, media representatives, and members of the public who value honest numbers should not trust the cost estimates presented by infrastructure promoters and forecasters. Another important implication is that institutional checks and balances—including financial, professional, or even criminal penalties for consistent or foreseeable estimation errors—should be developed to ensure the production of less deceptive cost estimates. The work of designing such checks and balances has been begun elsewhere, with a focus on four basic instruments of accountability: (1) increased transparency, (2) the use of performance specifications, (3) explicit formulation of the regulatory regimes that apply to project development and implementation, and (4) the involvement of private risk capital, even in public projects (Bruzelius et al., 1998; Flyvbjerg et al., in press).

ACKNOWLEDGMENTS

The authors wish to thank Martin Wachs, Don Pickrell, and three anonymous *JAPA* referees for valuable comments on an earlier draft of the article. Research for the article was supported by the Danish Transport Council and Aalborg University, Denmark.

NOTES

1. Merewitz's (1973a, 1973b) study compared cost overrun in urban rapid transit projects, especially the San Francisco Bay Area Rapid Transit (BART) system, with overrun in other types of public works projects. Merewitz's aims were thus different from ours, and his sample of transportation projects was substantially smaller: 17 rapid transit projects and 49 highway projects, compared with our 58 rail projects, 167 highway projects, and 33 bridge or tunnel projects. In addition to issues of a small sample, in our attempt to replicate Merewitz's analysis we found that his handling of data raises a number of other issues. First, Merewitz did not correct his cost data for inflation, i.e., current prices were used instead of fixed ones. This is known to be a major source of error due to varying inflation rates between projects and varying duration of construction periods. Second, in statistical tests, Merewitz compared the mean cost overrun of subgroups of projects (e.g., rapid transit) with the grand mean of overrun for all projects, thus making the error of comparing projects with themselves. Subgroups should be tested directly against other subgroups in deciding whether they differ at all and, if so, which ones differ. Third, Merewitz's two reports (1973a, 1973b) are inconsistent. One (1973a) calculates the grand mean of cost overrun as the average of means for subgroups; that is, the grand mean is unweighted, where common practice is to use the weighted mean, as appears to be the approach taken in the other (1973b). Fourth, due to insufficient information, the p-values calculated by Merewitz are difficult to verify; most likely they are flawed, however, and Merewitz's one-sided p-values are misleading. Finally, Merewitz used a debatable assumption about symmetry, which has more impact for the nonparametric test used than nonnormality has for parametric methods. Despite these shortcomings, the approach taken in Merewitz's study was innovative for its time and in principle pointed in the right direction regarding how to analyze cost escalation in public works projects. The study cannot be said to be a true large-sample study for transportation infrastructure, however, and its statistical significance is unclear.
2. The Mâitre d'Oeuvre was an organization established to monitor project planning and implementation for the Channel tunnel. It was established in 1985, and until 1988 it represented the owners. In 1988 it was reverted to an impartial position (Major Projects Association, 1994, pp. 151–153).

REFERENCES

Arditi, D., Akan, G. T., & Gurdamar, S. (1985). Cost overruns in public projects. *International Journal of Project Management, 3*(4), 218–225.

Ascher, W. (1978). *Forecasting: An appraisal for policy-makers and planners.* Baltimore: Johns Hopkins University Press.

Blake, C., Cox, D., & Fraize, W. (1976). *Analysis of projected vs. actual costs for nuclear and coal-fired power plants* (Report prepared for the United States Energy Research and Development Administration). McLean, VA: Mitre Corporation.

Bok, S. (1979). *Lying: Moral choice in public and private life.* New York: Vintage.

Bruzelius, N., Flyvbjerg, B., & Rothengatter, W. (1998). Big decisions, big risks: Improving accountability in mega projects. *International Review of Administrative Sciences, 64* (3), 423–440.

Canaday, H. T. (1980). *Construction cost overruns in electric utilities: Some trends and implications* (Occasional Paper No. 3). Columbus: National Regulatory Research Institute, Ohio State University.

Cliffe, L., Ramsey, M., & Bartlett, D. (2000). *The politics of lying: Implications for democracy.* London: Macmillan.

Commission of the European Union. (1993). *Growth, competitiveness, employment: The challenges and ways forward into the 21st century* (White Paper). Brussels: Author.

Davidson, F. P., & Huot, J.-C. (1989). Management trends for major projects. *Project Appraisal, 4* (3), 133–142.

Department of Energy Study Group. (1975). *North Sea costs escalation study* (Energy Paper No. 8). London: Department of Energy.

Dlakwa, M. M., & Culpin, M. F. (1990). Reasons for overrun in public sector construction projects in Nigeria. *International Journal of Project Management, 8* (4), 237–240.

Flyvbjerg, B. (1996). The dark side of planning: Rationality and *Realrationalität.* In S. Mandelbaum, L. Mazza, & R. Burchell (Eds.), *Explorations in planning theory* (pp. 383–394). New Brunswick, NJ: Center for Urban Policy Research Press.

Flyvbjerg, B. (1998). *Rationality and power: Democracy in practice.* Chicago: University of Chicago Press.

Flyvbjerg, B., Bruzelius, N., & Rothengatter, W. (in press). *Megaprojects and risk: An anatomy of ambition.* Cambridge, UK: Cambridge University Press.

Fouracre, P. R., Allport, R. J., & Thomson, J. M. (1990). *The performance and impact of rail mass transit in developing countries* (TRRL Research Report 278). Crowthorne, UK: Transport and Road Research Laboratory.

Fraser, R. M. (1990). Compensation for extra preliminary and general (P & G) costs arising from delays, variations and disruptions: The palmiet pumped storage scheme. *Tunneling and Underground Space Technology, 5* (3), 205–216.

Hall, P. (1980). *Great planning disasters.* Harmondsworth, UK: Penguin Books.

Hall, P. (n.d.). Great planning disasters revisited. Unpublished manuscript, Bartlett School, University College, London.

Healey, J. M. (1964). Errors in project cost estimates. *Indian Economic Journal, 12* (1), 44–52.

Henderson, P. D. (1977). Two British errors: Their probable size and some possible lessons. *Oxford Economic Papers, 29* (2), 159–205.

Holm, M. K. S. (1999). *Inaccuracy of traffic forecasts and cost estimates in Swedish road and rail projects.* Unpublished manuscript, Aalborg University, Department of Development and Planning.

Hufschmidt, M. M., & Gerin, J. (1970). Systematic errors in cost estimates for public investment projects. In J. Margolis (Ed.), *The analysis of public output* (pp. 267–315). New York: Columbia University Press.

Kain, J. F. (1990). Deception in Dallas: Strategic misrepresentation in rail transit promotion and evaluation. *Journal of the American Planning Association, 56* (2), 184–196.

Leavitt, D., Ennis, S., & McGovern, P. (1993). *The cost escalation of rail projects: Using previous experience to re-evaluate the calspeed estimates* (Working Paper No. 567). Berkeley: Institute of Urban and Regional Development, University of California.

Lewis, H. (1986). *The metro report: The impact of metro and public transport integration in Tyne and Wear.* Newcastle, UK: Tyne and Wear Passenger Transport Executive.

Mackie, P., & Preston, J. (1998). Twenty-one sources of error and bias in transport project appraisal. *Transport Policy, 5* (1), 1–7.

Major Projects Association. (1994). *Beyond 2000: A source book for major projects.* Oxford, UK: Author.

Merewitz, L. (1973a). *How do urban rapid transit projects compare in cost estimate experience?* (Reprint No. 104). Berkeley: Institute of Urban and Regional Development, University of California.

Merewitz, L. (1973b). Cost overruns in public works. In W. Niskanen, A. C. Hansen, R. H. Havemann, R. Turvey, & R. Zeckhauser (Eds.), *Benefit cost and policy analysis* (pp. 277–295). Chicago: Aldine.

Merrow, E. W. (1988). *Understanding the outcomes for megaprojects: A quantitative analysis of very large civilian projects.* Santa Monica, CA: RAND Corporation.

Morris, P. W. G., & Hough, G. H. (1987). *The anatomy of major projects: A study of the reality of project management.* New York: John Wiley and Sons.

National Audit Office, Department of Transport. (1985). *Expenditure on motorways and trunk roads.* London: National Audit Office.

National Audit Office, Department of Transport. (1992). *Contracting for roads.* London: National Audit Office.

National Audit Office, Department of Transport; Scottish Development Department; & Welsh Office. (1988). *Road planning.* London: Her Majesty's Stationary Office.

Nijkamp, P., & Ubbels, B. (1999). How reliable are estimates of infrastructure costs? A comparative analysis. *International Journal of Transport Economics, 26* (1), 23–53.

Pickrell, D. H. (1990). *Urban rail transit projects: Forecast versus actual ridership and cost.* Washington, DC: U.S. Department of Transportation.

Pickrell, D. H. (1992). A desire named streetcar: Fantasy and fact in rail transit planning. *Journal of the American Planning Association, 58* (2), 158–176.

Riksrevisionsverket. (1994). *Infrastrukturinvesteringar: En kostnadsjäörelse mellan plan och utfall i 15 större projekt inom Vägverket och Banverket.* Stockholm: Author.

Simon, J. (1991). Let's make forecast and actual comparisons fair. *TR News, 156,* 6–9.

Skamris, M. K., & Flyvbjerg, B. (1997). Inaccuracy of traffic forecasts and cost estimates on large transport projects. *Transport Policy, 4* (3), 141–146.

Summers, R. (1967). Cost estimates as predictors of actual costs: A statistical study of military developments. In T. Marschak, T. K. Glennan, & R. Summers (Eds), *Strategy for R&D: Studies in the microeconomics of development* (pp. 140–189). Berlin: Springer-Verlag.

Szyliowicz, J. S., & Goetz, A. R. (1995). Getting realistic about megaproject planning: The case of the new Denver International Airport. *Policy Sciences, 28* (4), 347–367.

Under water, over budget. (1989, October 7). *The Economist,* pp. 37–38.

Vejdirektoratet. (1995). *Notat om anlægsregnskaber.* Copenhagen: Danish Road Directorate.

Wachs, M. (1986). Technique vs. advocacy in forecasting: A study of rail rapid transit. *Urban Resources, 4* (1), 23–30.

Wachs, M. (1989). When planners lie with numbers. *Journal of the American Planning Association, 55* (4), 476–479.

Wachs, M. (1990). Ethics and advocacy in forecasting for public policy. *Business and Professional Ethics Journal, 9* (1–2), 141–157.

Walmsley, D. A., & Pickett, M. W. (1992). *The cost and patronage of rapid transit systems compared with forecasts* (Research Report 352). Crowthorne, UK: Transport Research Laboratory.

World Bank. (1994). *World development report 1994: Infrastructure for development.* Oxford, UK: Oxford University Press.

World Bank, (n.d.). *Economic analysis of projects: Towards a results-oriented approach to evaluation* (ECON Report). Washington, DC: Author.

APPENDIX

The first task of the research reported in this paper was to establish a sample of infrastructure projects substantially larger than what is common in this area of research, a sample large enough to allow statistical analyses of costs. Here a first problem was that data on actual costs in transportation infrastructure projects are relatively difficult to come by. One reason is that it is quite time consuming to produce such data. For public sector projects, funding and accounting procedures are typically unfit for keeping track of the multiple and complex changes that occur in total project costs over time. For large projects, the relevant time frame may cover 5, 10, or more fiscal years from decision to build, until construction starts, until the project is completed and operations begin. Reconstructing the actual total costs of a public project, therefore, typically entails long and difficult archival work and complex accounting. For private projects, even if funding and accounting practices may be more conducive to producing data on actual total costs, such data are often classified to keep them from the hands of competitors. Unfortunately, this also tends to keep data from the hands of scholars. And for both public and private projects, data on actual costs may be held back by project owners because more often than not, actual costs reveal substantial cost escalation, and cost escalation is normally considered somewhat of an embarrassment to promoters and owners. In sum, establishing reliable data on actual costs for even a single transportation infrastructure project is often highly time consuming or simply impossible.

This state of affairs explains why small-sample studies dominate scholarship in this field of research. But despite the problems mentioned, after 4 years of data collection and refinement, we were able to establish a sample of 258 transportation infrastructure projects with data on both actual construction costs and estimated costs at the time of decision to build. The project portfolio is worth approximately US$90 billion (1995 prices). The project types are bridges, tunnels, highways, freeways, high-speed rail, urban rail, and conventional (interurban) rail. The projects are located in 20 countries on 5 continents, including both developed and developing nations. The projects were completed between 1927 and 1998. Older projects were included in the sample in order to test whether the accuracy of estimated costs improved over time. The construction costs of projects range from US$1.5 million to US$8.5 billion (1995 prices), with the smallest projects typically being stretches of roads in larger road schemes, and the largest projects being rail links, tunnels, and bridges. As far as we know, this is the largest sample of projects with data on cost development that has been established in this field of research.

In statistical analysis, data should be a sample from a larger population, and the sample should represent the population properly. These requirements are ideally satisfied by drawing the sample by randomized lot. Randomization ensures with high probability that factors that cannot be controlled are equalized. A sample should also be designed such that the representation of subgroups corresponds to their occurrence and importance in the population. In studies of human affairs, however, where controlled laboratory experiments often cannot be conducted, it is frequently impossible to meet these ideal conditions. This is also the case for the current study, and we therefore had to take a different approach to sampling and statistical analysis.

We selected the projects for the sample on the basis of data availability. All projects that we knew of for which data on construction cost development were obtainable were considered for inclusion in the sample. Cost development is defined as the difference between actual and estimated costs in percentage of estimated costs, with all costs measured in fixed prices. Actual costs are defined as real, accounted costs determined at the time of completing a project. Estimated costs are defined as budgeted, or forecasted, costs at the time of decision to build. Even if the project planning process varies with project type, country, and time, it is typically possible to locate for any given project a specific point in the process that can be identified as the time of decision to build. Usually a cost estimate was available for this point in time. If not, the closest available estimate was used, typically a later estimate resulting in a conservative bias in our measurement of cost development. Cost data were collected from a variety of sources, including annual project accounts, questionnaires, interviews, and other studies.

Data on cost development were available for 343 projects. We then rejected 85 projects because of insufficient data quality. For instance, for some projects we could not obtain a clear answer regarding what was included in costs, or whether cost data were given in current or fixed prices, or which price level (year) had been used in estimating and discounting costs. More specifically, of those 85 projects, we rejected 27 because we could not establish whether or not cost data were valid and reliable. We rejected 12 projects because they had been completed before 1915 and no reliable indices were available for discounting costs to the present. Finally, we excluded 46 projects because cost development for them turned out to have been calculated before construction was completed and operations begun; therefore, the actual final costs for these projects may be different from the cost estimates used to calculate cost development, and no information was available on actual final costs. In addition to the 85 rejected projects mentioned here, we also rejected a number of projects to avoid double counting of projects. This typically involved projects from other studies that appeared in more than one study or where we had a strong suspicion that this might be the case. In sum, all projects for which data were considered valid and reliable were included in the sample. This covers both projects for which we ourselves collected the data and projects for which other researchers in other studies did the data collection (Fouracre et al., 1990; Hall, 1980; Leavitt et al., 1993; Lewis, 1986; Merewitz, 1973a; National Audit Office, Department of Transport, 1985, 1992; National Audit Office, Department of Transport, 1985, 1992; National Audit Office, Department of Transport, Scottish

Development Department, & Welsh Office, 1988; Pickrell, 1990; Riksrevisionsverket, 1994; Vejdirektoratet, 1995; Walmsley & Pickett, 1992). Cost data were made comparable across projects by discounting prices to the 1995 level and calculating them in Euros, using the appropriate geographical, sectoral, and historical indices for discounting and the appropriate exchange rates for conversion between currencies.

Our own data collection concentrated on large European projects because too few data existed for this type of project to allow comparative studies. For instance, for projects with actual construction costs larger than 500 million Euros (1995 prices; EUR1 = US$1.29 in 1995), we were initially able to identify from other studies only two European projects for which data were available on both actual and estimated costs. If we lowered the project size and looked at projects larger than 100 million Euros, we were able to identify such data for eight European projects. We saw the lack of reliable cost data for European projects as particularly problematic since the Commission of the European Union had just launched its policy for establishing the so-called trans-European transport networks, which would involve the construction of a large number of major transportation infrastructure projects across Europe at an initial cost of 220 billion Euros (Commission of the European Union, 1993, p. 75). As regards costs, we concluded that the knowledge base for the Commission's policy was less than well developed, and we hoped to help remedy this situation through our data collection. Our efforts on this point proved successful. We collected primary data on cost for 37 projects in Denmark, France, Germany, Sweden, and the U.K. and were thus able to greatly increase the number of large European projects with reliable data for both actual and estimated costs, allowing for the first time a comparative study for this type of project in which statistical methods could be applied.

As for any sample, a key question is whether the sample is representative of the population. Here the question is whether the projects included in the sample are representative of the population of transportation infrastructure projects. Since the criterion for sampling was data availability, this question translates into one of whether projects with available data are representative. There are four reasons why this is probably not the case. First, it may be speculated that projects that are managed well with respect to data availability may also be managed well in other respects, resulting in better than average (i.e., nonrepresentative) performance for such projects. Second, it has been argued that the very existence of data that make the evaluation of performance possible may contribute to improved performance when such data are used by project management to monitor projects (World Bank, 1994, p. 17). Again, such projects would not be representative of the project population. Third, we might speculate that managers of projects with a particularly bad track record regarding cost escalation have an interest in not making cost data available, which would then result in underrepresentation of such projects in the sample. Conversely, managers of projects with a good track record for costs might be interested in making this public, resulting in overrepresentation of these projects. Fourth, and finally, even where managers have made cost data available, they may have chosen to give out data that present their projects in as favorable a light as possible. Often there are several estimates of costs to choose from and several calculations of actual costs for a given project at a given time. If researchers collect data by means of survey questionnaires, as is often the case, there might be a temptation for managers to choose the combination of actual and estimated costs that suits them best, possibly a combination that makes their projects look good.

The available data do not allow an exact, empirical assessment of the magnitude of the problem of misrepresentation. But the few data that exist that shed light on this problem support the thesis that data are biased. When we compared data from the Swedish Auditor General for a subsample of road projects, for which the problems of misrepresentation did not seem to be an issue, with data for all road projects, for which the problems of misrepresentation did not seem to be an issue, with data for all road projects in our sample, we found that cost escalation in the Swedish subsample is significantly higher than for all projects (Holm, 1999, pp. 11–15). We conclude, for the reasons given above, that most likely the sample is biased and the bias is conservative. In other words, the difference between actual and estimated costs derived from the sample is likely to be lower than the difference in the project population. This should be kept in mind when interpreting the results from statistical analyses of the sample. The sample is not perfect by any means. Still it is the best obtainable sample given the current state of the art in this field of research.

In the statistical analyses, percentage cost development in the sample is considered normally distributed unless otherwise stated. Residual plots, not shown here, indicate that normal distribution might not be completely satisfied, the distributions being somewhat skewed with larger upper tails. However, transformations (e.g., the logarithmic one) do not improve this significantly. For simplicity, therefore, no transformation has been made, unless otherwise stated.

The subdivisions of the sample implemented as part of analyses entail methodological problems of their own. Thus the representation of observations in different combinations of subgroups is quite skewed for the data considered. The analysis would be improved considerably if the representation were more even. Partial and complete confounding occur; that is, if a combination of two or more effects is significant, it is sometimes difficult to decide whether one, the other, or both cause the difference. For interactions, often not all the combinations are represented, or the representations can be quite scarce. We have adapted our interpretations of the data to these limitations, needless to say. If better data could be gathered, sharper conclusions could be made.

The statistical models used are linear normal models (i.e., analysis of variance and regression analysis with the appropriate F-tests and t-tests). The tests of hypotheses concerning mean values are known to be robust to deviations from normality. Also, chi-square tests for independence have been used for count data. For each test, the p-value has been reported. This value is a measure for rareness if identity of groups is assumed. Traditionally, a p-value less than 0.01 is considered highly significant and less than 0.05 significant, whereas a large p-value means that the deviation could be due to chance.

Flyvbjerg is a professor of planning with the Department of Development and Planning, Aalborg University, Denmark. He is founder and director of the university's research program on transportation infrastructure planning and was twice a Visiting Fulbright Scholar to the U.S. His latest books are *Rationality and Power* (University of Chicago Press, 1998) and *Making Social Science Matter* (Cambridge University Press, 2001). He is currently working on a book about megaprojects and risk (Cambridge University Press). **Holm** is an assistant professor of planning with the Department of Development and Planning, Aalborg University, and a research associate with the university's research program on transportation infrastructure planning. Her main interest is economic appraisal of projects. **Buhl** is an associate professor with the Department of Mathematics, Aalborg University, and an associate statistician with the university's research program on transportation infrastructure planning.

From *Journal of the American Planning Association,* Vol. 68, No. 3, Summer 2002, pp. 279-295.

Roadblocks in Reforming Corrupt Agencies: The Case of The New York City School Custodians

Reformers have traditionally assumed that agencies can combat corruption through controls such as tighter oversight, increased regulation, internal audits, reorganizations, and performance accountability mechanisms. But this case study of the New York City school custodial system shows how a corrupt agency can derail these devices. New York City's $500,000,000 custodial system, responsible for maintaining its 1,200 schools, has been unleashing scandals since the 1920s despite decades of regulations, multiple reorganizations, and layers of oversight. Its history shows that a deviant culture—a management "captured" by special interests—and an infrastructure enmeshed in abusive policies will resist controls, no matter how well-crafted. True reform requires tackling institutionalized corruption through strategies like overhauling management, eradicating special interests, and aggressively punishing misconduct.

Lydia Segal
John Jay College

Introduction

This article examines one of the most perplexing problems in public administration today—how to reform chronically corrupt agencies. It highlights the roadblocks that can derail traditional control and redress devices through a case study of the New York City school custodial system, a deeply corrupt system that has resisted decades of reform efforts.

Much of the scholarship on organizational corruption—or systemic wrongdoing by employees who violate society's norms with the support of their organization's internal norms (Ermann and Lundman 1982)—assumes that corruption can be reduced through accountability devices such as oversight, surveillance, audits, performance evaluations, sanctions and structural reorganizations (Sherman 1978; Susan Rose-Ackerman 1993; Maynard-Moody, Stull, and Mitchell 1986). The conventional belief is that, if adequate controls exist, managers will enforce them and subordinates will follow them (Gardiner and Lyman 1993; Ward and McCormack 1987). That is why so much of the debate in the literature revolves around issues such as the types of audits needed to achieve different levels of fiscal accountability (Sheldon 1996), the deterrent value of criminal and civil sanctions (Walt and Laufer 1992; Coffee 1980), and the role of inspectors general (Gates and Moore 1986). If scandals continue despite these reforms, experts usually recommend tightening existing controls (Anechiarico and Jacobs 1996; Segal 1999).

But corruption may not result merely because an organization's internal accountability mechanisms are not tight or numerous enough. The history of the New York City custodial system, the subdivision of the city's board of education (BOE) that is responsible for cleaning and maintaining its 1,200 schools, shows that the assumptions underlying traditional corruption controls do not allow for organizations whose cultures are so deviant and whose missions have been so twisted that managers can barely recognize conduct that is deviant and employees regard wrongdoing as their right.

In the custodial system, exposés dating to 1924 paint a picture of "custodians," or school superintendents, who control thousands of dollars in building maintenance budgets and employ dozens of "helpers" such as cleaners and handymen, systematically transforming their schools into enterprises for bribery, extortion, theft, and nepotism. (BOE 1924; *People v. Cappeta* 86 A.D.2D 876, 447 N.Y.S.2d 293 [1982]; SCI 1992). With little accountability and broad discretion over budgets and staff, custodians gave family and lovers no-show jobs as helpers and handed them thousands of dollars in fraudulent overtime. They used school maintenance budgets to renovate their homes.

They extorted kickbacks from emergency contractors (*People v. John Manfredi* 166 A.D.2d 460, 560 N.Y.S.2d 679[1990]). A number did not even maintain a presence at their schools, pursuing second jobs instead. Meanwhile, supervisors turned a blind eye to custodians' abuses and sometimes shared in the kickbacks from contractors.

Repeated scandals put pressure on top officials at the BOE and the Division of School Facilities (DSF), the BOE subdivision responsible for overseeing the system's 1,000 custodians, to try traditional internal corruption controls, including stripping custodians of discretion, tightening central oversight, and auditing custodians' financial records (BOE 1977a; NYC Comptroller 1989). But most of these initiatives turned to dust in the custodial system's daily operation as managers failed to enforce them, custodians and their supervisors refused to follow the rules, and incentives for corruption remained embedded in the agency infrastructure.

In 1993, in the wake of a highly publicized investigation, the state passed a law changing custodians' incentives. It stripped them of some of their civil service protections and tried to make them accountable for performance to principals. But scandals persisted because the law did not change the culture or fix the broken DSF bureaucracy that was supposed to oversee custodians.

The case of the New York City custodians challenges the commonly held assumption that when an agency repeatedly proves unable to police itself, *external* agents (such as prosecutors) will clean it up. The custodial system shows how a corrupt agency can escape such controls by, among other things, sanitizing wrongdoing through collective bargaining.

The custodial system's ability to elude internal and external controls is intriguing in light of how destructive corruption has been to the agency's core mission. Unlike some forms of corruption such as police perjury, which arguably further the agency's mission, custodial misconduct directly undercuts its central purpose: to maintain a clean, safe learning environment. As custodians diverted resources, children sat in filthy classrooms surrounded by peeling paint, falling plaster, and broken windows (BOE 1911/13; SCI 1992, 20–21). Water dripped on their desks from holes in the ceilings; rodents sometimes ran over their feet (NYC 1949, 159–249; Advocates 1999). Nails stuck out of floors; wires hung from walls (Willen 1993). As one commission put it, schools were "more suitable to prisoners than academics" (Levy 1995, 5). Sometimes these conditions even became dangerous: A toppling cinderblock killed one girl, leaky furnaces sickened dozens of pupils (Kolbert 1998).

The reform pitfalls highlighted in this case study are not unique. Many agencies, from hospitals to police departments, and many of the country's large public school custodial systems, from Chicago to Detroit to Los Angeles, face patterns of ingrained wrongdoing that have not responded to traditional corruption redress devices. As experts in these agencies grapple with how to reduce fraud, they should consider the lessons of the New York City custodian case. This article examines the types of controls tried in the custodial system, the reasons they failed, and the broader implications for corruption reform around the nation.

Research Methods

Research for this article was based on extensive examination of more than 30 reports issued by government and not-for-profit entities, hundreds of newspaper articles, and Freedom of Information Law requests. The government documents studied include city and state audits, grand jury reports, reports issued by city and state investigative offices and legislative committees, and transcripts of conversations that government informants secretly recorded with custodians for investigators.

The research was also based on a number of interviews with top- and mid-level managers at the DSF and the BOE, principals, auditors, investigators and city officials. Many interviewees requested confidentiality. All corroborated various aspects of published findings. A number said the reports described only a fraction of existing abuses.

Lastly, this article was informed by firsthand observations in my capacity as special counsel for the Special Commissioner of Investigation (SCI) for the New York City School District, where I led numerous investigations into corruption for three years and conducted many interviews with witnesses and informants at all levels of the school system.

The New York City Custodial System: A Recipe for Abuse

The Custodial System until the Passage of the 1993 State Law

With an annual budget of a half a billion dollars and a workforce of 8,500 employees, including 1,000 custodians, 6,500 helpers, 1,025 skilled trade mechanics, and 450 administrators, New York City's custodial system is the biggest, most expensive school cleaning enterprise in the nation, offering multiple incentives and opportunities for wrongdoing (Hay Group 1990). Much of the money flowing through the system is susceptible to theft. Since the BOE began hiring custodians in 1856, it has maximized their discretion to enable them to respond quickly and with minimal red tape. Accordingly, it established a managerial system known as the "indirect system," which granted custodians broad professional deference with little supervision (BOE 1977a).

Under this system, each custodian controlled his own annual school maintenance budget, which today ranges from $80,000 to over $1.2 million, depending on the school's size. Custodians were expected to use the money to buy supplies and to hire helpers, such as firemen who operate heating systems, handymen who perform repairs, watchmen who provide security, and cleaners. Custodians had discretion to pay helpers as much overtime as their budgets afforded (BOE 1977a, 63–64). They also negotiated wage and fringe benefits with their helpers' unions.

Although the BOE's budget allocation formula assumed that the bigger a custodian's school, the more helpers and supplies he would need, custodians did not have to hire a particular number of helpers or buy a particular amount of supplies. So long as they complied with the BOE's cleaning standards, how they spent their money was up to them (NYS Comptroller 1977a). But BOE cleaning standards, a bare-bones list of custodians' minimal duties, granted them total latitude in deciding how hard to work beyond the mandated minimum. In effect, the only way the BOE could know where custodians' money went was by auditing their expenditures after the fact (Lonergan 1998a, 26).

Custodians were also expected to pay themselves a salary from whatever was left over in their budgets after cleaning and maintenance expenses (*Beck v. NYC BOE* 52 N.Y.S.2d 712 [1945]). Administrators hoped that allowing custodians to determine their earnings would encourage them be frugal and efficient. They reasoned that custodians would not waste money because, the more they wasted, the more they would have to spend to clean their schools, which would mean they would have less for their salaries (NYS Comptroller 1977a, 28). Since 1964, when a scandal revealed that custodians earned more than most U.S. governors and mayors (Michalak 1964), the BOE has imposed caps on custodians' salaries (BOE 1977). The size of a custodian's cap was proportional to the size of his budget. Custodians were required to return any balance remaining above their caps at the end of the year to the BOE.

Flawed Accountability Mechanisms

Giving custodians broad discretion may have made sense when the BOE first hired them in 1856 because they lived in schools and had incentives to care for their buildings as they would their own homes (Lonergan 1998a). But once custodians moved out around 1900, their incentives became similar to those of independent contractors, who also control funds, hire their own workers, and buy supplies. But while contractors—like many regular government employees—are held in check by performance accountability and bureaucratic oversight (Romzek and Dubnick 1987; Light 1993), constraints on custodians were nonexistent or too flawed to be meaningful.

Bureaucratic Oversight and Work Standards. In the case of independent contractors, supervisors see that they comply with standards that ensure satisfactory service. But in the custodial system, oversight mechanisms did not ensure compliance, and BOE standards did not guarantee clean or well-maintained buildings, even if custodians followed them to the letter.

One reason was that the standards, known as "work rules," describe custodians' minimal tasks and serve as guides to inspire them to do more work (BOE 1903). While work rules have been minimal since the BOE first started issuing them in 1903, they have become increasingly so since the 1960s, as the BOE pared them down further and further in successive collective bargaining sessions with the custodian union, Local 891 of the International Union of Operating Engineers. Work rules issued in the 1970s and 1980s, for instance, required custodians to scrub toilets and mop cafeteria floors no more than once a week (BOE 1977b, §IV) and sweep classrooms only every other day (MOU 1987).

Adding to the inadequacy of the work rules, custodians used them, not as an inspiration to work harder, as administrators had hoped, but as an excuse to do no more than the mandated minimum (NYS Comptroller 1977a, 79 ff). So if a child threw up in the bathroom on a day when toilets were not due to be scrubbed, or spilled food in the lunchroom when it was not due to be mopped, custodians did not see this as their problem. Indeed, Local 891 would threaten custodians who volunteered to do more than was in the work rules. Its position was that, if the BOE wanted more, it would have to pay for it (SCI 1992, 64–65).

At the same time, the BOE's mechanisms for ensuring that custodians complied with work rules were marred in several respects. First, conflicts of interest between custodians and their immediate supervisors, known as "plant managers," compromised oversight. Plant managers were supposed to inspect custodians regularly and evaluate them annually (MOU 1987, §8). But until 1993, plant managers belonged to the same local as custodians and had "friendships and loyalties" to them (SCI 1992, 10). As a result, they rarely inspected custodians and gave them excellent ratings even when they were absent, engaged in fraud, or their schools were filthy (SCI 1992, 11–15, 77, 88).

Second, DSF, which was supposed to oversee custodians and plant managers, was too big and too removed from schools to supervise effectively. DSF's 450 administrators were headquartered in two high-rise office buildings in Queens, far from many city schools. Moreover, as civil servants not promoted on the basis of schools' physical condition, they had little incentive to ensure custodians were performing well (Lonergan 1999).

Needless to say, DSF rarely responded to complaints about custodians. Unless a problem was an emergency, had the potential to attract negative press, or was brought to top management's attention by prominent individuals with political clout, managers were unlikely to learn about it (Maire 1991). In one school, for instance, parents repeatedly complained to DSF for six months that their children were feeling faint because the school had no ventilation and that they could not use bathrooms because toilet bowls were missing. Until parents contacted their city councilman, who called the director of DSF to arrange a public meeting with reporters, DSF did not respond.

Internal Surveillance. The BOE also had no reliable machinery to police custodians for fraud and abuse. Although it had in-house investigators, exposés showed they were so dependent on BOE management for their jobs and raises, that, to avoid embarrassing their bosses, they usually swept findings under the carpet (JCI 1990; SCI 1999b).

The BOE also had in-house auditors, but they did not aggressively ferret out fraud either. Although they audited each custodian yearly, their audits were "compliance" audits not "fraud" audits (SCI 1999a). While fraud audits require auditors to visit schools to verify whether signatures on receipts are genuine and items were delivered, compliance audits merely require auditors to check paperwork to see that the proper forms were filed and signed in a timely manner (Lonergan 1998a, 56–57). Since fraud audits were rare, custodians knew they could usually avoid detection for fraud by supplying auditors with phony canceled checks and receipts (SCI 1992).

Moreover, unless auditors found evidence of theft that could be proved beyond a reasonable doubt in court, the BOE did not punish custodians whose money was missing (SCI 1999a). It simply required them to pay the money back without interest—in effect, rewarding sloppy and possibly crooked custodians with interest-free loans (SCI 1992).

Performance Accountability. Unlike independent contractors, who are held in check by the risk of being fired for poor performance, custodians faced no such risk. Until 1993, custodians enjoyed full civil service protection, making it practically impossible to fire them for abuse. In one case, the BOE fired a custodian who regularly locked teachers out of school. But after four years of administrative proceedings, the court held that the BOE had to hire him back because it had not documented its case for a long enough period (18 months) under state civil service laws (OATH 1995/96).

Second, custodians were not truly accountable to "customers," or those who *used* schools, such as students and principals. Regarding pupils, there was no formal mechanism to solicit their views on custodians (Fager 1994). As for principals, although the BOE had methods to solicit their views, it was widely understood to be "a waste of time" for them to state them (Daley 1988).

First, although principals could evaluate custodians once a year, until 1993, their input in these evaluations was limited. Principals could rate custodians only either satisfactory or unsatisfactory on *one* question—the custodian's "cooperation with principal"—out of many questions on the evaluation (SCI 1992, 10). All other questions were completed by the custodian's plant manager, whose objectivity was questionable. Therefore, a custodian could easily get high marks even if his principal thought he was unscrupulous (BOE 1977, 26–27).

Second, evaluations had no impact on what mattered most to custodians—their ability to transfer to schools with bigger budgets where they could earn higher salaries. Seniority, not merit, counted for this (SCI 1992).

But principals' evaluations were meaningless for yet another reason: Most principals were terrified of what they dubbed custodians' "reigns of terror" (SCI 1992, 21). If a principal became at all troublesome, the custodian could "fix" her in various ways. He could, for example, turn off the heat or hot water (22), lock auditoriums and bathrooms when after-school concerts were scheduled (30), leave school when a flood broke out, or tear down instructional materials that teachers had spent hours designing (30, 39). Some custodians even intimidated their principals physically. In one school, for instance, the custodian had his boiler operator curse at the principal and block her path whenever she walked through the halls (22–23). The upshot was that most principals gave their custodians the highest ratings regardless of performance.

Political Accountability. Finally, custodians and their higher-ups at DSF were not politically accountable to voters in significant ways. The executive director of DSF reported to the BOE chancellor, who answered to a seven-member central board of education in charge of the entire city school system. But the members of this board were appointed by so many politicians with different constituencies that voters could not realistically hold any single board member or politician responsible for school problems (Ravitch 1974). Each of the city's five elected borough presidents appointed one member to the board, while the mayor appointed the remaining two members. If voters were unhappy with the condition of the schools in their borough, they could not expect to have much impact by refusing to re-elect the mayor or their borough president, because neither politician decisively controlled the board.

The Ensuing Corruption and Abuse

With so little accountability, a number of custodians used their freedom from red tape, not to improve efficiency, as reformers had hoped, but to profiteer. Instead of paying themselves a salary from what was left over after cleaning expenses, they pocketed the maximum permitted under their salary caps (FOIL 1999) and found myriad ways to enrich themselves from whatever remained in their budgets.

Until 1992, for instance, custodians could pocket money directly from their budgets because it was legal to commingle funds from their school accounts with their personal accounts (SCI 1992).

Custodians also diverted resources by using their staff to work on personal projects. One custodian had his helpers renovate his home, boat, deck and woodshed. They would "clock in" at school on their way to his house and "clock out" on their way back (SCI 1992, 56, 62, 63).

With discretion to hire whomever they wanted as helpers, custodians boosted family and friends' incomes by putting relatives and lovers on the payroll (SCI 1992, 32–36, 67–76). A 1977 audit found that three out of four custodians had at least one relative on the payroll (NYS Comptroller 1977b, 2).

Custodians further showered family and friends with no-show jobs and overtime, a lucrative perquisite that pays time-and-a-half in addition to a fixed minimum, just for showing up on weekends and holidays (MOU 1987, schedule XLIV[B]). One custodian, for instance, gave his son, who never showed up, overtime for working seven days a week, nine to ten hours a day, with no lunch break or vacation for a whole year (NYS Comptroller 1977a). Another custodian allowed a family member to bill an average of 97 hours a week—more than twice the regular 40-hour week (NYC Comptroller 1996b).

Custodians also took kickbacks from their staff in exchange for giving them overtime (NYC Comptroller 1996a). One custodian borrowed thousands of dollars from his fireman, paying him with fraudulent overtime until the loan and the income tax due on it was repaid (SCI 1992, 63–64).

Meanwhile, many custodians whose duties were minimal to begin with barely did any work. A 1990 study found they devoted less time to cleaning than custodians in any other U.S. school system (Hay Group 1990, 63). In fact, custodians did not necessarily maintain a presence at their schools. A 1992 investigation disclosed some of the activities they pursued while they were supposed to be at work. One custodian, for example, flew corporate jets and operated his own pay phone company (SCI 1992, 17–18). When investigators asked how he could tend to his Brooklyn school when he was miles away in the sky, he pointed to his "nationwide" beeper and explained that the school could beep him no matter where he was. Another custodian operated a real estate law practice, using his school staff to run court errands (27–25). Others relaxed on their yachts, visited mistresses, took drugs and alcohol at school, or engaged in target practice in their school basements (12). Some custodians resented coming to school even to pick up their paychecks. As one custodian remarked to another in a conversation secretly recorded for investigators, "All I do is sign checks," to which the other wistfully replied, "I remember the old days when we didn't even come in. We picked up our checks at the bar" (SCI 1992, 14).

The Continuing Saga of Corruption Control: Various Reform Strategies and the 1993 Law

To fight corruption and abuse, BOE administrators tried many reforms. For example, they passed rules to reduce an array of wrongs ranging from absenteeism and poor record keeping to nepotism and the commingling of funds between custodians' personal and school accounts.

Administrators also tried structural reorganizations. From 1900 through 1953, for instance, the BOE experimented with centralization. It stripped custodians of discretion at some schools and moved power to central headquarters. It hired custodial helpers, bought supplies, and gave custodians and helpers civil service status (BOE 1924). But the experiment proved to be too expensive: The BOE had to hire large numbers of personnel to oversee and process the paperwork for custodians and their helpers (BOE 1977, 9). By 1953, it had reverted to the indirect system, under which custodians bore responsibility for their staff and cleaning operations (NYS Comptroller 1981). Despite these reforms, scandals persisted (SCI 1999; NYC Comptroller 1989).

In 1993, after a highly publicized investigation, state legislators passed one of the most comprehensive anti-corruption laws in the history of the custodial system. To strengthen performance accountability, legislators gave principals major input in evaluating custodians (NY Ed Law, §2590-h(26)). Custodians could be fired for poor performance if their principals gave them two consecutive "unsatisfactory" ratings (MOU 1994, §6(d)(ii)(B)). Legislators streamlined the procedures for firing them (NY Civil Service Law §§201(75) and (76); MOU 1994, §6(b)). Additionally, lawmakers sought to improve oversight by stripping plant managers, custodians' supervisors, of civil service status so that they would no longer belong to Local 891 (NY Civil Service Law §201(7)(g)).

The 1993 law was fleshed out in the BOE's 1994 custodian contract. That year, Mayor Rudolph Giuliani, a former U.S. attorney who owed little to organized labor, broke with the city tradition of acquiescing to whatever agreement the BOE struck with Local 891, and became directly involved in negotiations (Jones 1994). The 1994 contract accordingly put a premium on making custodians accountable to principals and strengthened existing prohibitions against many custodial abuses.

To curb theft, for instance, the 1994 contract required custodians to record their expenditures, itemizing quantity, vendor, and check number, and to keep original receipts (MOU 1994). The contract also prohibited custodians from commingling personal and school accounts. To stop absenteeism, custodians had to record the times they arrived and left school and notify their principal before leaving. To curb fraudulent overtime, custodians had to file timely records of their staff's overtime schedules with the DSF at the end of each pay period.

But the 1993 law and 1994 contract did not appear to stem the flow of scandal. Two years after the contract went into effect, investigators caught custodians giving each other fraudulent overtime to work on personal projects. Custodians also used staff to work on their homes and looked the other way as helpers falsified time cards, tampered with time clocks, and worked on private projects during school (SCI 1996). A year earlier, city auditors uncovered that, in 1994 alone, helpers racked up $31 million in questionable overtime, doubling and tripling their salaries (NYC Comptroller 1996b, 7). Needless to say, custodians' record keeping was still nonexistent or inaccurate. And 34 percent of custodians continued to mingle personal with school funds (NYC Comptroller 1996a).

Meanwhile, maintenance costs soared (*New York Times* 1996), schools were still dirty, toilets were chronically clogged, sinks did not work, and bathrooms lacked soap and paper (Advocates 1999).

Why does corruption persist after all these reforms? Conventional wisdom would probably blame loopholes in the 1993 law and 1994 contract. But the history of custodial reform suggests that even if controls were tighter, abuses would continue. After all, the DSF already had earlier versions of most of the anti-corruption rules in the 1994 contract on its books. Custodians have had to record their hours and notify principals before leaving their buildings since at least 1903 (BOE 1903). They have had to keep records of their expenditures and their staff's schedules since the 1920s (BOE 1927). Nepotism had been banned since 1978 (BOE 1977/78). Commingling personal and school funds has been prohibited since 1992 (NYC Comptroller 1992).

Deeper Obstacles to Internal Control in Corrupt Agencies

The Role of Management in Frustrating Reform

In chronically corrupt agencies, there are many often-overlooked impediments that can derail even well-crafted reforms. One of these obstacles can be management itself. DSF managers, for instance, repeatedly failed to enforce existing rules and use available tools to reduce corruption, sometimes even after multiple warnings from auditors.

Classical organizational theory presumes that upper management has a stake in meeting official objectives, identifies with those objectives (Meyer and Zucker 1989, 23; Weber 1946); and will at least *try* to implement reforms that reduce corruption, particularly when it *harms* the agency's core mission. Indeed, a good deal of the literature on implementation assumes just this as it dispenses advice on how top officials can ensure that their initiatives are implemented (Matland 1995)—such as by simplifying rules (Lowi 1969), reducing the actors involved in enforcement (Pressman and Wildavsky 1973), or securing sufficient resources (Van Meter and Van Horn 1975).

But if top officials do *not identify* with agency objectives for whatever reason, they may not enforce anti-corruption rules, regardless of how clear and simple rules may be or how many resources they have. DSF managers, for instance, often failed to enforce rules that were clear, simple, easy to enforce, and would have *added* money to the system's coffers. For example, they rarely enforced rules requiring custodians to return money they owed to the BOE (NYC Comptroller 1975, 7).

One reason top managers may not enforce anti-corruption rules is that they are influenced by groups with agendas that conflict with those of the agency (Merton 1968). These groups, sometimes called the "dominant coalition" (Sherman 1978), gain power over official decision making and set an organization's real agenda to reflect their own, not the public, interest. If corruption controls threaten its power, the dominant coalition will seek to block the enforcement of those controls.

How Special Interests Can Capture Power: Local 891's Rise at the DSF. While the ease with which a dominant coalition can mobilize depends on many factors (Blau and Schoenherr 1971), public agencies may be particularly vulnerable to exploitation by special interests because managers may not have strong enough incentives to safeguard the public interest. (Segal 1999). The ease with which a dominant coalition can use such weaknesses is illustrated by the rise to power of one of the most prominent unions in the custodial system, Local 891.

The custodians' union began exerting influence on DSF well before it was recognized as a union for official collective bargaining purposes in the early 1960s. In 1930, the association that became Local 891 bargained informally with the BOE and DSF on custodians' behalf (Lonergan 1998a, 17–18). But while DSF and the BOE had few incentives to protect students' and taxpayers' interests, they had many reasons to placate the union.

Consider DSF's incentives to defend the public interest. Managers were not evaluated on agency performance and suffered no consequences if it fared poorly. Because the system was a virtual monopoly, parents would not remove their children, the system would not shut down, and officials would not be out of jobs if schools deteriorated.

Additionally, unlike union negotiators, whose jobs and salaries depend on striking deals favorable to their members, public officials are insulated from the consequences of making concessions unfavorable to their customers. No one ever demoted a BOE negotiator for striking a poor labor deal. In fact, BOE officials could afford to make abusive concessions because, as public-choice theorists point out, monopolistic agencies such as public schools can ask the legislature for more money without having to compete seriously with other providers (Niskanen 1971).

Further, until the early 1970s, the BOE could make concessions behind closed doors because few paid attention (Fager 1994). Before Watergate, the media probed the pubic sector less aggressively than it does today. The BOE, moreover, was even more insulated from scrutiny than most agencies because, as neither a mayoral nor a state agency, it enjoyed a quasi-independent political status (Viteritti 1983). So the mayor did not usually bring the force of his clout to the negotiating table, as he did for regular mayoral agencies.

Contrast this with DSF's incentives to appease Local 891. First, satisfying it assured labor peace and averted school shutdowns. Even when lawmakers passed the Fair Employment Practices Act (§200 ff), thus restricting custodians' ability to strike, custodians could still intimidate DSF with school shutdowns because they could persuade their staff—many of whom were their relatives and were *not* covered by the act—to strike.

Second, DSF had reason to placate the union because a number of its managers were former union members. Local 891 gradually infiltrated DSF as current and former members worked their way to top positions there. Historically, for example, the executive director and deputy director of DSF's Bureau of Plant Operations—the office responsible for overseeing custodians—have been former Local 891 members[1] (BOE 1977, 11). While "revolving door" legislation blocks public employees from taking jobs in the private sector within certain time periods after leaving their agencies (18 USCS §207 [1997]), nothing prevents former union members from assuming jobs in the agencies they worked for, or vice versa. Although custodians would lose their membership in Local 891 as they were promoted into upper management, to the extent that they remained loyal to their union, they assured it of a voice in policy making.

Local 891 even secured a foothold in BOE collective bargaining because some top DSF officials who used to belong to Local 891 would help the BOE's Office of Labor Relations negotiate contracts against the very union they once belonged to. For example, one high DSF official, who had been a member of the custodian union's executive board, helped the BOE negotiate its 1988 custodial contract. Not surprisingly, the contract, though trumpeted as a "historic settlement" with the union, was filled with false promises (NYC Comptroller 1989; Guttenplan 1990).

The union's capture of DSF did not result from a conspiracy to systematically exploit management's weaknesses. Rather, as opportunities presented themselves and as the union won concessions, victory fed itself: The more the union won, the more formidable it became at the negotiating table. The more formidable it became, the more DSF treated it as a partner in policy making, eventually losing the ability to recognize what was in students' best interests (Levy 1995). In one example of just how much managers saw themselves as Local 891 's ally, when auditors recommended they contract out custodial services to save money, they said they could not make such a decision without consulting the union (NYC Comptroller 1977, 14).

One of the union's biggest early victories came in the 1950s. During the BOE's experiment with centralization, it made custodians civil servants. But in a coup for custodians, when it gave them back their autonomy in 1953 after centralization proved to be too expensive, instead of revoking custodians' civil service status, the BOE let them keep it. This gave custodians the best of both worlds: the freedom of independent contractors with the job security of civil servants. After this triumph, Local 891 easily won many others, ranging from unlimited sick days to free Jeeps to free income tax return preparation (BOE 1977; MOU 1987).

Management's alienation from its mission eventually reached the point that it would side with the union against even the most sensible law enforcement suggestions to reduce abuse. When auditors advised DSF to prohibit custodians from cashing personal checks against their school accounts in order to reduce theft, for instance, DSF objected. Taking the union's part, it insisted that custodians *needed* to pay local vendors cash—even though, as auditors noted, most local vendors knew their custodians personally and would most likely have accepted their checks (NYC Comptroller 1996a, 34-35). Even during one of the toughest financial periods the BOE faced—New York City's fiscal crisis in the mid-1970s—DSF refused to cut perquisites that auditors said were wasteful, such as free preparation of custodians' income tax returns (NYC Comptroller 1975, 13). Although its budget had been cut and it had reduced custodians' duties, DSF insisted on keeping this unusual frill.

How Managers Can Frustrate Controls while Concealing that They Do So. Once captured, management can frustrate corruption controls and disguise what it is doing in many ways. One way DSF did this was by pretending to embrace reforms, but then failing to implement them after the pressure subsided. In 1988, after exposés of waste, for instance, the BOE publicly announced it would no longer give custodians free Jeeps (NYC Comptroller 1989). In fact, however, it merely imposed a one-year moratorium on the practice, during which it was to study the problem (Fager 1994). After the media attention died down, the BOE never completed the study and allotted $2.5 million to buy 200 Jeeps for custodians during the following two years (Fager 1990).

Managers used similar tactics to stall auditors. For example, they explicitly assured auditors they would implement various reforms, but then did not. After audits revealed that custodians' records of their helpers' schedules were nonexistent, auditors asked DSF to discipline custodians who did not comply with record-keeping rules (NYC Comptroller 1975). DSF explicitly agreed (11). But almost 20 years later, custodians' records were still nonexistent or so poor as to be "audit-proof," as DSF had never properly checked them, let alone disciplined custodians (SCI 1992, 74).

Even if controls were implemented, managers sabotaged them in various ways. For example, one year after the 1993 law made it more likely that plant managers would evaluate custodians objectively—by preventing them from belonging to Local 891—DSF emasculated plant managers by ensuring their evaluations would have no impact on whether custodians were promoted, disciplined, fired, or denied transfers to larger schools (MOU 1994).

A graphic illustration of how managers could subvert their own reforms was DSF's pilot program to privatize custodial services. Auditors had long urged DSF to contract out custodial services (NYS Comptroller 1976, 3, 4, 60; NYS Comptroller 1981, 10). They hoped that DSF would learn how private contractors saved money and force their own custodians to copy them (BOE 1976, 2–4).

Local 891, however, opposed contracting out and demanded that DSF not conduct studies comparing contractors to BOE custodians (EPP 1976). Managers resisted privatization as long as they could (NYC Comptroller 1977, 14). When pressure finally forced them to try it in 1963, they implemented it so as to minimize any threat to BOE custodians.

First, officials made it nearly impossible to compare private custodians to BOE custodians (NYS Comptroller 1981, 10, 11). Until the mid-1980s, DSF privatized at too few schools to provide a statistically significant basis for comparison. DSF also gave private custodians many more duties than BOE custodians, making comparison difficult (FOIL 1999).

Even more telling, the BOE refused to cooperate with auditors trying to compare BOE custodians to contractors (NYC Comptroller 1989). It also inexplicably stopped a study that its in-house auditors had begun to compare the two (George 1999). For that reason, after nearly 40 years, DSF still cannot say whether contractors are more efficient than its own custodians (Lonergan 1998a, 71).

Second, DSF prevented contractors from being as successful as they might have, thus lessening their potential to make BOE custodians look bad. For example, managers required contractors to hire skilled mechanics at the same rates as DSF's civil service mechanics, although the non-civil service mechanics that contractors wanted to hire would have been cheaper (Lonergan 1997). DSF also gave private contractors no choice in selecting their buildings, so often they received schools in neighborhoods where vandalism put them at a comparative disadvantage to BOE custodians, who had a choice (NYS Comptroller 1981).

Further undermining the program's success, DSF would sometimes re-hire the same contractors whose contracts it had previously refused to renew due to incompetence (NYS Comptroller 1976, 2) Perhaps due to all these impediments, DSF has been unable to attract many qualified bidders, creating yet another obstacle to successful privatization. Today, as in the first 12 years after the start of the program, only two corporations offer the BOE custodial services (FOIL 1999).

The Role of "Culture" in Undermining Reform

Another hidden barrier to reforming corrupt agencies is their culture, or shared values about appropriate behavior (Rainey and Steinbauer 1999). A deviant culture can foster resistance to reform, in many ways. It can encourage employees to regard wrongdoing as their prerogative. Or it can make them fearful of trying change and new powers. The more entrenched the culture and the more alienated employees are from society's values, the more fiercely they will fight corruption controls.

Many factors can contribute to the tenacity and virulence of a deviant culture. Management, for instance, can set a corrupt example. In one telling instance of how rank-and-file workers absorbed DSF managers' skewed priorities, employees in the custodial payroll unit saw themselves primarily as serving Local 891—to the point they would return telephone calls of union officials but not of BOE higher-ups who were not directly involved in the custodial system (NYS Comptroller 1977a, 85).

Management can also fuel a culture of deviance and estrangement from society's norms by not punishing misconduct. After years of getting away with abuses, many custodians could barely even conceive that their conduct might be considered objectionable from society's perspective. A window into that alienation is provided by the brazenness of one custodian, who announced to his principal shortly after he was transferred to her school that, since he had two other jobs, she should contact his secretary, not him, if she needed anything (SCI 1992, 20). Another insight is offered by a custodian who let his boiler operator store his gun collection near the lunchroom and live in the basement, where he slept, entertained women, and kept a dog (22–23). Yet another example is a custodian who used his school basement to raise chickens for cockfighting, telling inspectors that the hundreds of labeled eggs he was incubating there were to feed students (Lonergan 1999).

Culture has foiled many custodial reforms. Culture was, for instance, an important reason that legislators' measures to improve custodial accountability for performance did not work. The 1993 law gave principals more power than ever before to evaluate and affect custodians' careers (Sack 1993). But after years of watching DSF do nothing as principals suffered the consequences of standing up to derelict custodians, principals refused to use their new power to evaluate custodians honestly because they still feared reprisals and had little faith that DSF would support them (Lonergan 1998). Custodians, after all, remain in their schools while dismissal proceedings are pending, creating an even worse nightmare for the principal should the custodian not be fired. If the custodian is fired, moreover, the principal cannot choose his successor—DSF does.

Not surprisingly, surveys conducted after 1993 show that principals continue to give custodians top ratings, mostly likely without regard to performance (Lonergan 1998a, 37–40). While 15 principals gave their custodians two consecutive unsatisfactory evaluations shortly after the law went into effect, these principals all capitulated when forced to confront their custodians during arbitration and raised their ratings. Administrative hearings accordingly found the custodians competent, and most returned to their schools, while a few transferred to new ones. (Rothman 1999). Needless to say, out of a workforce of 1,000, not one custodian has been fired for incompetence or abuse since the 1993 law was passed.

The culture of fear, moreover, is self-perpetuating, making it an even more potent obstacle to reform. The more principals retreat from giving custodians unsatisfactory ratings, the less likely it is that custodians will be fired, further feeding principals' fear that they are invincible. In fact, the easiest way for principals to get rid of custodians is to give them high marks, which helps them to transfer to bigger schools. The worst thing principals could do is give custodians average or below-average marks, which would be low enough to antagonize them and dim their transfer prospects, but not low enough to fire them (Lonergan 1997).

In addition to managers' conduct, history and the size of the profits at stake can also foster a deviant culture. In the custodial system, history has reinforced custodians' notion that certain misconduct was their prerogative, while the large sums of money to be gained strengthened their determination to persist in wrongdoing. These factors buttressed the culture of corruption to such a degree that even when managers *wanted* to enforce controls, the culture blocked them.

Consider how culture foiled DSF's efforts to fight nepotism. Nepotism has been an integral part of custodians' lives since the 1850s, when their families, who lived in schools with them, helped with school chores (Lonergan 1998a, 11–12). Sons apprenticed with their fathers, learning skills such as how to operate school coal furnaces. Indeed, some custodians today have forefathers who trace their custodial lineage back to the Civil War. Nepotism, furthermore, was lucrative. Experts estimate that, in 1991 alone, nepotism cost the BOE about $4 million and boosted an individual custodian's family income by thousands of dollars yearly (Fager 1991).

When DSF passed a rule in 1978 prohibiting custodians from hiring their wives (BOE 1977/78), custodians got around it by hiring each other's wives (SCI 1992, 60, 75). In these deals, referred to as "wife swapping," one custodian would hire a second's wife, and the second would hire the first's wife (NYS Comptroller 1981, 17). In 1994, the BOE prohibited wife swapping between two custodians (MOU 1994, §11(b)), but custodians found ways to circumvent this rule, too. Many swapped wives among *three* custodians: The first custodian would hire the second one's wife, the second would hire the third's wife, and the third would hire the first's wife (Kong 1995).

Impediments to Structural "Reorganizations"

One of the most revered strategies in the literature on public administration for turning around corrupt agencies is to "reorganize" them by replacing the dominant coalition with honest personnel (March and Olsen 1983). Research certainly suggests that leaders are crucial to an agency's success (Yukl 1998; Behn 1991), and removing the old guard is important to changing its culture (Sherman 1978). In fact, the criticism leveled at most reorganizations is that they do not go far enough. Other than in small agencies (Sherman, 99–101), simply replacing the executive and his deputies is generally not sufficient to neutralize a dominant coalition (Ermann and Lundman 1982).

The consequences of shallow reorganizations are illustrated by various chancellors' efforts to reinvigorate DSF by replacing its executive director. Consider former Chancellor Green's hiring of a new DSF head in 1988 (Guttenplan 1990). Despite high expectations for this Yale University graduate, she was frozen out of major policy decisions by powerful subordinates who refused to share information with her. DSF's entrenched bureaucracy refused to carry out her initiatives. When she tried, for instance, to make it easier for custodians to obtain specialized tools from central shops controlled by skilled mechanics, personnel would not cooperate (Lonergan 1997). She eventually ceded real control to the head of the DSF Bureau of Plant Operations. However, as a former high-ranking union official, he did not want to challenge the status quo. Finally, forced to face her inability to change the system, she resigned.

The Difficulty of Removing the Entire Dominant Coalition

It can, however, be difficult to remove an agency's entire dominant coalition, especially if it is large and protected by civil service. The extraordinary efforts required for such an endeavor are highlighted in a study of the Kansas Department of Health and Environment (Maynard-Moody, Stull, and Mitchell 1986). This agency underwent 17 reorganizations without changing significantly because none involved more than the top layer of personnel. Only after a new executive redefined every managerial position, removed authority from the old guard, and filled every opening with new people, did the subculture finally change. Even greater efforts would be required to affect the dominant coalition in the custodial system, which is bigger than that in the Kansas agency and includes many dozens of upper- and mid-level civil service managers at DSF and the BOE.

Removing All Corrupt Personnel Is Not Enough: Special Interests Remain Embedded in Infrastructure

But even if reformers can neutralize an agency's dominant coalition, roadblocks may remain. In the custodial system, for instance, even if DSF could have started with an entirely new slate of people, special interests, deeply embedded in the system's policies and modus operandi, would have trumped reforms. At a certain point, the problem with an agency whose management has long been captive to special interests becomes bigger than the dominant coalition or any interest group. The sheer accumulation of concessions that reflect special interests creates an organizational infrastructure so enmeshed in its own selfish advantage that it takes more than new personnel to change it.

Consider how various union concessions undermined legislators' 1993 efforts to require custodians to be evaluated on the overall condition of their buildings (NY Ed. Law §2590-h(26)). The reality was that custodians could *not* take responsibility for their buildings because DSF, in a concession to the 15 unions that represent the "skilled trade mechanics" such as electricians, plumbers, and carpenters, precluded custodians from handling any "major" repairs. These repairs were to be the exclusive domain of the civil service skilled trade mechanics who worked at DSF (Rothman 1999).

Many so-called "major" repairs, however, were basic to the operation of schools and could easily have been handled by custodians—at a fraction of the cost of skilled mechanics. For example, while a custodian could replace a regular light bulb, only a skilled electrician who cost $32 an hour could replace a fluorescent bulb—although a custodial handyman, who cost $15 an hour, could easily have done it (Lonergan 1998b). While a custodian could patch a hole in a wall if its diameter was less than three inches, if the hole was bigger, a carpenter at $45 an hour was required. And should a skilled mechanic have needed an assistant to hold up his ladder or shine a flashlight, he was entitled to a skilled maintenance worker, who cost twice as much as a handyman but did essentially the same work.

These restrictive labor policies often made it *impossible* for custodians to keep their buildings in good condition, for several reasons. First, the policies prohibited custodians from making many fundamental repairs even if they had *wanted* to (*Newsday* 1993). Skilled trade unions, with jobs and union dues at stake, fiercely guarded their members' work fiefdoms (Lonergan 1999).

Second, although custodians could request skilled trade mechanics to make repairs at their schools, it could take years for them to arrive (NYS Comptroller 1993). Custodians had to fill out a work order, which had to be reviewed and signed by various supervisors before it was sent to DSF. There it would go into a queue behind a backlog of over 35,000 other orders (Lonergan 1997).

Custodians' dependence on skilled trade mechanics directly hampered their ability to maintain schools, as illustrated by their painting duties. Custodians were allowed to paint only up to a height of eight feet on exterior walls and 10 feet or the picture molding on interior walls, whichever was lower (MOU 1987, 102). Anything higher required a skilled painter. But because 40 percent of schools had interior and exterior walls over 10 feet (NYC Comptroller 1989, 34), and because it usually took long for painters to arrive, walls looked half-done for months. One custodian, for instance, could not paint over the upper parts of graffiti on a wall because it went above the permissible limit.

Abusive Policies Bolstered by Decades of Arbitration Decisions

But can't a new slate of managers simply repeal these union concessions? This brings up yet another, usually ignored impediment to reform: Arbitrators limit management's ability to unilaterally revoke anything that has become a "policy and practice" without going through collective bargaining. This may apply even if a concession was never included in a labor agreement. When DSF tried, for example, to discontinue custodians' free coffee machines, coffee and tea—perquisites never mentioned in any contract—arbitrators held they could not do so because these frills had become "policy and practice" over the years (AAA 1996, 10).

As for repealing union concessions through collective bargaining, new managers in corrupt agencies may have little to offer labor in exchange. As one administrator explained about DSF, previous managers had "given away so much… there was nothing left to give" (Lonergan 1998b).

Eluding External Criminal Sanctions

The usual presumption for agencies as corrupt as the custodial system is that prosecutors will step in, clean them up, and remove the "rotten apples" (Anechiarico and Jacobs 1996). But the custodian case shows that corrupt agencies can sometimes elude criminal sanction—even in cities with a vibrant media like New York.

Consider how the custodial system has largely escaped criminal sanction. Despite the city's establishment in 1990 of SCI, a powerful, independent school inspector general, prosecutors have focused on "major" custodial crimes such as extortion and bribery (*People v. Cappeta* 86 A.D.2D 876,447 N.Y.S.2d 293 [1982] [grand larceny and fraud]; *People v. Manfredi* 166 A.D.2d 460, 560 N.Y.S. 2d 679 [1990] [grand larceny and bribery]), but not on the "minor" corruption that is more prevalent, more costly, and more central to what makes the agency systemically corrupt.

There are several masons for this. First, some misconduct, no matter how abusive or costly, is not necessarily criminal (Segal 1998). In the custodial system, some of the most prevalent and costly abuses, such as nepotism, are administrative violations but not crimes.

Second, other misconduct that *ought* to be criminal has been sanitized through collective bargaining, arbitration decisions, discretion, and tradition. In most agencies, for example, employees who take equipment home—even old, broken equipment—can be prosecuted for theft. But until 1994, the custodial contract permitted custodians to keep millions of dollars in capital equipment, such as jeeps and snowplows, after five years' use (NYC Comptroller 1975).

Third, conduct that *is clearly criminal* may escape prosecution because it does not appeal to prosecutors. The most prevalent custodial crimes are hard to prove, resource-intensive to investigate, and easy to conceal. To determine whether a custodian is hiring relatives, for instance, investigators need to scour payroll records that are often illegible or nonexistent. Custodians can easily hide phony overtime by handing it out during holidays when few witnesses are around (SCI 1992, 74, 89). With the keys to clean time clocks, they can also easily cheat schools on time worked (85–88).

Broader Implications for Corruption Reform

The reform pitfalls highlighted in the New York City custodian case have implications for many agencies battling systemic corruption. An ingrained culture of deviance and management's failure to enforce rules, rather than their absence or inadequacy, for example, can help explain the persistence of corruption in agencies ranging from the New York Police Department, where scandals crest every 20 years or so despite decades of various corruption controls (Mollen 1994), to Medicare programs, where the FBI has been fighting fraud for over a decade with little sign that it is diminishing (Pear 2001).

The consequences that flow from this observation—the futility of relying exclusively on traditional redress devices in deeply corrupt organizations—are also widely apparent. Consider the Facilities Management Division of the Los Angeles Unified School District (LAUSD), which is responsible for building and maintaining the city's public schools. Despite a multitude of state laws to guard against the construction of schools on toxic sites, despite fiscal controls and accounting standards, and despite replacing the division director three times in eight years, the division was beset with bid rigging, bribery, and fiscal abuse (Mullinax 1999a, b; Gittrich 1999a). Officials poured $200 million to partially complete the most expensive high school in California history, the Belmont Learning Complex, atop an oil field emanating explosive gases. They had abandoned accounting procedures and fiscal controls and covered up the project's hazards and true costs (Mullinax 1999b; California State Auditor 1999). As investigators found, management was steeped in a culture of "turf rivalry" (Mullinax 1999a, 4) where personal aggrandizement came before protecting the public interest and telling the truth (Gittrich 1999b). Neither more regulations nor new directors alone could change this culture.

Other insights of the New York City custodian case also have broad application. Consider the lesson about how unions can block corruption control by co-opting management and imposing abusive work rules on an agency. The custodian union's effort to control DSF for its own ends is actually consistent with a broader trend in unionism harking back to the 1960s, when unions saw themselves as management's adversaries and went all out to win benefits for their members without regard for the impact on agency efficiency or the quality of services (Johnson and Kardos 2000). Management, not the union, was supposed to safeguard efficiency, quality of services, and customer interests.

The problem was that, with weak incentives to protect customers, agencies were vulnerable to unions' setting the agenda and, if they wished, hampering corruption control. Unions succeeded in controlling policy to different degrees in different agencies. But the custodian union's enormous success in blocking reform at DSF was not unique. It reflects what happened in a number of institutions such as the construction industry, where unions thwarted crime controls by pressuring managers to adopt and keep work rules that facilitated organized crime (Goldstock et al. 1990).

But perhaps one of the most vivid illustrations of how much some agencies can share the reform roadblocks of the New York City custodian system is the Chicago public school custodial system.

With broad discretion over school maintenance budgets and a history going back to the nineteenth century, Chicago custodial engineers, known as "engineers," had a record of abuses reminiscent of their New York City counterparts: theft, kickbacks, bribery, absenteeism, questionable overtime, waste, and recalcitrance (Vander Weele 1994; Rossi 1994). Schools were filthy and decrepit (Rossi 1996a; Mitchell 1996). One engineer let pigeons live in his school, (Reyes 2000) while another stopped painters from painting his school because they had not started with his office first (Rossi 1996a). As in New York City, principals complained about not having power over delinquent engineers, who reported to the unresponsive central BOE Division of Facilities, now called the Division of Operations (Johnson 1993; Kostopulos 2000). Meanwhile, questionable overtime was rampant (Vander Weele 1993), while salaries were second highest among the nation's public school custodians, after New York City's (Vander Weele 1991a).

Until 1995, reformers tried to fix the problem with shallow reorganizations and traditional controls. They replaced the director of the Facilities Division in 1994 (Katz, Fine, and Simon 1997) and issued an array of controls such as labeling equipment with bar codes to prevent theft (Vander Weele 1995).

Corruption, however, persisted. The reasons highlight key insights of the New York City custodian case. The Facilities Division was controlled by the engineers union, which used it as its clubhouse. James Harney, the division director from 1986 to 1994, had been an engineer in nearly 50 schools and was regarded as the union's de facto head (Vander Weele 2000). The division routinely awarded millions of dollars of work to companies run by former engineers (Vander Weele 1995). Companies would submit bills without detailing work done, and administrators would pay them without asking questions, often in exchange for bribes, to an estimated loss of over $7 million yearly. As Harney would later explain to a federal judge, "The deal—the thinking was, as we did the work we'd share the profits" (O'Connor 1996).

Moreover, as in New York City, costly, counterproductive work rules had become entrenched (Vander Weele 1991b). Overtime pay, for example, was built into engineer pay schedules, so they would receive it any time their school was open before or after regular hours, regardless of whether they could have avoided it through better scheduling (Banas and Davidson 1985).

With the Facilities Division immersed in a culture of profiteering, issuing more corruption controls and replacing the division director accomplished little. Managers did not use the tools available to effect reform. Audits remained spotty. When abuses were uncovered, no one was punished. After two schools allegedly "lost" more than $400,000 in custodial equipment, managers promoted all three employees responsible for overseeing the equipment (Vander Weele 1995). Management also seemed reluctant to cooperate with law enforcement. When the school inspector general requested records for an investigation, he said it took three tries and the threat of a subpoena before anyone produced the information (Rossi 1994).

What We Can Learn from Agencies that Have Overcome Roadblocks to Corruption Reform

Some agencies appear to have overcome the reform pitfalls highlighted in the New York City case. One of the most instructive examples is, again, the Chicago custodial system. While it may be premature to make definitive conclusions about it because its reforms are still recent, the record so far is encouraging and informative.

Corruption started to decline in the Chicago custodial system in 1995, when the Illinois legislature passed a sweeping amendment to the Chicago School Reform Act, giving a new school chief executive selected by the mayor vast powers to privatize entire classes of unionized employees (Katz, Fine, and Simon 1997, 117). While audits found $7 million in theft and overcharges in 1995, they unearthed less than $500,000 in overcharges in 1996 (Oclander 1996).

With the mayor's support and a mandate to reform the school system, Chief Executive Officer Paul Vallas used privatization to sweep away the old guard and its entrenched work rules. He hired about 100 new people loyal to his initiatives, fired or transferred many existing administrators (Katz, Fine, and Simon 1997), and privatized all of the BOE's 400 skilled trade workers (Rossi 1996a) and 75 percent of engineers' janitorial staff (Reyes 2000). The result: Top managers and a significant portion of middle management were new hires who shared his vision for reform. With respect to engineers, Vallas won numerous concessions and eliminated many work rules simply by threatening to privatize (Martinez 1996; Rossi 1996a).

Reformers additionally took extensive steps to infuse accountability for performance in the school system. The 1995 state law made engineers accountable to principals, allowing them to discipline them for poor performance. Principals, who were stripped of tenure and hired on four-year performance contracts, were accountable to parents and teachers. The chief executive and central school board were accountable to the mayor. Vallas also hired different companies that were accountable to him to help oversee and monitor engineers and their staff (McCabe 2000).

Chicago's success can be attributed to yet another strategy implied by the New York City case: deterring wrong-doing by establishing a strong office to investigate wrong-doing and inviting prosecution and disciplinary sanctions. If rogues think they will be caught and punished, they will have reason to change—and so will the people around them who see the consequences. Vallas doubled the size of the school inspector general, established a fraud hotline, and privatized the school internal audit unit to ensure it would perform rigorous monthly compliance and fraud audits (Ilagan 2000; Rossi 1996b). Further, the school board reached out to the Cook County state attorney's office, making an agreement to pay it to dedicate a team of attorneys to prosecute school fraud (Rossi 1997). In January 1996, in one of the biggest city school crackdowns in 20 years, Vallas announced plans to fire 32 employees and discipline 12 others for wrongdoing (Rossi 1996c). In May 1996, he moved to blacklist 40 school repair vendors who had overcharged the system. Adding to the message of no tolerance for corruption, in 1996, former Facilities director James Harney was sentenced to 41 months in federal prison for extortion and kickbacks (Mitchell 1996).

While it may be difficult to replicate all the tactics that Chicago employed, its success suggests the importance of a minimum of three broad reform strategies. The first is to launch tough, publicized law enforcement initiatives that include investigations, compliance and fraud audits, and punishment for wrongdoers. Although most agency executives dread having corruption exposed on their watches, welcoming outside prosecutors, as Chicago did, can be crucial to changing a deeply deviant culture. Some other agencies, such as the LAUSD, have begun to adopt such measures.

The second strategy is to oust as much of the dominant coalition as possible, not just the top layer, and any work rules that block reform. Executives must use whatever power is available to privatize, demote, transfer, and redefine managerial jobs to remove old guard members protected by civil service and to build a loyal base. If necessary, reformers should lobby for legislation to declassify as many posts as possible.

The third strategy is to hold managers accountable for performance to the agency executive and customers and to provide meaningful consequences for failure. In Chicago, large numbers of personnel, from principals, engineers, and private contractors to the chief executive himself, can be replaced if they do not meet performance standards. Performance accountability that carries real consequences for failure helps address one of the key underlying reasons agencies have been vulnerable to takeover by special interests: weak incentives to safeguard customer interests. Holding managers accountable to customers gives them stronger incentives to resist agendas that conflict with those goals and to ensure that resources go where they were intended (Segal 1997).

Reformers should additionally give different interest groups with a stake in the agency mission formal opportunities to put their views before management (Meier 1993). One way to achieve this in beleaguered school custodial systems around the nation is to allow parents to bring television camera crews into schools, giving them the power to embarrass management and force it to respond.

Without such minimal reform strategies, merely tightening existing controls, issuing more rules or instituting shallow reorganizations in chronically corrupt agencies will merely create the illusion of change without the reality.

Postscript

In December 2001, 11 custodians were charged with rigging contracts for washing school windows in return for 10 percent cash kickbacks. One custodian pocketed $62,000. In most cases, the windows were never washed (Williams 2001). Months earlier, in April, another custodian was charged for using his school budget as a credit line to pay his taxes, mortgage, and trips to Atlantic City. (SCI 2001).

Acknowledgments

I am grateful to the Smith Richardson and John M. Olin Foundations for their generous research support. I am also grateful to Professors James Jacobs, John Kleinig, and Patrick O'Hara for their valuable insights and helpful comments.

My deepest thanks also go to Jim Lonergan at DSF, who, as a manager dedicated to improving his agency, has shared innumerable insights about it.

Note

1. The current director and his deputy are the first offices in recent memory not to have risen to their posts as former custodians.

References

Advocates for Children of New York, Inc. 1999. *Neglected Buildings, Damaged Health: A Snapshot of New York City Public School Environmental Conditions*. New York City: Advocates for Children.

American Arbitration Association (AAA). 1996. *In the Matter of the Arbitration Between the NYC BOE and Local 891*. Case #130 39000709 96, December 18. New York: American Arbitration Association.

Anechiarico, Frank, and James Jacobs. 1996. *The Pursuit of Absolute Integrity*. Chicago: University of Chicago Press.

Banas, Casey, and Jean Davidson. 1985. City Schools Back in Business: 2-year Teacher Contract Links State Aid, Raises. *Chicago Tribune*, September 5, C1.

Behn, Robert D. 1991. *Leadership Counts*. Cambridge, MA: Harvard University Press.

Blau, Peter, and Richard Schoenherr. 1971. *The Structure of Organizations*. New York: Basic Books.

Board of Education (BOE). 1903. *Rules and Regulations for the Custodial Workforce*. New York: BOE.

——. 1911–13. *Final Report: Educational Investigation Committee on School Inquiry, 1911–13*. Vol. 3. New York: BOE.

——. 1927. *Rules and Regulations for the Custodial Workforce*. New York: BOE.

——. 1976. *Report on Contract Custodial Services: 1964 to 1976*. New York: Division of School Buildings.

——. 1977a. *A Source Document on Custodians and Custodial Helpers*. New York: BOE.

——. 1977b. *Rules and Regulations for the Custodial Force in the Public Schools of NYC*. New York: BOE.

——. 1977/78. *Hiring of Custodial Relatives*. Chancellor's Circular #1. New York: BOE.

California State Auditor/Bureau of State Audits. 1999. *Los Angeles Unified School District: Its School Site Selection Process Fails to Provide Information Necessary for Decision Making and to Effectively Engage the Community*. Report No. 99123.

Chicago Sun-Times. 1995. School Bribe Charges Shocking—and Sad. Editorial, December 3, 41.

Coffee, J. 1980. Making the Punishment Fit the Corporation: The Problem of Finding the Optimal Corporate Criminal Sanction. *Northern Illinois University Law Review* 1(3): 3–36.

Daley, Suzanne. 1988. Custodian vs. Principal: Stacked Deck. *New York Times*, February 25, B1.

Education Priorities Panel (EPP). 1976. *NYC School Custodial and Maintenance Costs*. New York: EPP.

Ermann, M. David, and Richard J. Lundman. 1982. *Corporate and Governmental Deviance: Problems of Organizational Behavior in Contemporary Society*. 2nd ed. New York: Oxford University Press.

Fager, John. 1990. About Education: Getting Tough with Custodians. *New York Newsday*, July 6, 60.

——. 1991. Study on School Custodians Doesn't Even Scratch the Surface. *New York Times*, April 9, A24.

——. 1994. And I'll Turn on The Heat When I'm Done Cleaning My Yacht. *Washington Monthly*, July, 24, 60.

Freedom of Information Law (FOIL). 1999. *Response to FOIL Request #1935 Concerning Various School Facilities Financial Data*. Reference No. 1999–303. New York: BOE.

Gardiner, John A., and Theodore Lyman. 1993. The Logic of Corruption Control. In *Political Corruption: A Handbook*, edited by Arnold J. Heidenheimer, Michael Johnston, and Victor T. Levine, 827–40. New Brunswick, NJ: Transaction Publishers.

Gates, Margaret, and Mark Moore. 1986. *Inspectors-General: Junkyard Dogs or Man's Best Friend? Social Research Perspectives*. New York: Russell Sage Foundation.

George, Tim. 1999. Interview. Deputy director of plant operations, Division of School Facilities, Board of Education, New York City, July 15.

Gittrich, Greg. 1999a. Workers Indicted in Scam Case: Millions in Prop BB, Federal Funds Involved. *Los Angeles Daily News*, June 18, N3.

——. 1999b. Fiscal Abuse Widespread, Prober Says. *Los Angeles Daily News*, December 15, N1.

Goldstock, Ronald, Martin Marcus, Thomas Thacher II, and James B. Jacobs. 1990. *New York State Organized Crime Task Force: Corruption and Racketeering in the New York City Construction Industry: Final Report to Governor Mario M. Cuomo*. New York: New York University Press.

Guttenplan, D.D. 1990. *School Custodians Willing to Let Other Unions Take Lead*. New York Newsday, October 22, 19.

Hay Group. 1990. *Preliminary Report of Findings and Recommendations for the NYC Public School System Plant Operations Study*. New York: Hay Group.

Ilagan, Sandy. 2000. Interview. Manager, KPMG Internal Audit Unit, Board of Education, New York City, November 10.

Johnson, Mary A. 1993. Structure and Leadership: Question of Who is Boss Still Debated. *Chicago Sun-Times*, March 28, 24.

Johnson, Susan Moore, and Susan M. Kardos. 2000. Reform Bargaining and Its Promise for School Improvement. In *Conflicting Missions? Teachers Unions and Educational Reform*, edited by Tom Loveless, 7–46. Washington, DC: Brookings Institution.

Joint Commission on Integrity in the Public Schools (JCI). 1990. *Investigating the Investigators*. March. New York: Joint Commission.

Jones, Charisse. 1994. Pact Breaks Grip of New York School Custodians. *New York Times*, May 5, A1.

Katz, Michael B., Michelle Fine, and Elaine Simon. 1997. *Poking Around: Outsiders View Chicago School Reform*. New York: Columbia University, Teachers College.

Kolbert, Elizabeth. 1998. Schools Face Tough Choice about Repairs. *New York Times*, February 9, B1.

Kong, Yvonne P. 1995. *A System Like No Other—School Custodians*. Masters thesis, City University of New York.

Kostopulos, Margaret. 2000. Interview. Director of labor relations, Board of Education, Chicago, IL, November 3.

Levy, Harold. 1995. *Report of the Commission on School Facilities and Maintenance Reform*. New York State.

Light, Paul C. 1993. *Monitoring Government: Inspectors General and the Search for Accountability*. Washington, DC: Brookings Institution.

Lonergan, James. 1997. Interview. Director of building services, Division of School Facilities, Board of Education, New York City, October 17.

——. 1998a. *Custodial Contract Between BOE and Local 891: An Analysis*. Masters thesis, Queens College, City University of New York.

——.1998b. Interview. Director of building services, Division of School Facilities, Board of Education, New York City, December 16.

——. 1999. Lecture at John Jay College of Criminal Justice, City University of New York, February 18.

Lowi, Theodore. 1969. *The End of Liberalism*. New York: W.W. Norton.

Maire, Kathy. 1991. A Triple Tax On Toilets? *New York Newsday*, June 20, 60.

March, James, and Johan Olsen. 1983. Organizing Political Life: What Administrative Reorganizations Tell Us about Government. *American Political Science Review* 72(June): 281–96.

Martinez, Michael. 1996. Schools, Janitors Reach Accord: Building Engineers' Jobs Safe for Now. *Chicago Tribune*, July 22, N3.

Matland, Richard. 1995. Synthesizing the Implementation Literature: The Ambiguity-Conflict Model of Policy Implementation. *Journal of Public Administration Research and Theory* 5(2): 145.

Maynard-Moody, S., D.D. Stull, and J. Mitchell. 1986. Reorganization as a Status Drama: Building, Maintaining, and Displacing Dominant Subcultures. *Public Administration Review* 46(4): 301–10.

McCabe, Paula. 2000. Interview. Director, Department of Operations (oversees engineers), Board of Education, Chicago, IL November 3.

Meier, Kenneth J. 1993. *Politics and the Bureaucracy*. Pacific Grove, CA: Brooks/Cole.

Merton, Robert. 1968. *Social Theory and Social Structure*. New York: Free Press.

Meyer, Marshall W., and Lynne G. Zucker. 1989. *Permanently Failing Organizations*. Thousand Oaks, CA: Sage Publications.

Michalak, Joseph. 1964. Custodians Pay Still in Top Bracket. *New York Herald Tribune*, October 19.

Mitchell, Mary. 1996. Ex-School Aide Sentenced for Extortion. *Chicago Sun-Times*, May 18, 4.

Mollen, Milton. 1994. *Report of the New York City Commission to Investigate Allegations of Police Corruption and the Anti-Corruption Procedures of the Police Department*. New York: City of New York.

Memorandum of Understanding (MOU). 1987. *Memorandum of Understanding between the Board of Education of the City School District of the City of New York and Local 891*. New York: BOE.

——. 1994. *Memorandum of Understanding between the Board of Education of the City School District of the City of New York and Local 891*. New York: BOE.

Mullinax, Don. 1999a. *Report of Findings: Belmont Learning Complex*, OSI 99–12, September 13.

——. 1999b. *Report of Findings—Part II: Belmont Learning Complex*, OSI 99–20, December 13.

Newsday. 1993. Fall Guys for the BOE. Editorial, November 30, 122.

New York Times. 1996. The Ripoff Continues. Editorial, March 30, 22.

New York City (NYC). 1949. Louis E. Yavner and George D. Strayer. *Interim Report*, Chapter VII, 159–249. New York: Management Committee, Mayor's Office.

New York City Comptroller. 1975. *Board of Education Financial and Operating Practices Pertaining to Custodial Services—1975*. New York: NYC Comptroller.

——. 1977. *Report on the Financial and Operating Practices of the Board of Education Pertaining to Custodial Services For the Calendar Year 1975*. January 19. New York: NYC Comptroller.

——. 1989. *The School Custodians' Contract: An Evaluation of the Reforms of 1985 and 1988*. December. New York: NYC Comptroller.

——. 1992. *Directive #11*. New York: NYC Comptroller.

——. 1996a. *Audit Report on the New York City Board of Education Controls over Custodial Hiring Practices and Use of Separate Bank Accounts*. June 27. New York: NYC Comptroller.

——. 1996b. *Audit Report on the New York City Board of Education Controls over Custodial Employees Work Hours*. March 14. New York: NYC Comptroller.

New York State Comptroller. 1976 *Tentative Draft Audit Report, Bureau of Plant Operation Contracted Custodial Services*. June 29. New York State.

——. 1977a. *Custodial Service At a Certain High School—NYC BOE*. January 28. Report #NYC-4–77.

——. 1977b. *Financial and Operating Practices, Bureau of Plant Operations—Custodial Services, New York City Board of Education: July 1, 1974 to January 31,1977*. Report #NYC-64–77.

——. 1981. *Bureau of Plant Operations Custodial Services Follow-Up, New York City Board of Education*. October 9. Report #NYC-21–80.

Niskanen, William A. 1971. *Bureaucracy and Representative Government*. Chicago: Aldine-Atherton.

Oclander, Jorge. 1996. School Billing Racket: Firms, Employees Still Scam System. *Chicago Sun-Times*, May 22, 1.

O'Connor, Matt. 1996. Ex-School Bureaucrat Took Bribes He Admits Trading Contracts for Favors. *Chicago Tribune*, March 1, N3.

Office of Administrative Trials and Hearings (OATH). 1995/96. *In Re Luther Drakeford*. New York: OATH.

Pear, Robert. 2001. Financial Problems in Government are Rife, Nation's Top Auditor Says. *New York Times*, January 18, A12.

Pressman, Jeffrey, and Aaron Wildavsky. 1973. *Implementation*. Berkeley, CA: University of California Press.

Rainey, Hal, and Paula Steinbauer. 1999. Galloping Elephants: Developing Elements of a Theory of Effective Government Organizations. *Journal of Public Administration Research and Theory* 9(1): 1–33.

Ravitch, Diane. 1974. *The Great School Wars: New York City, 1805–1973*. New York: Basic Books.

Reyes, Ben. 2000. Interview. Former operations chief, Board of Education, Chicago, IL, November 3.

Romzek, Barbara S., and Melvin J. Dubnick. 1987. Accountability in the Public Sector: Lessons from the Challenger Tragedy. *Public Administration Review* 47(3): 227–39.

Rose-Ackerman, Susan. 1993. Which Bureaucracies Are Less Corruptible? In *Political Corruption: A Handbook*, edited by Arnold J. Heindenheimer, Michael Johnston, and Victor LeVine, 803–18. New Brunswick, NJ: Transaction Publishers.

Rossi, Rosalind. 1994. School Board Tightens Purchasing Procedure. *Chicago Sun-Times*, July 19, 12.

——. 1996a. School Engineers Get Warning. *Chicago SunTimes*, May 25, 4.

——. 1996b. Schools Put 40 Vendors On Notice: Vallas to Bar 8 Contractors Suspected of Overcharges. *Chicago SunTimes*, May 23, 6.

——. 1996c. Schools Target 32 for Firing: Biggest Crackdown Ever, Officials Say. *Chicago Sun-Times*, January 23, 1.

——.1997. Special Unit to Probe School Fraud: Service "Bought" from State's Attorney. *Chicago Sun-Times*, September 25, 12.

Rothman, Jerry. 1999. Interview. Associate attorney, Office of Labor Relations, Board of Education, New York City, February 22.

Sack, Kevin. 1993. Cuomo Signs Bill on Control of School Custodians. *New York Times*, November 27, 25.

Segal, Lydia. 1997. The Pitfalls of Political Decentralization and Proposals for Reform: The Case of the New York City Schools. *Public Administration Review* 57 (2): 141–49.

——. 1998. Can We Fight the New Tammany Hall? Difficulties of Prosecuting Political Patronage and Suggestions for Reform. *Rutgers Law Review* 50(2): 507–62.

——. 1999. Corruption Moves to the Center: An Analysis of New York's 1996 School Governance Law. *Harvard Journal on Legislation* 36(2): 323–67.

Sheldon, D.R. 1996. *Achieving Accountability in Business and Government: Managing for Efficiency, Effectiveness, and Economy.* Westport, CT: Quorum Books.

Sherman, W. Lawrence. 1978. *Scandal and Reform: Controlling Police Corruption.* Berkeley, CA: University of California Press.

Special Commissioner of Investigation for the New York City School District (SCI). 1992. *A System Like No Other: Fraud and Misconduct by New York City School Custodians.* New York: SCI.

——. 1996. *Taking Their Time: An Investigation into BOE Custodial Employee Time Abuse.* New York: SCI.

——. 1999a. Case no. 97-0520 *Re Irwin Crespi*, January 28. New York: SCI.

——. 1999b. *Cheating the Children.* New York: SCI.

Vander Weele, Maribeth. 1991a. Overtime for Maintenance Staff at City Schools Tops $6 Million. *Chicago Sun-Times*, September 11, 35.

——. 1991b. Schools Feel OT Pinch: Private Custodial Pacts Studied. *Chicago Sun-Times*, April 29, 1.

——. 1993. Union Rules Don't Stop Principal. *Chicago SunTimes*, March 28, 26.

——. 1994. *Reclaiming Our Schools: The Struggle for Chicago School Reform.* Chicago: Loyola University Press.

——. 1995. System of Fixing Buildings Needs Repair. *Chicago Sun-Times*, March 13, 18.

——. 2000. Interview. Inspector general for the Chicago Board of Trustees, Chicago, IL, October 27.

——. 2001. Investigation Re Steven J. McGuire. Case no. 99-0428, April 5. New York: SCI.

Viteritti, Joseph. 1983. *Across the River: Politics and Education in the City.* New York: Holmes and Meier.

Walt, Steven, and William Laufer. 1992. Corporate Criminal Liability and the Comparative Mix of Sanctions. In *White-Collar Crime Reconsidered*, edited by Kip Schlegel and David Weisburd, 309–31. Boston: Northeastern University Press.

Ward, Richard H., and Robert McCormack. 1987. *Managing Police Corruption: International Perspectives.* Chicago: University of Illinois Press.

Weber, Max. 1946. Bureaucracy. In *Max Weber: Essays in Sociology*, edited by H.H. Gerth and C. Wright Mills, Oxford: Oxford University Press.

Willen, Liz. 1993. 10 Worst Schools Cry "Repair Us." *New York Newsday*, October 21, 4.

Williams, Joe. 2001. Nab 11 Janitors in School Scam. *New York Daily News*, December 12, 40.

Yukl, G. 1998. *Leadership in Organizations.* Upper Saddle River, NJ: Prentice Hall.

***Lydia Segal** is an assistant professor at John Jay College of Criminal Justice, City University of New York, with law degrees from Harvard Law School and Oxford University. She was counsel to the special commissioner of investigation for the New York City Schools, where she directed investigations into a broad range of wrongdoing. She has since written many articles on public corruption and a forthcoming book on corruption and reform in the New York City schools. Email:* **lydiagsegal@hotmail.com**.

UNIT 3

Human Resources Administration

Unit Selections

11. **Is Your Performance Evaluation Fair for All?** Katy Mohler Fodchuk
12. **Preventing Workplace Harassment: A Fact Sheet for Employees**, *Bureau of National Affairs*
13. **Drug and Alcohol Testing in the Workplace: An Overview and Practical Guide for Cities**, Omniah Ebeid
14. **Double-Dip Dilemma**, Anya Sostek

Key Points to Consider

- Identify and discuss the criteria necessary for a fair performance evaluation. Review the performance evaluation instrument and process in your organization, and identify some improvements that would improve them.
- Review the fact sheet on workplace harassment. Also review the policies and the training regarding sexual harassment in your organization. If you are not currently employed, select a public organization and review their information on sexual harassment. What did you learn from your review? What changes (if any) do you think are necessary to improve the organization's policies and training procedures?
- Review the policies and procedures that are related to drug and alcohol testing in your workplace. Identify those procedures that are necessary to ensure that your organization's policies are consistent with the Americans With Disabilities Act (ADA). In your opinion, what actions should be taken by your organization to ensure that the procedures are ADA compliant?

Links: www.dushkin.com/online/
These sites are annotated in the World Wide Web pages.

Sexual Harassment in the Workplace: A Primer
http://www.uakron.edu/lawrev/robert1.html

Skill-Based Pay
http://www.bizcenter.com/skillpay.htm

U.S. Department of Labor
http://www.dol.gov/index.htm

Zigon Performance Group
http://www.zigonperf.com

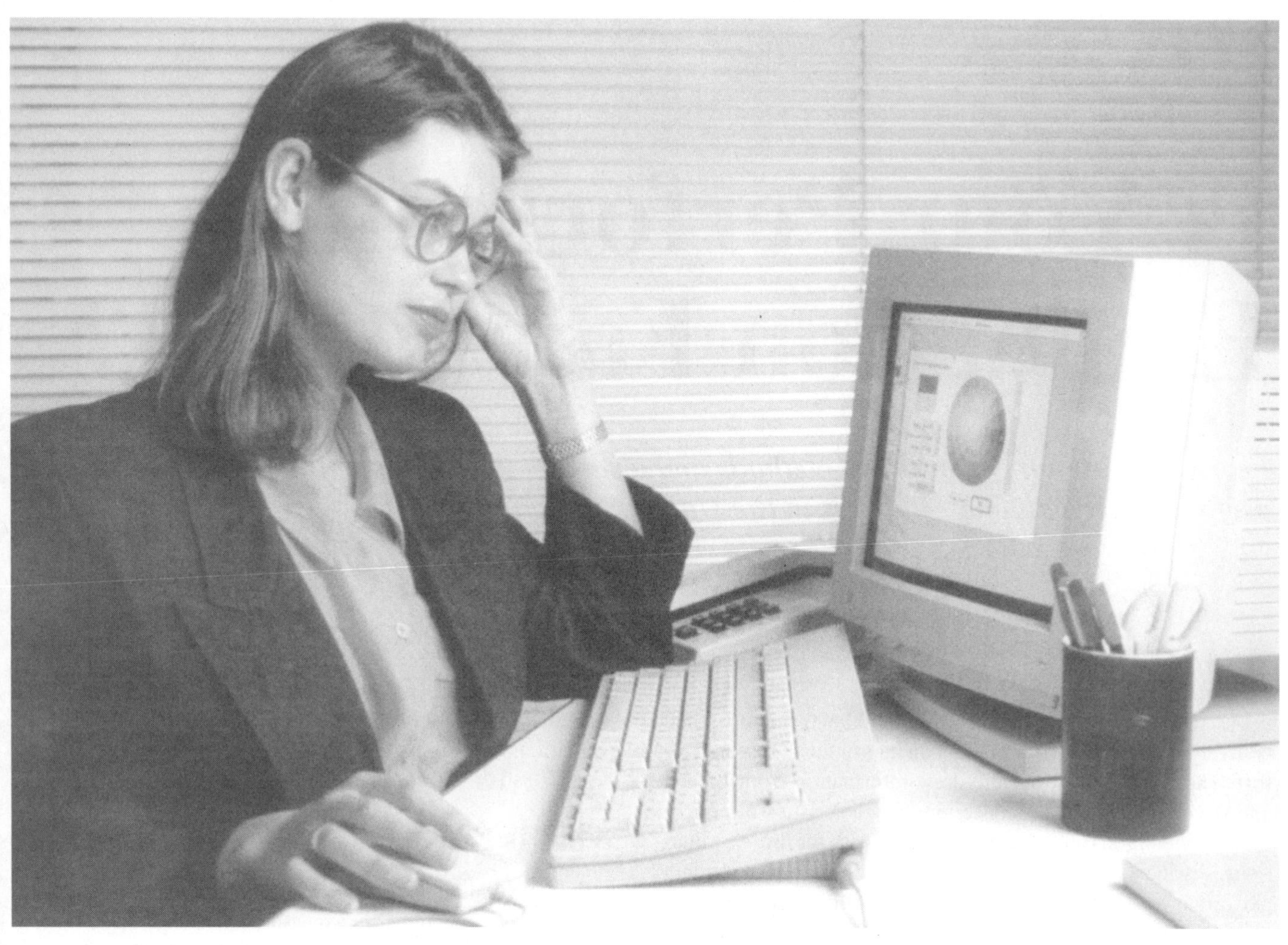

Each article in this section has been selected to provide the reader with an understanding of the complexities faced by human resource administrators in the public sector. The articles focus on the areas of performance evaluation, retirement, employee terminations, and workplace and sexual harassment. In addition, the expansion of charitable choice and faith-based initiatives is also explored.

"Is Your Performance Evaluation Fair for All?" by Katy Fodchuk reviews the performance evaluation process in the United States and compares it with the same process in France. In addition, this comparative public administration article suggests methods for incorporating fairness into a performance evaluation instrument.

The Bureau of National Affairs handout "Preventing Workplace Harassment: A Fact Sheet for Employees" provides definitions of sexual and other workplace harassment, identifies employee responsibilities for preventing harassment, and outlines a chronology of the development of workplace harassment law.

In the article "Drug and Alcohol Testing in the Workplace: An Overview and Practical Guide for Cities," Omniah Ebeid provides an overview of the laws regarding drug-testing policies and programs and outlines a practical guide for public sector employers to follow in enacting or amending current drug testing policies and procedures to make them consistent with laws such as the Americans With Disabilities Act (ADA).

Anya Sostek, in her article "Double-Dip Dilemma, points out that state legislatures are continuing to pass return-to-work or "retire-rehire" laws. This article explores the benefits and disadvantages of "double-dipping" or allowing public employees, who have retired and are collecting a pension, to return to work and draw a salary.

Is Your Performance Evaluation Fair for All?

Learn more about comparative methods and a sample tool for examining performance evaluation fairness in the United States and France.

KATY MOHLER FODCHUK

In March of this year, the National Academy of Public Administration's Center for Human Resources Management invited consortium members to take part in an international research effort. The project questionnaire drew information from French and American employees concerning characteristics of performance evaluations and perceptions of fairness for those evaluations. As most managers are sure to know, compensation and performance evaluations are both sensitive subjects for employees, even for a relatively non-diverse workforce. When a company has a diverse population of employees, it becomes even more important for managers to understand culturally sensitive ways to create and implement procedures for evaluating and allocating resources to employees.

United States and France

The current study analyzed the differences concerning the types of methods used to evaluate employees in the United States and France and, in addition, investigated French and American employees' perceptions of whether they think these procedures are fair, known in industrial/organizational psychology as "procedural justice perceptions." Findings showed interesting similarities and differences concerning the types of evaluations used and emphasis on different aspects of fairness for each country. While the scope of this article cannot cover the results of the study, readers are invited to peruse the survey findings at the Web address listed at the end of the article.

This article presents an adaptation of the survey for readers to survey their own employees. It can be used to discover the extent to which existing performance evaluation procedures incorporate fairness and to identify what aspects are most important to a particular workforce. In addition, the article offers suggested methods for incorporating fairness in a performance evaluation.

What Is Fair?

Before discussing the survey, it is important to first identify how fairness perceptions were measured. In a study which specifically examined employee perceptions of fairness in performance appraisals, Greenberg (1986) questioned a group of managers concerning circumstances in which they received an especially fair or unfair performance appraisal and requested they report precisely what made it so fair or unfair. After Greenberg analyzed the survey results, two factors that accounted for most of the variance were apparent. The first, the procedural justice factor, showed significant emphasis on the following five variables:

- soliciting input prior to evaluation and using it;
- two-way communication during the interview;
- ability to challenge/rebut evaluations;
- rater familiarity with ratee's work; and
- consistent application of standards.

The second factor that fell under the category of distributive justice also became apparent, with significant emphasis on the following two variables: receipt of rating based on performance achieved; and recommendation of salary/promotion based on rating. This second category of distributive justice concerns whether or not resources (pay, benefits, bonuses, etc.) are perceived as fairly distributed, while the first category of procedural justice concerns whether the procedures used to determine those allocations are fair. For example, if an employee receives a smaller raise than her coworker she may perceive that the distribution of resources was unfair resulting in lower distributive justice perceptions. In addition, suppose the employee feels that the evaluation procedure was inconsistent and did not accurately measure performance. This would result in low procedural justice perceptions.

Why Be Concerned with Procedural Justice?

This article specifically focuses on procedural justice perceptions. One reason procedural justice is often the focus of research is that it is pliable and tangible as procedures can be adapted and altered to fit the needs of employers who can attempt to produce changes in ineffective existing practices. Further reason for focusing on procedural justice is offered by Cropanzano and Greenberg (1997) who cite several studies that show that fair treatment in procedures makes individuals more accommodating when changes in organizations take place. Studies examined everything from acceptance of smoking bans to pay systems to disciplinary actions. All studies yielded similar results in that employees were more accepting of decisions that incorporated fair procedures as opposed to those that incorporated unfair procedures.

Procedural justice rules were first examined in 1980 and then combined in 2001 into a framework for analyzing fairness perceptions across cultures. These procedural rules include:

- the consistency rule (allocation procedures should be consistently applied to all persons across time);
- the bias suppression rule (following procedures that are free of personal self-interest and devotion to dogmatic views);
- the accuracy rule (basing decisions on as much good information and informed opinion as possible);
- the correctability rule (allowing for decisions to be modified or reversed if needed);
- the representativeness rule (incorporating the basic concerns, values, and outlook of all concerned parties);
- the ethicality rule (following existing ethical and moral principles);
- voice (the ability to participate and voice opinions);
- information justification (information given to evaluated party concerning evaluation process); and
- social sensitivity (receiving dignified and respectful treatment).

Examining Your Performance Evaluation System for Fairness

Now that procedural justice rules have been discussed, how does one apply this information to his/her current system? The following section presents an approach which can be used to identify employee expectations for performance evaluation procedures, and areas where your current system is not incorporating procedural justice rules.

Survey for Employees

When trying to determine employee expectations for performance evaluation procedures, the following survey—which addresses expectations for each procedural justice rule—can be administered. Also included in the survey are questions drawing information concerning whether the employee feels that procedural justice rules are incorporated in the existing evaluation.

Survey Administration

The left column of Table 1 presents the various procedural justice rules along with questions managers should ask when analyzing their organization's performance evaluation. The column on the right contains two sections, the first of which contains the subheading "Existence of Rule in Current Evaluation Procedure." Below this heading questions address the extent to which rules are incorporated in performance evaluations. Under the second subheading "Expectation for Rule Incorporation in Evaluation Procedure," questions measure employee expectation for procedural justice rules. It is suggested that the statements be included with a five-point scale in order to show relative agreement to these statements (i.e., 1-strongly disagree, 2-disagree, 3-neither agree nor disagree, 4-agree, 5-strongly agree).

When administering the above survey it is important that employees' participation and responses are voluntary, confidential, and where possible, anonymous. If it is not possible to have anonymous responses (e.g., small workforce), employees' responses should in no way influence future performance evaluations. The use of a nonpartial, third person party to administer, analyze, and make recommendations concerning the survey results is suggested.

Inspection for and Incorporation of Procedural Justice

In addition to surveying employees it is also important to conduct a careful inspection of your organization's current procedure, and implement any missing components that would allow for the incorporation of relevant procedural justice rules. The left column on the chart offers helpful questions to ask during this inspection. The following sections suggest components and methods for evaluating employees while incorporating procedural justice rules.

Voice and Correctibility Rule Incorporation

If initial inspection of the performance evaluation indicates a lack of employee participation opportunity, the situation can be remedied by incorporating additional components or adjusting the components that already exist. Performance evaluations should always include a scheduled results discussion meeting between the evaluated employee and his/her evaluator. This meeting should entail a genuine exchange of dialogue and follow a predetermined schedule. For example, results can be

Table 1
Procedural Justice Rules and Sample Survey Questions

Procedural Justice Rule	Employee Survey Statement
Voice: Are evaluated employees allowed and/or encouraged to vocally participate in evaluations?	**Existence of Rule in Current Evaluation Procedure?** • There is an exchange of dialogue between my evaluator and me during the evaluation process. • My evaluator asks me to give input concerning my performance when performance evaluations are conducted. • I am able to express my opinions concerning my evaluation during the evaluation process. **Expectation for Rule Incorporation in Evaluation Procedure.** • I feel that an evaluation process, which limits my participation, is unfair. • I would be upset if others evaluated me without considering my opinions concerning my performance.
Consistency: Do evaluated employees receive the same treatment at all times?	**Existence of rule in Current Evaluation Procedure?** • Employees in similar jobs are evaluated using the same criteria. • Evaluators use a consistent evaluation procedure for all employees. **Expectation for Rule Incorporation in Evaluation Procedure.** • I think it is important for employees to be evaluated using similar and consistent procedures.
Bias-suppression: Does bias result against evaluated employee's group (e.g., sex, race, age, etc)?	**Existence of rule in Current Evaluation Procedure?** • The evaluation of my performance is conducted in an objective manner. • I feel my evaluator judges me on job related factors only. **Expectation for Rule Incorporation in Evaluation Procedure.** • I think it is unacceptable for an evaluator to allow personal biases to influence the results of an employee's performance evaluation.
Accuracy: Is the evaluator using accurate information and is the evaluator competent?	**Existence of rule in Current Evaluation Procedure?** • The performance evaluation reflects true performance levels. • My evaluator keeps accurate records of my performance during the performance evaluation period. **Expectation for Rule Incorporation in Evaluation Procedure.** • I would be disappointed if my evaluator was not aware of my performance and accomplishments during my evaluation period.
Correctability: Does the evaluated employee have the ability to correct or change results by presenting relevant information?	**Existence of rule in Current Evaluation Procedure?** • If I offer legitimate concerns about the results of my evaluation, they can be changed. • If I have any concerns about the results of my evaluation, I feel comfortable telling my evaluator. **Expectation for Rule Incorporation in Evaluation Procedure.** • If an employee feels their performance evaluation results are unfair that employee should have the opportunity to offer legitimate information in order to change the results of a performance evaluation.
Representativeness: Will the evaluated employee's interests be taken into account?	**Existence of rule in Current Evaluation Procedure?** • I feel my evaluator is aware of my career needs and goals. • I feel as though my evaluator understands and takes into account certain barriers, which may hinder my performance during the evaluation period (e.g., lack of resources, personal health problems, infeasible deadlines, etc.). **Expectation for Rule Incorporation in Evaluation Procedure.** • I expect my evaluator to take my individual circumstances and obstacles into account when evaluating my performance.
Social Sensitivity: Is the evaluated employee treated with dignity and respect?	**Existence of rule in Current Evaluation Procedure?** • My evaluator praises or compliments me for my performance during the performance evaluation. • My evaluator shows me respect during the performance evaluation. **Expectation for Rule Incorporation in Evaluation Procedure.** • If my evaluator showed me little respect during my evaluation procedure I would be really upset.

Table 1 continued

Information Justification: Is the evaluated employee provided with information concerning how the evaluation results were determined?	**Existence of rule in Current Evaluation Procedure?** • I understand the procedure used to evaluate me. • I am given information on the manner in which the results of my evaluation are determined. **Expectation for Rule Incorporation in Evaluation Procedure.** • Employees who are being evaluated for their performance should be given information as to how the results are determined.
Ethicality: Are the evaluated employee's moral and ethical values respected?	**Existence of rule in Current Evaluation Procedure?** • There are certain aspects of the evaluation process in my company which I find unethical. • The performance evaluations at this organization are conducted using an approach which contradicts my principles. **Expectation for Rule Incorporation in Evaluation Procedure.** • Performance evaluations which violate moral and ethical values should not be used.

presented by the evaluator and should give examples of work behaviors to justify the conclusions. Another excellent way to incorporate voice is with the use of self-ratings. This allows the evaluated employee, or "evaluatee" to participate in the evaluation process while offering examples of work behavior and work products that lead to above or below average ratings.

To incorporate the rule of correctibility, the evaluatee should have the opportunity to offer additional information that the evaluator does not take into account. The evaluatee should also feel comfortable in questioning any results that do not correspond with the evaluatee's perceptions or records concerning his/her performance. By allowing for active participation in the evaluation procedure the evaluatee is encouraged to become more accountable for keeping track of on-the-job challenges and accomplishments.

Consistency and Accuracy

The consistency of performance evaluation procedures use across employees is an imperative characteristic of a fair performance evaluation. For example, suppose one employee receives a casual evaluation that is mostly based on his/her most recent successful work product, while his/her colleague receives an extensive review of performance relating to client contact, all work products from the preceding year, and programming skills. While it is understood that employees in different positions will be evaluated using different criteria it is still desirable for the structure of the evaluation to be similar across employees. Therefore, if one employee participates in the evaluation by detailing self-ratings for job-related work behaviors and products, it would be inconsistent if his/her co-worker had no say in his/her results and was evaluated only by a supervisor.

Accuracy can be implemented in an evaluation by careful recording of the evaluatee's job-related behaviors and work products. During the evaluation period evaluators should keep a written log of accomplishments, improvement, as well as areas where the employee is having difficulty meeting goals. Evaluatee self-ratings are definitely a good complement to the evaluator's log as it allows for two separate accounts of the employee's performance that can later be compared when discussing results. Given the amount of employment litigation in the United States, this type of record keeping is also essential as a means for justifying differences in pay across incumbents in similar job categories.

Bias Suppression and Social Sensitivity

One method for possibly reducing the influence of an evaluator's potential bias against the evaluatee's group membership (race, sex, age, creed, national origin, etc.) is to require the evaluator to record work-related behaviors as mentioned above for accuracy. The recordings should be specific, dated, objective, and focus on job-related behaviors as opposed to subjective opinions. For example, suppose Janet is not meeting goals concerning duties that entail customer service. Further, suppose her evaluator writes as a log entry, "Janet is a real pistol. I can't stand the way she flies off the handle with customers all the time!" This does not say much about Janet's observable work behavior. Instead the evaluator would offer more objective and documented information by stating the following:

> On March 23, 2002, while taking a client call from Company X, I overheard Janet using inappropriate language and a hostile tone with the client. On a follow-up phone call, the client expressed reluctance to work with our company due to Janet's behavior. Several other client complaints are listed with corresponding names and dates below.

If employees should challenge or question the results, accurate information and non-biased information must available for justification. In addition the use of more than one evaluator potentially can help offset personal biases by holding evaluators more accountable for justifying their results to other evaluators as well as allowing for the generation of more information on the evaluatee's performance record.

Social sensitivity can be incorporated in an evaluation procedure by creating a format where evaluatees are treated with respect. Oftentimes performance evaluations act as a discussion ground for areas where evaluatees need improvement. Given the sensitive topics, evaluators need to be trained in offering constructive criticisms without trampling employee feelings and confidence. Again evaluators should always focus on the work behavior and not the personality of the evaluatee. For example, during Janet's evaluation her supervisor says:

> You are horrible at customer relations! I don't know how you expect to succeed in technical support with that attitude of yours. Because you are so hopeless in this area I gave you the worst rating possible.

Instead a better approach would be to bring it back to work behaviors or outcomes, for example:

> As you know I have spoken with three clients who were upset by tech support calls directed by you. Specifically, they complained that the treatment they received was impolite and abrasive and their questions were not answered. This is why you received such a low evaluation rating for client contact.

This type of language is much more descriptive in identifying shortcomings and allows for an easier discussion to follow on methods for improving the evaluatee's performance.

Information Justification

Research shows that when employees have an understanding of how an employment decision is derived they are more likely to perceive it as fair (Daly & Geyer, 1995, Greenberg 1986). All evaluatees should be provided with adequate information concerning how they will be evaluated. Adequate information includes a description of all the processes within the evaluation procedure (e.g., employee self-rating, evaluator review of self-ratings, discussion of results, pay increase, etc.) as well as the standards by which the employee will be evaluated (e.g., number of products sold, product enhancement goals met, completion of employee manual, etc.) This information should be provided as soon as the employee begins a new position as not only will it foster understanding of the evaluation procedure, the employee also will learn the goals toward which he/she will need to work in the subsequent performance evaluation period.

Representativeness

Representativeness is perceived when the evaluator is aware of the employee's career needs and goals. The representativeness rule can be implemented by ensuring that evaluatees have the option to discuss obstacles that have been impeding their ability to adequately perform the job. Obstacles can be personal problems such as an ailing family member, marital difficulties, or health problems. It is understood that the employer has little control over the employee's personal obstacles. However, on-the-job barriers such as lack of office supplies, need for training, supplier delays, inefficient and unproductive co-workers or subordinates, and infeasible deadlines should be addressed and taken into account when evaluating an employee. Provisions should be made by the employer to eliminate legitimate on-the-job barriers (e.g., training seminars, reevaluation of deadlines, etc.). A discussion of barriers should be incorporated in the evaluation procedure and employees should be encouraged to generate solutions to problems.

REFERENCES

Greenberg, Jerald. "Determinants of Perceived Fairness of Performance Evaluations." *Journal of Applied Psychology*, (71 (2) 1986), pp. 317–372.

Leventhal, Gerald. "What Should be Done with Equity Theory? New approaches to the study of fairness in social relationships." K.S.Gergen, M.S. Greenberg, and R.H. Willis, eds. *Social Exchange: Advances in Theory and Research* (New York, Henum Press: 1980).

Miceli, M. P. and Jerald Greenberg. "Justice and Pay System Satisfaction." R. Cropanzano, ed. *Justice in the Workplace: Approaching Fairness in Human Resource Management* (Hillsdale, NJ, Erlbaum: 1993), pp. 257–283.

Steiner, Dirk. "Cultural Influences on Perceptions of Distributive and Procedural Justice." Gilliliand, Steven, Dirk Steiner, and Skarlicki, D. eds. *Theoretical and Cultural Perspectives on Organizational Justice*. (2001): pp. 111–136.

Katy Mohler Fodchuk *is completing her master's degree in industrial/organizational psychology at California State University, Sacramento. Mrs. Fodchuk received the 2001–2002 Fulbright Advanced Student Scholarship to conduct international research concerning procedural justice perceptions and performance evaluations at the Université de Nice, Sophia-Antipolis in Nice, France. Full study findings, including bibliography, can be found at:* www.geocities.com/performanceevaluation2002.

PREVENTING WORKPLACE HARASSMENT: A FACT SHEET FOR EMPLOYEES

Inside This Fact Sheet You'll Find:

Definition of Sexual and Other Workplace Harassment

- what harassing behavior is
- when a workplace environment becomes hostile
- how to tell if conduct is unwelcome

Employee Responsibilities for Preventing Sexual and Other Workplace Harassment

- appropriate responses
- participating in an investigation

Chronology of Development of Workplace Harassment Law

THIS FACT SHEET... explains what workplace harassment is under federal law and what it is not, the kinds of behavior that may be interpreted as harassment in the workplace, how a workplace environment can become "hostile," how to avoid harassment of co-workers, how to deal with harassment if it arises, and what to do if you become involved in a harassment investigation.

This publication was prepared by David Kadue, a partner in the law firm of Seyfarth Shaw. It is current through December 31, 2002, and emphasizes not only explicitly sexual and gender-based harassment but also harassment that is based on protected statuses other than sex. This fact sheet provides accurate and authoritative information regarding harassment but is not legal advice. For legal advice or other expert assistance, seek the services of a competent professional.

What Is Workplace Harassment?

Workplace harassment occurs whenever unwelcome conduct on the basis of gender or other legally protected status affects a person's job.

Sexual harassment. Sexual harassment is defined by the Equal Employment Opportunity Commission (EEOC) as unwelcome sexual advances, requests for sexual favors, and other verbal or physical conduct of a sexual nature when:

- submission to the conduct is made either explicitly or implicitly a term or condition of an individual's employment, or
- submission to or rejection of the conduct by an individual is used as a basis for employment decisions affecting such individual, or
- the conduct has the purpose or effect of unreasonably interfering with an individual's work performance or creating an intimidating, hostile, or offensive working environment.

The U.S. Supreme Court has explained that there are two basic types of unlawful sexual harassment. The first type involves harassment that results in a tangible employment action. An example would be a supervisor who fires a subordinate for refusing to be sexually cooperative. The imposition of this crude "put out or get out" bargain is often referred to as *quid pro quo* ("this for that").

This kind of sexual harassment can be committed only by someone who can make or effectively influence employment actions (such as firing, demotion, and denial of promotion) that will affect the victim.

A second type of unlawful sexual harassment is referred to as *hostile environment.* Unlike a *quid pro quo,* which only a supervisor can impose, a hostile environment can result from the gender-based unwelcome conduct of supervisors, co-workers, customers, vendors, or anyone else with whom the victim interacts on the job. The behaviors that have contributed to a hostile environment have included:

- unfulfilled threats to impose a sexual *quid pro quo;*
- discussing sexual activities;
- telling off-color jokes;
- unnecessary touching;
- commenting on physical attributes;
- displaying sexually suggestive pictures;
- using demeaning or inappropriate terms, such as "Babe";
- using indecent gestures;
- sabotaging the victim's work;
- engaging in hostile physical conduct;
- granting job favors to those who participate in consensual sexual activity; or
- using crude and offensive language.

These behaviors can create liability if they are based on the affected employee's gender and are severe or pervasive, as explained in the next section. Nonetheless, even if unwelcome conduct falls short of a legal violation, employers have moral and organizational reasons as well as legal incentives to address and correct that conduct at its earliest stages.

The conduct constituting sexual harassment is not always sexual in nature. One court held that a man's violent physical assault on a woman was sexual harassment because the assault was based on the woman's gender, even though there was nothing sexual about the assault itself. Suppose, for example, that men sabotage the work of a female co-worker because she is a woman. Even if the men don't engage in sexual behavior, such as telling off-color jokes or displaying pornographic photos on the walls, their behavior is sexual harassment because the behavior is based on the woman's gender.

Harassment on bases other than sex. The *quid pro quo* type of harassment described above happens only with respect to sexual harassment, and perhaps religious harassment (if an employer requires an employee to participate in religious activities as a condition of employment). The hostile environment type of harassment described above can happen with respect to not only gender-based conduct, but also conduct based on other protected statuses, such as race, color, religion, national origin, age, and disability.

As to hostile environment harassment, the same principles that apply to harassment based on gender apply to harassment that is based on other protected statuses. In each case, the questions will be whether there was unwelcome conduct, whether the conduct was based on an employee's protected status, whether the conduct was severe or pervasive enough to affect the employee's employment, and whether the employer will be liable for harassment. These issues are addressed in the remainder of this fact sheet.

When Does a Work Environment Become Hostile?

To create a hostile environment, unwelcome conduct based on a protected status must meet two additional requirements: (1) it must be subjectively abusive to the person(s) affected, and (2) it must be objectively severe or pervasive enough to create a work environment that a reasonable person would find abusive.

To determine whether behavior is severe or pervasive enough to create a hostile environment, the finder of fact (a court or a jury) considers these factors:

- the frequency of the unwelcome discriminatory conduct;
- the severity of the conduct;
- whether the conduct was physically threatening or humiliating, or a mere offensive utterance;
- whether the conduct unreasonably interfered with work performance;
- the effect on the employee's psychological well-being; and
- whether the harasser was a superior in the organization.

Each factor is relevant—no single factor is required to establish that there is a hostile environment. Relatively trivial, isolated incidents generally do not create a hostile work environment. For example, one court found no legal violation where a woman's supervisor, over the course of a few months, had asked her out on dates, called her a "dumb blonde," placed his hand on her shoulder, placed "I love you" signs in her work area, and attempted to kiss her.

Hostile environment sexual harassment also was not found where women were asked for a couple of dates by co-workers, subjected to three offensive incidents over 18 months, or subjected to only occasional teasing or isolated crude jokes and sexual remarks.

Sexual harassment was found, on the other hand, where women were touched in a sexually offensive manner while in a confined work space, subjected to a long pattern of ridicule and abuse on the basis of their gender, or forced to endure repeated unwelcome sexual advances.

These examples simply illustrate how severe or pervasive gender-based conduct must be to be legally actionable (and how blurred the line between lawful and unlawful conduct sometimes is). Given this uncertainty, prudent employers will address incidents of unwelcome gender-based conduct long before they approach the level of severity or pervasiveness that would create a hostile environment as a legal matter.

Is It Really Harassment?

Hostile environment cases are often difficult to recognize. The particular facts of each situation determine whether offensive conduct has "crossed the line" from simply boorish or childish behavior to unlawful harassment. One factor to consider is the reasonable sensibilities of the person affected. Some courts state that men and women, as a general rule, have different levels of sensitivity—conduct that does not offend most reasonable men might offend most reasonable women. In one study, two-thirds of the men surveyed said they would be flattered by a sexual approach in the workplace, while only 15 percent would be insulted. The figures were reversed for the women responding. Differing general levels of sensitivity have led some courts to adopt a "reasonable woman" standard for judging cases of sexual harassment. Under the standard, if a reasonable woman would feel harassed, harassment may have occurred even if a reasonable man might not see it that way.

Because the boundaries are so poorly marked, the best course of action is to avoid all sexually charged conduct in the workplace. You should be aware that your conduct might be offensive to a co-worker and govern your behavior accordingly. If you're not absolutely sure that behavior is sexual harassment, ask yourself these questions:

- Is this verbal or physical behavior of a sexual nature?
- Is the conduct offensive to the persons who witness it?
- Is the behavior being initiated by only one of the parties who has power over the other?
- Might the employee feel that he or she must tolerate that type of conduct in order to keep his or her job?
- Might the conduct make the employee's job environment unpleasant?

If the answer to these questions is "yes," put a stop to the conduct.

How Can You Tell if Conduct Is Unwelcome?

Only *unwelcome* conduct can be harassment. Joking, comments, and touching, for example, are not harassment if they are welcomed by the persons involved.

Conduct is *unwelcome* if the recipient did not initiate it and regards it as offensive. Some sexual advances ("come here Babe and give me some of that") are so crude and blatant that the advance itself shows its unwelcomeness. Similarly, use of a racist epithet or display of a noose (to suggest lynching) could be so obviously offensive that no additional proof of unwelcomeness is needed. Often, however, the welcomeness of the conduct will depend on the recipient's reaction to it.

Outright rejection. The clearest case is when an employee tells a potential harasser that conduct is unwelcome and makes the employee uncomfortable. It is very difficult for a harasser to explain away offensive conduct by saying, "She said no, but I know that she really meant yes." A second-best approach is for the offended employee to consistently refuse to participate in the unwelcome conduct.

Ambiguous rejection. Matters are more complicated when an offended employee fails to communicate clearly. All of us, for reasons of politeness, fear, or indecision, sometimes fail to make our true feelings known.

Soured romance. Sexual relationships among employees often raise difficult issues as to whether continuing sexual advances are still welcome. Employees have the right to end such relationships at any time without fear of retaliation on the job, so that conduct that once was welcome is now unwelcome. However, because of the previous relationship, it is important that the unwelcomeness of further sexual advances be made very clear.

What not to do. Sending "mixed signals" can defeat a case of sexual harassment. Complaints of sexual harassment have failed because the victim:

- invited the alleged harasser to lunch or dinner or to parties after the supposedly offensive conduct occurred;
- flirted with the alleged harasser;
- wore sexually provocative clothing and used sexual mannerisms around the alleged harasser; and
- participated with others in vulgar language and horseplay in the workplace.

For these reasons, if you find conduct offensive, you should make your displeasure clearly and promptly known. Remember that some offenders may be unaware of how their actions are being perceived. Others may be insensitive to the reactions of fellow workers. Tell the harasser that the behavior is not acceptable and is unwelcomed by you. At the very least, refuse to participate in the behavior.

Even if you do not find the conduct personally offensive, remember that some of your co-workers might, and avoid behavior that is in any way demeaning on the basis of a protected status such as gender, race, or religion. In determining if your own conduct might be unwelcome, ask yourself these questions:

- Would my behavior change if someone from my family was in the room?

- Would I want someone from my family to be treated this way?

EMPLOYEE RESPONSIBILITY FOR PREVENTING WORKPLACE HARASSMENT

You and your employer share a stake in maintaining a harassment-free work environment. Many organizations have written policies, distributed to all employees, that contain examples of prohibited conduct and describe procedures for handing complaints. These policies may forbid conduct that falls short of unlawful workplace harassment. It's important to learn about your own employer's policy.

Retaliation against any employee who reports harassment or who cooperates when the employer investigates a claim of harassment is prohibited. The employer will want to conduct a prompt and thorough investigation of all complaints, and matters will be kept as confidential as possible.

Employer policies typically provide that any employee found to have violated the policy will be subject to discipline, up to and including immediate discharge, and that the complaining employee will be told whether action has been taken, even if not told specifically what was done.

Respond Appropriately When you Encounter Workplace Harassment

If you experience harassment or witness it, you should make a report to the appropriate official. You do not have to report the incident to your supervisor first, especially if that is the person doing the harassing.

Remember that harassment is an organizational problem, and the employer wants to know about it so it can take prompt and appropriate action to ensure that no further incidents occur, with the present victim or other employees, in the future. Report incidents immediately, especially if they are recurring.

Employees who promptly report harassing conduct can help their organization as well as themselves. One comprehensive survey by the American Management Association reported that roughly two-thirds of internal reports result in some kind of discipline being imposed on the alleged harasser, with even more internal reports resulting in either discipline or counseling.

Participating in an Investigation

All employees have a responsibility to cooperate fully with the investigation of a harassment complaint. Investigations will vary from case to case, depending on a variety of circumstances. While not every investigation will follow the same format, in every case you need to keep certain things in mind.

Keep it confidential. First, whether you are the accused employee, the complaining one, or merely a potential witness, bear in mind that confidentiality is crucial. Two people have their reputations on the line, and you may or may not know all the facts. In the typical situation, the employer will keep the information it gathers as confidential as possible, consistent with state and federal laws, and both the accused and the complainant will have a chance to present their cases.

Don't be afraid to cooperate. There can be no retaliation against anyone for complaining about harassment, for helping someone else complain, or for providing information regarding a complaint. The law protects employees who participate in any way in administrative complaints, and employer policies protect employees who honestly participate in in-house investigations. If you are afraid to cooperate, you should be very frank about your concerns when talking to the employer's investigator.

Answer the questions completely.

As the complainant —If you are making the complaint, the investigator will need to know *all* the details, unpleasant though they will be to recount. The investigator has a duty to be fair to everyone involved and needs as much information as possible. Be prepared to give the following information:

- the names of everyone who might have seen or heard about the offensive conduct;
- the names of everyone who may have had a similar experience with the alleged harasser;
- a chronology—when and where each incident occurred;
- the reasons why you did not report the incidents earlier (if you have delayed at all); and
- your thoughts on what the employer should do to correct the problem and maintain a harassment-free environment.

The investigator may need to talk with you several times while other employees are questioned and information is gathered.

As the accused —If you are the person accused of harassment, you must remember that you have a duty to cooperate in the investigation, regardless of whether you believe the allegations to be true or false. You will be expected to answer questions completely and honesty.

You may be asked not to communicate with certain individuals during the course of the investigation. You must remember that you are not to retaliate against the person who made the complaint or against anyone who participates in any way in the investigation. You must treat them in the same fair and even-handed manner you would if no complaint had ever been raised.

Failure to abide by these rules may result in discipline against you, even if the investigation shows that no harassment occurred. Indeed, retaliation against the complainant may violate the law even if the underlying complaint of harassment cannot be substantiated.

You should expect to be asked to confirm or deny each of the specific allegations made against you. It is possible that the allegations are gross exaggerations or downright lies, but it is important to remain calm and keep your responses factual. You may be asked to provide any facts that might explain why the complainant would be motivated to exaggerate or fabricate the charges. The investigator might need to talk to you several times while other employees are questioned and information is gathered.

As a potential witness —You may be asked to provide details concerning alleged harassment between other employees. You have a duty to respond truthfully to the questions concerning these allegations.

The natural tendency after an interview by an investigator is to share with co-workers the more interesting details. Remember that the employer's policy is to keep the interviews as confidential as possible. Gossip about allegations can unfairly damage the reputation of co-workers.

Keep the lines of communication open. The object of the employer's investigation is to find out what happened. The investigator may conclude that harassment occurred, that it did not occur, or that it is impossible to tell what really happened.

As the complainant or as the accused, you have the right to know in general terms what the organization's conclusion is, and you should ask if you are not told. Do not assume that the matter is settled until you have been told so directly.

If you are the complaining party, it is important to promptly report any new incidents of harassment that occur after your first talk with the investigator, and to tell the investigator about anything you may have forgotten or overlooked. Do not be discouraged by the fact that the employer takes time to act, and bear in mind that the more information you provide, the better chance there is for decisive action by the employer.

If you are the accused, do not be discouraged if the employer's investigation fails to completely clear your name. It is not uncommon to conclude that there is no way to tell what really happened. Remember, harassment complaints often involve one-on-one situations where it is difficult to determine the truth. Moreover, two people can have totally different perceptions of the same incident. The best you can do in such a situation is to avoid future situations where your words or conduct can be used as evidence of harassment.

Expect adequate remedial action. If the employer finds that harassment did occur (or even some inappropriate conduct falling short of harassment), expect the employer to take some remedial action. A variety of disciplinary measures may be used, including:

- an oral or written warning;
- deferral of a raise or promotion;
- demotion;
- suspension; or
- discharge.

The action taken in any particular case is within the organization's discretion. The precise nature of the discipline is often kept confidential to ensure that the privacy of individuals is protected. One aim of the action is to deter any future acts of harassment. If you, as the complaining party, feel that the harasser is retaliating against you for complaining or is continuing to harass you, you should immediately use the employer's procedures to report the conduct so that the employer can take whatever further action is appropriate.

If the employer does not have enough evidence to reach a conclusion about harassment, it still might take other actions, such as separating the parties, holding training sessions on preventing harassment, or having the affected employees certify that they have read again and fully understand the employer's policy against harassment.

Note: Many organizations forbid conduct that falls short of unlawful harassment, and do impose discipline for conduct that comes to their attention as the result of a harassment complaint, even if the conduct does not violate the law or the organization's antiharassment policy. For example, a manager who makes sexual advances to subordinates might be disciplined for exercising poor judgment, even if the advances were welcome; and an employee who engages in a single incident of offensive conduct might be disciplined for inappropriate conduct, even if the incident was not severe enough to create a hostile environment. The fact that an employer imposes discipline in response to a complaint of harassment is not an admission, therefore that any unlawful harassment has occurred.

DEVELOPMENT OF THE LAW OF WORKPLACE HARASSMENT

1964...

The Civil Rights Act of 1964 became law. Title VII prohibits employment discrimination on the basis of race, color, religion, national origin, and sex. There is no mention of harassment in the law or its legislative history.

1967...

The Age Discrimination in Employment Act becomes law. It forbids employers to discriminate against individuals, over age 40, on the basis of their age, without specifically addressing harassment on the basis of age.

1968...

The Equal Employment Opportunity Commission (EEOC), the agency that enforces federal antidiscrimination laws, finds that an employer violated the Title VII ban on national origin discrimination by permitting employees to harass a Polish-born co-worker with demeaning conduct that included making him the butt of "Polish" jokes. Case No. CL 68-12-431EU, 2 FEP Cases 295.

1972...

A U.S. appeals court consider the race-based harassment of an employee that involved no tangible job action but that undermined her psychological stability. The court rules that Title VII forbids working environments "heavily charged with ethnic or racial discrimination." *Rogers v. EEOC,* 4 FEP Cases 92 (5th Cir.)

1974...

A female employee claims she was retaliated against for rejecting her boss's sexual advances. There was no sex discrimination, a trial court decides. The male supervisor, the court says, merely solicited his subordinate because he found her "attractive" and then retaliated because he felt "rejected." *Barnes v. Train,* 13 FEP Cases 123 (D.D.C.)

1975...

An atheist who resigned to avoid mandatory staff meetings featuring religious talk and prayers could claim an unlawful constructive discharge on the basis of religion, a U.S. appeals court rules. *Young v. Southwestern Sav. & Loan Ass'n,* 10 FEP Cases 522, 524–25 (5th Cir.)

1976...

The humiliation and termination of a female employee by her male supervisor because she rejected his sexual advances, if proven, would be sex discrimination, a court rules, because it was an artificial barrier to employment placed before one gender and not the other. *Williams v. Saxbe,* 413 F. Supp. 654, 12 FEP Cases 1093 (D.D.C.)

1977...

Reversing the 1974 *Barnes v. Train* case, appealed under a different name, a U.S. appeals court rules that if a female employee was retaliated against for rejecting sexual advances of her boss, this is sex discrimination in violation of Title VII. *Barnes v. Costle,* 561 F.2d 983, 15 FEP Cases 345 (D.C. Cir.)

1980...

The EEOC issues guidelines interpreting Title VII to forbid sexual harassment as a form of sex discrimination. 29 C.R.F. § 1604.11

1981...

For the first time a U.S. appeals court endorses the EEOC's position that Title VII liability can exist for sexual insults and propositions that create a "sexually hostile environment," even if the employee lost no tangible job benefits as a result. *Bundy v. Jackson,* 641 F.2d 934, 24 FEP Cases 1155 (D.C. Cir.)

Another U.S. appeals court recognizes that African-American employees subjected to a "steady barrage of opprobrious racial comment" by co-workers and supervisors can sue for racial discrimination under Title VII, though they must show the comments were more than sporadic. *Johnson v. Bunny Bread Co.,* 25 FEP Cases 1326, 1331–32 (8th Cir.)

1983...

An employer is held liable for the sexist name-calling of a female air traffic controller because it failed to take corrective action when the employee complained. *Katz v. Dole,* 709 F.2d 251, 31 FEP Cases 1521 (4th Cir.)

1985...

Physical violence can be sexual harassment, a U.S. appeals court says, even if the conduct is not overtly sexual: all that is necessary is that the unwelcome conduct be on the basis of the victim's gender. *McKinney v. Dole,* 765 F.2d 1129, 38 FEP Cases 364 (D.C. Cir.)

1986...

Addressing the sexual harassment issue for the first time, the U.S. Supreme Court rules that a woman who allegedly had sex with her boss a number of times, because she feared losing her job if she did not, could sue for sexual harassment. The question is not whether the employee's conduct was voluntary, but whether the boss's conduct was unwelcome, the Court explains. An employer can be held liable for sexual harassment committed by supervisors if it knew or should have known about the conduct and did nothing to correct it, the Court adds. *Meritor Savings Bank v. Vinson,* 477 U.S. 57, 40 FEP Cases 1822.

1988...

When male construction workers hazed three female colleagues, even if the conduct was not specifically sexual in nature, it was gender-based harassment prohibited by the law, a U.S. appeals court finds. *Hall v. Gus Construction Co.*, 842 F.2d 1010, 46 FEP Cases 57 (8th Cir.)

1989...

Addressing a claim of age-based harassment, a U.S. appeals court assumes that the principles forbidding sexual harassment also apply to claims of harassment based on age over 40. *Young v. Will County Dep't of Public Aid*, 50 FEP Cases 1089, 1093 (7th Cir.)

1990...

The EEOC issues a policy statement saying that sexual favoritism can be sexual harassment. Isolated incidents of consensual favoritism do not violate Title VII, but sexual favoritism does violate the law if advances are unwelcome or favoritism is so widespread that it has become an unspoken condition of employment, the EEOC says.

The Americans with Disability Act (ADA) becomes law. It forbids employees to discriminate against individuals on the basis of a disability, without specifically addressing harassment on the basis of disability.

1991...

A sexually hostile environment violating Title VII is found where women were a small minority of the work force and crude language, sexual graffiti, and pornography pervaded the workplace. Title VII is "a sword to battle such conditions," not a shield to protect preexisting abusive environments, the court declares. *Robinson v. Jacksonville Shipyards*, 760 F. Supp. 1486, 57 FEP Cases 971 (M.D. Fla.)

A court finds that because male and female sensibilities differ, the appropriate standard to use in sexual harassment cases is that of a "reasonable woman" rather than a "reasonable person." The conduct in question—a man's unsolicited love letters and unwanted attention—might seem inoffensive to the average man, but might be so offensive to the average woman that it creates a hostile working environment, the court rules. *Ellison v. Brady*, 924 F.2d 872, 54 FEP Cases 1346 (9th Cir.)

The Senate Judiciary Committee conducts hearings on the nomination of Judge Clarence Thomas to Associate Justice of the United States Supreme Court. One issue is whether, while chairman of the EEOC, Thomas sexually harassed female assistant Anita Hill. Although some senators believe Hill's charges, the Senate votes to give Thomas a seat on the Court. The hearings highlight the issue of sexual harassment and spark debate over just what harassment is and what should be done about it.

The Civil Rights Act of 1991 becomes law, providing for jury trials and for increased damages under Title VII.

1992...

Sexual harassment returns to front-page status with reports of the Navy's Tailhook scandal. The Navy investigates allegations that women attending a convention of naval personnel at a Las Vegas hotel were forced to run through a gauntlet of male personnel and subject themselves to unwelcome touching. The investigation leads to the discipline of several high-ranking naval officers for permitting the situation to occur.

1993...

In its second decision on sexual harassment in employment, the Supreme Court rules that a discriminatorily abusive work environment is unlawful even if it does not affect an employee's psychological well-being. It is enough if (1) the employee subjectively perceives a hostile work environment as a result of gender-based conduct, and (2) the conduct was severe or pervasive enough to create an objectively hostile work environment—one that a reasonable person would find hostile. *Harris v. Forklift Sys.*, 114 S. Ct. 367, 63 FEP Cases 225

A mining company in northern Minnesota is found liable in the first successful sexual harassment lawsuit by a class of women victimized by sexual harassment. *Jensen v. Eveleth Taconite Co.*, 61 FEP Cases 1252 (D. Minn.)

The fact that a woman posed nude for two motorcycle magazines does not affect her claim that she found workplace conduct to be offensive, for her wild private life did not mean she acquiesced to unwanted sexual advances at work. *Burns v. McGregor Elecs. Indus.*, 989 F.2d 959, 61 FEP Cases 592 (8th Cir.)

The EEOC issues proposed guidelines clarifying that harassment on any basis protected by employment law is unlawful. The guidelines are later withdrawn because of controversy over how they would be applied to religious activities in the workplace. 58 Fed. Reg. 51,266

1994...

A state high court rules that an employee who quits and then sues for "constructive discharge" (to hold the employer responsible for terminating employment even though the employee quit) must prove that the employee informed the employer of intolerable conditions and gave it a chance to correct them before resignation. *Turner v. Anheuser-Busch, Inc.*, 7 Cal. 4th 1238, 1248–50 (Cal.)

1995...

A federal district court dismisses the reverse discrimination suit of a male supervisor who was fired for participating in an office party in which a female subordinate received a sexual device as a birthday gift. The court holds it was not discriminatory for the male supervisor to be held to a higher standard as to conduct that led to only a "slap on the wrist" for the female subordinate. *Castleberry v. Boeing Co.*, 880 F. Supp. 1435 (D. Kan.)

1996...

A federal court upholds the dismissal of a manager who was fired for disregarding his boss's order not to discuss an ongoing sexual harassment investigation with other employees. The court rejects the manager's argument that the manager, in discussing the investigation with another employee, had been engaged in activity protected by law. *Morris v. Boston Edison Co.*, 942 F. Supp. 65 (D. Mass.)

A federal appeals court throws out a sexual harassment claim based on a handful of sexually suggestive comments made over a three-month period. This behavior was not severe or pervasive enough to be unlawful harassment, even though the victimized employee subjectively perceived the behavior as harassing. *McKenzie v. Illinois Dep't of Transp.*, 92 F.3d 473, 167 Daily Lab. Rep. (BNA) E-1 (7th Cir.)

1997...

A U.S. appeals court rules that a sexual harassment investigation need not be perfect and that the employer need not take the action the complainant suggests, so long as the action is reasonably calculated to prevent harassment. *Knabe v. Boury Corp.*, 73 FEP Cases 1877 (3d Cir.)

Another U.S. appeals court rules that a police dispatcher can sue for religious harassment on the basis of claims that the police chief scolded her for being sinful, told her she needed salvation, and threatened to fire her unless she "saved" herself. *Venters v. City of Delphi*, 74 FEP Cases 1095 (7th Cir.)

1998...

The California Supreme Court rules that an employer would have had "good cause" to fire an employee for sexual harassment even though a jury had ruled that the alleged misconduct did not occur, so long as the employer reached a conclusion "supported by substantial evidence gathered through an adequate investigation that includes notice of the claimed misconduct and a chance for the employee to respond." *Cotran v. Rollins Hudig Hall Int'l Inc.*, 75 FEP Cases 1074 (Cal.)

In its third case addressing liability standards for harassment in employment, the Supreme Court holds that men as well as women can bring sexual harassment claims and that Title VII applies to "same-sex" harassment. An oil platform worker alleged that male co-workers subjected him to sexual assaults and threatened him with rape. He quit and sued the company for failing to stop this conduct. The Court holds that even though Title VII does not specifically protect men from gender-based harassment by other men, the general principles of sex discrimination and harassment do apply to that conduct. This does not mean that Title VII creates a "general civility code for the American workplace," for "social context" and "common sense" will still control whether particular gender-based conduct is severe enough to create a hostile environment for a reasonable person under the circumstances. *Oncale v. Sundowner Offshore Servs., Inc.*, 76 FEP Cases 221

In two more cases addressing harassment in employment, the Supreme Court creates a new rule for employer liability where a supervisor creates a hostile environment for a subordinate. Under this rule, an employer is liable for an actionable hostile environment created by a supervisor who has immediate (or successively higher) authority over the victimized employee if the harassment results in a tangible employment action, such as a dismissal, a demotion, or a denial of promotion. The employer is also liable for a hostile environment created by a supervisor even where no tangible employment action has occurred, unless (1) the employer has taken reasonable care to prevent and correct sexual harassment, and (2) the employee unreasonably has failed to avoid harm. Proof that an employee failed to use the employer's complaint procedure usually will be enough to show an unreasonable failure by the employee to avoid harm. *Burlington Indus. v. Ellerth*, 77 FEP Cases 1; *Faragher v. City of Boca Raton*, 77 FEP Cases 14

1999...

To give an employer adequate notice of sexual harassment by a co-worker, the complaining employee must provide "enough information to raise a probability of sexual harassment in the mind of a reasonable employer." It is not enough simply to say that a co-worker is "staring" or "name-calling" or that he will not leave the complainant alone. *Kunin v. Sears Roebuck & Co.*, 175 F.3d 289, 79 FEP Cases 1350 (3d Cir.)

A sexually harassed school teacher lost her case under the *Ellerth/Faragher* rule, because she misled investigators and did not report all the harassment that had occurred when she was first interviewed. *Scrivener v. Socorro Indep. Sch. Dist.*, 169 F.3d 969, 79 FEP Cases 429 (5th Cir.)

Responding to a complaint that a male employee had made crude sexual remarks to a female subordinate, an employer avoided liability for sexual harassment by promptly giving him a written reprimand, suspending him without pay for a week, and bringing the harassment to a complete halt. A U.S. appeals court holds that this action was appropriate under the circumstances. *Indest v. Freeman Decorating, Inc.*, 164 F.3d 258, 78 FEP Cases 1527 (5th Cir.)

2000...

The need to show unwelcome conduct

A female sales representative who alleged foul sexual language lost her case because she herself used this type of language around co-workers and thus failed to show unwelcomeness. *Hocevar v. Purdue Frederick Co.*, 216 F.3d 745 (8th Cir.)

Sexual content not necessary to show gender basis

A female employee won her case of sexual harassment because the unwelcome conduct—including sabotage of work and personal isolation—was based on animosity toward her because of her gender, even though it was not sexually explicit. *Pollard v. E. I. DuPont de Nemours Co.*, 213 F.3d 933 (6th Cir.)

Employers must take effective remedial measures, and can be responsible for nonemployee's conduct

A sexual harassment plaintiff prevailed where the employer failed to investigate allegations of co-worker harassment, and was liable even for behavior by nonemployees, because employees encouraged the harassment. *Slayton v. Ohio Dep't of Youth Servs.*, 206 F.3d 669 (6th Cir.)

A female employee was permitted to pursue her sexual harassment claim even though the employer transferred her to end the harassment, because her new location was inconvenient and arguably left her worse off; remedial measures that make the victim worse off are necessarily "ineffective." *Hostetler v. Quality Dining, Inc.*, 218 F.3d 798, 810–11 (7th Cir.)

An employer prevailed against a female electrician whose male co-workers harassed her, because the employer investigated promptly, redistributed the sexual harassment policy, and offered transfer to a different department. This response was reasonable given (1) the time elapsed between notice and response, (2) the options available to the employer, (3) the disciplinary steps taken, and (4) that the response ended the harassment. *Stuart v. GMC*, 217 F.3d 621, 633 (8th Cir.)

Employee must use avenues available

A male employee lost this case because his "off the record" discussion did not imply sexual harassment and he endured 15 unwelcome sexual propositions before finally reporting. *Casiano v. AT&T Corp.*, 213 F.3d 278, 286–87 (5th Cir.)

An employee lost her case because her anonymous letter of complaint, which she then disavowed, was not a reasonable use of the sexual harassment policy. *Hill v. American General Fin.*, 218 F.3d 639, 643 (7th Cir.)

Female store clerks lost their case because they failed to use designated avenues to complain to the designated person, and also failed to reasonably use Open Door Policy because they did not fully inform managers of harassment or request that action be taken. *Madray v. Publix Supermkts., Inc.*, 208 F.3d 1290, 1300 (11th Cir.)

A female employee lost her case because she assured supervisors that everything was fine and did not seek reassignment for herself or the harasser. *Coates v. Sundor Brands*, 164 F.3d 1361 (11th Cir. 1999)

2001...

Disability harassment

In affirming a jury verdict for a medical assistant who is harassed because of her HIV-positive status, a U.S. appeals court becomes the first to state affirmatively that an employee can sue for disability-based harassment under the ADA. *Flowers v. Southern Regional Physician Servs., Inc.*, 247 F.3d 229, 232–33 (5th Cir.)

An invitation to some sexual conduct does not excuse other unwelcome conduct.

An assistant manager prevailed in a case where her supervisor touched her breasts; her speaking in "sexually suggestive terms" did not show she welcomed having her breasts touched. *Beard v. Flying J, Inc.*, 266 F.3d 792 (8th Cir.)

Words alone can be enough

A court permitted female restaurant employees to go to trial where their manager allegedly subjected them to "incessant put-downs, innuendos, and leers." EEOC v. R&R Ventures, 244 F.3d 334 (4th Cir.)

Employers are well positioned when they have adequate policies

Ruling for an employer, a court held that distributing an antiharassment policy will prove that the employer took reasonable care, unless the policy was adopted in "bad faith" or was "otherwise defective or dysfunctional." *Barrett v. Applied Radiant Energy Corp.*, 240 F.3d 262, 266 (4th Cir.)

Employee must use avenues available

Courts have continued to reject employee excuses for failing to report sexual harassment. Among the excuses rejected have been generalized fears of retaliation or futility, and subjective fears of confrontation or unpleasantness. *See Barrett v. Applied Radiant Energy Corp.*, 240 F. 3d 262 (4th Cir.) and Leopold v. Baccarat, Inc., 239 F.3d 243 (2d Cir.)

The First Amendment does not protect harassment

Female firefighters won a sexual harassment case when the court rejected the argument of their city employer that male firefighters had a First Amendment right to view pornography in public areas of the fire station. *O'Rourke v. City of Providence*, 235 F.3d 713, 735 (1st Cir.)

2002...

The Supreme Court addresses the statute of limitations in harassment cases. The Court recognizes that hostile environment claims based on other protected statuses use the same general standards as are used in sexual harassment cases. As to all harassment claims, one can consider "behavior alleged outside the statutory period... so long as any act contributing to [the] hostile environment takes place within the statutory time period," but an employee cannot recover for remote events if the incident within the filing period has "no relation" to events preceding the filing period or if the employer has engaged in "intervening action" to address the earlier harassment. *National R. R. Passenger Corp. v. Morgan*, 122 S. Ct. 2061, 2068, 2074 n. 10, 2075

Physical gay-bashing forbidden by Title VII

In a lawsuit by a gay hotel butler alleging that his co-workers grabbed his crotch, poked his anus, and called him "sweetheart," a controversial U.S. appeals court opinion holds that Title VII can forbid anti-gay harassment when the conduct involves physical sexual assault, with one of the plurality opinions reasoning that anti-gay harassment may also be forbidden under Title VII on the theory that the victimized employee can show gender bias by proving "gender stereotyping harassment," *Rene v. MGM Grand Hotel, Inc.*, 305 F.3d 1061, 1064, 1068–70 (9th Cir.) (en banc)

2003...

A U.S. appeals court rules that an Hispanic employee can sue for national-origin harassment consisting of a long pattern of rude conduct—such as making noises, laughing, and calling Hispanics "stupid." *Diaz v. Swift-Eckrich, Inc.*, 318 F.3d 796 (8th Cir.)

Understanding Workplace Harassment

After having read this fact sheet, you should have a pretty good understanding of what workplace harassment is, how to prevent it, and what to do if you see it. For review and general guidance, here are some of the most commonly asked questions about harassment. For more specific information, contact the human resources office.

Q. Doesn't sexual harassment have to involve sexual advances or other conduct sexual in nature?

A. No. The 1980 EEOC Guidelines on Sexual Harassment do suggest that conduct constituting sexual harassment must be "conduct of a sexual nature," but it is just as wrong and just as unlawful to harass people with gender-based conduct of a non-sexual nature. Consider, for example, a man and a woman each holding the same kind of job in an organization. If their supervisor gives demeaning and inappropriate assignments (such as serving coffee, picking up dry cleaning, emptying a wastebasket) to the woman, but not to the man, because of the woman's gender, that conduct, if sufficiently severe or pervasive, could amount to harassment on the basis of sex even though the assignments are not sexual in nature. The key question here is not whether the conduct was sexual in nature but whether it was based on the victim's gender.

Q. Isn't sexual harassment limited to situations where supervisors make sexual demands on subordinates?

A. No. Sexual power plays by supervisors constitute the most widely publicized and easily understood form of sexual harassment. But harassment also occurs when supervisors, co-workers, or even nonemployees create a hostile environment through unwelcome sexual advances or demeaning gender-based conduct. There have even been cases where a subordinate has sexually harassed a supervisor.

Regarding harassment by nonemployees (clients, customers, vendors, consultants, independent contractors, and the like), the employer's ability to police unwelcome conduct may be more limited than with employees. For example, it is easier to investigate and discipline an employee than a customer. The employer still must take reasonable steps to address the situation once the matter comes to its attention.

Q. Can harassment occur without physical touching or a threat to the employee's job?

A. Yes. The nature of harassment may be purely verbal or visual (pornographic photos or graffiti on workplace walls, for example), and it does not have to involve any job loss. Any conduct based on a protected status that creates a work environment that a reasonable person would consider hostile may amount to harassment.

Q. Isn't there a right to free speech?

A. The First Amendment protects some forms of expression, even in the workplace, but the verbal threats and name calling often involved in harassment are not protected as free speech. For example, the First Amendment would not protect, as free speech, a supervisor's threat to a subordinate that she will lose her job if she does not sleep with her boss. Nor will the First Amendment protect verbal conduct that offends and intimidates other employees to the point that their work is affected, creating a hostile environment.

Q. Is sexual harassment of men, either by women or by other men, unlawful?

A. Yes. Although sexual harassment generally is perpetrated by men against women, any form of unwelcome sexual advance against employees of either gender may be the basis for a case of unlawful sexual harassment.

Q. Can individuals be legally liable for harassment, or just employers?

A. Some courts have held that individual employees cannot be liable under Title VII. Some state laws, however, do impose personal liability on individuals for perpetrating harassment. While employers often provide a legal defense for employees in a lawsuit, an employer may be entitled, after a court decision against it, to recover damages and legal expenses from an employee whose unauthorized conducted created the problem.

Q. I'm so mad at the person who harassed me and at my employer that I just want to sue. Should I even bother to complain under my employer's harassment policy?

A. Yes. You owe it to your employer and to your coworkers to report through the organization's channels to give the employer a chance to solve the problem promptly, before others are affected.

A prompt complaint is also something that you owe yourself, even if your sole concern is to sue your employer. If you ail to use internal procedures, the employer's defense team will be sure to use that fact to argue that (1) the conduct complained of never occurred, (2) the conduct was not really unwelcome, (3) the conduct was not severe or pervasive enough to create a hostile work environment, or (4) the employer cannot be held responsible for preventing or correcting harassment that it did not know about.

Furthermore, under the 1998 decisions by the U.S. Supreme Court in *Ellerth* and *Faragher*, if the employer has an effective antiharassment policy that the employee unreasonably fails to use, the employer may win a hostile environment lawsuit on that ground alone.

Failing to complain can be particularly harmful to your legal interests if you claim that harassment forced you to quit. It is hard to blame your employer for forcing you off the job if it could have corrected the conduct but was never given the opportunity to do so.

Drug and Alcohol Testing in the Workplace:

An Overview and Practical Guide for Cities

In the 1990's, the nation declared a war on drug abuse in the workplace. Since then, the courts have grappled with defining and redefining the parameters within which employers may prohibit the use and abuse of drugs through drug testing policies in the workplace. This paper will attempt to provide an overview of the law regarding drug testing policies and programs, and will provide a practical guide to cities as employers in enacting or amending current policies.

By Omniah Ebeid

TML Legal Counsel

Alcohol Testing

Drug and alcohol testing policies generally raise constitutional issues such as right to privacy and the right against unreasonable searches and seizures. In addition to these constitutional rights, testing policies must, under some circumstances, pass muster with the Americans with Disabilities Act (ADA).

With regard to alcohol testing, the Equal Employment Opportunity Commission (EEOC) has interpreted the ADA's application to drug and alcohol testing policies, and concluded that alcohol testing is considered a medical examination under the Act. A medical examination is generally defined as a procedure that seeks information about a person's physical or mental impairments or health. Accordingly, any alcohol testing conducted by employers to determine whether or how much alcohol an individual has consumed is medical in nature and is therefore prohibited. This prohibition, however, applies only in the pre-job offer stage. Therefore, employers are only prohibited from requiring alcohol testing intended to detect whether or not an applicant has used or is currently consuming alcohol prior to extending to the applicant a conditional offer of employment. The Act, however, does permit an employer to make pre-employment inquiries into the ability of an applicant to perform job-related functions. These inquiries must be relevant, consistent with a business necessity, and narrowly tailored for the job in question.

With regard to testing current employees, the law does not prohibit alcohol testing as long as the test is job-related and is administered consistently with a business necessity. For example, an employee who shows up to work under the influence of alcohol and whose job performance is compromised as a result of such intoxication may be subjected to an alcohol test pursuant to a testing policy. However, it would not be permissible to require all employees to undergo random alcohol testing.

Practical Guide to Implementing Alcohol Testing Policies

When drafting an alcohol testing policy, employers are advised to prohibit only the use or possession of alcohol or intoxication during the course and scope of employment. A critical step in drafting or amending an alcohol testing policy is to include a clear and precise definition of the term "intoxicated" that is clearly consistent with the Texas Labor Code. Therein, intoxication is defined as: 1) having a blood alcohol concentration level of 0.10 or more; or (2) not having the normal use of one's mental or physical faculties, resulting from the voluntary introduction into the body of an alcoholic beverage, a controlled substance, a dangerous drug, an abusable glue or aerosol paint or any similar substance, the use of which is regulated under the law.

Second, a policy should prohibit employees from being under the influence of alcohol in the workplace, and may give employers the authority to conduct alcohol testing as long as the employer has a reasonable belief that an employee has been drinking during work hours. With regard to periodic alcoholic testing, employers may not generally require it of their employees. However, employees who have been in an alcoholic rehabilitation program may be required to undergo periodic alcohol testing provided that the employer has reasonable belief that the employee may pose a direct threat to other employees in the absence of such testing. In determining whether an employee should be subjected to such periodic testing, the employer should consider the safety risks associated with the employee's position, the consequences of the employee's inability or impaired ability to do his or her job, and the reason(s) that the employer believes the employee may or will pose a direct threat to the other employees.

Third, employers must comply with the ADA by ensuring that any and all results of alcohol tests be kept in a confidential file that is separate and apart from the employee's personnel file.

Drug Testing

Drug testing policies are generally much more complicated than alcohol testing policies, and require a more careful analysis. Nevertheless, employers need not consider certain ADA ramifications because (1) the ADA specifically establishes that tests to determine the current illegal use of controlled substances are not considered "medical examinations," so testing of job applicants is not prohibited; and (2) current drug users are not considered to be "individuals with disabilities" under the Act, so the testing of such individuals does not have to pass ADA muster. Employers must, however, comply with ADA when dealing with the results of such tests. As with alcohol testing, employers are required to keep drug test results in a separate file (apart from an employee's personnel file) that must remain confidential.

What makes drug testing policies more complicated are constitutional questions that center around an employee's right to privacy, the right against unreasonable search and seizure by the government under the Fourth Amendment, and the consequent constitutional restrictions imposed on a governmental entity's actions.

Privacy Rights

Generally, the right to privacy precludes governmental intrusion into the life of an individual. This right is said to emanate from specific guarantees found in the Bill of Rights, and involves one's autonomy in his or her body, freedom from unwanted governmental intrusions in decisions about one's life, and the right to not be required to disclose certain personal facts. However, though recognized by the United States and Texas Supreme Courts, the right to privacy is not absolute, and some regulations may be justified.

It has been established by the courts during the past 20 years that drug testing is one of the areas in which the right to privacy of an employee or applicant will sometimes yield to governmental intrusion. When presented with invasion of privacy claims, however, Texas courts have consistently upheld random testing and have refused to create a public policy exception based on invasion of privacy. In reality, in the majority of cases, employees find it hard to establish an invasion of privacy claim because they are not forced into taking the drug tests. Accordingly, unless the test is conducted in a manner that is, in itself, an invasion of privacy, the employer will have an absolute defense to an invasion of privacy claim. This should not be construed, however, as a total defense in all cases, and employers must certainly ensure that the dignity of the employee is maintained during testing.

With that said, however, a drug testing policy must still meet other tests in order to pass constitutional muster. The government must demonstrate that: (1) the intrusion is warranted to achieve a compelling governmental objective; and (2) the objective of the test cannot be achieved by less intrusive, more reasonable means. In analyzing the constitutionality of testing programs, the United States Supreme Court has stated that in some cases an employee's privacy expectations may be lowered if his or her position already entails going through some sort of background investigations, medical examinations, or other such intrusions. For instance, the privacy rights of security guards were reduced because they were already subjected to extensive medical examinations and background checks. In another case, employees at a chemical plant were found to have a lower level of privacy expectation because they were already subjected to annual drug testing. The testing of athletes in schools was upheld under a similar theory.

Employees have attempted to redefine the limits of their privacy rights under a negligence theory. This was addressed in Texas in 1998 in *Quintanilla v. K-Bin, Inc.*, in which an employee argued that his employer was negligent for failing to evaluate his explanation for a positive drug test result because the consent form gave the employer "the power to terminate him if his drug test revealed an unexplained presence of a drug and/or alcohol." The court rejected this argument and dismissed the employee's negligence and gross negligence claim. In reaching its conclusion, the court reasoned that in order to maintain a negligence claim, there must be a duty owed to the plaintiff, but that no such legal duty exists in the context of an employment-at-will relationship.

To summarize, even though employees have had difficulty challenging drug testing policies in Texas by arguing invasion of privacy, employers must nevertheless ensure that: (1) if they require testing, the employee's dignity during the testing is maintained; (2) that they use reasonable care in administering the tests; and (3) the governmental body has a compelling objective it wishes to achieve by drug testing.

Fourth Amendment Rights—Random Testing

The second constitutional issue that employers must consider when dealing with drug testing policies is the right of protection from unreasonable searches and seizures pursuant to the Fourth Amendment of the United States Constitution. The type of drug testing that poses the greatest risk in connection with the Fourth Amendment is random or suspicionless testing.

The Fourth Amendment establishes "[t]he right of the people to be secure in their persons, houses, papers, and effects, against unreasonable searches and seizure" and states that such rights "shall not be violated, and no Warrants shall issue, but upon probable cause." Fourth Amendment protection extends to individuals even when the government acts as their employer, but does not strip the government of the power to safeguard its vital interests by limiting the individuals' rights to privacy. With regard to drug testing, it is well established that urinalysis drug tests invade the reasonable expectations of privacy of an employee and are "searches" within the meaning of the Fourth Amendment.

Pursuant to the Fourth Amendment a search must normally be accompanied by a valid warrant that is issued based on probable cause. However, the courts have ruled that neither a showing of probable cause nor a warrant will be required for drug testing. The question then becomes whether such searches are "reasonable."

A search or seizure is usually unreasonable unless there is an individualized suspicion of wrongdoing. However, it is often impractical and ineffective to allow drug testing based on an individualized suspicion, especially where the government's interest in having random testing would be jeopardized by requiring individual suspicion in each case. Accordingly, the courts have recognized an exception under which random or suspicionless testing is allowed. This exception provides that a governmental entity may randomly drug test employees if it can show that it has "special needs, beyond the normal need for law enforcement." In other words, the governmental entity must have a need that is different than the enforcement of anti-drug laws.

If the employing entity establishes a valid special need, the courts are then required to undertake a "context-specific" inquiry, which entails close examination of the competing private and public interests advanced by the policy. In order to be upheld, the special need of the government must be "substantial—important enough to override the individual's acknowledged privacy interest, sufficiently vital to suppress the Fourth Amendment's normal requirement of individualized suspicion."

Courts have grappled with the meaning of the term "special need," and the methods of defining it has evolved into two distinct categories. Under the first approach, a "special need" has been found to exist in cases where the individual subject to the tests performed a highly regulated function concerning public safety or a special governmental role. As stated by the United States Supreme Court, if the risk to public safety is substantial and real, or where "public safety is genuinely in jeopardy" then suspicionless drug testing may be considered reasonable for Fourth Amendment purposes. Mere desire to sustain or provide public confidence, instilling some kind of symbolic feeling of public integrity, upholding the global goal of prevention of substance abuse, or a display of commitment to the struggle against drug abuse have all been rejected by the courts as insufficient special needs that will not withstand a constitutional challenge.

The second way of showing a "special need" is by a showing of exigent circumstances coupled with continued failure in attempts to alleviate the problem. For example, in *Vernonia*, the Supreme Court upheld random drug testing of student athletes because the school was in crisis, a large part of the student body was in rebellion and athletes were leaders of the drug culture, the athletes were held to have a lower expectation of privacy than the rest of the student population, and there was an increased risk of sports-related injuries. Evidence of prior drug use, even if demonstrative of a drug epidemic or problem, is not sufficient, standing alone, to show special need. There must be a showing of more than mere symbolic desire to alleviate drug use.

Assuming a special need can be shown, an employer must also be able to make a showing of causation in order for the random testing policy to withstand a constitutional challenge. This requires the employer to establish a "clear and direct nexus... between the nature of the employee's duty and the nature of the feared violation." In the *Cheney* case, the Army instituted a compulsory drug testing program for certain civilian employees. The labor unions sued the Army, and the Court held that the Army established a nexus in some cases, but that no nexus was established between the duties of lab technicians or other employees in the chain of custody and the nature of the feared harm. Therefore, the drug testing policy could not be upheld for such jobs.

Fourth Amendment Rights—Non-Random Testing

Many employers maintain programs that allow testing only if a reasonable suspicion of drug use exists. These policies must also be analyzed in terms of constitutional restraints, but do not pose the same level of difficulties found in random testing policies. Similar to random testing, no search warrants are required. Rather, the validity of the government's policy is determined by "balancing its intrusion on the [employees'] Fourth Amendment interests against its promotion of legitimate governmental interest." "When the balance of [these] interests precludes insistence on a showing of probable cause,... some quantum of [reasonable or] individualized suspicion must be shown before a search may be deemed reasonable under the Fourth Amendment." As stated in the *Yeutter* case, employees who did not hold safety-sensitive or security-sensitive positions could not be tested unless the government had a reasonable suspicion of drug use. In other words, if the government has a legitimate public health, safety, or national security interest in confirming whether an employee is using illegal drugs on or off-duty, the existence of reasonable suspicion weighs in favor of finding that a resulting search is reasonable.

Similar to testing based on suspicion of drug use, post-accident testing and pre-employment or applicant testing has been upheld under certain circumstances. Although upheld, the courts have established that the government must have a compelling security or safety interest in order to allow this type of testing. The decision in the case allowing these tests revolved around the fact that in addition to the government's interest, the jobs in question were already in a heavily regulated industry, and the employees were also already subject to a higher level of scrutiny than other employees.

The Texas Workers' Compensation Act

In addition to the forgoing constitutional restrictions, Texas law contains an additional requirement that applies to many employers. The Texas Workers' Compensation Act requires an employer that has fifteen (15) or more employees and is providing workers' compensation insurance coverage to adopt a policy "designed to eliminate drug abuse and its effects in the workplace." The employer is legally required to provide a written copy of the policy to each and every employee on or before the first day of employment or within thirty (30) days of adopting the policy. Pursuant to the Texas Workers' Compensation Commission regulations, the employer must maintain a written policy that not only covers drugs, but also covers inhalants and alcohol. The plan must specifically include the following:

1. a statement of purpose and scope;
2. a description of the consequence for violations;
3. a description of available treatment programs, insurance coverage, and rehabilitation programs;
4. a description of available drug and alcohol abuse training programs; and
5. a description of any drug testing policy.

Summary

Employers who wish to conduct random drug testing must make certain that they perform a balancing of the employee's interests against the government's interests in order to determine the constitutionality of the policy. When drafting or amending its drug testing policy, a city must analyze it in terms of its invasion on the employees' privacy rights and rights under the Fourth Amendment against unreasonable search and seizure. When dealing with an employee's privacy rights, a city must ensure that its policy does not unreasonably and unnecessarily intrude into the employee's privacy; that any intrusion is warranted by a compelling governmental objective; and that such objective cannot be achieved by a less intrusive more reasonable means. Although not all employees will enjoy the same level of privacy, depending on the nature of their jobs, a city must nonetheless ensure that the integrity of employees and the testing is maintained. The integrity of the testing may usually and easily be maintained by hiring or contracting with a reputable outside or independent company specializing in administering drug tests.

The validity of the governmental action will also ultimately rest on "balancing its intrusion on the employees' Fourth Amendment interests against its promotion of legitimate governmental interests." Accordingly, in examining Fourth Amendment ramifications, a city is advised to conduct a two-part analysis: (1) the city must first consider whether the testing will serve a special governmental need that is beyond the need for law enforcement; and (2) assuming that such a need exists, the city must determine whether its interests in testing its employees are sufficient to outweigh the privacy interest expectations of its employees. Indeed, there have been circumstances where an employee's constitutional rights were found to be minimal compared to the government's interest, and if this conclusion is reached, the courts will, in all likelihood, conclude that the test or search is reasonable despite the absence of suspicion. Undoubtedly, without a finding of a sufficient "special need," a testing policy will most likely not be upheld by a court.

Furthermore, cities must be cognizant of the fact that the burden of establishing the nexus between the employees' duties and the testing rests on them. The Fourth Amendment requires that the government connect its interest in random drug testing to the particular job duties of the applicants it wished to test. On a practical note, cities are accordingly advised to list all the positions and the specific duties that would justify random drug testing. Again, this must be done to establish the nexus required to pass constitutional muster. The policy must also identify those safety sensitive jobs as well as non-safety sensitive jobs.

In addition, and with all forms of drug testing, the intrusion on the employees must be minimized and all testing must be carried out in a non-arbitrary and non oppressive manner. Employers may include provision that provide advance notice of testing to applicants that they will be required to undergo random or post offer testing. This is advisable because notice will reduce the element of surprise and diminish the applicant's expectation of privacy. In addition, cities must ensure that all employees and applicants are made aware of any testing policy and its requirements. Policies must be strictly and consistently followed. If a city amends its policy, it must ensure that all current employees are made aware of the changes, which may not be retroactive. Finally, because public employment alone is not a "sufficient predicate for mandatory" testing, the bottom line is that cities must show a compelling interest in order to compel drug and alcohol testing in the workplace.

Double-Dip Dilemma

Should public employees who have retired and collect a pension be able to return to work and draw a salary?

BY ANYA SOSTEK

In Vancouver, Washington, it's become a common practice for teachers to retire from the local school system and then begin new teaching careers just across the Columbia River, in Portland, Oregon. The benefits are simple: a full salary in addition to their pension benefits.

Bill Fromhold, who represents the Vancouver area in the Washington legislature, is well aware of this trend. And when he learned there was a shortage of teachers in Vancouver a few years ago, he had a brainstorm: If teachers were allowed to collect a salary after retirement and continue working in Washington State, the shortage might be averted. "We had a maturing teacher population and shortages in critical areas like math-science education," says Fromhold. "We needed to provide some incentive to retain teaching staff."

Fromhold's bill, which passed the legislature in 2001, is one of a number of return-to-work or "retire-rehire" laws enacted in recent years. Previously, this practice was condemned as double dipping—and shunned by pension designers with an almost religious intensity. But primarily because of teacher shortages, about half of the states have started allowing retired employees to come back to work full-time, enabling them to earn a salary on top of their pension benefits.

At their best, the laws work in the way Fromhold envisioned: as a powerful tool to attract qualified retirees back into the workforce to fill critical shortages. But they also have been tarnished by some individuals who can't resist a sweet deal. As retire-rehire laws become more popular, states are learning that their success depends largely on targeted language and airtight implementation.

Nowhere is this lesson clearer than in Washington State. Although the bill was written with teachers in mind, the legislature decided to apply the law to all state employees because of shortages in other areas, such as court hearing officers. And aware that current employees might be tempted to use the new law just to fatten their paychecks, the legislature stipulated that employees needed to be retired for at least 30 days. To ensure that retirees would need to compete for their old positions, the bill also outlawed written agreements to rehire someone for a job from which they had just retired.

Initially, the law was lauded. In the first year, about 500 employees used it, and a *Seattle Times* article noted that "lawmakers and educators alike are already hailing the 'retire-rehire' legislation… as a success." In particular, principals praised the legislation for enabling them to fill shortages in secondary school math and science positions.

But one year after the law's passage, the tide started to turn. The *Seattle Times* reported that two top employees in the state Code Reviser's Office had "retired" for the mandatory 30-day period, and then immediately returned to work. Their desks were never cleaned out, nor were their positions ever advertised. Furthermore, even though written rehire agreements were prohibited, both employees had verbal agreements that they would be rehired. Both employees earn nearly $100,000 a year in salary alone, and are now also collecting sizable pensions. After the *Times* report, legislators and the public felt "a very strong sense of outrage," as Fromhold puts it. But there wasn't much that anyone could do about it. Under the law, their actions were perfectly legal.

With public sentiment now against the law, the legislature took up the issue again this spring. Convinced that the actions of a few should not spoil the potential good of the program, the legislature decided not to scrap the law but to add more safeguards against abuses. Eventually, a bill passed lengthening the retirement time to 90 days, prohibiting verbal rehire commitments and imposing a three-year limit for using the program. But the legislature decided not to restrict the program to teachers, or to teachers in shortage areas, as other states have done.

UNINTENDED CONSEQUENCES

Washington State is not the only place to learn the hard way about the unintended consequences of retire-rehire. In Louisiana, a law meant to bring retirees back for short-term help was used by almost 200 current, full-time employees in the Department of Corrections. An oversight in the writing of the law even allowed "retired" employees to continue accruing money into their pension plans.

In New Hampshire, the legislature passed a law that applied only to top-level officials and required no mandatory retirement period. After several officials took immediate advantage, the law was derided as a "golden parachute" and quickly repealed. During the period between the legislature's vote on the repeal and the time that the repeal went into effect, however, several other officials also "retired." They include Secretary of State Bill Gardner, who remains on the job and is running for re-election in November.

This is not to say that all states have had problems. In West Virginia, school districts are required to prove that there is a shortage before they are allowed to rehire a retired employee—thus eliminating a good deal of abuse. In other states, a portion of the workers' pension money is put into an escrow account for use after they truly stop working.

In order for retire-rehire laws to accomplish their objectives, states must take measures to prevent current employees from retiring just to get the benefits. "You need to tailor it to make it clear that it's for shortages," says Jeannie Markoe Raymond, executive director of the National Association of State Retirement Administrators. "You need to make sure that these rules do not prompt a change in retirement patterns."

PHILOSOPHICAL DEBATE

Even if states are able to craft a law that will fulfill the desired intent, retire-rehire laws are not without controversy. The pension traditionalists feel that the pension system should be used only after employees stop working. Others, however, view pension money as a pot that could be tapped before one's working days are over.

"Retirement systems were meant for retirement, not for retainment of personnel," says state Representative Henry Mock, who led the effort to repeal New Hampshire's law. "If they have teacher shortages and more money will keep them, give them more money—don't do it under the disguise of retirement."

Gone Today, Back Tomorrow

School district employees in Washington State who retired and then were rehired

POSITION	RETIRE/REHIRES 2001-02	RETIRE/REHIRES 2002-03
Superintendent	8 (1.6%)	25 (2.4%)
Central Office	27 (5.4%)	58.5 (5.6%)
Principals	41.5 (8.3%)	59.5 (5.7%)
Vice Principals	7 (1.4%)	25 (2.4%)
Teachers	413 (82.1%)	801 (76.9%)
Classified	6 (1.2%)	72.5 (7%)
Total	502.5 (100%)	1,041.5 (100%)

Source: Washington Association of School Administrators

Proponents of the idea argue that as long as employees have reached retirement age, they have earned the money. If they would like to start withdrawing that money, and it doesn't cost the state any additional dollars, it should be their choice. A decade ago, that view would have been seen as radical. But now, the practice is widespread in the federal government. And last year the IRS—which technically prohibits retire-rehire laws but does not really enforce the ban—started to study more liberal options

In Washington State, Fromhold brings the argument back to the individual teachers: If nobody has a problem with their going to Oregon after they've retired, why can't they just stay in Washington? "The bottom line is, the person has earned their pension and they're entitled to collect it," he says. "We're not an island unto ourselves and it made little sense to me to have rules in place that don't recognize reality." Fromhold notes that some of the legislators who oppose retire-rehire laws have themselves retired from one profession and are currently collecting a legislative salary.

Hypothetically, then, would there be a problem with allowing everyone to collect a pension at the same time as a salary once they reached retirement age? To some extent, it depends on the design of the pension system. Many systems rely on people paying into the system to fund payouts to those who have retired. Once a retire-rehire arrangement goes into effect, those employees stop paying in. If retire-rehire laws are used on a limited basis, as they are now, pension systems can easily handle it. If everyone started using it, however, some systems could be destabilized

An even bigger issue than actuarial concerns, however, is the public reaction to "double-dipping." Even if it doesn't cost the state any additional money, it often just doesn't pass the smell test. "The public often view the people who go back to work and collect a salary and pension as doing something shady," says Ron Snell, director of the economic and fiscal division for the National Conference of State Legislatures. "They think they're feathering their nest at the public expense."

Regardless of whether or not those employees are actually doing anything wrong, the mere appearance of wrongdoing is enough to keep retire-rehire laws fairly limited. "Somebody coined the term double-dipping and it seems to have stuck," says Raymond, of the retirement administrators' association. "Truly, they're not doing anything illegal. But there's an alarmist, knee-jerk reaction against it."

UNIT 4

Finance and Budgeting

Unit Selections

Key Points to Consider

- What are some of the reasons that federal budget forecasts are so inaccurate? Given the problems with accuracy, what are some of the things that policy makers should do to compensate? Also, what are some of the things that can be done to improve the accuracy?
- Discuss the differences between entitlement and discretionary spending. How does Congress divide up the discretionary funds in the federal budget?
- What are some of the major decisions that have to be made by administrators when they cut a city's budget? What factors have to be taken into consideration?
- Identify and discuss at least three things that you learned from doing the exercise, "The Budget Game."
- Identify and discuss the use of public bonds to finance big projects. What are the major benefits of using public bonds to fund these projects?

Links: www.dushkin.com/online/
These sites are annotated in the World Wide Web pages.

FirstGov
http://www.firstgov.gov

Giving Federal Workers the Tools They Need to Do Their Jobs
http://acts.poly.edu/cd/npr/npr-3-3.htm

Performance Measurement Page (City of Grand Prairie)
http://www.cityofgp.com/citygov/bettergov/perform/perform.htm

The U.S. Chief Financial Officers Council
http://www.cfoc.gov

Articles in this unit focus on financial management issues such as uncertain budget forecasts, cuts in services for state and local governments, fiscal tricks to alleviate fiscal stress, and how to operate an effective budget office during periods of cutbacks.

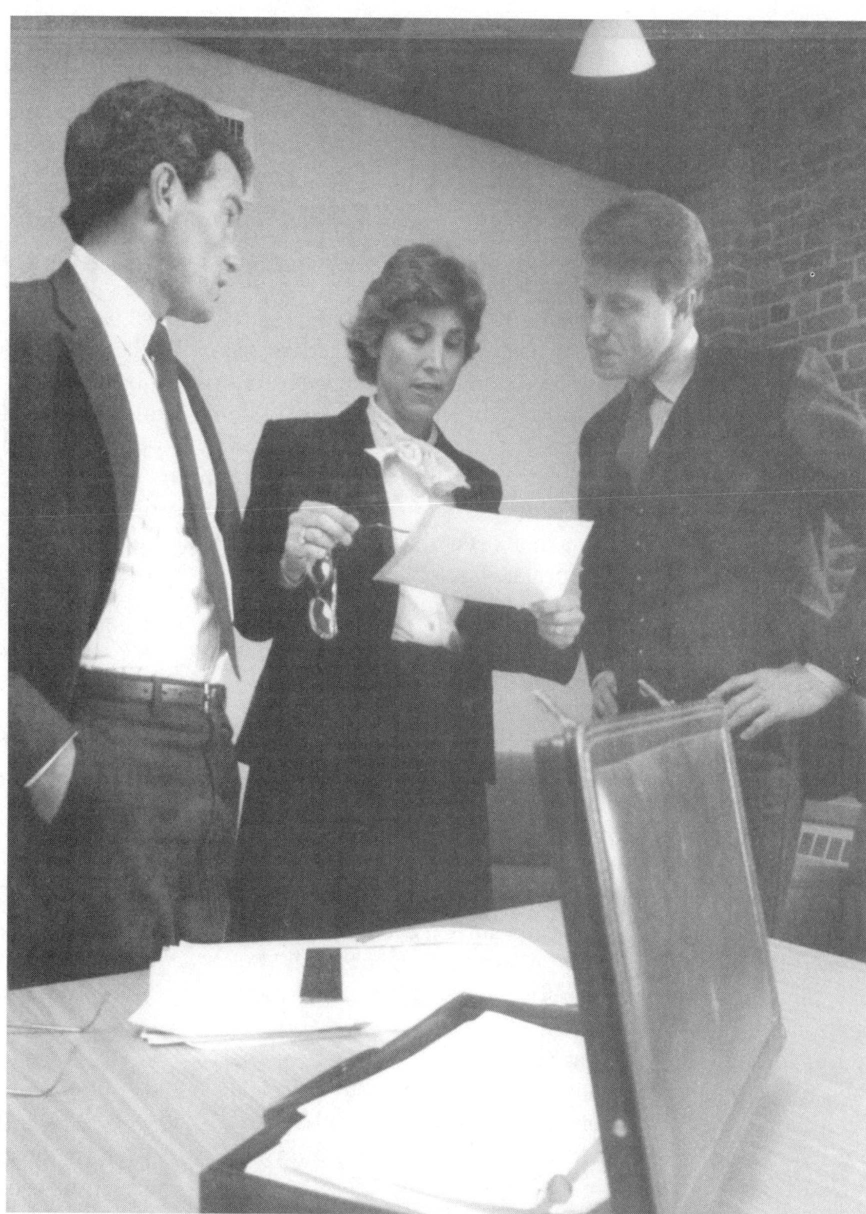

"Dealing With Uncertain Budget Forecasts," by Rudolph Penner, reviews the history of past budget projections by the Congressional Budget Office (CBO). The author finds that the budget forecasts and projections have been extremely inaccurate because of errors in the choice of economic and technical assumptions. The errors grow rapidly as the projection's period is lengthened. The author concludes that the projections are unlikely to get better soon and suggests that projections made for more than 5 years be de-emphasized by policy and decision makers.

"How Congress Divides Our Money," by Chuck Lindell, reviews how congressional power players divide up the dollars. According to the author, the appropriations game involves instinct, timing, and good friends. Congress doles out only one-third of the $2.2 trillion federal budget. The rest is mandatory spending for interest on the federal debt and on entitlement programs such as Social Security and Medicare.

Stephen Scheibal's article, "City of Austin's Budget Crisis," reviews the city's need to cut $29 million from its budget. Review the dilemma of the staff—to solve the city's budget shortfall without eliminating necessary services. Cities across the country are now in fiscal stress and are dealing with similar problems and issues.

"The Budget Game" is an exercise that was published in the newspaper *The Austin-American Statesman*. The exercise gives the reader an opportunity to play state lawmaker and to try to eliminate the state of Texas's potential financial deficit and close the budget shortfall. The goal is to bridge the projected $9.9 billion gap between the state's expected revenue and what the state must spend to maintain existing services. But watch out. Every move comes with a political cost.

"Deferrals: Gimmick or Usual Budget Math?," by Gary Susswein, provides some additional fiscal tricks by which state and local governments are trying to overcome fiscal stress and cover budget deficits.

Dealing with Uncertain Budget Forecasts

The article reviews the history of past budget projections by the Congressional Budget Office (CBO). The projections have been extremely inaccurate because of errors in the choice of economic and technical assumptions. The errors grow rapidly as the projection's period is lengthened. The projections are unlikely to get better soon. Therefore, the question becomes how CBO, the Congress, and the media should react to the extraordinary uncertainty that must be attached to the budget outlook. Among other things, the author suggests de-emphasizing projections made for periods longer than five years, because such projections are only a little better than random noise. He also points out the futility of aiming for rigorously enforced numerical targets for the budget balance, as was done in Gramm-Rudman and as has been proposed in various types of "lock box" legislation. The targets move around too rapidly to ever be hit.

RUDOLPH G. PENNER

Since budgeting is about the future, budget decisions regarding the allocation of resources must be based on forecasts. But budget forecasts are always wrong, and often they are wrong by a lot.[1] Indeed, changes in budget projections caused by alterations in economic forecasts and technical assumptions generally far exceed adjustments caused by changes in fiscal policies. A tax cut of $50 billion planned in the summer for the next fiscal year represents a politically important change in policy, but an identical change in the baseline surplus forecast for the next fiscal year is relatively minor compared to a typical forecasting error. Between April and July of 2000, for example, the Congressional Budget Office (CBO) adjusted the surplus estimated for 2001 upward by $95 billion for economic and technical reasons. The degree to which politicians are annoyed by such major adjustments is dampened only slightly by the fact that we are now enjoying the best budget outcomes of the last 70 years.

Forecasts are unlikely to become significantly more accurate in the future. They are compiled by skilled technicians who do their work conscientiously. Inaccuracy is partly due to the unscientific state of economic science. But economic and budget forecasting is also affected by bad forecasting in other fields. Forecasters are notoriously unreliable at predicting things like the next wave of technological change, the weather, and earthquakes, all of which can have significant economic and budget implications. Given that we cannot expect major improvements in the accuracy of forecasts, the question becomes how policymakers should use these highly inaccurate forecasts as effectively as possible and how journalists should report on them. But before tackling this difficult question, it is useful to examine the historical record.

SINS OF THE PAST

Surplus Projections

The budget surplus is of great interest to policymakers and the press. It provides an immediate, if crude, indicator of how the nation is doing fiscally. Errors in projecting the surplus seem inordinately large because budget forecasters do not project surpluses directly. They project two much larger numbers, receipts and outlays, and take the difference. As a result, relatively small percentage errors in projection receipts or outlays translate into very large percentage errors in projecting the surplus. For example, receipts in fiscal 2000 were $2,025 billion and outlays were $1,788 billion, so the surplus was $237 billion. Between 1980 and 2000, the average absolute error in projections of receipts and outlays for the next year was a little more than three percent.[2] Such an error in the forecast of receipts for 2000 would have implied a change of 26 percent in the surplus forecast.

Figure 1 examines the economic and technical errors made in forecasting the budget balance between the pro-

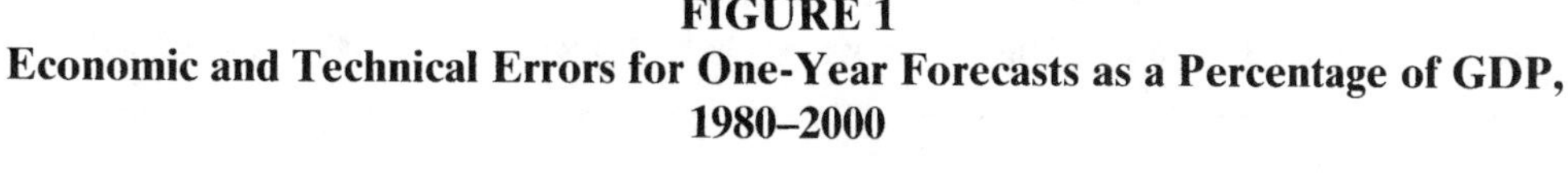

FIGURE 1
Economic and Technical Errors for One-Year Forecasts as a Percentage of GDP, 1980–2000

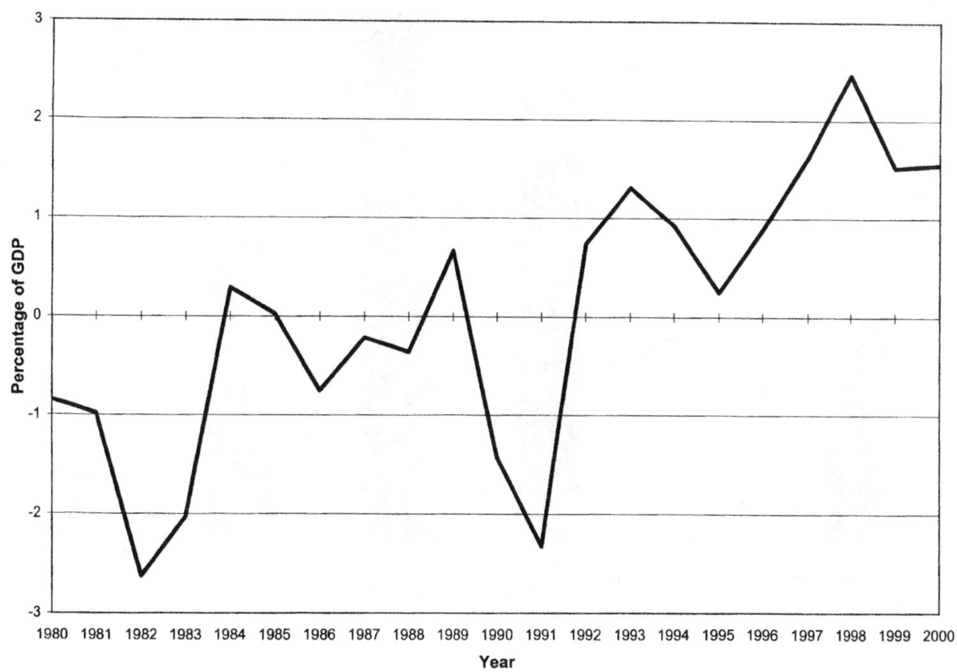

mulgation of CBO's baseline budget, which is usually prepared in March or April, and the final number for the subsequent fiscal year.[3] For example, the baseline estimate for fiscal 1998 (prepared in March 1997) is compared with the actual outcome in 1998 after the effects of legislative action between the two dates are removed.

Although CBO's first budget projection, generally produced in January, gets more publicity than the baseline forecast produced in the spring, it is the latter that serves as a foundation for congressional budget deliberations, so this analysis starts with the spring projection. Typically, the baseline differs only slightly from the January forecast, and those differences that exist come about mainly because CBO learns of administrative decisions in the president's budget that may affect receipts or expenditures. Sometimes the spring projections also correct errors found in the January projections. The economic assumptions are seldom changed between the two projections. Figure 1 shows the cumulative economic and technical errors between the baseline and the final outcome as a percentage of gross domestic product (GDP).

Two things about the figure stand out. First, the absolute errors during the three years from 1998 through 2000 were unusually large. The only other comparable errors occurred in 1982 and 1991, years affected by unpredicted recessions. Second, the earlier period, 1980 through 1991, is distinctly different from the later period, 1992 through 2000. In the earlier period, forecasts were overwhelmingly too optimistic, with only two years—1984 and 1989—that were slightly too pessimistic. In the latter period, forecasts have been overwhelmingly too pessimistic. If CBO is pessimistic (optimistic) in one year, it is highly probable that it will be pessimistic (optimistic) the next year as well. Statisticians refer to this as having a high serial correlation among the errors.

Figure 2 shows that smaller errors are more common than larger errors. A statistician would say that the errors appear to be normally distributed. It must be emphasized that there are only 21 years of experience in which errors have been computed consistently; it is difficult to reach statistically sound conclusions with such a small sample.

The most important point about the errors is that they can be very large: In 4 of 21 cases, they exceeded two percent of GDP. At current levels of GDP, that would imply an error of over $215 billion in the spring 2001 forecast of the 2002 surplus. The average absolute error is 1.1 percent, implying an error of about $120 billion for 2002.[4]

The available sample for errors made in five-year projections is extremely small. CBO has separated economic and technical forecasting errors from the effects of policy changes consistently only since the projection made for 1989 in the spring of 1984. Of course, the errors in the spring baseline projections for the fiscal year five years out are huge relative to the errors for the following fiscal year. The errors for five-year projections are shown in Figure 3.

FIGURE 2
Frequency Distribution of One-Year Errors as a Percentage of GDP, 1980–2000

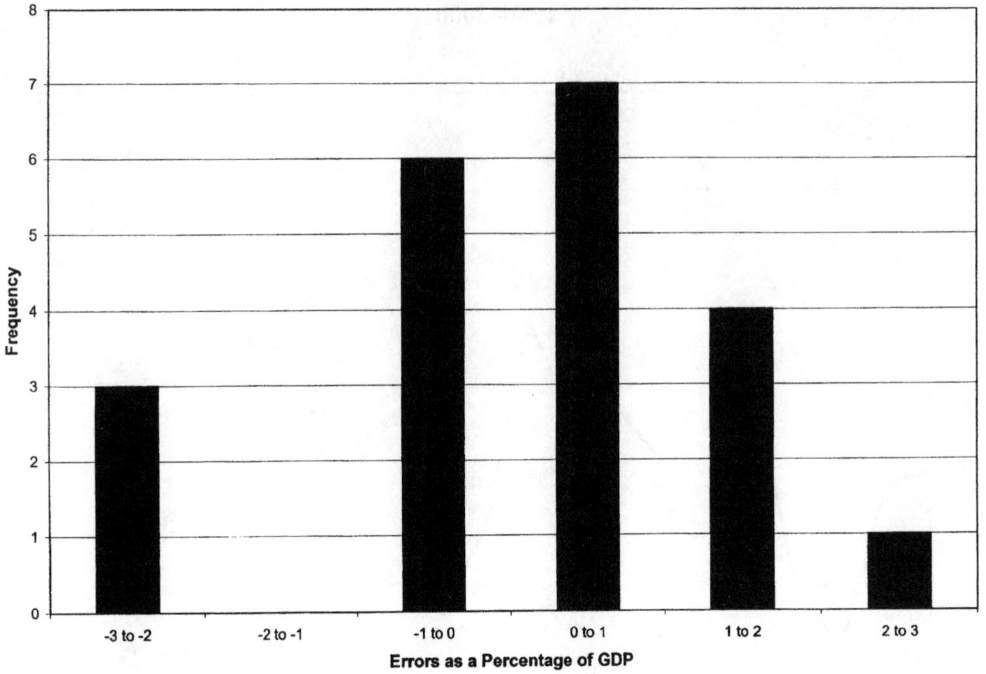

FIGURE 3
Economic and Technical Errors for Five-Year Forecasts as a Percentage of GDP, 1989–2000

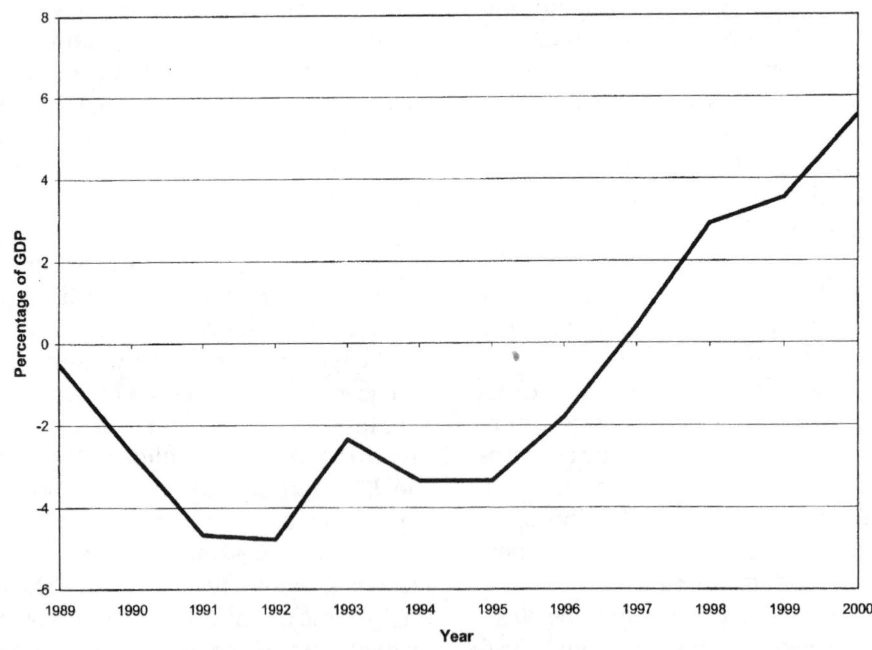

The most serious errors are for projections made in 1987 about fiscal 1992 and those made about fiscal 2000 in the spring of 1995. The errors exceeded five percent of GDP, equivalent to an error of over $660 billion in the budget balance forecast made for 2006 in the spring of 2001; the January 2001 projection of the 2006 surplus is only $505 billion. The average absolute error in the 12 observations in Figure 3 is about three percent of GDP,

FIGURE 4
Frequency Distribution of Five-Year Errors as a Percentage of GDP, 1989–2000

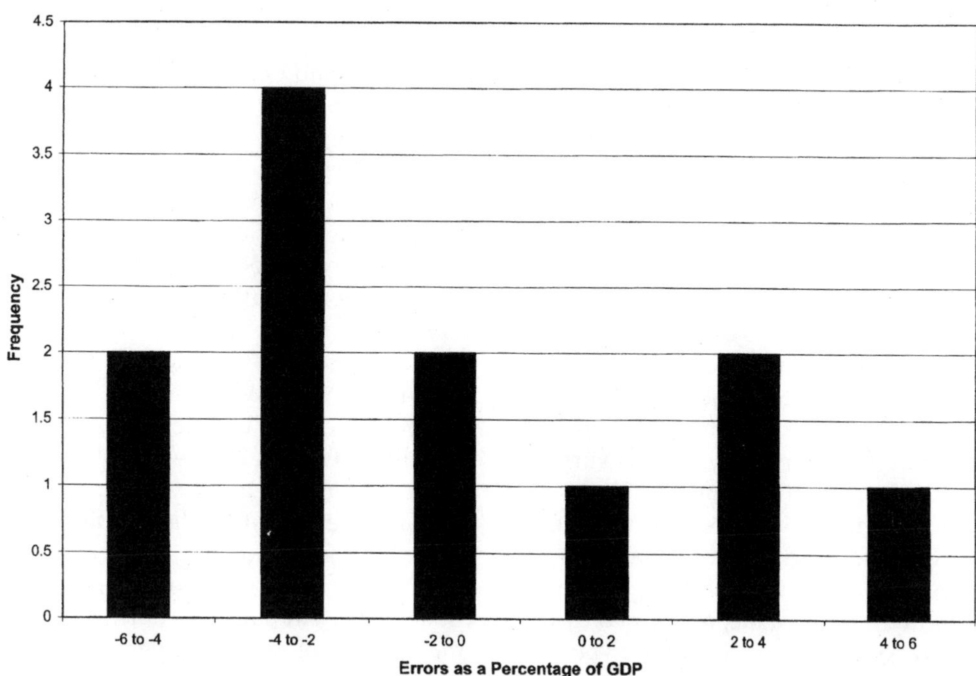

equivalent to an error of almost $400 billion in the spring 2001 projection for 2006.

The frequency distribution of the errors in five-year projections is not very revealing, since the sample is so small. Nevertheless, it is somewhat disturbing that small errors have been less likely than large errors, as shown in Figure 4.

Starting in the middle of 1996, CBO began making 10-year projections of the budget surplus. It is too early to test those projections against actual outcomes, but it is clear from adjustments made so far that those long-term projections will be extremely inaccurate. When the budget balance for 2007 was first projected, in the spring of 1997, the projection called for a deficit of $278 billion. By the summer of 2000, the projection had changed to a surplus of $523 billion, a difference of $801 billion. But policy changes used up some of the surplus in the interim, so the cumulative sum of economic and technical forecasting errors over the period was $844 billion, or over six percent of expected GDP. If errors continue to be serially correlated, the cumulative error will grow over time. If there is a shift toward pessimism, the cumulative error will shrink.

However, the change so far in the 2007 projection is huge relative to likely policy changes and is worth far more than the tax cut proposed by President George W. Bush. If the projections had not become so much more optimistic over time, it is unlikely that either presidential candidate would have promised substantial tax cuts during the campaign, and we probably would not be talking about policy initiatives such as a prescription drug benefit under Medicare. We can only hope that the projection does not become more pessimistic with equal rapidity. A comparable change over the next three years in our view of the 2011 budget balance would amount to over $1 trillion, an amount greater than the total 2011 surplus forecast in CBO's January 2001 report.

Projections of Receipts and Outlays

Errors in forecasting receipts are only slightly more important than errors in forecasting outlays in explaining the errors in one-year forecasts of the deficit. The absolute average error in forecasting receipts from 1980 to 2000 was 0.7 percent of GDP, and the average absolute error in forecasting outlays was 0.5 percent.[5] Simply adding up the positive and negative errors makes it clear that there is no statistically significant bias in forecasting outlays or receipts over the entire period, a proposition Auerbach's rigorous analysis confirms for receipts.[6]

Errors in forecasting receipts and outlays can go in the same direction or in opposite directions, depending on the event that catches forecasters by surprise and results in the error. For example, a surprising rise in inflation will raise both receipts and outlays, whereas a surprising recession will lower receipts but raise outlays on safety net programs. From 1980 to 2000, the sum of economic and technical errors on the receipts and outlay sides of the budget reinforced the effect of each on the budget balance in 15 of the 21 years.

In his careful analysis of errors in forecasting receipts, Auerbach documents the same serial correlation in these errors as discussed above for the budget balance. He divides the 1986–1999 period into pre-Clinton (1986–1993) and post-Clinton (1994–1999) eras, showing persistent optimism in the earlier period and persistent pessimism in the latter. The same type of persistence can be shown for errors in outlay forecasts, albeit with a somewhat different dividing line. Between 1980 and 1991, economic and technical errors caused actual outlays to exceed forecast outlays in all but 2 of the 12 years. Between 1992 and 2000, actual outlays fell short of the forecast in every year.

The examples described above imply that outlay and receipts forecasting errors reinforced each other in creating the serial correlation in the errors in the budget forecast. Although receipts and outlay errors were, on average, of similar relative importance between 1980 and 2000, very large errors in predicting receipts were the main reason for the surprising emergence of the surplus in 1998. Large errors occurred both because GDP growth was understated and because revenues rose unexpectedly as a share of GDP. The unpredicted rise in the stock market led to a surge in revenues from capital gains taxation, and a rapid rise in the share of income earned by the very rich raised the average individual tax rate. The corporate profit share of GDP also exceeded CBO's expectations and added to corporate tax collections.

The five-year projections of receipts and outlays show similar patterns, in that forecasts tend to be persistently optimistic early in the period and persistently pessimistic later. The errors, of course, grow as the forecast period lengthens. These longer-run forecasts will not be examined in detail here. The long-run errors in receipts and outlay projections manifest themselves in the very large errors discussed above for five-year projections of the budget balance.

THE FORECASTING PROCESS

The procedures for forecasting budget totals are very similar at CBO and at the Office of Management and Budget (OMB), so it is not surprising that their past errors have also been very similar.[7] The process begins with an economic forecast, because economic variables are crucial in projecting most types of outlays and receipts. At OMB, the economic forecast is produced by the "Troika," economists drawn from the Council of Economic Advisers, the Department of the Treasury, and OMB. In preparing their forecasts, economic forecasters in the administration and at CBO pay close attention to the forecasts made by business economists and private forecasting companies such as DRI and Macroeconomic Advisors. CBO, in particular, does not want to deviate far from the consensus and receives input from a diverse set of academic and business advisers. To deviate significantly from the consensus would be considered to be partisan in one direction or the other.[8] During the Reagan and Bush administrations, OMB forecasts were often, but not always, somewhat more optimistic than the consensus forecasts, but during the Clinton administration, forecasts were much more conventional, and so far, the Bush administration seems to be following this precedent.

Theoretically, one would expect to see differences between CBO and OMB forecasts, since CBO bases its forecast on the fiscal stance implied by current policy, whereas the OMB forecast is based on the assumption that all presidential recommendations are adopted. Because most of the president's policy proposals are aimed at improving the state of the economy, one would expect the differences in policy assumptions to make the president's economic outlook more optimistic than CBO's. As a practical matter, however, other uncertainties in the forecasting process tend to overwhelm these differences in policy assumptions.

CBO carefully characterizes its estimates for the current and the next calendar year as a "forecast" and estimates for subsequent years as projections. The projections assume that GDP follows a linear trend from the end of the forecast period to a point on the potential growth path of the economy ten years hence. The potential or full-capacity growth path is deemed to be consistent with an unemployment rate of 5.2 percent toward the end of the period. CBO explicitly notes that it does not mean to rule out business cycles that could cause GDP to vary above and below the potential growth path.

However, business cycles do not have a major long-run impact on the budget balance. When the economy recovers from a recession, the budget will as well. The only major lasting difference is an increase in the interest bill on the debt, because the reduced budget balance while the economy was depressed adds to the outstanding debt.

The budget balance projected for the longer run is crucially dependent on the rate at which it is assumed the economy can grow without provoking inflation. If that rate falls from the currently assumed 3.3 percent to rates below the 2.5 percent commonly assumed in the 1980s, a very large proportion of the projected unified budget surplus disappears.

Dozens of experts have some input into the forecast; for example, energy experts comment on oil prices and agricultural experts suggest farm prices. In checking the forecast, forecasters make considerable use of accounting and other definitions. For example, accounting definitions are supposed to yield equal numbers for total domestic and net foreign investment and the total amount of domestic saving. Any forecast that caused the two numbers to deviate significantly would have been viewed with some suspicion in the past. Unfortunately, a large discrepancy between reported investment and saving has emerged in recent years. This indicates imperfections in the data-gathering system, because the data should show them to be equal. The imperfection means that CBO must forecast a statistical discrepancy, which is a bit like forecasting a random number. This is just one of many problems that make economic forecasting challenging.

Once economic forecasters have produced forecasts for variables like the consumer price index, unemployment, interest rates, and corporate profits, the analysts who compute program outlays and different types of receipts go to work. For example, specialists in the Medicaid program are responsible for projecting its costs. Medicaid is the third-largest entitlement program, and in the past errors in projecting its costs have been quite large. Medicaid costs depend on the number of people eligible for the program, a number that may be influenced by many factors, including the unemployment rate. Then the analysts must estimate the proportion of eligibles who will actually enroll in the program, Medicaid enrollees' per capita consumption of health services, and the cost of those services. Medical prices will, of course, be influenced by the overall inflation rate.

Errors are inevitable in each step of the budget forecasting process, which involves making estimates for hundreds of programs and sources of revenues. A good forecast, which emerges if the hundreds of errors offset each other, is largely a matter of luck. Highly competent analysts making hundreds of tiny errors that generally go in the same direction can make the forecasters of budget aggregates appear highly incompetent, whereas true incompetence may yield a satisfactory forecast, so long as individual analysts are incompetent in opposite directions.

WHY IS THE DIRECTION OF FORECAST ERRORS SO PERSISTENT?

The analysis in this section is highly subjective. It is based on many years of watching budget analysts at work from the sanctity of think tanks and from my own participation in the forecasting process as chief economist at OMB from 1974 to 1977 and as director of CBO from 1983 to 1987. Based on this personal experience, I believe that there are a number of powerful forces that push forecasters in the same direction. As a result, an error in one direction in one year makes it highly probable that analysts will make an error in the same direction the next year.

There may be purely statistical reasons for this phenomenon. In some program and revenue estimating areas, analysts rely heavily on equations whose parameters are estimated on the basis of historical data. Typically, the equations are re-estimated periodically as new information comes in. However, adding one year's new data, even if it is highly unusual, does not change the estimates of the parameters very much. Consequently, if some important structural change has occurred in relationships among variables, it may not be recognized for many years, and forecasting errors in the interim are likely to all go in the same direction. Although such statistical phenomena may be of some importance, I suspect that the more informal judgments that analysts introduce into their forecasts are at least equally important. These judgments are often motivated by psychological and political factors that enhance the tendency for errors to go persistently in one direction or another.

In the Medicaid example used above, analysts attempt to model different components of the problem. They may modify the results of the models based on judgments about the effects of factors that are difficult to model. The important point is that they will consider all the information available to them and ultimately produce a forecast. Say, for example, that they decide that Medicaid outlays will rise eight percent next year but later find that the actual outcome is an increase of four percent. It will not be easy to identify the reason for the discrepancy quickly, because the requisite administrative and other data will be available only after a long time lag. Having used all the available information to produce the original forecast of eight percent, there is a natural human tendency for forecasters to believe that the discrepancy must have been the result of an anomaly. If their techniques again yielded an estimate of eight percent outlay growth for the following year, the analysts might think up some excuse for lowering the forecast to seven percent, just in case some unknown factor were working to depress Medicaid costs, but unless they were certain that something important was changing, they would be very slow to adjust their estimates downward. They would not dream of lowering their forecast all the way to four percent.

This is not an irrational approach to forecasting. A whole branch of statistics, called Bayesian statistics, relies on just such an approach. Analysts allow previously held views, presumably based on good information, to restrain statistical estimates of relationships among variables, thereby protecting the analyst against aberrations in the sample. If the restrained estimates do not work very well over time, prior views are adjusted, but the process of finding truth works slowly.

The models used by program analysts and revenue forecasters are often fairly crude and sometimes are little more than a collection of rules of thumb. Analysts seldom have time to construct highly sophisticated models. Moreover, it may not be worth trying to be highly sophisticated. Policy changes and changes in underlying economic relationships can cause the most sophisticated model to go astray. In other words, sophistication does not necessarily improve accuracy. Consequently, the art of forecasting may involve constantly adjusting crude models in a way that corrects the direction of errors very slowly.

Another, and perhaps the most important, psychological factor that intensifies the propensity for the errors' direction to persist afflicts everyone from technical analysts to the directors of CBO and OMB. If forecasting techniques and assumptions are changed significantly every time an error is made, long-run budget projections will jump all over the map from year to year, making the analysts appear incompetent and infuriating policymakers. Consequently, analysts or directors demand convincing proof that something fundamental has changed before significantly changing forecasting techniques or assumptions. Because it takes time to gather evidence of fundamental change, forecasting techniques and assumptions are likely to change more slowly than reality, and that lag may be the most important reason that errors persist for so long. The resulting slow change sounds much like the result of the Bayesian process described above. But the reluctance to make too many changes too quickly is an added factor that slows the adjustment of forecasts to reality. It might be called a political factor, but it is nonpartisan and simply reflects a desire not to become too unpopular too fast.

THE USEFULNESS OF FLAWED FORECASTS

The damage done by forecast errors depends on how forecasts are used. For some purposes, inaccuracy is not much of a problem. In other contexts, an inaccurate forecast can badly mislead policymakers and media pundits.

Forecasts serve two important purposes in the budget process. They indicate the fiscal health of the nation, and they provide assumptions that can be used to help evaluate tax and expenditure policies.

It has been shown that forecasts become rapidly less reliable as the forecast period is extended. Forecasts for periods beyond five years are not totally misleading, but it would be foolish to believe that they provide anything but the crudest indication of the nation's fiscal health. Given constant policies, the surplus for 2011 was projected in January 2001 to be $889 billion, or 5.3 percent of GDP. There is, however, a good chance that the final outcome could be twice that figure or zero, even without any policy changes. On the other hand, there is only the tiniest possibility that 2011 could see a deficit in the range experienced between 1982 and 1986, when the unified deficit varied between 4.0 and 6.1 percent of GDP. Although the uncertainty is enormous, the estimates indicate that the nation's budget is very likely to remain healthy or at least not become extremely unhealthy for the next ten years, even if the large tax cut of 2001 is extended beyond its current termination date.

Given that the long-run estimates provide some information, regardless of how crude it may be, they should continue to be produced. However, they need not be given the prominence that they now receive.

If ten-year forecasts are too inaccurate to be displayed prominently, what are we to make of the 75-year time horizon used to evaluate the financial well-being of the Social Security system or the comparably long projections of budget aggregates periodically published by CBO, GAO, and OMB? Such forecasts are incredibly inaccurate. However, they serve a useful purpose. They illustrate that current policy is not sustainable. The retirement of the baby boomers and increases in life expectancy will cause the costs of Social Security, Medicare, and Medicaid to grow so rapidly that deficits soar and interest costs explode around the middle of the century. Whether this happens in the 2030s or the 2060s depends on one's assumptions, but the point is that it does happen using a wide range of models and assumptions. Certainly the precise numbers should not be taken seriously. It is sobering to remember that demographers failed to forecast either the postwar baby boom or the baby dearth that followed.

It was noted above that budget estimates provide assumptions for evaluating policy changes. This is known as scorekeeping, a crucial part of the budget process. Policymakers must have estimates of the dollar value of policy changes. It is particularly important for them to know whether a change in an entitlement program will cost a great deal more in the long run than it does in the first few years, and, similarly, whether the long-run revenue effects of a change in tax law will dwarf its short-run effects. It is impossible to make such judgments without a long-run forecast.

CBO extended its forecast period from five to ten years when the Senate extended the time horizon for applying its pay-as-you-go rule from five to ten years. That rule insisted that tax cuts or entitlement increases be paid for by tax increases or entitlement cuts. When the pay-as-you-go rule was applied with a five-year horizon, it became common for legislators to propose phased-in tax cuts or spending increases that cost much less annually during the first five years than they did in the longer run. Ten-year scorekeeping was introduced to limit such gaming.[9] The estimate of the precise quantitative effect of the policy change in years 5 and 6 may be inaccurate, but even so, an assessment of the qualitative nature of the pattern of effects is unlikely to be badly misleading. This is especially true if a policy has been designed to delay its effects until after the time horizon used for scorekeeping, because then the change in the time path of effects is very apparent.

If a five-year scorekeeping horizon encourages gaming between years 5 and 6, it is natural to ask whether a ten-year horizon will encourage gaming between years 10 and 11. It probably will, and it did with a vengeance in designing the recent tax cut that sunset after year 10, but as the scorekeeping horizon lengthens, gaming of this type becomes less of a concern. A policy change enacted this year is likely to be altered many times over a ten-year period and may not even be recognizable by year 11. Moreover, if the largest effects of a policy change are long delayed, it will be much less attractive politically.

Although attempts at gaming and other reasons for large swings in the costs of a policy change are likely to be identified even if estimates are based on a bad forecast, a bad forecast may, of course, sometimes substantially misrepresent the time pattern of a policy change's budget effects. For example, the time pattern of the effects of a change in the taxation of capital gains will obviously depend on the time pattern of capital gains realizations, which are notoriously difficult to forecast. Our view of the cost path for a new entitlement may be badly distorted if we inaccurately forecast the participation rate of those who are eligible. But in general, the problems bad forecasts pose for scorekeeping are minor relative to the value of having a rough idea of how the costs or savings associated with a policy change are likely to vary over the long run.

SUGGESTIONS FOR THE CONGRESSIONAL BUDGET OFFICE

CBO should de-emphasize forecasts produced for the second five years of the 1-year forecast period.

CBO should show the estimates for years 5 through 10 of the projection period in an appendix, rather than in the main body of its reports, to indicate that it regards the later projections as being considerably less reliable than shorter-run forecasts. The division of the forecasts into two five-year periods is somewhat arbitrary, because the reliability of the forecast declines steadily as the period lengthens (i.e., the forecast for year 5 is only somewhat more accurate than the forecast for year 6). However, the tradition that a five-year projection is appropriate was established by the Budget and Impoundment Control Act of 1974, and five years is a reasonable projection period, even though a five-year projection may contain very large errors.

CBO should not provide a cumulative value for the budget balance or policy changes.

Even if the projection period that is given prominence is only five years, it is extremely misleading to add the surplus projection for year 5 to the surplus for year 1 to provide an estimate of the cumulative surplus. The process of adding up surpluses give equal weight to longer and shorter projections, implying that the estimate for year 5 is as reliable as the estimate for year 1. In truth, however, longer-term projections are much more uncertain.

CBO should continue to publish and refine estimates of the degree of confidence that should be attached to estimates of the budget balance.

In the past, CBO has found it difficult to describe the degree of uncertainty that should be attached to its estimates. In its report of January 2001, CBO introduced a more effective approach, providing a distribution of the probabilities of different outcomes, given the baseline estimates. Because CBO's history is not long enough to provide a large sample of past errors, any probability distribution based on the historical record is necessarily crude, but it is nonetheless extremely valuable. The CBO report also describes the budget implications of different economic scenarios, and it includes sensitivity tables showing the impact that errors in the economic forecast might have on the budget. For example, the tables show the effects of a 0.1 percent annual error in the assumed growth rate and of errors in estimating specific amounts of inflation. The scenarios and sensitivity tables are interesting, but their usefulness is limited by the difficulty of assessing the probability of different scenarios or specific changes in economic variables.

SUGGESTIONS FOR CONGRESS

Congress should not insert quantitative targets into laws governing the budget process.

Forecasting is not accurate enough to support laws that set quantitative targets for budget totals. The Gramm-Rudman-Hollings Act of 1985 (GRH) required Congress to balance the unified budget within five years and specified a precise path of declining deficits on the way to the ultimate target. If targets were not met, spending would be cut according to a complex formula. The law was bound to fail, and it did. When the economy failed to perform as well as forecast, the size of the tax cuts or spending reductions necessary to meet the targets became totally implausible, as was doing so entirely on the spending side using cuts determined by an automatic formula.[10]

The same fate will await any of the "lock box" laws recently discussed in Congress. They would make it illegal to run deficits outside the Social Security system, presumably enforcing the goal with some type of automatic mechanism. It will be no easier to balance the budget under this definition than it was to balance the unified budget under GRH.

So how do states manage to create the balanced budgets mandated by their laws or constitutions? Sometimes they do it honestly, with real tax increases and spending cuts, but often they use bookkeeping changes and artificial changes in the timing of expenditures and revenues.[11]

Congress should devote more effort to analyzing the risks of outcomes that may occur because the forecast is wrong.

Because of the uncertainty that must be attached to projections, policymakers proposing a specific policy change should not only assess its desirability given the current set of budget and economic projections, they should also examine its implications if current projections turn out to be far too optimistic or pessimistic.

Today, the budget risks are much more symmetrical than they were in the 1980s when the deficit threatened to get out of hand in the sense the interest costs might grow faster than taxes could be raised or spending cut. Now we may end up saving too much or too little because of a flawed forecast, but the welfare loss will be similar regardless of the direction of the error.

Congress should seek to improve the quality of economic statistics.

A last suggestion for Congress is a favorite of economists but has few other constituencies: The statistical agencies of the government need larger budgets. The agencies currently cannot do the research necessary to adjust their data-gathering practices to rapid changes in the structure of the economy or to otherwise improve the quality of data used in forecasting efforts. In addition, very small increases in the statistical budgets of operating agencies could improve the quality and timeliness of administrative data generated by spending programs and the tax system. Forecasts will still be wrong, because our theoretical ignorance of how the economy works is a more serious problem than errors in the numbers, but there would, at least, be marginal improvements.

SUGGESTIONS FOR THE MEDIA

The media should change the language it uses to describe budget totals and policy changes.

Although the language of the policy debate seems to be fairly set in the media lexicon, the media should consider the fact that the discussions of budget totals or the budget effects of tax and spending policies that are cumulated over long periods are misleading and would not be very descriptive even if they were not misleading. As was noted previously, adding the projected surplus for 2006 makes little sense, because the two numbers differ so much in their reliability.

More generally, recent reporting on spending and tax issues leaves much to be desired, especially in terms of conveying a sense of how much uncertainty should be attached to estimates of the value of tax and spending proposals relative to projected surpluses. Much is made regarding differences between the CBO and OMB forecasts of surpluses that are trivial relative to typical forecasting errors.

Quantitative comparisons of tax and spending proposals should not be avoided entirely, but they should be reported with much more caution. There are ways of reporting the size of tax or spending initiatives that are less susceptible to forecast error than is an absolute dollar sum. For example, instead of saying that a tax cut is worth $1.35 trillion—a figure that must mean little to most Americans—the cut could be reported as equal to about five percent of projected revenues through 2011. Because most surprising economic events will push total revenues and the size of the tax cut in the same direction, a report of the percentage cut is likely to be less susceptible to forecast errors than a dollar figure. Similarly, the cost of a prescription drug plan could be reported as a percentage of total outlays or as a percentage of current Medicare outlays.

The media should place more emphasis on the qualitative characteristics of proposed policies.

Given that numerical estimates are extremely unreliable, it would be instructive to place more emphasis on debates regarding the qualitative merits of policy proposals rather than discussing whose numbers are correct. Issues of equity or economic efficiency are not easily resolved, but it is much easier for readers to understand the relevant arguments. For example, discussion of tax proposals should ask whether the tax cuts simplify or complicate the system. Are they efficient? Are they fair? If they are targeted, are they likely to be effective?

CONCLUSIONS

Because budget projections tend to be highly inaccurate and are unlikely to get better soon, policymakers, policy analysts, and the media must live with tremendous uncertainty. That uncertainty should be recognized more explicitly than it has been in the past, and the dialogue regarding policy decisions should pay more attention to the risks of being wrong. Almost everyone involved in the policymaking process recognizes this intellectually, but their time is scarce, and it is difficult enough to analyze policies under the assumption that the future is certain. Nevertheless, relatively simple changes in language, more caution in discussing and legalizing precise quantitative targets, and a more detailed discussion of the risks associated with bad forecasts have the potential to significantly improve the policy dialogue.

ADDENDUM ON TECHNICAL ISSUES

Because of the size of the errors in past forecasts, there are sometimes calls for radical changes in the forecasting techniques used by CBO and OMB. As noted above, the budget forecast process begins with an economic forecast that usually relies heavily on results derived from complex structural models of the economy. Robert Lucas won a Nobel Prize for critiquing such models.[12] He argued that the structure of the economy is constantly changing as decision makers learn more about how the economy functions and as important changes continually occur in technologies and other relationships. In particular, as people learn more about how policies are formulated, their reactions to policy changes will be altered. For example, if people come to expect that government will provide a tax incentive for investment during recessions, they might delay investments in order to enjoy the tax advantage if a recession appears imminent. Such behavior would, of course, make a recession more likely.

Lucas concluded that forecasts derived from the assumption that people do not learn such things and that the structure of behavior is constant were bound to be wrong. The fact that practical forecasters constantly make judgment changes to individual equations in structural models was taken as evidence that they are accommodating structural changes in the economy.

The alternative to using structural models is to use analyses of variables over time that are not restrained by specific structural assumptions. Past patterns in time series may be able to tell us something about future patterns. Using these new techniques, it might be possible to forecast things like personal income tax revenues and Medicare outlays directly without going through the step of first making an explicit, detailed economic forecast.

CBO experimented with such techniques in the mid-1980s—specifically with vector auto regression approaches—but they yielded totally implausible forecasts. By comparison, forecasts based on structural models did not look so bad.

When practical forecasters judgmentally adjust equations in a structural model in the hope of improving the model's forecast, it is unlikely that many believe that they are adjusting for changes in the basic structure of the economy. Even if the economy's structure is constant, it would be remarkable if it could be described with complete accuracy by a system of equations. Because of problems in describing the economy and fitting the equations to historical data, a blind run of a complex model will probably provide implausible results for particular variables. If the forecast for, say, business equipment investment is not credible, analysts will adjust the relevant equations. The beauty of a structural model is that one can quickly assess the effects of an adjustment in one place on all other variables in the system. If correcting an absurdity in one area creates a problem in another area, the analyst quickly returns to the drawing board and makes more adjustments. Forecasting becomes an iterative process, and although the forecast may turn out to be wildly wrong, it is, at least, logical.

Most time series analysis does not provide the same checks on the forecaster's judgment as a structural model does. Despite my earlier contention that the serial correlation of errors often occurs because analysts take a long time to recognize fundamental structural changes in economic relationships, I cannot imagine relying heavily on time series analysis, given the current state of the art. Unfortunately, we are a very long way from having a solution for this problem in which the cure is not worse than the disease.

I once suggested reforming the process in a radically different direction.[13] Given that forecasts were so inaccurate, I thought it might be preferable to rely on projections based on simple rules of thumb. My specific suggestion was a simple extrapolation of the last five years of history. The process would be simple, transparent, and immune from political influence and the biases of technical analysts. It would avoid creating the illusion that we could forecast with accuracy.

Unfortunately, the suggestion was made at a time that revealed the proposal's weakness. In the early 1980s, the rampant inflation of the late 1970s came to an end much more quickly than anyone thought possible. Basing the budget projections of the early 1980s on an extrapolation of the inflation rates of the late 1970s would have been more wildly misleading than the most inaccurate forecast imaginable.

A similar break in historical trends occurred in the late 1990s, when economists constantly raised the rate at which they assumed the economy could grow without provoking inflation. Again, budget projections based on historical economic trends would have been even worse than the forecasts that were actually used.

It seems evident that there is no easy way of improving on current procedures. CBO and OMB should continue to experiment with novel approaches, including time series analyses, but it is unlikely that we will see old-fashioned structural models of the economy abandoned any time soon. CBO, OMB, and private forecasters all rely on them to a considerable degree, and none of the proposed alternatives is significantly more accurate than any of the others, either in the two-year forecasts so important to the budget process or in their five-year projections. If there were better ways to forecast, private forecasting companies would clearly have a very powerful incentive to adopt them.[14]

NOTES

The Urban Institute is a nonprofit, nonpartisan policy research and educational organization that examines the social, economic, and governance problems facing the nation. The views expressed are those of the author and should not be attributed to the Urban Institute, its trustees, or its funders. The author would like to thank Barry Anderson, Joseph Antos, Alan Auerbach, William Hoagland, Arlene Holen, Richard Kogan, and Carol Wait for extremely useful comments. He would also like to thank the Smith Richardson Foundation for financial support. This article is an amended version of an occasional paper published by the Urban Institute in May 2001.

1. Henry J. Aaron, "Presidential Address—Seeing through the Fog: Policymaking with Uncertain Forecasts," *Journal of Policy Analysis and Management* 19, no. 2 (2000): 193–206.
2. Since this analysis was completed, CBO has altered its techniques for estimating errors in outlay projections. All changes in projections of discretionary spending are now defined as legislative, reducing the measured forecast error on the outlay side of the budget. Whether this change is appropriate involves a number of complex issues that will not be discussed here. The basic point is that the division of changes in the projections into legislative, economic, and technical changes is somewhat arbitrary. Different approaches yield somewhat different results, but changes in definitions do not alter the conclusion that errors are very large.
3. There are gaps in CBO's records that prevent a completely accurate separation of the effects of policy changes on the budget deficit from the effects of economic forecasting and technical errors made in the early 1980s. However, the gaps are small, and it is unlikely any of the important

conclusions of this analysis would be altered if discrepancies in the data were completely resolved.

4. Because of the change in the definition of forecast error reported in note 2, CBO reports a somewhat smaller possible error using a similar sample period. See CBO, *The Budget and Economic Outlook* (Washington, DC: U.S. Government Printing Office, 1987–2001).
5. CBO reports that outlay errors are considerably smaller relative to revenue because of the change in definitions reported in note 2.
6. Alan J. Auerbach, "On the Performance and Use of Government Revenue Forecasts," *National Tax Journal* 52, no. 4 (1999): 767–82.
7. The accuracy of the economic forecasts of the two agencies are compared in CBO, *The Budget and Economic Outlook: An Update* (Washington, DC: U.S. Government Printing Office, July 2000). Appendix B.
8. Indeed, as director of CBO, I sometimes semiseriously characterized our process as forecasting what the consensus forecast would be several months hence, when we would be defending our forecast before Congress.
9. Section 303 of the Congressional Budget Act provides a point of order against having any provisions, including phase-ins, effective beyond the time period covered by the budget resolution. However, the provision does not apply to revenue measures in the House and can be waived by a majority of senators. The provision has not been effective in the past and ironically played a role in inducing the Congress to sunset the recent tax cut at the end of calendar 2010, thus making it appear smaller than it is likely to be in the long run. Ten-year scorekeeping can, at least, identify the gaming that this provision tries to prevent.
10. For a more favorable account of the effects of GRH, see Edward M. Gramlich, "U.S. Federal Budget Deficits and Gramm-Rudman-Hollings," *American Economic Review* 80, no. 2 (1990): 75–80.
11. General Accounting Office, *Balanced Budget Requirements: State Experience and Implications for the Federal Government*, GAO/AFMD-93-58BR (Washington, DC, 1993).
12. Robert E. Lucas, "Econometric Policy Evaluation: A Critique," in *The Phillips Curve and Labor Markets*, Carnegie-Rochester Conference Series on Public Policy (1), ed. Karl Brunner and Alan Meltzer (Amsterdam: North Holland, 1976); "Methods and Problems in Business Cycle Theory," *Journal of Money, Credit and Banking* 12, no. 2 (1980): 696–713; Robert E. Lucas and Thomas Sargent, "After the Phillips Curve," in *Rational Expectations and Econometric Practice*, ed. Robert E. Lucas and Thomas Sargent (Minneapolis: University of Minnesota Press, 1978).
13. Rudolph Penner, "Forecasting Budget Totals: Why Can't We Get It Right?" in *The Federal Budget: Economics and Politics*, ed. A. Wildavsky and M. Boskin (San Francisco: Institute for Contemporary Studies, 1982), 89–110.
14. Daniel Bachman provides an excellent description of how practical, private forecasters approach their task in *What Economic Forecasters Really Do* (Bala Cynwyd, PA: The WEFA Group, 1996).

Rudolph G. Penner is a Senior Fellow at the Urban Institute and was Director of the Congressional Budget Office from 1983 to 1987. His most recent book, with Isabel Sawhill and Timothy Taylor, is *Updating America's Social Contract*. Correspondence concerning this article should be addressed to him at The Urban Institute, 2100 M Street, NW, Washington, DC 20037. He can be reached by e-mail at rpenner@ui.urban.org.

From *Public Budgeting & Finance,* Vol. 22, No. 1, Spring 2002, pp. 1-18.

How Congress Divides Our Money

How Congress' power players divvy dollars. Appropriations game involves instinct, timing and good friends.

By Chuck Lindell

WASHINGTON—U.S. Rep. Chet Edwards dropped a $1 million calling card on Williamson County this month, welcoming 48,000 new voters to his district with a display of clout that said: "I can bring home the bacon."

Some might call $1 million for a Lake Georgetown hike-and-bike trail park, a budget-inflating bone thrown to the home district to buy jobs or popularity. But you can bet a $600 hammer that those critics share two traits: They live in another district, and they wanted that money for their local project. Money is power, trite but true, but you need power to get the money. And in Congress that power churns in the House and Senate appropriations committees, where Edwards and 93 congressional confederates dole out billions in a process so complex and so mysterious that it inspires awe in the most jaded corners of the capital.

That process lurches to an inelegant climax with the approach to Tuesday, when the U.S. fiscal year beings. Congress has yet to pass any of its 13 spending bills, provoking bitter partisan sniping last week when both houses passed a four-day budget extension to keep the government running. Another extension will be needed by week's end as unfinished business piles up, and adjournment is expected to be pushed into December instead of October, as planned. "Even if we were agreeing with each other, these decisions would take a while," said James Dyer, staff director for the House Appropriations Committee.

Through it all, the appropriations committees endure as the province of egos and jealousy, expert gamesmanship and midnight deals—and a dirty little secret called bipartisanship. Even party affiliations crumble with about $760 billion at stake. Add the zeroes to fully appreciate the sum: $760,000,000,000. The figure has doubled since 1984, and it's not enough. "For every request that's approved, there are probably 10 that are turned down," said Edwards, D-Waco.

Competition among lawmakers is furious and behind the scenes, with success depending on political instinct, timing and whom you know. It's one of the least understood aspects of Congress, even among some lawmakers. Only one-third of the $2.2 trillion federal budget gets doled out by Congress; the rest is mandatory spending for interest on the federal debt and on programs such as Social Security and Medicare.

Who gets the discretionary money? Members of the appropriations committees get first priority, then dignitaries such as the speaker of the House and Senate majority leader, then heads of other committees and members with seniority. The rest gets picked over by nonapproriators, for whom a friend on an appropriations committee is a friend indeed. In practice, the process is anything but simple.

The situation galls Sen. Phil Gramm, R-Texas, a frequent budget critic. Gramm's drawling voice rises an octave as he complains that spending has grown almost four times faster than the inflation rate since 1998. "The plain truth is, we have been on a spending binge since the surplus, since 1998. The surplus just burned a hole in Congress' pocket," he said. Gramm was on the Senate Appropriations Committee in the early 1990s and recalls sitting around a table as senators listed their priorities—$70 million here, $30 million there—until they came to Gramm, who said he wanted to spend $8 billion less. "After everyone had a good laugh, they went on about their business," he said. "My problem as an appropriator came because disputes in appropriations are solved by spending money," Gramm said. "I get what I want by helping everyone else get money for their projects." Edwards offers a different interpretation. "We see in greater detail of importance of so many of these programs, whether it's improving military housing for Army soldiers at Fort Hood or funding a research program at the University of Texas," he said. Careful study is essential, because if you can't justify a project, a opportunistic rival will swoop in for the kill, Edwards said. Also important is the satisfaction that follows shaping priorities and influencing lives.

Sen. Kay Bailey Hutchison said she has steered $500 million to colonias, Mexican border towns beset by poor sanitation and limited utility service. "Not one federal dollar had been spent for colonia cleanup until I came to the committee," she said. Last year, Edwards successfully fought the Bush administration and leading appropriators to add $226 million toward securing nuclear weapons in Russia. "My hope is through that one effort alone, I've justified the space I've taken up in this world," Edwards said.

Power Plays

U.S. Rep. Henry Bonilla is a Republican from San Antonio, but to thousands of lobbyists, industry representatives and interest groups, he goes by a different title: cardinal.

Bonilla and the 12 other leaders of House appropriations subcommittees each write one of the 13 spending bills that fund the entire federal government. With their Senate counterparts, they exercise so much authority that their power is linked to that of Roman Catholic cardinals, sometimes called the princes of the church.

"If you want a hospital built, an agriculture research project or a conservation project, there is only one way you're going to get it, and that's if the chairman decides you're going to get it," a congressional staff member said. Each of the 13 bills, if well written, will emerge from its subcommittee with few notable changes. That makes it essential to gain the chairman's attention, because it's easier to protect your money than to take somebody else's. There are limits to that power, however.

"No one exists here running their own private little empire," said Bonilla, chairman of the agriculture subcommittee. An overtly political bill or one that ignores Democrats will not pass. Bonilla walks a careful line, juggling competing interests from 434 other representatives of varying shades of importance. "There is no formula. You don't find the process written down. You just get a feel for it," he said. The operation begins with the eagerly awaited arrival of the president's proposed budget in January. Congressional offices scan the document line by line to decide where to tweak or attack in search of money for their priorities and pet projects.

Then it's time to write letters—detailed wish lists—to the 13 subcommittee chairmen. This is where the game gets interesting. The letters are an art form in themselves, created after months of meetings with lobbyists, interest groups and delegations from home—each with projects that need money. If you misjudge your clout and ask for too much, the projects that get funded may not be your highest priorities. Seek too little and you waste an opportunity.

Bonilla received about 2,700 separate requests, many signed by multiple lawmakers, last spring. With supporting documents, they stacked almost two feet tall.

Next, the requests are assigned priorities. Anything the chairman wants, the chairman gets. The same is usually true with the subcommittee's leading Democrat, whose blessing carries considerable weight with other party members.

Myriad other factors, too numerous to include, also get stirred into the pot. Seniority is important. So is reputation. A trusted friend will outshine a political agitator or a lawmaker who made unrealistic requests in the past. "After you've been around here awhile, you know who those people are," Bonilla said.

Election-year politics also enter the mix. Well-liked legislators in danger of losing their seats often find a boost from appropriations, giving them something to write home about. But until the chairman's bill is unveiled, few know how their projects will fare.

Team Texas

There's an added dimension in the complex tug-of-war for federal dollars: loyalty to home. Bonilla and Edwards pay close attention to their home districts and the people who sent them to Congress. "We fight as hard as we know how to see that Texas, and in my case, Central Texas, gets its fair share of the tax dollars we sent to Washington," Edwards said.

ON THE WEB: Senate Appropriations Committee: www.senate.gov/~appropriations
House Appropriations Committee: www.house.gov/appropriations

Budget Breakdown

The federal government's budget grew 172 percent in 20 years, fueled largely by Social Security, Medicare and other mandatory spending. Discretionary spending grew at a slower pace, creating hotter competition in the annual fight for dollars in Congress.

U.S. Budget

In trillions
1981: $0.72 1991: $1.43 2001: $1.95
Limiting Congress's options
In trillions
1981: Mandatory: $339 (47%) Discretionary: $308 (43%) Interest in debt: $69 (10%)
1991: Mandatory: $703 (49%) Discretionary: $533 (38%) Interest in debt: $194 (14%)
2001: Mandatory: $1,095 (56%) Discretionary: $649 (33%) Interest in debt: $205 (11%)

Source: Congressional Budget Office.

They also feel responsible for the state, working with fellow Texans Tom Delay and Kay Granger to field requests from all 26 Texas representatives not on the House Appropriations Committee. Watching above them all is Hutchison, the Republican senator who has made it clear that partisan politics stop when a Texas district, industry or city needs money.

"I can't say enough about Senator Hutchison," Edwards said. "We've worked very closely together on Fort Hood, the Houston Ship Channel, the Trinity River in Dallas. (These) are not Republican or Democratic programs. They are investments in the future." Said Hutchison: "If a House member misses getting something in a bill, then they will call me, and I will try to help. And they do the same."

The Texans do have a reputation for cooperation, said Leo Coco, a senior policy adviser for the lobbying arm of Powell Goldstein Frazer & Murphy LLP law firm in Washington. "They communicate well, and the delegation is... very large, so the tentacles of that delegation are through all the different power bases throughout Congress," Coco said. This "Texas Team" attitude, by the way, is not news to those who play the budget game.

The president's proposed military construction budget included steep spending cuts for Texas and California, an obvious low-ball offer worked up by the Defense Department and the Office of Management and Budget. Sen. Dianne Feinstein, D-Calif., is chairwoman of the military construction subcommittee, and Texan Hutchison is the leading Republican. Budget writers knew the senators would protect their home states, so they packed money into projects elsewhere. And they were right. Hutchison was able to add $31 million in Texas projects, a 25 percent increase.

A Difficult Year

Once money gets into a spending bill, an appropriator's work isn't done. Changes can happen in full committee. And on the floor nonappropriators typically can offer unlimited amendments—but here, bills are protected by a simple procedure. Any money added to a project must be subtracted from somewhere else, a move sure to infuriate at least one lawmaker. Success is rare.

Then it's on to conference committee, where often vast differences between House and Senate versions must be reconciled, frequently by cutting money or entire projects. Finally, the president can sign or veto. At best, it's an arduous process, but this has been a particularly complicated year.

Homeland security and the war on terror have drained time and money. Also, five years of surpluses have dried up because of a slow economy, last year's tax cut and higher defense spending, according to the Center on Budget and Policy Priorities, a nonpartisan research group. With the government again spending more money than it has, three things are happening:

- Instead of paying off the national debt by next decade, congressional estimates predict a $3.2 trillion debt by 2011.
- Almost $2 trillion will be spent on interest payments over the next decade, more than will be spent on defense.
- Congress is being pressured to hold down spending. President Bush is backing the House, which is operating with a $759 billion cap, while the Senate is looking to spend about $9 billion more.

With major fights looming in conference committee, Congress trudges on. This week, the House and Senate will consider a second "continuing resolution" to keep the government running at 2002 levels for a set period of time. The solution isn't ideal—no new projects can start, and no increases planned for next year can occur—but it keeps the wheels turning. Meantime, the House has passed five spending bills, the Senate three. The rest are working through the process, including the water-energy spending bill in which Edwards recently found money for local projects.

Edwards originally allocated $1.9 million for a home-district ground-water study that was no longer needed, so he redistributed $1 million to Lake Georgetown, $500,000 to renovate a Lake Belton park and $400,000 to a flood-control study on the Colorado River.

The committee deferred to Edwards because all the projects were in or near his district, and there was no impact on the bottom line. As one House staff member put it: "It's all a matter of getting your priorities put ahead of other priorities."

clindell@statesman.com, (202) 887-8329

City of Austin's Budget Crisis

In search of $29 million Austin can do without

By Stephen Scheibal

Pretend you have to cut $29 million from the City of Austin's budget.

There are rules, of course—such as the deadline: You have until July 31. That's when beleaguered budget writers will present to the City Council the toughest budget they've written in more than a decade.

Next, most of the $1.9 billion that the city spent and collected this year is off-limits. Three-fourths of that pays off debt, runs utilities or covers the budgets of operations that pay for themselves.

That leaves the general fund, a catch-all account that pays for police, libraries, parks and other basics that's expected to total $449 million next year.

You can't cut from all parts of that fund, either. More than half of it will go to police, fire and Emergency Medical Services.

With a new police labor contract and security costs, the three public safety departments will eat up more than $255 million—almost all of the sales and property taxes the city collects next year.

That leaves you with less than $200 million from which to squeeze $29 million, the gap between the money the city expects to take in and pay out next year as sales tax receipts and other revenues continue suffering from the sluggish economy.

You must take it from neighborhood and traffic planning, road work, Smart Growth planning, emergency rooms, library books, sports and arts programs, building inspections and hundreds of other programs that link the city to your life.

Tax bills will go up. If you can stand dirty looks from neighbors and voters, you can raise the tax rate even higher. You should avoid layoffs if you can.

And remember: You have until the end of July to present the budget to the council, which will vote on the plan in September.

"Right up until the end, we're going to be balancing the needs of one department against another and the needs of one constituency against another," said John Stephens, acting assistant city manager who, with City Manager Toby Futrell, is presiding over the process. "At some point, you're going to need to get a budget out."

Stephens, Futrell and the council have already made the job a lot easier. Last month, council members gave their tacit blessing to a menu of cost-saving strategies that would cut the budget gap from $72 million to $29 million.

The staff plans to leave the tax rate where it is, increasing bills for homeowners whose property values rose this year. An additional tax rate increase that would generate an additional $7 million got a cold reception among council members last month.

Stephens pledged to "make sure we can very clearly communicate to the council the effects of that budget.

"The policy decision is up to them, as to whether they want to live with what that budget would do."

So where do you look for $29 million?

You could start with the obvious targets, the ones that catch flak whenever people look to save city money.

Cancel the Austin Music Network, which broadcasts regional musicians 24 hours a day. Dump the bike and pedestrian coordinator's office, which builds and improves sidewalks and bike lanes. Delete the Art in Public Places program, which uses city money to install, well, art in public places.

Combined, those three programs cost less than $1 million.

Even those frequently criticized programs have strong defenders. They say the music channel bolsters Austin's "Live Music Capital of the World" claim even as longstanding venues die off, while the bike and pedestrian coordinator makes it safer for people to move about without adding traffic or ozone.

Subject to Cuts?

A sampling of city programs (and their department) receiving general fund money in the 2001–02 budget. Austin officials said these programs may face reductions next year, but few, if any, will be eliminated altogether:

- Neighborhood development plans coordination (Neighborhood Planning & Zoning): $1 million
- Academy on building strong neighborhoods (Neighborhood Planning & Zoning): $180,000
- Smart Growth redevelopment planning (Transportation Planning & Sustainability): $1.4 million
- Water conservation promotion (Transportation Planning & Sustainability): $1.2 million
- Bicycle and pedestrian coordination (Transportation Planning & Sustainability): $149,000
- Slowing speeders in neighborhoods (Transportation Planning & Sustainability): $260,000
- Victim trauma counseling (Police): $1.2 million
- Health Connection mobile counseling (Health & Human Services): $149,000
- Disease and injury prevention (Health & Human Services): $233,000
- Youth reading programs (Libraries): $1.2 million
- Community recreation programs (Parks): $5.7 million
- Roving Leader youth outreach (Parks): $671,000
- Senior recreation services (Parks): $1.5 million
- Totally Cool, Totally Art teen education (Parks): $262,000

Source: City of Austin

The general fund

The preliminary 2002–03 budget will be released next month. Here are highlights showing how the City of Austin budgeted its discretionary general fund for 2001–02:

- Police: $141 million
- Fire: $79 million
- Emergency medical service: $19 million
- Neighborhood planning and zoning: $4 million
- Watershed protection and development review: $8 million
- Transportation, planning and design: $10 million
- Health and human services: $26 million
- Parks and recreation: $31 million
- Libraries: $19 million
- Total: $466 million

Potential savings

City Council-endorsed policies that might be used to cut Austin's budget gap from $72 million to $29 million:

- Devote half of this year's ending balance to next year's budget: $13 million
- Increase Austin Energy's transfer to the general fund: $2.5 million
- Redirect excess hospital fund money: $6.5 million
- Cut vehicle replacement money by half: $3.9 million
- Increase fees to reflect costs of services: $2.4 million
- Consolidate departments and functions: $1.8 million
- Adjust pay and benefits package: $3.8 million
- Reduce administrative support costs: $2.4 million
- Eliminate half of the positions frozen to cover this year's budget: $6 million

Cuts only get harder from there. Do you—or do your neighbors and voters—want to do away with seniors' services at recreation centers? Neighborhood development plans? Water conservation promotions?

Losing those three would save $4 million, and each enjoys more political support than Art in Public Places.

Programs that don't protect people's lives probably will get less money next year, Stephens said, but few face oblivion. Instead, the city is spreading the cuts around departments and focusing on functions people are less likely to miss, particularly administrative jobs.

As a starting point, city department heads have been asked for savings plans keyed on specific targets. Stephens declined to say who's been asked to cut what, saying he doesn't want to alarm people with cuts that may not happen.

Hundreds of positions have been held vacant to cover this year's budget shortfall, and budget officials want to eliminate half of those jobs altogether. They'll talk with department directors over the next several months about what departments want to maintain, where they can cut and how Austinites will notice the consequences.

"It comes down to an analysis of where you're going to do the least damage to the city as a whole," Stephens said.

Austan Librach, director of Transportation Planning and Sustainability, said he is trying to eliminate 10 percent of his administrative costs and 10 percent of everything that remains. He expects to purge 15 vacant positions, saving $800,000 to $900,000.

The department probably will have to tighten spending on road signs or street paint, Librach said, quickly adding that it will not sacrifice traffic safety. He also said departmental studies may take longer to complete, and crews will build fewer miles of sidewalks than in past years.

"We'll be stretching our staff a little thinner," Librach said. "Its real tough. It's also compressed. We're trying to get a lot of work done here in a little bit of time."

Some departments say they are already lean to the point of emaciation.

Austin's libraries have shut branches an extra day a week to save $323,000 through the summer. The hiring freeze took such a toll that branches couldn't always provide reliable service.

Austin/Travis County Health and Human Services Director David Lurie said his staff has already worked several years to whittle its budget. He said he does not know where the department, which handles such functions as disease control, preventive health programs and child care, will find the cuts. He does not think the reductions will escape people's notice.

"These are all pretty significant programs and services. It's certainly not an easy process for pinpointing areas for reductions," Lurie said. "It's pretty evident that you can't absorb that strictly through your indirect costs. You've got to look at some of your direct services."

Toolbox rummaging

As you cut, you will want tools that help other cities stretch their dollars. Some don't exist here. Others are almost maxed out.

Dallas, Houston, Fort Worth and San Antonio all have tax-supported districts that pay for public hospitals and clinics that treat the poor. But Austin will spend about $20 million, with no help from the neighboring cities and counties that use Brackenridge Hospital, to cover indigent health-care costs.

Austin also boasts a lower property tax rate than other big Texas cities. San Antonio, which carries the second-lowest rate in the group, would have to cut its rate 20 percent to match Austin's.

The saviors, for budget planners and taxpayers, are city utilities. Austin Energy and the water utility gave $90 million in dividends to the general fund this year.

Budget officials plan to take more money from Austin Energy next year, up to the maximum allowed by city policy. Transferring more than 9.1 percent of the utility's revenues to the city's general fund might worry the utility's bondholders.

The city has all but abandoned an increase in the amount of water utility money shifted to general uses.

Austin is bracing to spend hundreds of millions of dollars on a new water treatment plant and repairs to aging water and sewer pipes. Those improvements will require higher water and sewer rates this year or next.

Stephens expects those increases in 2004. Between the failing economy and the budget cuts, he said, 2003 will be tough enough.

Betty Dunkerley, the city's former finance director who won a City Council seat last month, said she hopes to make it through budget season without raising the property tax rate.

But she doesn't know what will have to be cut to afford that. She doubts the city will shed $29 million without anyone noticing.

"I think (residents) will notice that some things will not be done as quickly as they were in the past," Dunkerley said.

"I can't tell yet what's going to have to be done. There's not just one thing you do. You do 50 things or 100 things."

Those things will define how the City of Austin serves its residents.

So how would you cut $29 million?

---

sscheibal@statesman.com; 445-3819

The Budget Game

Here's your chance to play state lawmaker. Your goal: Bridge the projected $9.9 billion gap between the state's expected revenue and what Texas must spend to maintain existing programs.

But watch out. Every move comes with a political cost.

Good luck, and as our state leaders are fond of saying, God Bless Texas!

How to play

Make your choices for new revenue (left) and for savings from program cuts (right). Note: Leaders already say cuts alone aren't likely.

The game adds the revenue and cuts together. Your target is the $9.9 billion needed to balance the budget.

The game will tally the political costs of your decisions. Check the chart to see what voters are likely to say.

—Staff reporter Gary Susswein and State Editor Juan B. Elizondo Jr. contributed to this report.

New revenue

1. Personal income tax

Vote for a personal income tax. Under the Kansas model, the first $30,000 of income would be tax-exempt, the next $30,000 taxed at 3.5 percent and above that at 6.25 percent.

❑ $11.6 billion

Political cost: Most consider a state income tax downright un-Texan. So, unless you're very charismatic or extremely lucky, pack up your office. You're out of a job.

Political Points: 75

2. Tobacco money

Sell future rights to tobacco settlement money.

❑ $5.8 billion

Political cost: This could leave a bad taste in the mouths of health-care advocates and anti-smokers, but the political clout of those interested could be distracted and it could be hard to generate heat over the complicated issue.

Political Points: 4

3. Food tax

Charge sales tax on groceries.

❑ $2.6 billion

Political cost: Texans have come to believe most food will always be tax-free, so the bad public relations would be hard to overcome

Political Points: 9

Program cuts

1. Local school budgets

Cut aid to local school districts, including money for new textbooks.

❑ $1.8 billion

Political cost: Not much upsets Texans as much as cuts in public school funding, and it could cause local tax hikes.

Political Points: 50

2. Medicaid

Reduce Medicaid payments to doctors and hospitals by 33 percent.

❑ $1.5 billion

Political cost: Would mobilize the forces of politically potent health-care providers against you.

Political Points: 8

3. Teacher health insurance

Reduce yearly payment to teachers for health insurance from $1,000 to $500.

❑ $1.2 billion

Political cost: Teachers are well-organized but so are state employees, who have lately clashed with educators over compensation and benefits.

Political Points: 5

New revenue

4. State sales tax

4a: Increase by a half-cent to 6.75 percent; 4b: By a quarter-cent to 6.5 percent.

❑ 4a $2.2 billion

❑ 4b $1.1 billion

Political cost: Advocates for low- and middle-income Texans don't have the largest pots of political cash. But combined with the bad public perception of increasing a regressive tax, steam from other Texans who also won't want to pay more and an overall anti-tax sentiment, there'd be a fight. Even a smaller sales tax increase would be hard for voters to swallow.

Political Points 4a: 6
Political Points 4b: 4

5. Cigarette tax

Hike the cigarette tax by $1 per pack, to $1.41.

❑ $1.5 billion

Political cost: Smokers won't like it, but it can be easier to target them than to cut services for elderly and young Texans.

Political Points: 3

6. Rainy day fund

Empty the state's rainy day fund.

❑ $1 billion

Political cost: Supporters could be accused of using one-time money for recurring costs, but aside from Comptroller Carole Keeton Strayhorn, there's no significant effort to the protect the fund. Gov. Rick Perry wants a piece of it for a one-time economic development investment.

Political Points: 2

7. Gasoline tax

Add 5 cents to the 20-cents-a-gallon gasoline tax. Money from that tax is dedicated to roads and schools.

❑ $1 billion

Political cost: This would hit a broad swath of Texans, many of whom think gas is too expensive already.

Political Points: 6

8. Medicine tax

Charge sales tax on medicine.

❑ $830 million

Political cost: This would be another broad swipe at all Texans, and supporters easily could be branded as cruel and heartless.

Political Points: 9

Program cuts

4. Prisoner programs

Lay off 2,500 probation officers; eliminate offender treatment programs in prison.

❑ $800 million

Political cost: Texans are tough on crime and expect their politicians to be likewise.

Political Points: 8

5. Higher education

Don't pay for enrollment growth at universities and community colleges.

❑ $500 million

Political cost: Tens of thousands of Texans who depend on community colleges could see higher costs, but those aren't the most powerful political groups.

Political Points: 4

6. Elderly care

Eliminate community care for elderly Texans.

❑ $453 million

Political cost: These folks vote and so do their children and grandchildren.

Political Points: 7

7. Mental retardation services

Reduce services for mentally retarded Texans.

❑ $165 million

Political cost: Although Texans are sympathetic to this group, there are more powerful lobbies out there.

Political Points: 5

8. CHIP

Reduce eligibility for the Children's Health Insurance Program.

❑ $141 million

Political cost: Targeting children is never a wise political move.

Political Points: 6

New revenue

9. Internet tax

Approve an Internet sales tax.

❑ $400 million

Political cost: The growing field of online buyers won't like it, but other states are moving toward a uniform tax, so Texas would lose money if it doesn get on board.

Political Points: 4

10. The "Delaware sub"

Eliminate the "Deleware sub," a provision of state law that allows businesses incorporated in low-tax states, such as Delaware, to form business partnerships in Texas and avoid paying the state's franchise taxes.

❑ $360 million

Political cost: Could anger businesses, such as Dell Computer Corp. and SBC Corp., that don't pay the tax, but they aren't likely to protest very loudly. It also would sell well with taxpayers who believe companies should pay their fair share.

Political Points: 3

11. Business/personal property tax

Require businesses to accurately report and pay taxes on their personal property.

❑ $150 million

Political cost: There's little risk that affected companies would rally against paying what they really owe.

Political Points: 1

12. Multistate lottery

Introduce a multistate lottery game.

❑ $102 million

Political cost: Not popular with politically conservative or religious groups, but many see the lottery as a self-imposed tax. (You have to pay to play.)

Political Points: 3

Program cuts

9. Medicaid

Reduce Medicaid coverage for low-income pregnant women.

❑ $90 million

Political cost: This isn't a powerful political group, but there would be bad public relations and if health-care providers get nicked, watch out.

Political Points: 5

10. Foster care

Reduce financial support for foster care and adoptive families.

❑ $88 million

Political cost: This affects another less powerful political group, though expect some bad publicity from this vocal group.

Political Points: 2

11. Medical coverage

Reduce or eliminate medical coverage for people with HIV or epilepsy, and for children with special health-care needs.

❑ $60 million

Political cost: These Texans are tenacious in their fight for services. Be ready to face them at every turn.

Political Points: 5

12. Prescription drugs

Eliminate prescription drug benefits and treatment for mentally impaired probationers and parolees

❑ $22 million

Political cost: The law-and-order types will approve, but there is a risk. If one of these folks commits a terrible crime, be prepared to take the some heat

Political Points: 3

Budget scorecard

NEW REVENUE	You've found:	PROGRAM CUTS
1. ________ __	New Revenue money $_____	1. ________ __
2. ________ __	plus program cuts $_____	2. ________ __
3. ________ __	**Total money** $_____	3. ________ __
4a. ________ __	**The political cost is**	4. ________ __
4b. ________ __	Revenue points $_____	5. ________ __
5. ________ __	plus Cuts points $_____	6. ________ __
6. ________ __	**Total points** ____	7. ________ __
7. ________ __	**How did you do?**	8. ________ __
8. ________ __	**25 points or less:** You'll skate into another term.	9. ________ __
9. ________ __	**26–50:** A fair challenge awaits you at the polls.	10. ________ __
10. ________ __	**51–75:** Get ready for a tough battle, and dust off your résumé just in case.	11. ________ __
11. ________ __	**76 or more:** Save yourself the hassle; don't seek re-election.	12. ________ __
12. ________ __		**Total:** ________ __
Total: ________ __		

78TH LEGISLATURE

Deferrals: gimmick or usual budget math?

By Gary Susswein
AMERICAN-STATESMAN STAFF

State lawmakers say their plan to balance the 2004–05 budget by pushing off the payment of some of their bills to 2006 is a tried-and-true accounting method. But critics inside and outside government say it's nothing but a gimmick, and one suggests that the plan is reminiscent of the Enron scandals.

"This is a classic gimmick. The state has done it many times in the past," said Michael Granof, a University of Texas accounting professor and a leading expert on government finance. "You're pushing the cost of services that we, the taxpayers of today, are enjoying onto the taxpayers of tomorrow."

Although some of the problems at Enron Corp. stemmed from fraudulent accounting, Granof said, most came from "aggressive accounting" that took advantage of legal loopholes.

"That's what you're seeing here," he said of the Legislature's proposed budgets. "You're seeing budgetary measures which are perfectly legal but they are intended to circumvent spending restrictions."

The Senate and House have passed separate $118 billion budgets that cut state services and raise no new taxes. They also delay between $977 million and $1.76 billion in payments to school districts and other programs from August 2005, the last month of that fiscal year, to September, the first month of the next budget year, according to figures from the state comptroller's office.

Lawmakers say it's the only way to pass a balanced budget, as required by the constitution, without raising taxes or making deeper cuts that would hurt more Texans. And they're confident the economy will rebound by the time the bills come due in 2006.

But they still have to sell that argument to Texans whose retirement savings have been gutted by recent corporate accounting scandals and to officials such as Gov. Rick Perry and Comptroller Carole Keeton Strayhorn who have staked their political future on cutting state spending, not delaying it by a few days.

"It can be called smoke and mirrors, but what it is is an accounting method. And you know what, we've probably all used it in our own households," said Senate Finance Committee Vice Chairwoman Judith Zaffirini, D-Laredo. "Do I like it? No. Would I do it under different circumstances? No. But there are times when situations are so serious that you have to take exceptional behavior."

More of the same

The plan is actually pretty typical of state budgets. Over the past 20 years, both Democrats and Republicans have tweaked their spending plans so that no one necessarily gets less or more, they just get it all a little earlier or later.

The trend began in 1984 when then-Comptroller Bob Bullock moved up monthly sales tax collections by 10 days so the state could take in 13 months' of sales taxes during a tight year.

At the end of fiscal 1987, state government rolled a month's worth of salaries into the 1988 budget by switching the state's payday from the last day of the month to the first workday of the next month.

And then-Gov. George W. Bush and the Legislature paid for some of their 1999 tax cuts by pushing a month of Medicaid payments from the 1998–99 budget to the 2000–01 budget.

During the 2000 presidential election, Democrats shunned those deferred payments as smoke-and-mirror budgeting; Republicans defended them as legitimate accounting moves.

"They're both right," said Eva DeLuna Castro, a senior budget analyst at the Center for Public Policy Priorities, which advocates for low-income families. "If everybody remembers what they did and then undoes it as soon as they have money, there's no problem."

That happened in the mid-1990s when lawmakers made up for some of their early '90s deferrals. For example, they spent an extra $488 million in 1995 by moving payments to school districts and colleges back to their traditional due date.

But payday has never been moved back to the end of the month. And lawmakers have continued to roll one month of Medicaid to the next budget, never paying for 25 months in a 24-month budget to bring the payments in sync with services.

"It does make it really hard to understand what's going on in the budget," Castro said.

In the budgets approved last month—which are now being negotiated by a House-Senate committee—both chambers continue to delay the Medicaid payment and also delay about $800 million in payments to school districts.

Paying later

The state House and Senate have balanced their 2004–05 budgets by moving some state payments into the first days of the fiscal 2006 budget. The two budgets are currently being negotiated in conference committee. Figures are rounded.

House

- Delay one month of Medicaid payments: $177 million
- Delay payments to school districts: $800 million

Total: $977 million

Senate

- Delay one month of Medicaid payments: $177 million
- Delay payments to school districts: $800 million
- Delay contributions to Employees Retirement System: $14 million
- Delay contributions and payments to Teacher Retirement System: $355 million
- Delay mental health/mental retardation payments: $33 million
- Delay transfer of motor fuel tax revenue out of treasury: $376 million

Total: $1.76 billion

Source: Legislative Budget Board

The Senate plan goes even further, pushing off money for mental health services and for the employees and teachers retirement systems. It also holds motor fuel tax payments in the state's general fund for a few days before shifting them to the accounts that pay for schools and highways.

Perry and Strayhorn say putting off the payments is like running up a credit card bill, and they warn that Texas may not have enough money to pay up in 2006, especially since the Legislature is also tapping the state's rainy day fund this year.

But Perry signed a budget two years ago that pushed off a month of Medicaid payments. Strayhorn certified that budget and doesn't appear to have any authority to stop the deferrals.

Motivations

Some senators hint that the criticism is politically motivated. They note that the state's bond ratings stayed strong despite two decades of deferrals and say their plan is no different than renegotiating a car payment from the last day of the month to the first day.

The deferrals "are tried and true measures around the Legislature," said Senate Finance Committee Chairman Teel Bivins, R-Amarillo.

Several other states have also deferred payments to future budgets over the past two years, though not as much as Texas lawmakers are discussing, according to the National Conference on State Legislatures.

Texas and other states can defer the payments in part because they use accounting systems that record expenses when money is actually paid, not when services are rendered.

And it all suggests that writing a state budget is never just about balancing the ledger.

"It is a legitimate accounting procedure. All that means is there's a debit and credit, and they make sense from an accounting point of view," said Jan Gillespie, another University of Texas accounting professor. "Whether they make sense from a public policy point of view is a separate question."

---

gsusswein@statesman.com; 445-3654

UNIT 5

Technology and Information Systems

Unit Selections

Key Points to Consider

- Discuss the impact of information technology on the problems of representative government in the United States, specifically on citizens, elected representatives, and the media.
- Identify and discuss some of the ways in which the legal and judicial systems have been improved by the introduction of technology. Can you think of any downside to the introduction of technology in the courtroom?
- Identify and discuss some of the health problems associated with the introduction and improvement of technology in the workplace. What can be done to mitigate the health problems associated with the introduction of technology?
- What is "Web accessibility," and why is it an important concept? What is the relationship of Web accessibility to the Americans With Disabilities Act (ADA)?
- Identify and discuss some of the major problems associated with computer security, especially wireless computer security. What are some of the things that you can do to improve security in this area?

Links: www.dushkin.com/online/
These sites are annotated in the World Wide Web pages.

Activity-Based Costing (ABC)
http://www.esc-brest.fr/cg/cgkiosk3.htm

Alliance for Redesigning Government
http://www.napawash.org/pc_local_state/about.html

American Capital Strategies
http://www.americancapital.com/news/press_releases/pr/pr19961024.html

Brookings Institution
http://www.brook.edu

Center for Policy Research on Science and Technology (CPROST)
http://edie.cprost.sfu.ca

Economic Development Administration
http://12.39.209.165/xp/EDAPublic/Home/EDAHomePage.xml

Putting Technology to Work for America's Future
http://sunsite.unc.edu/darlene/tech/report3.html

Reason Foundation
http://www.reason.org/privatizationctr.html

The articles in this unit review the impact of technology on such diverse areas as democratic governance, the digital divide, the courts, and worker health. Additional articles also discuss security in a wireless world and Web accessibility for persons with disabilities.

"'Smart' Government Online, Not Inline," by Breena Coates, reviews the impact that information technology will have on the e-haves and e-have nots of society. In addition, commenting on the digital divide, the author explores public policy concerns such as privacy rights, e-security, and e-commerce.

"All Rise (and Power On)," by Sherri Day, illustrates how technology has reinvented the courtroom and the legal and judicial system. According to author Day, PowerPoint presentations and videoconferencing have helped to improve and speed up courtroom proceedings.

In "The Price of Progress?" author Tod Newcombe explores the improvements in technology in government but also notes that these improvements come with increased problems for employee health. Solutions include ergonomic design of equipment and voice recognition software systems.

"Doing the Right Thing," by Abhijeet Chavan and Chris Steins, reviews the concept of Web accessibility as not just a legal requirement under the Americans With Disabilities Act (ADA) but as a smart strategy for everyone to follow. The authors provide tips on how to make your Web site accessible for persons with disabilities.

"Wi-Fi Anxiety," by Christopher Swope, discusses problems with computer security. Improving computer security is not an easy task, especially when we are talking about wireless computer security. This article provides information and tips on how to keep intruders outside of your system.

"Smart" Government *On*line, Not *In*line

How will the digital divide affect less-advantaged areas and what are the implications on democracy, equity, gender, and freedom in terms of e-haves and e-have nots? Opportunities, challenges, and concerns.

BREENA E. COATES

Silicon Valley provides an example of one of the largest e-community projects in the nation. Known as "Smart Valley," it was implemented in 1993. It served 30 cities and towns and 1,200,000 people. It has created a series of programs in all sectors of the valley community. For example, "Smart Schools" has connected 10,000 classrooms to the Internet. "Smart Voter," a project led by the League of Women Voters, provides personalized ballots and information on candidates and initiatives. "Smart Permitting" assists cities to put building and other permits on the Web. Smart Valley's board of directors is a mixture of public and private-sector executives and professionals. This developing resource represents the best of Web-level bureaucracy and its hopes and dreams for promoting better government.

Introduction

The toolbox of bureaucracy has been expanded considerably in the Information Age. What implications do these new revolutionary tools have for government and its people? For one thing, the new tools are designed to provide better, cheaper, faster, and more responsive service, thereby diffusing the long-held beliefs that government is inefficient, expensive, slow, and unresponsive to social needs. Whether this hope is, in fact, a reality, or likely to become one soon, is a subject that is addressed below.

The use of electronic tools grew rapidly during the last decade of the 20th century. More people were connected to the World Wide Web and in turn government, the facilitator of technology, has begun to be the provider as well as user of e-services. By the year 2001, all states had installed e-bureaucracy—some in more limited forms than others. The following types of services appear to be the most frequently used e-government services:

- filing personal income tax returns;
- reserving campsites in a state park;
- applying for a state fishing or hunting license;
- renewing a professional license;
- submitting employment information;
- registering a complaint against a business or professional licensee;
- renewing a driver's license; and
- requesting a government loan.

In the drive toward total quality management, governments today report that they set up internal e-systems in order to provide the following benefits and services:

- streamlining bureaucratic operations;
- reduction in public-service costs;
- providing 24-hour a day service, 7-days a week;
- lessening the number of in-person bureaucratic contacts;
- delivery of bureaucratic services from any place to any place;
- providing bureaucratic control systems;
- delivery of informational transparency and de-territorialization of bureaucracy;
- flexibility of hierarchies within bureaucracies;
- effecting vertical as well as horizontal communication;
- facilitating inter-organizational cooperation; and
- providing the capacity for virtual simulations for aiding bureaucratic policy making.

Constraints of Traditional Bureaucracy

These e-services, although piecemeal in many cases, have attempted to refine the original Weberian form of rational-legal bureaucracy that has been the target of much criticism over the years. The criticisms of Weber's ideal type of bureaucracy, while harsh, are not always inappropriate. Nowhere in his ideal-type is mention made specifically of the need to produce ends that best serve the citizen-customers of government. Rather, its emphasis on rules and order focuses on how things must be done, rather than for whom these things should be done. It is this strategic value concept on "how" rather than "for whom" that has been the driver for bureaucrats and bureaucracies around the world.

> A new type of bureaucrat is showing up in government—the Web-level bureaucrat.

A number of arguments are used to illustrate this point: First, Weberian rule-based logic favors standardization over uniqueness of individual claims. For instance, even if unique treatment is reasonable and required in the circumstances at hand, bureaucracies will not likely permit it. Second, bureaucracy is constraining to its citizen-clientele and its personnel. Third, it is slow in response. Fourth, its rule-based logic is often cost-ineffective and wasteful. It is these and other flaws that a Web-based bureaucracy hopes to overcome. (For more on Weberian thoughts see Max Weber: Essays in Sociology. 1949 [translation]. Edited by H. H. Garth and C. W. Mills. Oxford University Press: U.K.)

Web-Level Bureaucracy

All of these flaws taken together create a general perception of lack of quality in bureaucratic outcomes. Web-level bureaucracy, by contrast, generates opportunities to overcome the challenges to Weberian forms, and even to exceed expectations of the role of US bureaucracies. The use of information technology (IT) on its own does not add any particular value to bureaucracy. In order for IT to function correctly, it must be part of an information system that includes e-bureaucrats who can implement and evaluate policy. It is they, not the technocrats, who must determine how useful the technology is to furthering given policy ends.

By adding this important additional dimension to Weberian bureaucracy, IT has both complicated and changed the nature of bureaucracy in several important domains. These include liberty and equality concerns and the elimination of slow deliberation. E-bureaucracy's very quickness that encourages instant responses (which are seen as a plus along with quality, innovation, etc.) can also be seen as a minus, for it discourages the very thing that the Founding Fathers wanted—slow and careful deliberation of policy issues and thoughtful exercise of democratic choice. Thus, despite the many opportunities that IT can provide to bureaucracies, there are also several threats becoming apparent as we live through the age of the new e-bureaucracy.

Public Policy Concerns

Privacy Rights

The policy implications of e-government, particularly the use of the Internet, have preoccupied policy makers in Washington in several significant ways in the last decade. Among these is the issue of the protection of civil liberties, such as privacy rights versus the public right to information. Government information that has been inaccessible in the past is becoming more and more available—internal memoranda, records, executive meeting sessions, and other electronic files that may contain sensitive, confidential, or potentially damaging information.

Another privacy issue involves the concern that network-based technologies can facilitate connections of multiple files in ways that could breach confidentiality. Thus, a street-level bureaucrat, e.g., a traffic cop, while giving a ticket, can, perhaps, also have the capability to inform the violator that he owes child-support, or has a delinquent property-tax payment on his record.

E-security and E-crime

E-security is a new area that public administration must consider. A constant concern is that e-security being a young, and as yet developing field (with dependability issues to sort out), that such data will fall into the wrong hands. Loss of protection of informational property rights such as copyrights to protect intellectual property and software copyrights are included in this category. Also, e-crime is becoming an increasing concern of lawmakers. The most familiar type of e-crime to most Americans is the problems of computer virus/worm attacks. Hackers, "crackers," other terrorists, and e-anarchists have victimized both the private sector and government. Such computer crimes involve sophisticated techniques. They are hard to trace, and of increasing concern to the e-bureaucracy because of their potential to inconvenience thousands of people simultaneously for indefinite periods of time.

Globalization of Local E-bureaucracy

Another policy issue has been posed by local government. Some communities have expressed fears of globalization of local e-bureaucracy. This involves the potential threat of outsourcing services—e.g., personnel management and financial services—to cheaper venues, outside the United States (such as in Asia).

Taxing E-commerce

Yet another issue arises regarding taxing of e-commerce. US governors have moved to tax the Internet, and a bill in the US House of Representatives has been passed to stop this movement.

Technology Without Policy

Other policy issues ensue from government bureaucracies across the United States that rush to use the new technology without first considering its long-term effects. An example of technology without policy comes from Fulton County, Georgia, where a popular Web-to-database searching method gave the public free access to land records. After a few months the private company that was supplying the service to the county decided to charge a fee. This meant that two systems were in place: a free over-the-counter service for citizens who came in to the county office and a fee-based system over the Web. The county commission voted to instruct the webmaster to discontinue the service because of this discrepancy. Because Fulton County had no policy in place for regulating fees for public information, the county had to withdraw a service that had become popular.

Web-Level Bureaucrats: The New Bureaucratic Elite

A new type of bureaucrat is showing up in government—the Web-level bureaucrat. This individual is the technocrat who has garnered a high degree of "expert" power. Much hope and expectation is being placed on this new Web-level bureaucrat and his/her emancipatory value in moving public organizations into the 21st century. However, today there is skepticism and even pessimism among many about the so-called emancipatory aspects of technology. Georgia's Director of the Technology Authority, Larry Singer, maintains that technology should be viewed merely as a tool to solve public problems. He notes that "technology projects should not be thought of as technology projects at all, they are business improvement projects, that happen to require an advanced set of tools to achieve business objectives." Computer professionals are thus helpful to the degree that they are able to translate their technical knowledge to help solve the "real" world problems encountered in bureaucracies.

One of the reasons that informational technology initiatives have failed in states is due to lack of "ownership" of the process by the very people—the program staffers—whose program is being automated. It is imperative that the staffers set the priorities and specifications and not the technologists, so as to ensure the end result will be improved services to the citizens. The Los Angeles County Sheriff's Department has used technology to support its criminal-justice mission. One way to ensure this, observed Chief Lee Davenport (head of the sheriff's technology division), is that the same officers who rely on the technology administer and develop its operation. Information critical to protect themselves and the public in tense, often violent situations is provided by the department's wide area network system that supports 15 criminal justice information applications linking 2,000 law enforcement computers together in SDN—the Sheriff's Data Network. This data network provides information and analyses of crime, geographic crime patterns, and other criminal justice information so that beat officers can safely enforce laws.

Bureaucracy, associated with stability, slowness, and limited outputs, has taken on an antithesis—flexibility.

Democracy and E-government

Electronic aids have been touted as having emancipatory potential for democracy. It has been suggested that e-technology will change the nature of American political activity by infusing into our nation a more efficient outreach system. Yet the old question of 1789 comes back to haunt us in the 21st century—is faster government truly better government in terms of our democratic values? The answer is that there is a clear "digital divide" in the 21st century. This divide leaves out many citizens who have no means to participate in the electronic revolution. Thus there is a growing concern as to whether citizens are able to participate and benefit equally from the benefits of the digital society.

The lack of access to information among segments of the American population needs to be addressed more strongly, if government is to become increasingly reliant on informational technology. The inability to purchase computers and software has created a new underclass in American society. Federal studies have indicated that "e-haves" and "e-have-nots" are class and race-based in nature.

Feminists often raise the issue about the role of women in e-business. We are recognizing that emergent social structures of the 21st century are increasingly organized around informational technology. Networks "constitute the new social morphology of our societies and the presence or absence of networks among groups determine power and domination in social settings." A large body of scholarly work specifically addressed toward gender issues and technology has emerged since the 1990s from all across the western world. While computers at first may seem to be gender-neutral devices, gender, class, race, and other issues show that these factors can influence and shape expectations of the new computer technology.

Studies of modern technocratic workplaces reveal that males fill 95 percent of technical jobs. While the disporportionality is less marked in the 21st century, there is a technology divide between genders in terms of experts and non-experts. Clerical jobs that have traditionally been filled by female workers are more likely to be replaced by technology in routine jobs. They constitute a more flexible group that can be dismissed via restructuring as needed. This thwarts affirmative action and equal employment opportunity for women that 20th century social laws have tried to eliminate.

Summary

Bureaucracy, which has been associated with stability, slowness, and limited outputs, has taken on its antithesis—flexibility, speed, and expansion of outputs in the electronic age. It is beginning to synthesize these two extremes surprisingly well so far. While criticisms still remain about issues like democracy and access, focus on them will likely help to accommodate these vital values in the 21st century.

The electronic toolbox of bureaucracies will more than likely continue to fill up, as governments make ever more ambitious plans to provide added value to American citizens. In concluding, this hopeful view of the future is provided by the state of Washington:

> Diane Doe has just moved to Washington. As soon as the movers unpack her personal computer, she logs on to the Access Washington Web site and chooses from a menu of common life events. She clicks on "Moving to Washington," which gives her a list of the chores one commonly has to do to settle into a new community and state. By clicking on those items that fit her situation, she can request new plates for her car, register to vote, enroll her son in the local school, send a change of address form to her old post office, and order a tag for Fi Doe, the dog. Because Washington has linked its databases and designed its application to have a common look and feel, Diane has to enter her personal information only once, and is able to choose her payment method from a number of options, all within a secure environment. She has just completed online in a few minutes what would have taken her days to accomplish standing in line. And because digital government is available to citizens around the clock, Diane is able to accomplish all of this in one evening, with no interruptions to her workday or time with her son. (See Washington State Web site.)

REFERENCES

Washington State Web Site (*www.wa.gov/dis/e-gov/plan/summary.html*).

California Legislative Analyst Report, "E-Government in California: Providing Services to Citizens Through the Internet," January 24, 2001.

Frissen, P. H., *Politics, Governance and Technology: A Post-modern Narrative on the Virtual State,* 1999, translated C. Emery, Cheltenham Publishers, UK.

O'Looney, J., "Local Government Online: Putting the Internet to Work," 2000, Management Association Publication, Washington, DC.

Digital readiness survey conducted by: The Center for Digital Government, the Progress and Freedom Foundation, and Government Technology Magazine (*http: www.centerdigitalgov.com/center/Final-Rank.doc*).

Breena E. Coates *teaches at the School of Public Administration and Urban Studies. San Diego State University.*

From *The Public Manager*, Vol. 30, No. 4, Winter 2001-02, pp. 37-40.

All Rise (and Power On)

Technology Comes to Courtrooms, Streamlining the Proceedings

By SHERRI DAY

As Judge Lewis A. Kaplan took his seat in Courtroom 12D in United States District Court in Manhattan, the plaintiff's lawyer sheepishly raised a question. He needed help connecting a laptop that contained a PowerPoint presentation that a witness would use during questioning. A court clerk sprang into action, and minutes later the cover page of the witness's presentation appeared on the courtroom's monitors.

As a result of an initiative by federal and state judges, Judge Kaplan's courtroom is one of many across the country where computer technology is becoming as much a fixture as the American flag.

When lawyers present and summarize a case, they need to do it "in a way that people now expect to see information presented to them," said James E. McMillan, a management consultant in technology services at the National Center for State Courts, a nonprofit organization in Williamsburg, Va. "We are a TV generation now."

These days, opening and closing arguments are often augmented with PowerPoint presentations and video clips from depositions that jurors can view on monitors in the jury box. Through audio conferencing, foreign language translators in remote locations can take part in courtroom proceedings.

In some cases, the courtroom itself is becoming outdated. More courtroom proceedings occur through videoconferences in which a camera transmits a judge's image to lawyers in offices elsewhere.

At a recent trial in Chattanooga, Tenn., in which Tyson Foods was acquitted of charges of smuggling immigrants, lawyers for the company and the federal government wore tiny wireless microphones on their lapels that amplified their voices. In Judge Kaplan's federal courtroom in Manhattan, lawyers who approach the judge's bench for a sidebar conversation are unlikely to be overheard by jurors because the judge can activate sound-neutralizing white noise in the jury box from a touch-screen panel that controls the court's audio and visual equipment.

LABORATORY With immersive virtual reality, the scene of a crime can be reconstructed with computer graphics and re-experienced by a witness who dons a headset and goggles. Students used the technology in a mock trial at the law school of the College of William and Mary.

The amount of evidence presented in court has increased strikingly in the last 40 years, Judge Kaplan said, and improved technology makes it easier for jurors to sift through the information.

"The benefit is that it makes the trial go a lot faster and thus enables us to do more in the same amount of time, and it is much clearer to the jury to be able to get information this way," Judge Kaplan said. "When it's well used, the juries love it."

Judge Kaplan is a member of a committee of the Judicial Conference of the United States that makes recommendations about improving technology in the federal courts. According to the Courtroom 21 Project, an experimental and demonstration site for students at the College of William and Mary law school in Virginia that is a testing ground for such technology, one-quarter of the courts in the nation's 94 federal districts have at least one high-tech courtroom. Such a courtroom is defined as one with advanced electronic presentation systems; real-time court reporting, in which court reporters' notes are available as they type; digital audio recording; and Internet access that allows the judge to research legal and administrative materials from the bench.

In Judge Kaplan's courtroom, which was outfitted last year, the jury box has nine flat-screen computer monitors that are shared by the jurors. Flat-screen monitors also sit on the desks of lawyers, the judge, the court clerk and the witness stand. The 15-inch monitors display evidence from the lawyers' laptops and serve as television screens when VHS tapes or digital clips are played. Judge Kaplan posts his instructions to the jury on the monitors rather than reading them out loud. (He still reads the jury its charge, however.)

Minutes before a hearing began in Judge Kaplan's courtroom last week, the court clerk, Andrew Mohan, offered to show lawyers how to operate the courtroom equipment. Eight lawyers surrounded a presentation machine, an electronic imaging device that functions as a projector but also has a video camera on top that allows exhibits like weapons to be shown on monitors in the courtroom.

"Just put your object there on the screen underneath the camera," said Mr. Mohan, placing a ring of keys on the screen to demonstrate. The keys instantly appeared on four monitors on the lawyers' tables and on a 42-inch plasma screen.

The lawyers need only master two buttons, one for zooming in on an object and another that shows it at a distance, Mr. Mohan said. With the presentation machine, lawyers no longer have to walk around the courtroom to display evidence.

Highlighting capabilities on the flat-screen monitors at the lawyers' lectern and in the witness box allow information to be entered into evidence quickly. Lawyers and witnesses can use their fingers to underline or circle text or images. The highlighted document appears immediately on the monitors throughout the courtroom and is entered into evidence after it emerges from a small printer beneath the lawyers' lectern. Ballpoint pens and markers are no longer needed.

"I'm a big believer in technology in the courtroom," said Kathleen M. McKenna, a partner with the New York law firm of Proskauer Rose who recently tried a case in Judge Kaplan's courtroom. "I think jurors expect it. They're used to talking heads with things moving behind them. They're used to seeing bulleted points even when they see magazine news shows."

Ms. McKenna added, "Lawyers who don't come prepared to use the technology do their clients a disservice and, in the eyes of the jurors, appear less prepared and less sophisticated."

Courtrooms will probably never have the latest equipment because technology is always evolving and is too expensive for the government to try to keep up, said Judge James Robertson, a federal judge in Washington who heads the Judicial Conference's information technology committee. "It doesn't sound like space-age stuff, but I tell jurors that what they see—for the judiciary—is state of the art," he said. "For the rest of the world, it's pretty ordinary."

PowerPoint charts and video clips augment lawyers' presentations.

Federal and state judges are keeping a close watch on developments at Courtroom 21, the experimental court at William and Mary, which is said to be the most technologically developed courtroom in the country. Founded in 1993 as a joint project with the National Center for State Courts, the courtroom is a harbinger of technology that could one day show up in courts across the nation.

This spring, students at the school tried a case involving questions of law in the United States, England and Australia. Judges in each of the three countries presided through videoconferencing. Students also recently conducted a trial using immersive virtual reality, reconstructing the scene of a crime with computer graphics. Wearing headsets and goggles, witnesses were able to view the scene as if they were there. Those in court were able to see the scene though the witness's eyes, said Frederic I. Lederer, a law professor at William and Mary who developed Courtroom 21.

Professor Lederer foresees a substantial increase in remote appearances by trial judges, lawyers and witnesses. More evidence will also be presented electronically, he said, and entire court cases and exhibits will be filed over the Internet. Court reporters' notes could also be made available instantly on the Internet.

Legal experts say the use of electronic equipment raises new questions, like whether testimony from a witness who is not present to be sworn in is admissible. Moreover, they say, the posting of evidence on the Internet could compromise a judge's control over what information leaves the courtroom.

"Technology is only a means to an end; it is not an end in itself," Professor Lederer said. "The goal is justice at all times, not technology."

THE Pri¢e OF Progre$$?

As technology continues to proliferate in government, so do problems with worker health.

BY TOD NEWCOMBE

An operator working in the Rochester, N.Y., Office of Emergency Communications had such acute pain in her fingers, she was forced to leave her job. And she wasn't alone; at one point, more than one-third of Rochester 911's work force was diagnosed with musculo-skeletal disorders that included numbness in the hands, wrists and elbows.

The culprit is ergonomics, or lack thereof. Staff members handling emergency calls in the office were using new technology without ergonomically designed furniture or equipment. The situation was resolved when the workers' union and city management collaborated to design an entirely new facility that accommodated workers' physical needs, including workstations with adjustable keyboards and screens.

Not every computer-related health problem becomes so extreme, nor do all situations require a top-to-bottom overhaul of everything from workstations to lighting. But illness and injury from computers is an all-too-real problem that's costing workers their health, while government loses productivity and tax dollars.

"Poor ergonomics is a significant issue in the workplace," said Hank Austin, senior vice president for ErgoTeam, a consulting firm specializing in ergonomics. "People working with computers can develop a wide range of problems that affect every part of the body."

It's not just happening in high-stress work situations, but in any government agency with computers. For example, nearly 96 percent of public employees who are members of the American Federation of Teachers (AFT) use computers or technology equipment at work. Of those, 26 percent have developed health problems using computer-related equipment.

The Bureau of Labor Statistics (BLS) reported that more than 600,000 workers suffered serious workplace injuries caused by ergonomic hazards in 1999, the most recent year for statistics. The National Academy of Sciences puts the injuries from repetitive stress at 1 million annually.

Neither government agency breaks down the number of injuries due directly to computer use, but in 1999 the BLS reported about 28,000 cases of carpal tunnel syndrome, which is often related to computers. The debilitating condition, which can occur over years, is also one of the most costly. Because so many people with carpal tunnel receive surgery, it is the leading cause of lost workdays, and the average cost is more than $13,000 per case. But ergonomic experts say the true cost is triple that amount.

Workplace Design

Austin has nearly 20 years of experience in the field of ergonomics and worker safety. To spot ergonomic troubles in any office, he suggests taking a look at the workers. "See how many are rubbing their wrists, how many have small pillows behind their backs while they sit. That will begin to give you an idea of the ergonomic conditions," he said.

Wrists and backs aren't all that hurt when workers use computers—vision blurs, and hips, thighs and even ankles throb with pain. Less obvious problems with poor computer ergonomics include what Austin calls "psycho-social issues," which arise when workers are in constant discomfort or pain. The psy-

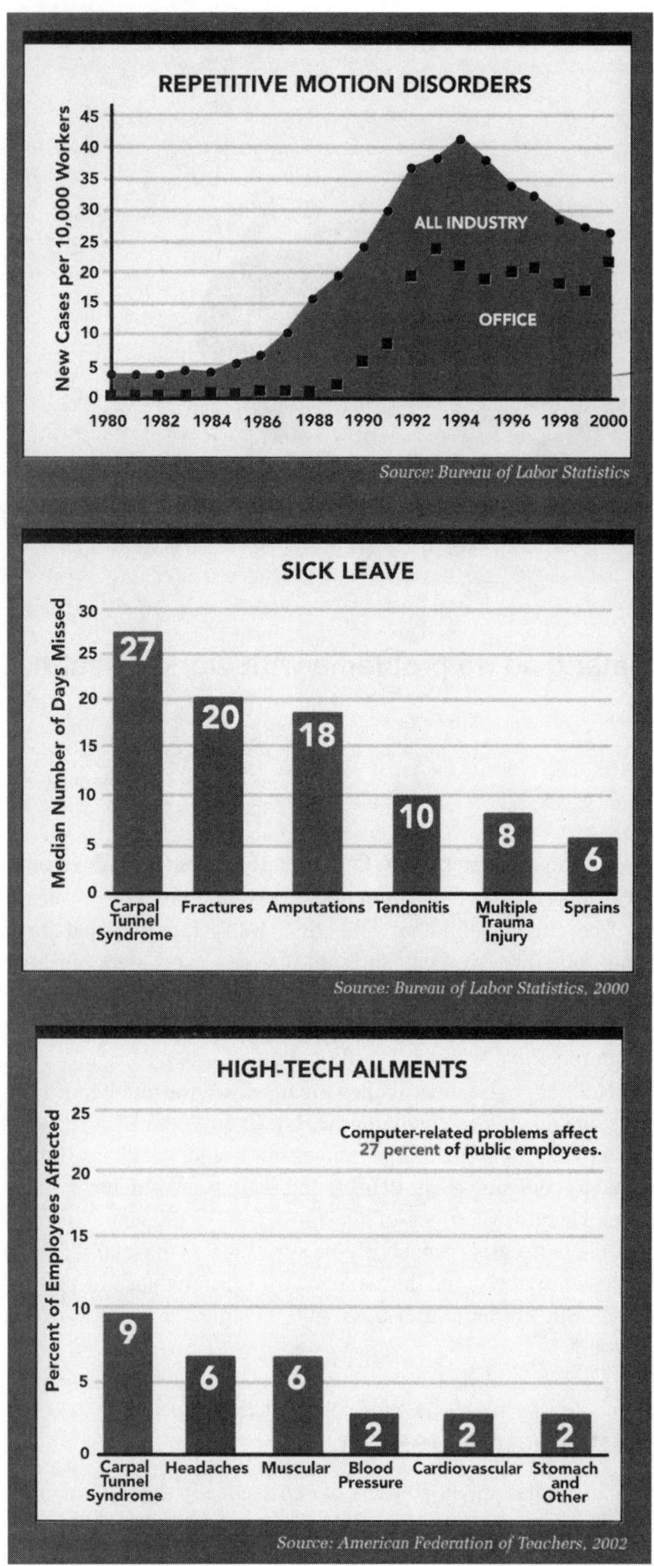

Source: Bureau of Labor Statistics

Source: Bureau of Labor Statistics, 2000

Source: American Federation of Teachers, 2002

chological effect of poor ergonomics can be especially acute for workers in customer service, or those who feel they have little control over their situation.

"The impact can start with lost workdays as workers stay home to recuperate mentally and physically," Austin said. The problems can grow into morale issues and eventually lead to valued employees quitting their jobs. Unfortunately, managers are often the last to realize what's going on because workers are reluctant to complain about a sore wrist or fatigue from using a computer. Meanwhile, public-sector employees report more stress and stress-related illnesses today than they did 25 years ago, according to the AFT.

Most people think poorly designed keyboards or computer monitors that are too high, too low or too close to the workers are causes. Nonadjustable chairs and desks also are reasons workers suffer while using computers. Other factors that contribute include poor lighting and ventilation.

Another significant concern centers on bad software design. For example, Austin cites mainframe database programs that require workers to use "F" keys to execute commands. Software that forces users to move their fingers all over the keyboard can be just as damaging physically as a nonadjustable chair. Poorly designed Web-based software programs, which may call for extensive use of both the keyboard and the mouse, can also lead to repetitive stress injuries.

Growing Concern

With the proliferation of IT throughout government, public-sector workers have grown concerned about health risks from overuse of computers. In response, some organizations are taking a variety of measures to combat the problem. First, they are evaluating working situations individually and in groups to resolve immediate ergonomic issues. These steps include teaching workers better ways to sit and use their computers, and providing more worker-friendly equipment, such as adjustable chairs and monitors.

Second, organizations are hiring ergonomic experts to evaluate office workflow processes and alleviate a wide range of potential health risks. Austin calls this approach industrial engineering. "We try to remove any unnecessary steps in the workflow and look at the best way for them to perform their job ergonomically."

Other solutions include the use of technology tools. Voice recognition software, which is mentioned repeatedly, converts human speech into text that can be edited and stored on the computer. While the software reduces the need for a keyboard, its accuracy can vary depending on how it's used.

Other software tools attempt to prevent injuries before they occur. For example, Magnitude Information Systems produces ergonomic management software that uses an algorithm to measure and monitor workers' computer use, and alerts them when it's time to take a rest, especially after they engaged in repetitive motions that may lead to injury. Mark Fuller, Magnitude's senior vice president, said the software is designed to address the repetitive stress issue before it becomes a problem and causes injuries. "The software gives the worker microbreaks after so many keystrokes," he explained.

The firm recently announced the sale of an enterprise license to Lockheed Martin, which has 140,000 workers. Other customers include Exxon.... Mobil Corp. and an agency within the Department of Defense.

These approaches—especially re-engineering workflow—don't come cheap, and introducing new techniques for getting the job done can take time and temporarily reduce productivity as workers learn new ways of doing familiar tasks. During the dot-com boom, when good workers were hard to find, many firms spent the extra dollar to make employees more comfortable. But in today's sluggish economy, with unemployment rising, more workers are willing to labor under stressful conditions. It also leaves organizations with less money to spend on what they deem as low-priority needs, such as ergonomics.

Different Standards

Rather than wait for government agencies to introduce ergonomic solutions, public-sector workers, through their unions, are trying to fix things on the legal and regulatory front. The American Federation of State, County and Municipal Employees (AFSCME), and the American Federation of Government Employees—which represents workers in the federal sector—have been lobbying for years to get new ergonomic standards passed by the Occupational Safety and Health Administration (OSHA).

Since 1990, the U.S. Labor Department has been considering rules on ergonomics. The issue got a boost in 1998 when the National Academy of Sciences linked workplace injuries to awkward and repetitive motions, and estimated that businesses lose $50 billion a year from sick leave, decreased productivity and medical costs from repetitive motion injuries, such as carpal tunnel syndrome.

In 2000, the Clinton administration issued rules that would have covered more than 100 million workers and required employers to redesign jobs that involved a variety of repetitive motions, including typing. The same year, Washington became the first state to adopt its own ergonomic rules, which take effect July 1, 2004. In Washington state, 50,000 employees suffer from work-related musculo-skeletal injuries, costing the state more than $411 million a year in medical and worker's compensation claims, according to the Department of Labor and Industries.

But Congress repealed Clinton's national ergonomic standards in March 2001, and the Bush administration promised to set a new policy for workplace safety based on stepped-up enforcement, training, research and voluntary guidelines. But unions, including AFSCME, called the new measures, "too little, too late" and "a sham." Their chief concern is that the guidelines rely too much on voluntary efforts and not enough on government oversight.

Jim August, AFSCME's assistant director of research and collective bargaining, said workers in 27 states aren't covered by federal OSHA laws, though several have their own laws that apply to worker health and safety. August called the newly issued ergonomic standards in Washington state a "model" AFSCME would like to see other states follow. "What we want to see is one standard emerge, not 50 different ones," he said.

But that fragmentation may be what's happening. When the White House repealed OSHA's regulations, many states withdrew state-level regulatory proposals that were based on the federal standards set in 2000. Now, according to Ergoweb Inc., a news service for the ergonomics industry, at least two states—Alaska and Minnesota—are contemplating new laws of their own. Washington, and to a lesser degree California, also have established standards.

People like August are pushing for a national, proactive approach to ergonomic standards. "If you compare the costs of doing nothing with the cost of buying better equipment and for training, the benefits will always outweigh the expense," he said, stressing that state and local governments should push ahead despite the fiscal crisis in the public sector.

Others agree. An ounce of prevention is worth a pound of cure, according to Austin. "Preventive maintenance on workers is the same as preventive maintenance on equipment," he said. "Why have a maintenance program for machines and not one for humans?"

Doing the Right Thing

How to build socially responsible web infrastructure.

What is web accessibility and why is it so important?

By Abhijeet Chavan and Chris Steins

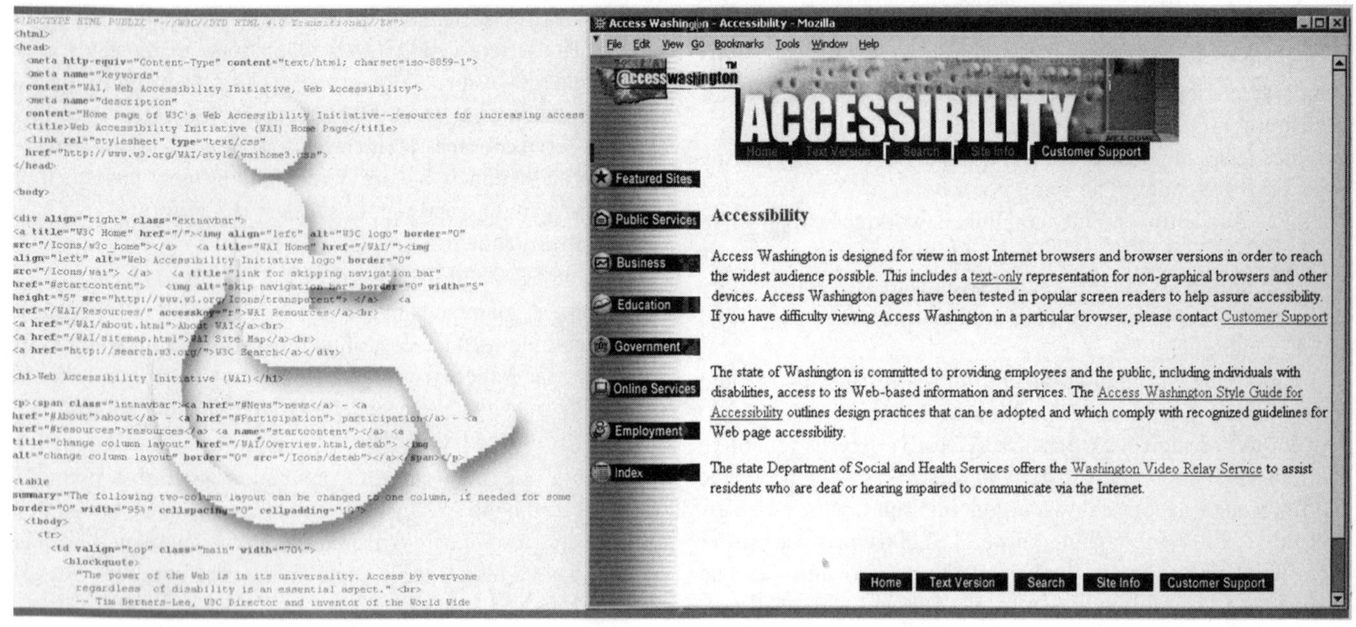

Access Washington - Accessibility - Mozilla
File Edit View Go Bookmarks Tools Window Help
access washington
ACCESSIBILITY
Home Text Version Search Site Info Customer Support
Featured Sites
Public Services
Business
Education
Government
Online Services
Employment
Index
Accessibility
Access Washington is designed for view in most Internet browsers and browser versions in order to reach the widest audience possible. This includes a text-only representation for non-graphical browsers and other devices. Access Washington pages have been tested in popular screen readers to help assure accessibility. If you have difficulty viewing Access Washington in a particular browser, please contact Customer Support
The state of Washington is committed to providing employees and the public, including individuals with disabilities, access to its Web-based information and services. The Access Washington Style Guide for Accessibility outlines design practices that can be adopted and which comply with recognized guidelines for Web page accessibility.
The state Department of Social and Health Services offers the Washington Video Relay Service to assist residents who are deaf or hearing impaired to communicate via the Internet.
Home Text Version Search Site Info Customer Support

Access Washington (access.wa.gov)

Adding an accessibility statement is an easy step but benefits all users.

For starters, it's the law. If your organization receives federal funding or has a federal contract for technology products and services, your website must be accessible to individuals with disabilities. That has been true since 2001, when Section 508 of the Rehabilitation Act of 1998 went into effect.

The law specifies that "members of the public with disabilities have access to and use of information and data, comparable to that of the... members of the public without disabilities."

Numerous people have disabilities—about one-fifth of the U.S. population, in fact. Individuals with visual, hearing, mobility, and cognitive impairments may not be able to visit inaccessible websites. And the growing population of senior citizens who are using the Internet also has special needs and re- web accessibility.

cessibility is not a new concept. Assistive technolo- ng persons with disabilities to access the web, have been available for some time. However, even as an increasing number of people are beginning to rely on the Internet for information, news, email, shopping, and entertainment, accessibility to the web is often neglected in the fast-moving world of web development. Just as the Americans with Disabilities Act of 1990 sets guidelines for accessibility in public places, Section 508 ensures that the benefits of the Internet are universally available by making web accessibility a requirement for federal or federally funded websites.

Section 508 has heightened public awareness of web accessibility. Arkansas, Connecticut, Kentucky, Missouri, North Carolina, North Dakota, Pennsylvania, Texas, and West Virginia are among the states with laws or policies in place for web accessibility. Even organizations not subject to federal website requirements, such as nonprofit organizations, educational institutions, and private businesses, are adopting Section 508 as a web accessibility standard.

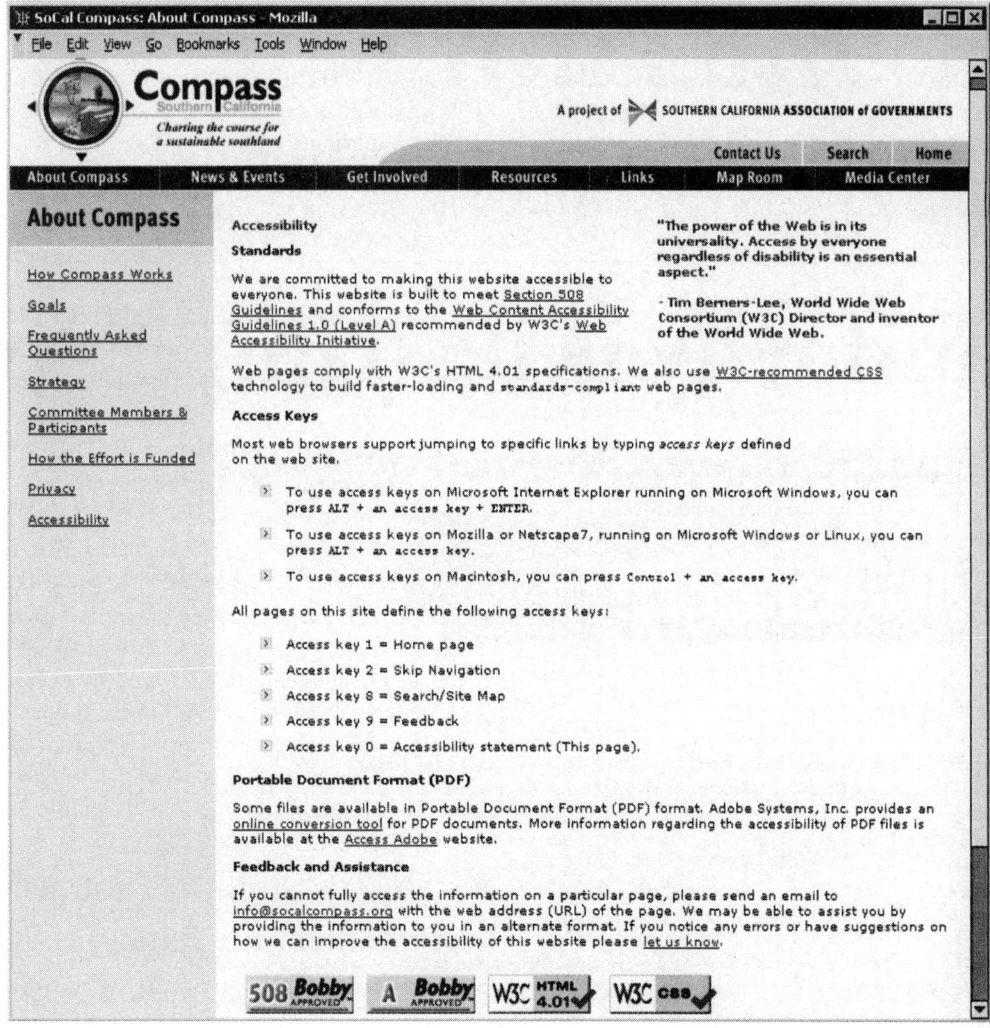

Southern California Compass (socalcompass.org)

One aid is to list and define access keys for most often used pages on a particular web site. This assists with navigation around the site.

The benefits

As the exciting possibilities of e-government slowly become reality, more citizens will depend on the web to access information, conduct transactions, and interact with their governments. Planners are building and using web infrastructure in the form of web applications, web-based mapping systems, and discussion boards to engage citizens in the planning process.

The Boston Indicators Project uses the web to measure the effectiveness of planning policies and makes this information available to citizens. The Neighborhood Knowledge California website enables citizens to access complex geographic data and spatial analysis using just a web browser. Both projects recognize that stakeholders should have equal access to planning information and processes made available via the web.

Just as a building's wheelchair-accessible ramp is useful to a parent with a baby stroller, accessibility enhancements, by improving a website's usability, provide benefits to all web users regardless of disability. Take the example of audio and video clips. Text alternatives for multimedia content are required by Section 508 guidelines. This makes the content available to search engines and data-mining software, thus improving a website's visibility on search engine listings. These text alternatives also make websites easier to read using a slower Internet connection and reduce a web server's load and bandwidth requirements.

Individuals using older computers or newer evolving technologies can also benefit from accessible websites. Text alternatives for multimedia content can be viewed using an old computer that cannot play sound files. Hand-held devices can pull in graphics-free, text-only versions of web pages over wireless connections.

Accessibility recommendations providing for clear navigation and direct, concise content are likely to benefit users for whom English is a second language or those with low literacy levels. By providing equal opportunities to all, accessible websites may also reduce legal liability. Raising awareness of the requirements of people with disabilities can reinforce your organization's socially responsible attitude and help create a workplace that is more welcoming to people with disabilities.

Is My Website Accessible? 6 Quick Tests

- Try browsing your website using only your computer's keyboard. Is it easy to navigate? Can you access all sections of your website?
- Turn off Javascript in your web browser and then visit your website. Can you still access all sections of your website?
- Does your website meet the Section 508 guidelines? Check your website's main page in WatchFire's online Bobby tool: www.cast.org/bobby.
- Does your website use valid HTML? Check your website using W3C's HTML online validator: validator.w3.org.
- Is your website readable to a person with color-blindness? Find out using VisCheck's online tool: www.vischeck.com/vischeck.
- How does your website look in a text browser? Find out Using LynxViewer: www.delorie.com/web/lynxview.html.

Strategies and solutions

Once a website has been built, it can be expensive to retrofit later. That is why it is important to make accessibility a requirement at the beginning of a new project. Clear policies and goals will make it easier to identify and implement accessibility features. Furthermore, if your project receives federal funding, accessibility is likely to be a funding requirement as well.

A common misconception is that accessibility can only be addressed by adding a separate text-only version of your website. Not so! Such text-only versions often end up being limited or outdated and are therefore not recommended unless as a last resort. Another assumption is that addressing accessibility considerations results in websites that are ugly or limited in functionality. You do not have to compromise aesthetics or functionality for accessibility. Web accessibility is not about removing features but about adding enhancements.

When several authors contribute to a website, it can be difficult to maintain consistent accessibility standards. A simple but effective solution is to develop page templates that implement the website's accessibility requirements. Make these templates available to your website authors and web developers, so that the pages they create will better meet your standards.

The State of Washington set accessibility standards for all state departments and agencies by creating accessible page templates. Software maker Macromedia offers ready-to-use accessible page templates that can be used to build accessible websites. The Illinois Technology Office is working with state agencies to create specially designed templates based on the Illinois Web Accessibility Standards, to help state agencies' web staffs easily create accessible, customizable web pages.

Many planning web applications that use dynamically generated maps, charts, tables, and diagrams to represent spatial data managed within a geographic information system (GIS) face unique accessibility challenges. Data tables with large amounts of information take a long time to read, and that can reduce accessibility for users with visual impairments. Color-blindness can also hinder people from viewing maps.

The technology to make digital maps accessible to all users with visual impairments does not exist yet. However, the information displayed in elaborate GIS maps could be made more accessible by incorporating the same data as a data table in text format.

For complex data, many federal agencies are offering email and telephone support so users can contact someone to get the information they cannot access over the web. "It's the data you [illegible] not the map," says Doug Wakefield, an accessibility specialist with the independent federal Access Board. For example, to make its mapping database meet accessibility requirements the U.S. Environmental Protection Agency website is planning to offer a telephone support system.

Five tips for accessibility

People use the web in very different ways. A website should therefore present information so that it can be accessed regardless of the hardware or software being used. Do not assume that everyone uses the same kinds of devices in the same way.

Most web accessibility problems can be fixed rather simply. (To find out if your website is accessible see the accompanying sidebar.) Images embedded in web pages can be annotated with alternate text. When accessed through devices that do not display images such as a screen-reader, this alternate text can be used to describe the image. Adding alternate text to all images (where possible) makes it more accessible to all users.

> Web accessibility is not just a legal requirement for some; it is a smart strategy with benefits for everyone.

A good place to start is the list of Quick Tips provided by W3C's Web Accessibility Initiative. An earlier article we wrote for *Planning* magazine ("A Web For Everyone: Creating Accessible Planning Websites," July 2001), also covered basic web accessibility techniques. Watchfire's Bobby and other testing software applications can test your website and reveal accessibility issues. Here are some additional tips for building accessible websites:

- Write for the web. Text suitable for a book may not be appropriate for a website. Usability expert Dr. Jakob Nielson of Nielson Norman Group recommends that no more than half the text you would have used in a hard-copy publication should be used on the website. Avoid long continuous blocks of text and use shorter paragraphs and bulleted lists, which are easier to scan for web users in a hurry. Split long pages containing a lot of information into multiple, shorter pages, and avoid phrases like "click here " or "click on arrow icon."
- Improve navigation. Poorly designed Javascript-based pop-up or pull-down menus can present serious accessibility obstacles. Make sure it is possible to navigate your website using alternate browsers, with or without Javascript, or without using a mouse. If you are uncertain, add a redundant set of text-only navigation links on every page.

A "site map" listing the contents makes a website more accessible. Provide a convenient link to this site map from every page of your website. All users will benefit from a site map, not just those with disabilities. For example, the website of the American Planning Association features a site map containing text links that can be easily reached via a link in the footer of every page.

Consistent navigation on every web page is a good practice, but it can present some accessibility challenges. Users with visual impairments browsing the web using a screen-reader may have to hear the same header and navigation links over and over again on every page they visit. Users that cannot use a mouse due to mobility impairments may be using the tab key to tab through all the navigation links on a page.

To understand the challenges faced by a user who has a mobility impairment, try navigating your favorite web sites without using your mouse. Instead, use only the keys on your keyboard to operate your web browser. You will quickly see how frustrating navigating websites can be.

The solution to this problem is simple yet extremely effective. Provide a "skip navigation" link to skip over header and navigation links will help users with this. For example, the website of the U.S. Geological Survey has a "navigation" link in the header of every page that allows the user to skip navigation links altogether.

• Make forms accessible. Inaccessible forms are a common cause for websites failing to meet the Section 508 requirements. A web form that looks great online may be confusing to someone listening to it when using a screen reader. To correct this problem, use the "label" tag to associate form fields with their labels. Group the form fields so that they make sense when heard using a screen-browser. Some web forms may be difficult to navigate for someone who cannot use a mouse. Use "Tabindex" attributes to set the tab order of the form fields.

• Define access keys. Keyboard access is important for users who cannot use a pointing device, such as a mouse. Access keys are essentially keyboard shortcuts that give a user quick and easy access to different sections of the website. You can define access keys for important or popular pages of your website. Here is a suggested scheme:

Access key 1 = Home page
Access key 2 = Skip navigation
Access key 8 = Site map (or Search page)
Access key 9 = Feedback
Access key 0 = Accessibility statement

Site-wide access keys are easy to implement and benefit all users. The website of the Southern California Compass project assigns access keys to frequently accessed pages of the website. (Disclosure: Urban Insight, the firm for which we work, was hired to develop this website.)

• Add an accessibility statement. This is probably the easiest step to take. An "accessibility statement" is a web page that clearly outlines the accessibility measures implemented on the website. List the accessibility standards met by the website. If you have defined "access keys" for the website, you can list them on this page. If you use any additional technologies such as documents in Portable Document Format (PDF) or multimedia content, provide links to necessary tools, browser plugins or instructions.

Be honest about which sections of the website may not be accessible. Provide the user with information on how to obtain the inaccessible content in an alternate format. List a phone number or a contact person that users can reach in case they need assistance. Access Washington features a statement that lists the accessibility measures taken by the State of Washington.

In the two years since Section 508 regulations were first implemented, it has become easier to build accessible websites. Professional web development software includes accessibility features. Auditing tools make it possible to test a website for accessibility. But it is up to us to encourage and implement good practices.

Web accessibility is not just a legal requirement for some; it is a smart strategy with benefits for everyone.

Resources

On the Web. Introduction to Web Accessibility, http://www.webaim.org/. W3C's Web Accessibility Initiative website: www.w3c.org/wai. Federal IT Accessibility Initiative: www.section508.org. Boston Indicators Project: www:bostonindicators.org. Neighborhood Knowledge California: www.nkca.ucla.edu. American Planning Association: www.planning.org. U.S. Geological Survey: www.usgs.gov. Southern California Compass: www.socalcompass.org. Access Washington: access.wa.gov. Macromedia Accessibility: www.macromedia.com/accessibility.

Abhijeet Chavan is the Chief Technology Officer of Urban Insight and Managing Editor of PLANetizen. Chris Steins is the organization's Chief Executive Officer and PLANetizen's Editor. Urban Insight, a Los Angeles-based web development firm, offers web accessibility consulting.

Article 24

GUIDE TO WIRELESS SECURITY

Wi-Fi Anxiety

Lock up your laptops. Secure your airwaves. In the wide-open world of wireless, it isn't easy to keep out intruders.

BY CHRISTOPHER SWOPE

For Kanawha County, West Virginia, the hacker's attack last December was a wireless nightmare. From a car parked outside the county courthouse, a silent intruder used a laptop with a wireless modem to ride the radio waves straight into the county's computer network. With a couple of keystrokes, he had seized control of the e-mail account of Kent Carper, one of the county's three elected commissioners, and sent county staffers a series of false and potentially damaging messages. He asked staffers to cut a $75 million check. Then, in an act of sheer bravado, the hacker took his tools inside the courthouse lobby, sat down between two state troopers and zipped off more bogus messages.

Nobody noticed a thing.

Fortunately this hacker meant no real harm. In fact, Kanawha officials paid him for the service. They wanted to find out how vulnerable their computer network, which included some snazzy new wireless components, was to attack. The answer—very vulnerable—forced the county to shut down the wireless portions of its network. Wireless networking, it seemed, left all the data in the county's computers free for the taking. "Wireless security? I call it wireless insecurity," says the real Kent Carper, who ordered the hacking test done. "It's like [illegible] the doors to the county courthouse [illegible]nlocked at night."

SPRINGING LEAKS

Wireless networks and gadgets are sweeping state and local government, but so is panic about wireless security. To be sure, the threat of hackers invading government networks is nothing new. But the new technology gives hackers, or "whackers" as wireless hacks are sometimes called, lots of new options. They can try to pluck sensitive government information literally out of the air. They might steal an employee's laptop or personal digital assistant for a front-door entrance into a network. Or they can wiggle the knobs of a number of wireless back doors, as Kanawha County's friendly hacker did. "You have to be really careful deploying wireless," says Tony Rosati, vice president of marketing at Certicom, a vendor specializing in wireless security. "The whole motivation for going wireless is better connectivity, but it gives that connectivity to everyone, including hackers."

Wireless worries among state and local agencies are so severe that many are holding back until a new generation of products comes out with stronger security features. They are following the lead of the federal government, which seems squeamish about using wireless, especially where national security concerns are at stake. The Pentagon in September extended a moratorium on the use of wireless devices for holding or transmitting classified information, citing the "exploitable vulnerabilities" of wireless technology. That finding was echoed by a November report from the National Institute of Standards and Technology, which recommended government agencies take a cautious approach to wireless security. "The technology's underlying communications medium, the airwave, is open to intruders," the report said.

Still, a growing number of state and local agencies feel confident they can keep the whackers out. And in any case, they're finding that the benefits of going wireless are well worth the risk. Police departments are starting to beam digital mug shots and fingerprints over the radio waves to laptops in squad cars. Auditors and inspectors are using PDAs to file reports from the field. Utility workers are using networked laptops to view maps on the scene during water main breaks. In all these cases, wireless offers a big productivity advantage: It saves mobile workers the hassle of making trips between the office and the field.

Wireless isn't just for field staff, though. It's increasingly popular in the traditional office environments of state buildings, courthouses and city halls. Even simple off-the-shelf hardware gives workers the freedom to haul their laptops to a conference room, for example, without having to plug in for Internet access or network connectivity. It's more than convenience that makes wireless local area networks, or LANs, attractive.

Must Reading

National Institute of Standards and Technology's report on Wireless Network Security: http://csrc.nist.gov/publications/nistpubs (listed under 800 series)

Public Safety Wireless Network's Communications Security Awareness Guide: http://www.pswn.gov/admin/library-docs/securitybooklet.pdf

Wi-Fi business and technology information: http://www.80211-planet.com

Information about wireless local area networks: http://www.wlana.org

Wireless hardware can prove much cheaper than lacing miles of cable through walls and under floors. And in historic buildings such as statehouses, where drilling holes through marble walls might prove difficult (or even illegal), wireless is sometimes the best networking option available.

Yet it is exactly this sort of in-the-office wireless that has the worst security track record. While "Wi-Fi" technology, also known commonly as 802.11, is usually intended for users inside a building, it also broadcasts the wireless signal out onto the street. Anyone can sniff out the location of a wireless network using commonly available programs with such odd names as "Airsnort" and "Netstumbler." It is a familiar game among computer geeks to take a laptop in a car on so-called "wardriving" trips around a city to find where these networks are. This is how the Kanawha hacker broke into the county's system so easily from the parking lot.

Wi-Fi equipment generally comes with security features, but some users simply forget to turn them on. Even when on, however, the security built into the current generation of basic Wi-Fi devices is so weak that any amateur can crack it. Unless information technology managers proactively layer in additional security features, hackers can somewhat easily gain carte blanche access to anything on the network. Not only can they steal sensitive government information, plant viruses and corrupt databases, but they can also pirate the government's systems to launch attacks on somebody else's computer network. Such an attack would falsely appear to be the work of a government employee rather than the hacker. "By default, these things are highly insecure," says Steven Jones, director of technology in Blacksburg, Virginia, where city officials have been using a wireless LAN to do some employee training. "You really need to put some time and energy into researching how to secure them."

The good news is that not all wireless devices are riddled with so many security holes. And the ones that are can be made secure enough to keep all but the most sophisticated hackers out. It takes some effort, though. Wireless networks require meticulous planning and relentless follow-up on the latest threats to break-ins and the newest methods for beefing up security. It's also a good idea to enforce strict policies about the laptops and handheld computers floating around in employees' hands—whether they're government-issue or not. "It's a matter of deterrence," Jones says. "You want to make your network difficult enough to break into that an intruder will say, 'The heck with this; I'll try someone else.'"

LAN LAW

Some of the earliest Wi-Fi adopters in state and local government were legislatures. Not long after the Internet became popular, lawmakers demanded the ability to tote laptops around their capitol buildings and log on without a wire. But they don't like to discuss their security policies with outsiders, fearing that hackers might game any hints to their advantage. "The first element of our security policy is that we won't share, publish or make available the details of our security policy," says Michael Adams, director of legislative information services for the Colorado General Assembly.

In Florida, Sean Johnson, the IT director for the Florida House, agrees to speak with a reporter about security—and only at the most rudimentary level—only after verifying his identity. "We're really concerned about 'social engineering' attacks where hackers call us posing as someone they're not and ask a lot of questions," Johnson says.

One reason why wireless LANs are a security problem is that they're not very complicated to set up. The basic off-the-shelf technology is pretty cheap. Laptop users must install a special wireless modem, while handheld computers usually have these built in. The modems send signals back and forth to a box, called an "access point," that connects directly into the network. Access points have a range of about 300 feet and can both transmit and pick up radio signals through walls. Setting up a statehouse for wireless access requires scattering a half-dozen or more access points throughout the building.

Securing a wireless LAN, Johnson says, happens at a number of different levels. First there's authentication. Wireless laptop users have to enter an ID and password to log on, just as they would on a wired network. Next, the data being passed between the laptops and the network is encrypted, so that even if it is plucked out of thin air, it won't be easily readable. Finally, there's a security layer with the wireless computers themselves: Each machine has a unique identifying number. If a lawmaker loses a laptop or it is stolen, Johnson can lock the machine out from accessing the network.

There's more. Any hacker attempt to cut through these security layers would show up on an "intrusion detection system" that Johnson's staff uses. And on the off chance an intruder gets through, he won't find much: Data on the wireless network are kept separate from the legislature's internal network. "Even if a hacker is smart enough to get through all those layers of security, he's only into

Rap Sheet

A little guidance to the latest terminology in wireless security:

LAN: A set of computers located near each other, linked together on a network. Wireless LAN is a set of computers connected without the trouble of stringing cable between them.

Access point: A box connected to the network that receives radio signals from computers that are specially equipped with a network interface card.

802.11b: The industry standard for an increasingly popular type of wireless networking equipment. Also known as Wi-Fi.

Wardriving: A game tech-geeks play to sniff the airwaves for wireless networks in an area. Armed with a laptop and easily available programs like Airsnort or Netstumbler, hackers can detect wireless systems. Then they can try to break in.

WEP: The built-in security with the current generation of Wi-Fi networks. Its encryption can be broken using easily-available computer tools such as WEPcrack.

802.11i: A new industry standard under development that aims to incorporate more robust security than is currently available. Work on the new standard is expected to be finished by the end of 2003.

FIPS 140-2: A seal of approval for wireless devices by the National Institute of Standards and Technology. Federal agencies are required to use FIPS-certified products when transmitting sensitive information over the airwaves.

the wireless part," Johnson says. "That's still bad, but it's nowhere near as bad as if he's into the rest of the network."

RISING TO THE CHALLENGE

Florida is reaching well beyond the notoriously weak security features that come with off-the-shelf equipment. Their system uses 128-bit encryption, which makes it much harder to intercept and descramble data than usual. The trouble with Wi-Fi comes when users rely on the technology's weak security—or forget to turn it on in the first place. Another problem: "rogue" access points. Wireless technology is so cheap now that tech-savvy employees might be tempted to buy it and install it themselves in their offices or cubicles. Such a setup can jeopardize a government's entire network without the IT staff even knowing about it.

Publicized examples of attacks on government systems are rare but not unheard of. For example, the civil courts in Harris County, Texas, were experimenting last year with using Wi-Fi to connect computer systems in two buildings. A former courts employee, who went on a wardriving mission around Houston, sniffed out the wireless network and found it was easy to break into. The hacker, who insists he had no malicious intent, pointed out the vulnerability to the county's IT director.

It's likely that Wi-Fi worries will fade as industry groups work out new security standards and a new generation of wireless products hits the market. Does this mean that agencies that are itching to use Wi-Fi now should wait? Not necessarily. It just means that they have to be extra diligent about layering in additional security features. And they must understand that managing a wireless network comes with considerably more challenges than a wired one. "Today's security is tomorrow's hole," says Colorado's Michael Adams. "We're constantly battling new developments in wireless security that come up."

PLAYING THE ODDS

Talk with Terry Lowe and you'll get the impression that wireless anxiety is overblown. Lowe is the systems project manager in Lincoln, Nebraska, where municipal employees are getting hooked on Palm Pilots. Animal control officers use them to help locate owners of lost dogs. Parking enforcers use them to cross-check for unpaid parking tickets. Cops use handhelds to run license plate numbers and search for outstanding warrants. Even arborists use them to update databases showing the condition of city trees.

As Lowe sees it, the first step to wireless security is assessing risk. In Lincoln, the bulk of the data that city employees pass through the airwaves is public information anyway. So the city took steps to tailor wireless security to each agency, depending on the sensitivity of the information. "Take sidewalk inspection data," Lowe says. "If someone wants to snatch that out of the air, more power to him. We just don't see risk in that."

Lincoln's handhelds, like many wireless devices on the market, have robust encryption systems built in. They meet a standard known as FIPS 140-2, which NIST recommends for government users of handheld devices. In addition, since Lincoln's Palm applications are Web-based, all transactions run through a secure Web server.

> Denver's Lieutenant John Pettinger says that everything available to Denver police officers on their desktops is now available to them in their squad cars.

Perhaps the biggest security problem with handhelds is that they are small enough to lose easily. According to University of Maryland marketing professor P.K. Kannan, who co-wrote a paper on mobile government, 80 percent of wireless security breaches happen when wireless devices are lost or stolen. Lowe has a solution for that, too. He keeps an inventory of serial numbers for each Palm in use. If an employee reports one lost or stolen, Lowe can block it from accessing Lincoln's network.

THE WEAKEST LINK

Police officers have been using laptops in squad cars to search criminal databases and do other simple tasks. Now departments are turning to a new generation of high-speed wireless networks that can send data-rich pictures through the airwaves. But there are security concerns. "The evolution toward automated, computer-controlled communications systems makes the threat of a system hacker more pressing," says a guide to communications security produced by the Public Safety Wireless Network, a federal initiative. "Depending on the system's features, hackers may infiltrate the system and reprogram radios, change security keys or reassign talk groups to different channels."

Police in Denver are testing a snazzy new wireless system where cops in their squad cars can use laptops to pull down mugshots, fingerprints, GIS maps and even detailed aerial photographs. The police officers can also receive and send e-mail from the field, something they couldn't do before. "Anything available to officers on their desktop is now available on the street," says tech chief Lieutenant John Pettinger, who is confident that his department has plugged the security holes.

Denver is using a service called Ricochet, which for many municipalities across the country is a name that echoes from the dot-com past. Ricochet runs on a network of transmitters hung mostly from streetlights, the leases for which a company called Metricom had negotiated with cities in 21 metro areas. Metricom later went belly-up, but in a fire sale, Denver-based Aerie Networks snatched up rights for the Ricochet network. Aerie is now negotiating with cities to light up the network again, so that it can sell service to private customers. And depending on the circumstances, the company is offering many cities free wireless access in exchange for using the light posts.

Denver was the first city to get Ricochet back on line (San Diego is the only other so far). It negotiated for 1,000 unlimited-access accounts, with modems, for free. The city is still figuring out how to divvy up the treasure trove among agencies, but police officials hope to have high-speed service in each of the city's 400 squad cars within months.

Pettinger seems unconcerned about security. The Ricochet signal does something called "frequency-hopping" from one light pole transmitter to the next, making it nearly impossible for hackers to grab data in mid-air. Ricochet also agreed to program the transmitters so that police data travel the airwaves in a different path than that of other private subscribers. Finally, Denver is using an encryption tool known as a "virtual private network," which industry experts agree only the most sophisticated hacker could crack.

Perhaps the greatest security risk is when cops stop for a break. They are prone to leave their squad cars unlocked when they dash in to buy coffee. Denver cops have had radios and shotguns stolen from their cars before. Are the laptops vulnerable? Pettinger has the ability to shut a lost or stolen machine out of the Denver Police computer network. Plus the thief would need to have—besides a ton of gumption—the cop's user name and password. "Whenever you bring information out to people, you get more risk," Pettinger says. "But I think it's a manageable risk. Given the benefits officers are telling me they get from this, it's well worth it."

UNIT 6

Public Policy, Planning, Intergovernmental Relations, and the Law

Unit Selections

25. **The Twin Challenges That Immigration Brings to Public Administrators**, Alexander Franco
26. **Deadly Strains**, Christopher Conte
27. **Winning the Water Wars**, Elaine Robbins
28. **A Mighty Wind**, Elinor Burkett
29. **Like Go-Go 1990s, Smart Growth's Time Had Passed**, Jonathan Osborne and Stephen Scheibal
30. **Tucson Fire Department's MMRS Exercise: A Bioterrorism Response Plan**, Les Caid
31. **How to Make Transit-Oriented Development Work**, Jeffrey Tumlin and Adam Millard-Ball
32. **The U.S. Supreme Court's New Federalism and Its Impact on Antidiscrimination Legislation**, Norma M. Riccucci
33. **TEA Time in Washington**, Jason Jordan

Key Points to Consider

- What are some of the short- and long-term challenges facing U.S. public administrators in dealing with immigration policy?
- Discuss the erosion of public health services that is occurring in the United States What are some of the major problems, and what are some of the proposed solutions to these problems?
- What are some of the major tradeoffs in the debate about using wind power as an alternative energy source?
- Identify and discuss some of the major lessons learned in the areas of emergency response and emergency preparedness.
- What is transit-oriented development (TOD), and how does it work to improve urban development?
- Discuss the concept of the "new federalism" as reflected in some recent U.S. Supreme Court decisions. What are the implications of these Court decisions for administration of human resources legislation?
- What is ISTEA, and what is the major benefit of this legislation? Do you believe that this legislation should be reauthorized?

Links: www.dushkin.com/online/
These sites are annotated in the World Wide Web pages.

Capitol Reports: Environmental News Link
http://www.caprep.com

Hopwood Reactions and Commentary
http://www.law.utexas.edu/hopwood/reaction.html

Innovation Groups (IG)
http://www.ig.org

National Association of Counties
http://www.naco.org/counties/index.cfm

National League of Cities
http://www.nlc.org

The articles in this unit focus on public policy issues, community and environmental planning, and intergovernmental relations and the law. In the area of policy we take a look into the future of the country when we see what is happening in California. That state has been traditionally a "crystal ball" into our future. Continuing a theme of "infrastructure breakdown" that was introduced in unit 2, related to power issues, we discover that our public health services infrastructure is also breaking down. Other policy areas explored are immigration policy and administration, foreign policy, and water policy.

Planning issues explored include environmental planning, growth and land use, including the use of codes, ordinances, and the development of emergency plans. In the area of intergovernmental relations and the law, we include an article on the U.S. Supreme Court's New Federalism and its impact on antidiscrimination legislation. Continuing a theme of reviewing public administration in the post–9/11 world, an article on organizing the federal system for homeland security included. Additional articles look at the 2003 Supreme Court decisions and their impact on the federal system, with a special emphasis on urban planning and property rights. Other articles look at planning issues such as transportation and model city charters.

Public Policy

"The Twin Challenges That Immigration Brings to Public Administrators," by Alexander Franco, reports that today there are more than 33 million immigrants (documented and undocumented) in the United States. The author focuses on the long-term challenges to public administrators dealing with immigration policy. One of these is correcting existing flaws within the current structure of the Immigration and Naturalization Services (INS). A second challenge is how to assist the public service infrastructures within many of the immigrant host communities that are currently experiencing fiscal and economic stress.

Christopher Conte, in his article "Deadly Strains," reports that SARS, West Nile virus, and bioterrorism are the big scares but that the greatest threat is the gradual erosion of public health services and health budgets at the state and local levels. He points out that the infrastructure for public health services is slowly falling apart due to overuse and decline of funds from all levels of government.

The article, "Winning the Water Wars" by Elaine Robbins, states that in the West they say, "water flows uphill to the money." Because water is such a scarce resource, cities are facing conflicts as they work to develop policies to meet their future needs. The author goes on to say that water planning is a must if cities are to solve their resource management problems.

Community and Environmental Planning

According to Elinor Burkett's article, "A Mighty Wind," alternative energy sources such as wind power are the hope of the future for environmental planners. The author asks what happens when a wind farm is planned for Cape Cod. The answer is that we have a clash of values between environmentalist planners who want a wind farm to be built and conservationists who say that the visual pollution that would result from such a project is unacceptable. It's all a matter of trade-offs!

Jonathan Osborne and Stephen Scheibal, in their article "Like the Go-Go 1990s, Smart Growth's Time Has Passed," review the history of "smart growth," an environmental planning term developed in the early 1990s. The purpose of the smart growth program was to encourage intelligent development within an urban area. Unfortunately, in Austin, Texas, according to the authors, it fell victim to a faltering economy and the "high tech" bust.

According to author Les Caid in his article, "Tucson Fire Department's MMRS Exercise: A Bioterrorism Response Plan," the city of Tucson conducted the nation's first large-scale exercise to test the city's emergency response and emergency preparedness in the event of a disaster or bioterrorist attack. The article reviews and analyzes the observations and the lessons learned from the exercise.

"How to Make Transit-Oriented Development Work," by Jeffrey Mumlin and Adam Millard-Ball, reports that "transit-oriented development (TOD)" seeks to improve the urban environment by promoting more compact development, less automobile dependence, and an improved quality of life. According to the authors, density and land use considerations are the key to successful transit-oriented development in an urban area.

Intergovernmental Relations and Public Law

"The U.S. Supreme Court's New Federalism and Its Impact on Antidiscrimination Legislation," by Norma M. Riccucci, reports that in recent years the U.S. Supreme Court has developed a new federalism policy that has reduced the powers of the U.S. Congress in favor of states' rights. This article addresses the implications of the Supreme Court's new federalism policy for the Americans With Disabilities Act (ADA) of 1990 and the Age Discrimination in Employment Act (ADEA) of 1967 as amended.

"TEA Time in Washington," by Jason Jordan, reviews the status of the landmark legislation for surface transportation planning in the United States, which is the Intermodal Surface Transportation Efficiency Act of 1991 (ISTEA). This legislation is scheduled for reauthorization. For smart growth proponents throughout the country, ISTEA reauthorization may be the most important piece of federal legislation facing Congress in the near future.

The Twin Challenges that Immigration Brings to Public Administrators

Post–September 11 Immigration Policy and Administration

From correcting flaws within immigration policy to immigration research and human trafficking, the issues facing immigration policy and administration range far and wide.

The following article attempts to bring some of these issues into focus.

Alexander Franco

Today there are over 33 million immigrants (documented and undocumented) in the United States—approximately 11.5 percent of the U.S. population. This number is unprecedented by historical standards. In 1910, at the peak of the early 20th century immigration wave, immigrants accounted for only 41 percent (13.5 million) of their number today.

The sheer numbers, particularly during the decade of the 1990s, have borne twin long-term challenges to public administrators. The first involves correcting existing flaws within the current administrative policies of the Immigration and Naturalization Services (INS) as well as reforming that organization's cultural environment. A recent study conducted by the Center for Immigration Studies found that, of 48 Islamic terrorists charged or involved in terrorism in the United States since 1993, 16 (one-third) were on temporary visas, 17 (one-third) were lawful residents or naturalized citizens, 12 (one-fourth) were illegal aliens and three were in the process of applying for asylum. In addition to the 12 with illegal status, another 10 had incurred significant violations of immigration laws prior to committing acts of terrorism, including living illegally in the United States at some point. The stay of some of these terrorists had been facilitated in some cases by fraudulent marriages and/or illegally held jobs.

Public administrators need to take a comprehensive look at the totality of the immigration system and to explore reform options involving the screening of visa applicants abroad, the processing of foreign citizens at our gateways, an effective but humane protection of our borders (north and south), and the enforcement of current immigration laws within the country.

The intense immigration of the 1990s also poses a comprehensive challenge to elected officials and public administrators in immigrant-host communities. According to the most recent statistics from the U.S. Census Bureau, the foreign-born are experiencing a poverty rate of 16.1 percent (about 5.2 million) as opposed to 11.1 percent for natives. If their U.S.-born children (under 18) are factored, the poverty rate for immigrants climbs to 17.6 percent (versus about 11 percent for natives and their children). About one-third of immigrants do not have health insurance, nearly 25 percent receive at least one major form of public assistance, and 30 percent do not have a high school education. The problem is particularly acute among Mexicans, the largest of all immigrant groups (about 30 percent of the total immigrant population). Census data indicates that about 24 percent of Mexican immigrants live in poverty and that 61.5 percent live in or near poverty ("near" defined as income under 200 percent of the poverty threshold).

The public service infrastructures within many of the immigrant-host communities are experiencing serious stress by way of increasing demand for public services accompanied by a declining tax base. The City of Miami, with a foreign-born population of 61 percent, is a dramatic example. According to the 2000 census, Miami is now the poorest city (i.e., cities with populations over 250,000) in the United States, with 32 percent of its residents living in poverty. This includes over 29,000 children and almost 18,000 elderly. A declining tax base and diminishing capitalization, due to white out-migration as well as corrupt practices and non-mainstream administrative policies that ignored a long-term orientation (such as economic development), resulted in a fiscal crisis and a budgetary collapse that forced the State of Florida to intervene with a financial oversight board. Both the City and the surrounding county (whose population is 51 percent foreign-born) face overcrowded schools surrounded by trailers, declining health and social services and severe traffic congestion due, in part, to a politically exploited and poorly administered mass transit system. The lack of economic development has created a community whose socio-economic dimensions resemble those of a developing world metropolis. As the recently departed city manager of Miami indicated, "This is a city of extremes. You have rich and very rich and you have a lot of poor people. What we don't have is a middle class."

Though the business leaders of the Cuban Exile enclave (which dominates the county) continue to propagate the mythology of the Exile's economic success story, census figures indicate that over 49 percent of all Cuban immigrants live in or near the poverty level, with 35 percent of their households (which tend to be extended households) receiving some major form of public assistance. Much of the Cuban enclave economy consists of minimum-wage jobs and of a significant informal economy that evades all levels of taxation and is devoid of minimum-wage enforcement as well as health and safety protections for workers.

Demographics is destiny! Political scientists have already written numerous studies on the political impact that naturalized immigrants have played in recent elections and they continue to write speculative studies about the future impact of the immigrant vote as it grows in number. Yet, studies by public administration researchers on the impact of immigration on our major metropolitan areas are scarce; others lack credibility since they were commissioned by local political interests. Some in the academic community stifle such endeavors since they feel this research belongs within the less important fields of comparative public administration and urban and regional studies. These areas, they argue, are plagued with mushy intangibles such as culture and assimilation, which, they claim, elude quantification. We can no longer afford to denigrate these fields of study. (And, in this era of globalization and the clashing of cultures, the same holds true for research on international studies of public administration.)

Information precedes action. Public administration researchers must focus more on the immigrant-host communities of this nation if government is to effectively meet many of the difficult domestic issues that currently confront us and which will continue to do so in the following decade. The Hispanic Research Center and the Metropolitan Research Policy Institute, (both at the University of Texas at San Antonio), serve as excellent examples of institutions that address and provide scholarly research of such long-term issues. Their work, and like-minded work, needs to be more liberally supported within the journals, conferences and institutions of public administration education.

ASPA member Alexander Franco is an assistant professor of public administration in the political science department of Southern Illinois University, Carbondale. Franco is an immigrant from Cuba. E-mail: franco@siu.edu

Deadly Strains

SARS, West Nile virus and bioterrorism are the big scares. But the greater threat is the gradual erosion of public health services.

By CHRISTOPHER CONTE

WHEN SEATTLE RECEIVED $2 MILLION IN FEDERAL money last year to prepare for a possible biological, chemical or radiological attack, public health director Alonzo Plough was relieved. Along with his counterparts around the country, Plough had watched new health threats multiply while public health budgets stagnated. Finally, he thought, the city would have funds to work out emergency procedures with area police departments, fire officials and other "first responders." He'd be able to hire new staff to help combat naturally emerging diseases as well.

Things haven't worked out as he planned. No sooner had he launched a terrorism-planning effort than he had to drop it because the federal government ordered its sweeping smallpox-vaccination program. That task tied up so much of Plough's staff that they were slow to detect a new outbreak of tuberculosis among Seattle's homeless population. As officials scrambled to catch up with that problem, SARS, or severe acute respiratory syndrome, emerged in China. Almost immediately, the mysterious disease started showing up in travelers returning from Asia. Plough had to divert staff from the unfinished smallpox and tuberculosis efforts and put them to work to keep the new disease from spreading in Seattle.

Plough's job has become a continuous exercise in triage. The reason: His department has too much to do and too few resources. "In my 20 years in public health, I have never seen such a layering of challenges, all with fairly equal urgency and all drawing on diminishing core funding," he says. "We aren't providing anything near the web of protection that's needed."

The problem isn't unique to Seattle. All over the country, local public health departments are struggling to keep on top of a growing list of health threats. Terrorism may turn out to be the least of their concerns. Changing patterns of land use are bringing people into contact with dangerous new microbes such as the West Nile virus and the coronavirus, which is believed to be the cause of SARS. Globalization is spreading these diseases more rapidly than human immune systems or modern science can build defenses. And many see a scenario in which the familiar influenza virus abruptly morphs into a deadly pandemic that the U.S. Centers for Disease Control and Prevention estimates could kill as many as 300,000 people. On top of that, old maladies such as tuberculosis have started appearing in drug-resistant strains; sexually transmitted diseases such as HIV and syphilis are on the rise because many people have become complacent about them; and chronic diseases such as asthma and diabetes are becoming more prevalent due to environmental and behavioral factors.

Local public health leaders widely agree with Plough that their tools and budgets haven't kept pace with these challenges. Despite the growing threat from communicable diseases, for instance, state health agencies employ fewer epidemiologists today (1,400) than they did in 1992 (1,700). When a professional association this fall and winter asked state health laboratory directors to rate their preparedness to handle a terrorist chemical attack, half scored their own facilities "1" or "2" on a scale of 1 to 10, with 1 being the poorest mark. And a Little Hoover Commission in California declared in April that the state's "public health infrastructure is in poor repair, providing less protection than it should against everyday hazards and unprepared to adequately protect us against the remote but substantial threats we now face." The commission noted, among other things, that only 20 percent of reportable diseases and conditions were actually reported to public health officials, and that at one key health laboratory, only 60 of 100 positions were filled.

As California goes, so goes the nation. Updating a 1988 report that concluded the country's entire public health system was in "disarray," the National Institute of Medicine said last

No Simple Task

Washington State's public health system is trying to meet five basic standards:

- **Promote understanding of health issues**—by assessing community health and disseminating findings.
- **Protect people from disease**—by maintaining surveillance and reporting systems, developing plans for handling communicable disease outbreaks, and establishing procedures for disease invstigation and control.
- **Assure a safe and healthy environment**—by educating the public, tracking environmental health risks and illnesses, enforcing health-related environmental regulations, and being prepared to respond to environmental disasters.
- **Promote healthy living**—by providing a prevention, early intervention and outreach services, and involving the community in efforts to prevent illness.
- **Help people get needed services**—by providing information to the public on existing health services, analyzing what factors affect access to critical services, and developing plans to reduce specific gaps in access.

For more: www.doh.wa.gov/standards/default.htm

fall that the system is plagued by "outdated and vulnerable technologies, lack of real-time surveillance and epidemiological systems, ineffective and fragmented communications networks, (and) incomplete domestic preparedness and emergency response capabilities."

STARVING THE SYSTEM

Policy makers are aware of the holes in the public health system. Last year, the U.S. Congress provided $940 million to help local health departments cope with emerging threats. Local health officials hoped to use the funds not only to prepare for terrorist attacks but also to improve their ability to conduct general surveillance and cope with natural outbreaks such as SARS.

The federal smallpox-vaccination program has absorbed nearly all of the funds so far, however, making "dual use" largely a chimera. Indeed, many local officials say the federal government hasn't even provided enough money for them to prepare adequately for possible terrorist attacks, let alone cope with naturally occurring diseases that already are killing people. In particular, the preoccupation with smallpox has set back efforts to plan defenses against a host of other potential biological weapons, including plague, tularemia, botulism toxin, and viral hemorrhagic fever; chemical agents such as ricin and sarin gas; and a possible "dirty bomb" laden with radioactive materials.

Many public health officials such as Plough also say they lack secure communications networks linking them with other first responders. On top of that, public health officials have received no money to start educating the public about what people should do if there is a biological or chemical attack. "We are writing plans, but plans by themselves don't automatically translate into increased capacity," says Jeffrey Duchin, chief of the Seattle health department's Communicable Disease Control, Epidemiology and Immunization section. "We aren't committing the resources needed to turn them into living documents."

Federal officials counter by saying that state and local agencies would have trouble absorbing many more funds than Congress has provided. But the increased federal funding has had an unintended side effect: Fiscally strapped states and localities have seized on it to cut their own public health spending. In Colorado's Larimer County, for instance, a $700,000 slash in state funds for public health more than erased a gain of $100,000 in federal money. Even with new federal funds, the Boston Public Health Commission has been forced to cut scores of positions.

"Overall, we are losing money in the public health budgets in the 50 states, despite funds for terrorism preparedness," says Dr. George Benjamin, executive director of the American Public Health Association. Benjamin formerly was health director for Maryland, which has received federal funds to increase its epidemiological staff but has been forced to cut its state-financed food safety program.

Perhaps more troubling, public health departments have had to rely increasingly on revenues that come with many strings attached. For years, they have sought wherever possible to support programs with grants or with user fees, such as charges for restaurant inspections. But you can't charge a mosquito when you test it for West Nile virus, and while you can persuade public and private grant-makers to provide funds for programs aimed at recognized ills such as breast cancer, nobody seems to want to pay for ongoing operations or general preparedness. "There is a much greater investment in public health and public health programs now than there was a decade ago," notes Mary Selecky, Washington State's secretary of health and president of the Association of State and Territorial Health Officers. "But there is far less flexibility in how the dollars are spent. We are driven by categorical funding."

Seattle's health department, considered by many to be dynamic and forward-looking, illustrates the problem. Its overall budget has grown impressively, reaching $187.9 million this year from $77.5 million in 1993. But almost all the increases have been in programs supported by user fees and grants. County government gives it $28 million to run its emergency medical services; a federal program provides $5 million to support AIDS victims (but not to help prevent spread of the HIV virus that causes AIDS); and the Robert Wood Johnson Foundation donated money for the development of a program to deal with asthma.

None of these funds pay for basic public health operations, including surveillance to detect new disease outbreaks, investigators to track the spread of diseases and a host of prevention-oriented activities. This year, funding for "core" activities totaled $30.9 million, barely up from $30.1 million 10 years ago. The current West Nile virus and TB outbreak alone would more than eat up that increase this year. And that doesn't take inflation or Seattle's substantial population growth into account. Per capita, core funding has dropped from $21.34 in 1997 to $16.67 today.

WAITING TIME

Behind those numbers lies a slow deterioration in the department's ability to address long-term problems or react quickly to changing conditions. When SARS hit this spring, for instance, the department couldn't follow up on a number of hepatitis B cases. The rate of childhood immunizations has fallen since 1998, while cases of measles and pertussis (whooping cough) have increased, and new TB cases are at a 30-year high.

When a team belatedly began combating the TB outbreak, it moved ahead in fits and starts. The key to stamping out such an outbreak is painstaking detective work: Investigators interview known victims, identify places they frequent and other people with whom they have come in contact, and then follow up those leads with additional screening and information-gathering. Eventually, such searches enable them to track a disease's movements, isolate it and stamp it out. By this spring, investigators had collected more than 50 pieces of information on each of some 528 actual or potential carriers. But the information lay unanalyzed for precious weeks because the outbreak team couldn't find an epidemiologist to work on it.

"Somewhere in there is the answer to where and how this got kicked off, and where it's going next," says Linda Lake, a consultant who leads the outbreak team and also chairs the Washington State Board of Health. "But the department is too busy dealing with SARS or other things. When you find somebody to help, it's always part-time, it's always for a short period of time, and it always takes them away from something else."

Outbreaks don't occur on a neat schedule, and there inevitably will be times that are busier than others. Even the most ardent public health advocates don't expect voters to pay to have public health workers waiting around for the next outbreak the way firefighters are paid to be available at all times. But there's a backlog of tasks that could keep the public health workforce busy when there are no emergencies.

Currently, the Seattle department can afford just 10 public health nurses for an intensive counseling program called "Best Beginnings," which has been proven to reduce a wide range of health problems affecting children of first-time teenage mothers. That's enough to reach only about one fourth of the mothers who need the service. Meanwhile, a strategy for working with schools to encourage teenagers to drink less soda and get more exercise—keys to reining in a near epidemic of juvenile diabetes—remains on the drawing boards for lack of funds, as does a major initiative to help Seattle's health providers incorporate ideas about safer behavior, better diets and exercise into their daily interactions with patients.

Although public health departments could make good use of additional funds, public skepticism about government and taxes usually trumps proposals to increase their resources. In Washington State, public health advocates were optimistic early this year after the Republican and Democratic leaders of the Senate co-sponsored a bill that would ask citizens to vote on whether to raise property taxes by $151 million to support local public health agencies. But health advocates lost heart after a poll commissioned by the Washington State Association of Counties and others showed the idea was far from assured of winning voter approval.

The lack of support demonstrates, in part, how reliance on categorical funding has become a political trap for public health

Detective Work

Is information technology the answer?

PUBLIC HEALTH DEPARTMENTS are harnessing computers to the task of identifying and tracking disease outbreaks, but they have a long way to go.

New York City and other jurisdictions are experimenting with "syndromic surveillance," which involves collecting information on symptoms from disparate sources—911 calls, emergency room visits, possibly even drugstore purchases—and using computers to search for patterns. A surge in drugstore sales of Pepto-Bismol, for instance, might indicate that the community has been hit by a new gastrointestinal disorder. "This could give us potentially an early-warning system," notes Dorothy Teeter, chief of health operations for the Public Health Department of Seattle and King County. But such fancy new computer systems may be unaffordable, especially at a time of tight budgets. Teeter estimates it would cost Seattle $10 million and take 10 years to create an effective system.

Costs aside, such ideas have their skeptics. "It's worth doing, but let's not put our eggs solely in the basket of automated systems," says Paul Wiesner, director of the DeKalb County Board of Health in Georgia. Weisner argues that medicine is still an "art," and that there is no substitute for the judgment and instincts of health professionals. Moreover, he adds, public health departments need much more than new software: "We need to focus on all aspects of infrastructure, including training."

Meanwhile, health departments coudl take less costly steps to improve their technological capabilities. The Kansas Department of Health has developed a Web-based communication system that enables it to exchange information on emerging health issues with local health departments. That's a step in the right direction, but many health departments don't even exchange information across the hallway, let alone across the state. While many epidemiologists use geographic information systems to track diseases, for instance, public health departments rarely integrate their efforts. "Agencies in all 50 states are using GIS for disease tracking, but their efforts aren't coordinated," says Bill Davenhall, a manager for the software company ESRI in Redland, California.

—C.C.

agencies. Victims of specific illness often lobby tirelessly and effectively for funds to address their afflictions, but it's hard to find citizens who feel the same degree of passion for quiet government activities that keep people healthy. Public health workers have the passion, but it doesn't get them very far. "People think they're just asking for a handout." says Pat Libbey, executive director of the National Association of County and City Health Officials.

REALITY CHECK

Clearly, voters expect more than they are willing to pay for. The Association of Counties poll showed, for instance, that 96 percent of Washington voters believe the services public health agencies provide are "very important." Yet the state Department of Health estimates that total public health spending in the state—about $507 million annually—amounts to only one third of what public health agencies need to do the job they currently are expected to do. The department says only one half of local public health agencies are doing reasonably well in meeting 202 performance measures developed for them.

For Carolyn Edmonds, a member of the county council for Seattle's King County and a former state legislator, the disparity between expectations and reality represents a political quandary. On one hand, she wonders whether advocates should present the budget situation in starker terms—by warning voters, for instance, that the current stringency is forcing public health officials to put fighting infectious diseases ahead of making sure children are immunized. "Public health has shied away from doing that," she says, "but maybe we're going to have to be more blatant" about what the trade-offs are.

On the other hand, Edmonds fears that voters won't believe leaders who say current budget and tax policy require such decisions: "People go to restaurants expecting that the food will be cooked properly. They go to a drinking fountain expecting that they won't get sick from the water. There is a built-in assumption that they will be taken care of."

Eventually, she says, the assumption will be disproved—maybe not in dramatic ways but slowly and less noticeably. "Response times will be slower. There will be fewer prevention measures," she says. "More people will get sick. People will die."

The end result, in Edmonds' view, may not be as shocking as, say, terrorists detonating a dirty bomb in a baseball stadium. Nevertheless, it will be very real and might have been avoided.

Article 27

Winning the Water Wars

In the West, they say that water flows uphill to money. In the 21st century, that is going to mean one thing: vast quantities of water moving from farms to fast-growing cities.

By Elaine Robbins

By all accounts, the cities will need it. Nearly a century after the infamous Los Angeles water grab dramatized in the movie *Chinatown*, many U.S. cities are facing interbasin conflicts as they search for water to meet their future needs. Rapid growth in the 1990s coupled with recent droughts have left communities wondering whether to limit growth because of water shortages.

A look at San Diego, San Antonio, and Atlanta—places that continue to attract new residents with their mild climates, robust job markets, and good quality of life—reveals that water supply will be one of their biggest ongoing challenges.

San Diego: How dry is dry?

On New Year's Day this year, San Diego received news that wasn't worth celebrating. At 8 a.m., two of the pumps that siphon its water from the Colorado River near Lake Havasu City, Arizona, were shut off and the last of San Diego's surplus allotment of Colorado River water went sluicing down the 242-mile aqueduct toward Southern California.

On January 1, the U.S. Department of the Interior shut down the pumps that siphon water from the Colorado River at Lake Havasu, cutting off the surplus allotment of water that has long gone to San Diego.

Interior Secretary Gale A. Norton had ordered Southern California's surplus water supply cut off because San Diego and the Imperial Irrigation District failed to meet a December 31 deadline to reach agreement on how to transfer water from the farm fields to the city. The agreement would have been a key piece of a scheme designed to wean California off its surplus allotments of Colorado River water.

It was only the latest volley in the battle over what Marc Reisner, in his 1986 book, *Cadillac Desert*, called "the most legislated, most debated, and most litigated river in the entire world." Along its 1,400-mile journey from its headwaters in Colorado to the point at which it discharges into the Gulf of California, the river is shared by seven states—Arizona, California, Colorado, Nevada, New Mexico, Utah, and Wyoming—as well as Mexico.

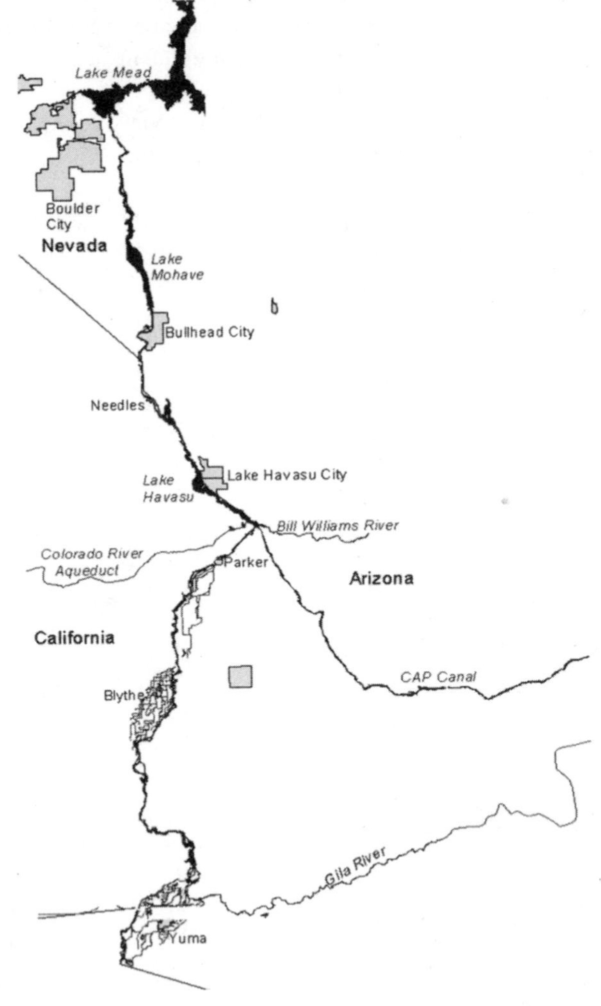

U.S. Department of the Interior

Seven states share water from the Colorado River, which travels 1,400 miles from its headwaters in Colorado to the Gulf of California

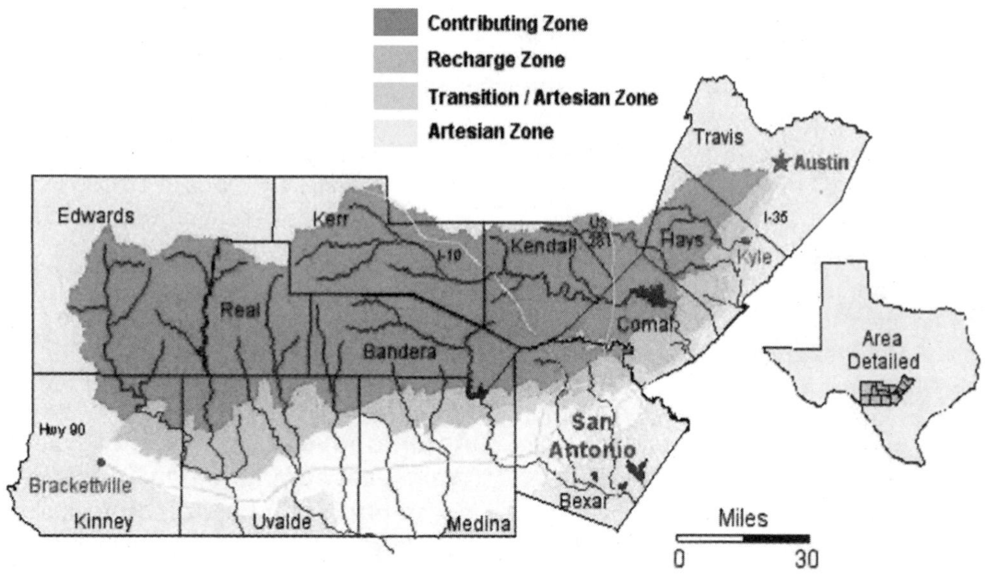

Map Greg Eckhardt

Due to growth, San Antonio must look beyond the Edwards Aquifer for fresh water. Sources include other aquifers as well as rivers. The price tag for these water transfers: over $500 million through 2005.

Ever since a 1964 U.S. Supreme Court decision that restricted California to 4.4 million acre-feet of river water, Los Angeles and San Diego have been allowed to use other states' unused apportionments. That's because many of those western states stayed relatively small while California boomed.

That situation has changed. Nevada, the fastest growing state, grew by 66 percent in the 1990s. Now the states that share the Colorado River with California are calling in their loans. They have demanded that the Interior Department take action to get California to live within its original 4.4 million acre-foot annual limit.

But in Southern California, the land of opportunity, "limits" has never been a part of the popular lexicon. That may be why San Diego's water planners are confronting the current water crisis with a can-do attitude.

"In San Diego, the question has always been, 'How can we accommodate the growth?'" says Joanna Salazar, associate regional planner for the San Diego Association of Governments (SANDAG), the regional planning agency. "The mission of the San Diego County Water Authority is and always has been to figure out what the growth is going to be and then figure out how to supply the water, as opposed to the other way around."

The city (pop. 1.2 million) has already lined up the water it needs to fill its immediate needs. "In the short term, the Metropolitan Water District—the big water provider for Southern California—has water in storage," says Dana Friehauf, water planner for San Diego. "They just completed construction of their Diamond Valley reservoir, which holds 800,000 acre-feet of water, so they'll use some of those supplies. They also have groundwater storage from the Central Valley. That's good for another two years or so."

When the city finally settles its differences with the Imperial Valley farmers, the Interior Department has agreed to restore its surplus Colorado River water—at least for now. Once that deal is made, San Diego plans to implement a 1998 agreement it made with the Imperial Irrigation District. In a move that will increasingly be adopted by thirsty U.S. cities, it will pay the farmers to conserve. The water that is freed up will be transferred to San Diego County.

In the long term, the city's approach is best described not by "limits" but by another word: diversification. "This year, especially because it was so dry out here, we were 90 percent reliant on imported water supplies," says Friehauf. "So what we're trying to do is diversify our supply through recycling, through more conservation, through groundwater, and through seawater desalinization."

The water authority's water plan calls for developing big quantities of water over the next 10 years: about 50,000 acre-feet each from desalinization, groundwater and recycling, and conservation. A desalinization plant to be built in the city of Carlsbad is scheduled to be up and running by 2008.

Concurrency in California?

Even in the land of opportunity, politicians are starting to realize that growth hinges on the availability of water. Under SB 610 and SB 211, two state laws that went into effect in 2001, developers must supply written documentation proving that sufficient water is available for their projects before they can get new housing developments approved.

"The intent of the new legislation is to link regional growth with water planning," says Salazar. "It has been pushing the idea that when some new project comes up, the land-use authorities have to provide documents that say yes, we will have enough water for that new development or we don't, in which case, they can't go ahead with the development. Those pieces of legislation have been for really large-scale development—500 units or more." Smaller scale development isn't covered, she says.

In the meantime, water planners will face a growing challenge to keep the water flowing. Eventually, they may come to appreciate the sentiments of William Mulholland, the politically savvy engineer who in the 1920s secured Los Angeles the water it needed to green its deserts. Reisner describes how Mulholland felt as he watched the city fathers' relentless push to lure newcomers to this promised land. "Mulholland begged the city fathers to end their abject deification of growth. The only way to solve the city's water problem, he grumbled aloud, was to kill the members of the Chamber of Commerce."

San Antonio: Texas-size thirst

Planners have traveled to San Antonio from as far away as South Africa to study the River Walk, a shady walkway lined with outdoor restaurants, historic hotels, and shops. Indeed, this riverside walkway—the crown jewel of the city's $4 billion a year tourism industry—is a leading example of successful urban revitalization.

But to truly understand the life source of this sunny, affordable city, you need to look not to the narrow San Antonio River but to a hidden underground cache of water called the Edwards Aquifer. Stored in a subterranean landscape of karst limestone, the Edwards Aquifer's cool, clear waters green the city's golf courses and the lawns in new subdivisions. The water allows San Antonio to continue to attract newcomers: The city's population grew by 20 percent in the 1990s—to 1.1 million.

Until recently the aquifer also gave San Antonio a strange claim to fame: It was the biggest city in the world solely dependent on an aquifer for its water needs. But that is about to change. The Edwards Aquifer Authority, the regulatory body created to manage the aquifer, recently granted a permit to the city to pump 159,000 acre-feet a year—about 20,000 acre-feet short of its normal usage. That shortfall—plus the fact that the population is expected to double in the next 50 years—means the aquifer will no longer suffice to meet San Antonio's needs.

So last year, the city began delivering its first non-Edwards water to some of its water customers—from the Trinity Aquifer to the north. By the end of this year, it will also begin pumping water from the Carrizo-Wilcox Aquifer to the southeast.

But those relatively small-scale transfers are just the beginning of a major shift in water policy. Since January 2001, when San Antonio began charging a separate water development fee on its utility bills, the city has been making deals that could radically transform the flow of water in South Texas.

Last year the city signed a $1 billion agreement with the Lower Colorado River Authority to pipe 150,000 acre-feet of water from the *other* Colorado River to meet the city's needs for the next 80 to 100 years. (This Colorado River originates and ends in Texas.) If approved, this deal would transfer vast quantities of water to the city—almost as much as it currently takes from the Edwards Aquifer.

The Edwards Aquifer was San Antonio's sole source of water until last year. Now recycled water is adding to the supply available to the San Antonio River along the city's famous River Walk. Last summer, local officials celebrated the completion of a new discharge area by pouring buckets of recycled water into the river.

Last year the city signed a deal to divert 94,500 acre-feet of water from the Guadalupe River. By the end of this year, the city will begin an aquifer storage project. It will pump extra water from the Edwards Aquifer in the winter months and inject it into the Carrizo-Wilcox Aquifer for storage. It will then pull that water out in summer, when demand is at its peak but flows are lowest due to lack of rainfall.

Starting in 2011, the city will start pumping water from the Gulf Coast Aquifer to the east. Payments to 34 rural landowners will start at $300,000 a year and go up from there.

These major water transfers carry a hefty price tag. They are expected to cost $519 million through 2005—a figure that could soar to at least $2.6 billion over the next 50 years.

What's more, several of the deals face opposition from environmentalists and other water users, which means the city may ultimately have difficulty getting the water it needs. Environmentalists are concerned about the impact of the Colorado River deal on Matagorda Bay, which serves as a key nursery and supports a $178 million fishing industry. Similarly, the Guadalupe River deal has alarmed people concerned about sufficient in-stream flow in the Guadalupe River, a popular river for canoeing, tubing, and fishing.

Where the Guadalupe discharges into San Antonio Bay, it provides an essential freshwater flow that affects salinity levels for the blue crab, an important food source for the endangered whooping crane. In an attempt to protect these resources, the San Marcos River Foundation has filed a request for instream flow.

There are also social costs to consider. As water moves from farms to cities, it is important to ensure that rural Texas communities don't dry up and blow away like tumbleweeds, as some did after the oil wells stopped pumping in the decades following World War II.

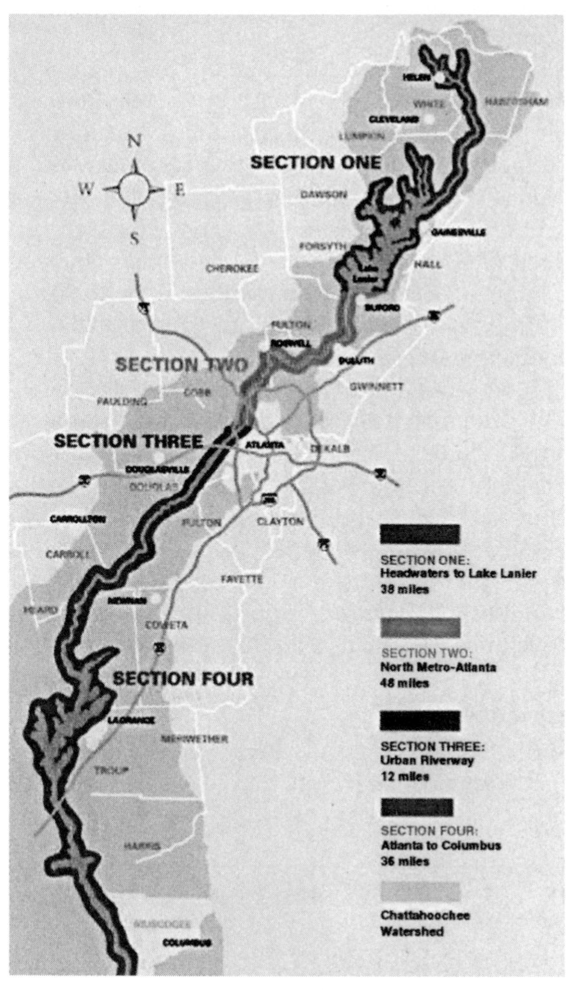

Trust for Public Land, Georgia office

Georgia, Alabama, and Florida all share water from the Chattahoochee River. But Atlanta is growing so quickly that downstream users are seeking legal help to guarantee water flows to critical areas.

A drop saved is a drop earned

One of the best ways to reduce all these impacts is conservation—a strategy that San Antonio has embraced. San Antonio uses less water than most other large cities in the West: 143 gallons per capita per day, compared with about 200 per capita in Denver, Dallas, and Houston.

"Water-use efficiency is of paramount importance to us," says Susan Butler, AICP, a planner who is director of water resources and conservation for the San Antonio Water System. "We've reduced our water use by about 30 to 35 percent over last 15 to 20 years." Much of that savings was achieved by replacing 6,000 toilets with low-flow models and from local industries' implementation of improved water-use technology.

Last year the city took another important stop toward conserving water. The development community agreed to support a new ordinance that will require all new homes to have low water-use landscapes. In a city where about 25 percent of the water goes to outdoor use—primarily lawn watering—this move will provide significant savings once it takes effect in 2006.

As water planners in other cities are discovering, conservation is also the cheapest source of new water, compared with the cost of dams or transfers. And as the population grows, conservation savings offer a key multiplier effect. "Looking out 50 years, when our population is expected to nearly double, we can create 100,000 acre-feet of new water through conservation," says Butler.

Even as it searches for new sources of water, San Antonio is also taking steps to protect the life-giving aquifer. Government Canyon State Natural Area, a 6,642-acre preserve bought in 1993 to protect the Edwards Aquifer recharge zone, is due to open for recreation soon. And last summer, when the city council approved a PGA Village golf resort in the recharge zone, local residents forced the city to pull out of the project.

Atlanta: A river runs through it

Atlanta seems to be sitting pretty. The Chattahoochee River, which supplies Atlanta with nearly all of its water, runs right through the city. And Atlanta is blessed with 50 inches of rain a year—compared with a mere 10 inches in San Diego, for example.

But in recent years, the Chattahoochee has been the focus of a debate more typical of the American West than the water-rich East. Atlanta's phenomenal growth and two drought-stricken summers have threatened the flow to downstream states. The shortage intensified a 10-year conflict over apportionment of the river's flows to Georgia, Alabama, and Florida.

Typically, Atlanta and surrounding towns have built reservoirs to capture water. "Frankly, the Chattahoochee is only as large as it is because of a Corps of Engineers dam," says Pat Stevens, chief of the Environmental Planning Division of the Atlanta Regional Commission. "If it wasn't for that reservoir [Lake Lanier], we could have walked across that river."

Atlanta's reservoir withdrawals are a concern for downstream users in Alabama and Florida. Downstream users were particularly alarmed last year, when Atlanta made a settlement agreement with the U.S. Army Corps of Engineers that allowed the city to increase its draws from Lake Lanier and the Chattahoochee by as much as 50 percent. In return, the city agreed to pay its fair share for the water so the area's power customers wouldn't carry most of the reservoir's expense.

In January, the Justice Department filed a suit to stop the settlement agreement. The agency feared the extra allotment to Atlanta could hamper a tri-state agreement that has been in the works for 10 years.

That agreement would guarantee flows into Florida's Apalachicola Bay, where it provides the freshwater flows needed to sustain a multimillion-dollar oyster and shrimp fishery. Diminished flows in recent years have made the famous oysters saltier, and oystermen worry about losing their livelihoods.

In a different legal action, environmental groups recently sued the Corps of Engineers over plans to build 17 more dams in the metro Atlanta area—schemes they say could have profound effects on the river's ecosystem.

But water planner Stevens thinks there is enough water to meet the needs of all of the river's current users. "Looking at some of the preliminary agreements," says Stevens, "we have plenty of water for the next 30 years, even with the allocations that Florida and Alabama wanted. There's a lot of discussion about what we do beyond then—or even up to that point. A lot of our future is going to involve very aggressive water conservation and recycling."

Atlanta has room for improvement in recycling: Despite its abundant rainfall, which keeps lawns green without constant watering, Atlanta uses 150 gallons of water per person per day, compared with 143 in San Antonio.

Even more challenging for this booming southern city than the tri-state agreement is how the city will divvy up its water allotment in the 16-county metro area. Atlanta grew by 40 percent in the 1990s, adding 1.2 million people. Two of the four fastest growing counties in the nation—Henry County to the south and Gwinnett County to the east—are in greater Atlanta. The other surrounding counties have either grown rapidly or are slated for future growth. In the traditional first come, first-served approach to water allocation, late-blooming communities are worried that they'll be left high and dry.

"Some of the communities that are just beginning the real rapid growth process are concerned that those larger communities may corner the resources that they might need if they're going to see similar kinds of growth," says Napoleon Caldwell, senior planner and policy adviser for the Environmental Protection Division of the Georgia Department of Natural Resources. "The major challenge if we're going to successfully use water within the confines of our limits is to come upon strategies that will result in more effective inter-jurisdictional cooperation. There's a very strong sense of independence on the part of the political jurisdictions that comprise the metro Atlanta area."

This is a challenge that other cities will face as populations begin to outstrip water supply. Instead of competing, cities and even states and nations will need to chart a new course toward regional management of water. "There's a lot of history that makes it very difficult for these entities to cooperate," says Caldwell. "Overcoming those histories is difficult, and it takes a lot of time."

Resources

Online. San Diego County Water Authority, www.sdcwa.org. San Antonio Water System, www.saws.org. Atlanta Regional Commission, www.altreg.com.

Elaine Robbins is a freelance writer in Austin, Texas.

A Mighty Wind

Time was when the ex-hippies and liberal stalwarts living on Cape Cod would have said that alternative energy was a force worth fighting for. But then someone actually proposed building 130 windmills in the ocean right off their beach.

By Elinor Burket

The buzz on Cape Cod is grim as summer approaches. There is little talk about beach permits or Kennedy sightings and much talk about dead birds littering beaches, jellyfish clogging waterways and tourism collapsing. Even Walter Cronkite, America's *éminence grise*, has issued a dire warning from his second home on Martha's Vineyard. "I'm very concerned about a private developer's plan to build an industrial energy complex across 24 square miles of publicly owned land," Cronkite intoned in a radio and television ad recently broadcast across the Cape.

The industrial energy complex in question is a wind farm. And the publicly owned land is really water—Nantucket Sound, which separates the Cape from Martha's Vineyard and Nantucket. That is where a Boston-based company called Cape Wind Associates hopes to build America's first offshore wind farm. At a cost in excess of $700 million, Cape Wind plans to spread 130 windmills, spaced a third to a half of a mile apart, across a shoal less than seven miles off the coast of Hyannis. Embedded in the ocean floor, each turbine would tower higher than the top of the Statue of Liberty's torch, its three 161-foot blades churning at 16 revolutions per minute. The wind forest promises to provide Cape Codders, on average, with 75 percent of their electricity, 1.8 percent of the total electrical needs of New England, without emitting a single microgram of greenhouse gases, carbon dioxide, nitrous oxide or mercury and without burning a single barrel of Middle Eastern oil.

The nation's leading environmental groups can barely control their enthusiasm. "We're bullish on wind," says Kert Davies, research director of Greenpeace USA. "Everybody has to ante up in the fight."

But like residents of dozens of communities where other wind-farm projects have been proposed, many Cape Codders have put aside their larger environmental sensitivities and are demanding that their home be exempt from such projects. As Cronkite puts it, "Our national treasures should be off limits to industrialization."

WIND IS THE WORLD'S fastest-growing energy resource, and after a decade of federal and state subsidies kick-starting the industry, creating enough power for more than a million American families in 27 states to tap into the breeze when they flick on their light switches. The country's oldest turbines have been part of the landscape on the Altamont Pass, east of San Francisco, for two decades. And Texans zooming along I-10 west to El Paso top a slight rise to the sight of a vast field of turbines stretching across the mesa. But energy providers in the Northeast, with its lack of wide open spaces, have long been consigned to dependence on oil, coal and natural gas, with only the occasional small-scale wind project.

Then Jim Gordon got restless. The president of Cape Wind, Gordon is a quixotic sort of energy executive. At the age of 22, he put aside his dream of becoming Francis Ford Coppola and instead started a small company that designed and installed heat-recovery systems for hospitals and factories. Ten years later, after a change in regulatory law opened a niche for independent power producers, he pioneered the building of natural-gas-generated electric plants in New England, a region long captive to highly polluting coal and oil.

Gordon eventually developed seven power plants throughout New England and became a very wealthy man. But with too much "creative juice," as he puts it, to rest on what he had already done, he went looking for the next challenge. Wind became his fixation.

"Imagine tapping into this inexhaustible supply of energy right here in our own state, lowering the cost of electricity, decreasing pollution, reducing reliance on foreign fuel," Gordon said recently as he paced his company's boardroom in downtown Boston. "We're feeding oil cartels whose whims move our economy and our armies. With wind, we can free ourselves from that."

In 1999, Gordon sold off his power plants. With a Department of Energy wind map in hand, he and his team began searching for a place to build dozens of technologically advanced turbines that would plug directly into the region's energy grid. If he had been building in the West, Gordon would have looked to the plains, what those in the wind industry call "the Saudi Arabia of wind." It being New England, he naturally looked to the mountains. But while the ridges of northern Maine offered plenty of gusts, he says, the transmission lines out of such underpopulated areas were already clogged. His eyes then fell on the sea.

Europeans had been constructing offshore wind farms for more than a decade. Just two miles outside of Copenhagen harbor, 20 turbines provide enough electricity for 32,000 homes. The British are developing more than a dozen wind projects in the Irish and North Seas. And a wind farm south of Dublin is expected to produce 10 percent of Ireland's electricity, reducing greenhouse gas emissions by 13 million tons per year.

"The Europeans are years ahead of us because they have had a consistent national policy to support wind power," Gordon said. Undaunted by the federal government's ambivalence toward alternative energy, Gordon sent his engineers out to find the perfect locale for a water-based wind farm. What they needed were fairly shallow waters, protection from the Atlantic's perfect storms, isolation from main shipping channels, easy access to the electrical grid and, of course, wind—an annual average of 18 miles per hour. The ideal spot, it turned out, is smack in the middle of Nantucket Sound, in the federal waters of Horseshoe Shoal, less than seven miles from the Kennedy compound.

CAPE CODDERS tend to be vain about their environmental sensitivities, so you would think they'd cheer the coming of alternative energy. But supporting the construction of dozens of towering turbines visible from their beaches, boats and waterfront homes is a very different thing from avoiding tern nesting grounds or attending a lecture on shoreline erosion. Even before Gordon finished his analysis of the shoal's sands, a forceful and well-connected army of opposition had formed.

Wayne Kurker, the owner of Hyannis Marina, set about issuing dire warnings of the "industrial park" being planned for the sound. When his neighbors ignored him, Kurker asked a graphic artist to create a mock-up of the proposed wind project and mailed it to thousands of boaters. His mantra was simple: "Windmills are probably great for the environment, but we shouldn't have to sacrifice the environment to build renewable energy."

Soon, the Alliance to Protect Nantucket Sound was filing lawsuits, mounting political pressure in Boston and Washington and, to bolster its legal case and maximize public anxiety, generating volumes of doomsaying critiques: The turbines will break up and the oil inside will spill into the sound, in a repeat of the Exxon Valdez disaster. Birds will be torn apart in "pole-mounted Cuisinarts." Whales will bump their heads. The annual Figawi race, the Memorial Day weekend Hyannis-to-Nantucket regatta, will have to be canceled. The pristine sound will become the world's 11th largest skyline, flashing 520 red and amber lights.

Representative William Delahunt spearheaded an effort to protect the sound by advocating that it be declared a national marine sanctuary. Robert F. Kennedy Jr. offered his name and voice to the struggle, despite the fact that the Natural Resources Defense Council, the environmental organization for which he is a senior attorney, is a strong advocate of offshore wind development. And the yacht-club set opened its checkbooks, donating money and stock to cover the $100,000-a-month bills for rent, three full-time salaries, television and radio time, two lobbyists and three law firms.

The alliance's legal strategists are basing their opposition to Cape Wind's proposal on what they say they believe is the absence of sufficient regulation of the private use of federal waters. "A for-profit company is taking advantage of a loophole in federal law," says Isaac Rosen, the Woody Allen-ish executive director of the alliance. "Developers cannot be allowed to swoop down, stick their shovels in the ground and claim a piece of the public waters for themselves. If they're allowed to do so, pretty soon we'll have liquid natural gas processing platforms in the sound, offshore casinos. It will be like the gold rush."

To bolster the legal struggle, Rosen also set about amassing a kind of Cape Cod-style Rainbow Coalition. He brought aboard commercial fishermen to decry the despoiling of their fishing grounds, motel owners worried about an eyesore that would send beachgoers north to Maine and boaters afraid that their small craft could crash up against the massive structures.

Environmentalists across the country chafe at what they see as the hypocrisy of those supposed Greens on the Cape who oppose the windmills. "The opponents of Cape Wind say they support renewable energy, but exactly what do they support?" asks Seth Kaplan of the Conservation Law Foundation, who admits he is more comfortable suing corporations than siding with them. "One or two turbines at town landfills? That's not going to solve global warming."

Kaplan, like many other environmental advocates, also challenges the alliance's penchant for overstatement:

whales will not be harmed, because their sonar allows them to avoid large objects; birds might be killed in the turbines, but at the rate of one or two per year; the turbines contain little oil, so a Valdez replay is impossible.

But nowhere has the alliance been more bitterly accused of peddling half-truths than in local environmental circles. "The sound is not pristine," says Matt Patrick, a member of the State Legislature whose support for the plan greatly compromised his re-election campaign. "You can't get to shore because it is lined with memorials to bad taste. Motorboats race around it, and if you go offshore in the summer, you look back and see yellow brown haze hanging over the mainland. And they make it sound as if Nantucket Sound will look like downtown New York, but the wind farm will be only a thumbnail on the horizon."

Dick Elrick, a Barnstable councilman who has been a ferryboat captain for two decades, is even angrier. "It's tough to listen to the same fishermen who have hurt the habitat by overdragging the bottom of the sound waving the flag of environmentalism," he says. "This isn't environmentalism; it's the not-in-my-backyard syndrome."

Walter Cronkite squirmed a bit at this characterization. "The problem really is Nimbyism," he admitted when I reached him by phone not long ago, "and it bothers me a great deal that I find myself in this position. I'm all for these factories, but there must be areas that are far less valuable than this place is." With prodding, he suggested the deserts of California. Then, perhaps realizing that might be a tad remote to serve New England's energy needs, he added, "Inland New England would substitute just as well."

As we talked, his discomfort was so keen that he interrupted his thought and pleaded, "Be kind to an old man," before summing up. "We have a lot of interesting wildlife, like porpoises and whales," he said. "It's a very important commercial fishing ground, and it's a marvelous boating area for recreational fishermen, for sailors. Last—but this is not inconsequential—it will be most unsightly for what is now open bay. Everybody will see it, anyone who wanders on the water, who has a home that faces the water."

This is a familiar refrain from wind-farm opponents across the country who insist on the intrinsic value of their neighborhoods. Activists in the mountains of Tennessee blocked the Tennessee Valley Authority from building 13 to 16 windmills on the ridgeline of Stone Mountain, despite the 33 metric tons of bomb-grade uranium that have been trucked in to nearby Erwin to power nuclear reactors. Their complaints? Up to 120 birds would be sucked into the turbines annually, and Weller's salamanders might be bombarded by spare electrons.

In Rosalia, Kan., residents pleaded the potential damage to native tall grass and the possible harm to the nesting grounds of prairie chickens. In Maine, hikers feared turbines would be within sight of a stretch of the Appalachian Trail. In rural Illinois, one farmer complained that it was "very annoying, seeing all this spinning around."

No matter how baseless the fears, everywhere the polemic is identical: we're not opposed to wind power, but this is not the right place.

"Traditionally, power plants were built in poor neighborhoods, so people living in nice neighborhoods weren't forced to confront the human cost of using electricity," said Greg Watson of the Massachusetts Technology Collaborative, an agency that administers Massachusetts's renewable energy trust. "But unlike coal, oil or natural gas, which you can truck, pipe or barge, Mother Nature dictates where you can locate a wind farm."

THIS IS NOT, like most anticorporate sagas, a David and Goliath tale. Despite the alliance's portrayal of Cape Wind as an "energy giant," nothing about Jim Gordon suggests evil capitalist or environmental rapist. During his 25 years in the energy business, he has never fallen afoul of the Environmental Protection Agency and has even won the admiration of notoriously feisty Greens. "Jim Gordon is the real thing," says Kert Davies of Greenpeace. "There aren't many entrepreneurs out there willing to take risks to clean up the environment."

The members of the alliance's board are similarly miscast in their self-assigned roles as small-town folk fighting corporate greed. Over the past several years, Wayne Kurker infuriated many Cape environmentalists when he expanded his Hyannis Marina by erecting corrugated metal hangars along the harbor. And the group's president, Doug Yearley, is a former C.E.O. of Phelps Dodge, one of the world's leading copper-mining companies. The alliance's lobbyist, John O'Brien, is a principal in a Boston firm that represents Exelon Generation, one of the largest fossil-fuel generating companies in the United States. Its Washington attorney is Guy Martin, a former assistant secretary of the interior. And, of course, there is the high-profile support of Robert Kennedy Jr.

'This is all about trade-offs,...' one environmentalist says. 'How heavily do you count yachting against the number of people who die from particulate matter?

"I am all for wind power," Kennedy insisted in a debate with Gordon on Boston's NPR affiliate. "The costs... on the people of this region are so huge,... the diminishment to property values, the diminishment to marinas, to businesses.... People go to the Cape because they want to connect themselves with the history and the culture. They want to see the same scenes the Pilgrims saw when they landed at Plymouth Rock." (It should be pointed out that the Pilgrims never saw Nantucket Sound, and if they had, they wouldn't have spied the Kennedy compound.)

Ultimately, though, the Kennedy that the alliance most wants on its side is Ted, but to date he has made only halting efforts on its behalf. It has managed to garner the support of Gov. Mitt Romney, and the state's attorney general, Tom Reilly, has also joined the antiwind brigade. But since Horseshoal Shoal is in federal waters, the state has little control, and opponents hold out scant hope that their junior senator, John Kerry, will lend them his aid. "Kerry's in a box," says Cliff Schechtman, editor of The Cape Cod Times. "He owns a house on Nantucket, but he's running for the presidency on a strong alternative energy platform." So they wait for Teddy to swoop in and introduce legislation that will bring Cape Wind's plans to a stop.

LIKE MANY SERIOUS environmentalists, Deborah Donovan of the Union of Concerned Scientists worries that the alliance's wish will come true and that Kennedy will intervene on its behalf. "Legislative intervention could go on and on every time there's a wind project that politically influential people don't like," she says. "I don't see how anybody would be willing to spend money on this industry."

Greenpeace's Davies suspects that might well be the alliance's real intention. "My gut reaction when I heard about them was that it was a front for the coal industry or some other power-industry sector that didn't want wind power to do well," he says. "And when I see who's on their board, I'm still not entirely sure. But I'm certain they're feeding the forces who want to discredit such technologies."

This sort of stance drives alliance supporters to distraction. "The others believe in green power above all," Yearley despairs. "I'm for trying to jump-start alternative energy, but we need to look at the costs. I don't know what the rush is. We're not going to solve global warming overnight."

The wind supporters at least agree with Yearley on one point: the struggle *is* ultimately about costs—it is about the costs of scattering turbines along ridgelines and sounds versus the costs of not doing so. To them, the national illusion that you can have electricity, clean air, a stable climate and independence from foreign oil without paying a steep price is ludicrous.

In fact, in late April, part of the price Cape Cod is already paying began washing up on its shores. En route to a power plant in Sandwich, on the northwest corner of the Cape, a leaking barge spilled 98,000 gallons of oil into Buzzards Bay. Shellfish beds were closed for a month. At least 370 birds died; 93 miles of coastline were tainted by thick globs of black oil.

"This is all about trade-offs," says Kaplan of the Conservation Law Foundation. "How much weight do you give aesthetics against the weight I give the reduction in CO_2? How heavily do you count yachting against the number of people who die from particulate matter? The opponents say they support renewable energy. But it's not acceptable to say that you're in favor of renewable energy only as long as you can't see it."

Kert Davies agrees. "It feels strange for Greenpeace to be fighting a grass-roots group," he says. "And it's sad for me to be arguing against the Kennedys, the only liberals left, and Cronkite, who is everybody's grandfather. But we, as environmental advocates, have to be consistent, and that includes the Kennedys and Cronkite. It's not fair to stump about how scary global warming is one week, then oppose this the next. It's not fair, in terms of environmental justice, for communities with cash to demand that projects they don't want be built somewhere else."

Elinor Burkett is the author of the coming book, "So Many Enemies, So Little Time: An American Woman in All the Wrong Places."

From the *New York Times* Magazine, June 15, 2003, pp. 48-51.

ANALYSIS

Like go-go 1990s, Smart Growth's time had passed

By Jonathan Osborne and Stephen Scheibal
AMERICAN-STATESMAN STAFF

In the end, Smart Growth passed away peacefully, and mostly unnoticed by the crowds that gathered earlier this month at City Hall. There were no tears; there were no eulogies.

And a City Council that once embraced Smart Growth so warmly in its infancy, essentially ushered it out of existence with a quick, unanimous vote, preceded by little substantive discussion.

In its final days, Smart Growth—an environmental development policy born in the late 1990s that, wrongly or rightly, came to mean so much more—had become a political scratching post within the city limits.

By the time the economy faltered, it had turned into a four-letter word—one that was used by those cursing everything from the loss of Liberty Lunch to the abandoned Intel Corp. project.

"You had people who were opposed to growth blaming Smart Growth, and you had people opposed to government intervention blaming Smart Growth," Mayor Will Wynn said. "It became very frustrating."

Yet in reality, Smart Growth was really nothing more than a product of its time.

The Smart Growth matrix, a system that awarded points and dollars to projects with certain desired elements, was never intended to do much more than lure developers from the suburbs and tempt them to build pedestrian-friendly projects with upfront fee waivers and cost reimbursements.

And at the very least, it played a part in doing so, though the role was probably relatively small next to an economic boom that brought almost 200,000 people to Austin in the 1990s.

About $500 million worth of development that is either finished, under construction or planned in downtown was aided by roughly $5 million in Smart Growth incentives—an amount the city should recoup through added value on the property tax roll alone in about five years.

The result is 1,275 new residences, and more than 1.2 million square feet of space for offices, shops and restaurants.

The Smart Growth philosophy also was applied to specific projects, including the Computer Science Corp. buildings and the Frost Bank tower, currently under construction at Fourth Street and Congress Avenue.

The Downtown Austin Alliance has even nominated the Smart Growth initiative for an international urban planning award, saying the program "served as a model for other cities and merits the highest recognition."

Nevertheless, the City Council undid the program at a meeting on June 12 and replaced it with a far more extensive economic development policy that will in part allow for incentive packages larger than could ever be awarded under Smart Growth. Although city leaders say the new policy incorporates many of the tenets of Smart Growth, they generally avoid those exact words.

"I think the phrase is tainted," said Austan Librach, head of the city's transportation, planning and sustainability department. "If nothing else, we should change the name and move on."

Better or worse?

Opinions about Smart Growth depend on whom you ask and what they remember about the late 1990s boom.

Most narrowly, Smart Growth stands for the fee waivers and utility reimbursements that the city used to lure developers downtown. Such incentives kept companies out of environmentally sensitive areas in Southwest Austin. They also paid for wider sidewalks, street-level shopping and other design details that would make downtown Austin a more pleasant place to work, to visit and—leaders hoped—to live.

"Smart Growth was introduced at a time when many believed we were having uncontrollable growth that wasn't conducive to keeping Austin Austin," said former Mayor Kirk Watson, who launched the program shortly after his election in 1997. "What Smart Growth was intended to do was to help us manage that growth."

Smart Growth was also an umbrella term that provided cover for a number of miscellaneous development initiatives.

It was the Computer Sciences Corp. deal that brought the company downtown and underwrote the new City Hall. It was Intel abandoning its habit of building in the suburbs with a new office

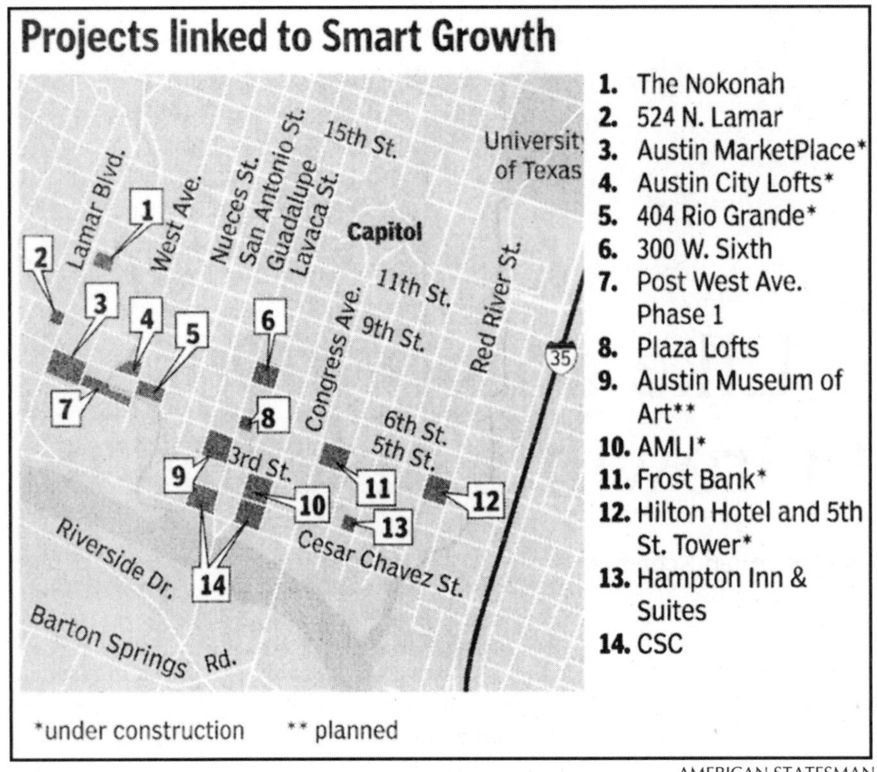

AMERICAN STATESMAN

building near the CSC blocks. It was the new art museum, new apartment buildings, new shops, new people—a dizzying array of novelty in what for years had been a largely derelict area.

"It was meant from the beginning to be lots of different kinds of things," Librach said. "The community thought of every effort to do something downtown as part of Smart Growth."

And it was, particularly toward the end, a catch-all lightning rod for Austinites who were disoriented and angry about the way their city was changing.

The concern began in neighborhoods, where some vocal residents feared they would trade peace and privacy for traffic and cramped quarters. It spread as the Liberty Lunch music club, Congress Avenue Booksellers, Waterloo Brewing Co. and other local institutions—for whatever reason—began to disappear.

Complaints hit a fever pitch as the boom economy collapsed. The Intel building sat unfinished and up for sale. CSC looked for tenants to fill its second downtown office building and scuttled plans for a third.

Opponents would point to the city money provided to the companies, lingering landmarks of failure such as the Intel skeleton, the defaced or vanished buildings where people used to drink beer or listen to music, and the general malaise running through an area that months before had seemed brimming with electric promise.

It all fit under the derisive, bitterly ironic heading of Smart Growth.

"People thought Smart Growth meant neighborhood sidewalks, transit-oriented development and a more livable community, but instead we got multimillion-dollar corporate subsidies and half-built or never-built buildings," said Mike Blizzard, a political consultant and an early critic of the subsidies initiative. "It was a PR disaster almost from the get-go, and I think people associate it far more with what we lost…than with whatever we may have gained."

Gains and losses

In reality, the city gained far more than it lost during the Smart Growth era.

But the degree to which Smart Growth played a role in those boom-time successes is equally up for debate.

"CSC's buildings are up and built and beautiful, a lot of CSC people are downtown, and the other projects that did receive Smart Growth incentives are exemplary projects," said Charlie Betts, executive director of the Downtown Austin Alliance. "Although you cannot unequivocally say that without those incentives none of those projects would have been built, the incentives were a factor and were a significant factor."

It's worth noting that the Smart Growth matrix was not actually used for the incentive packages that led to the Smart Growth-minded CSC buildings, a $64 million private investment or the Frost Bank project, which represents about $100 million in private investment. The Frost Bank building received a little more than $1 million in incentives, while CSC received about $10 million.

The seven Smart Growth matrix projects that are completed include the Nokonah Condominiums, the Plaza Lofts and the CarrAmerica building at 300 W. Sixth St. Together, those seven projects represent $219 million in private investment that received nearly $2.5 million in incentives.

"That's pretty effective leveraging," Betts said. This month, the council unanimously approved what are likely to be the last of the Smart Growth incentives, reimbursing and waiving fees for those existing projects and one new one, the Pedernales Live-Work project on East Sixth Street. Aside from a greater focus on creating jobs rather than placing buildings, the biggest difference between the old incentive system and the proposed new economic development policy is that developments would receive city money only after they are open and generating tax dollars.

The first example of the new policy in action came May 15 when the council approved a 20-year, $37 million investment in the Domain, a proposed North Austin urban village. It was the city's largest incentive package in five years and one that represents far more money than was ever waived through Smart Growth.

Watson said Smart Growth was always meant to change as the city changed. He sees the new policy as a reflection of the city's current economic trouble and an extension of Smart Growth principles: to enhance the economy while protecting the environment, avoiding the legal and legislative disputes that marked city politics through most of the 1990s.

"Think of the difference in our downtown now as opposed to 1996," the former mayor said. "The good news is even in a downturn economy, we set the foundation that allows this council to start dealing with it in different ways."

But even if Smart Growth principles remain for the foreseeable future, the name is history. Wynn, who was sworn in as mayor last week, will praise Smart Growth if asked, but he'd rather simply bury it.

"Politically," he said, Smart Growth's "shelf life clearly has expired."

---

josborne@statesman.com; 445-3621
sscheibal@statesman.com; 445-3819

Tucson Fire Department's MMRS Exercise: A Bioterrorism Response Plan

Les Caid

On September 11, 2001, life changed not only for the nation but also specifically for the United States' fire services. Amid the chaos of the aftermath of the attack, fire departments across the country started to take stock of their own capabilities, recognizing that the nation's firefighters and police would be the real first responders to any act of terrorism. Further examination by public safety departments found that they might be woefully unprepared to face large-scale acts of domestic terrorism.

With local government budgets being tightened, fire departments also are strained as they attempt to purchase chemical and biological detection equipment and pay for additional hazardous-material response training to meet potential threats. Systems must be built, and multiple agencies must coordinate, train, and drill together to enhance a community's ability to handle a surge of hospitalized patients or of victims who need decontamination or chemical-exposure antidotes and pharmaceuticals.

There is no institutional solution to this threat from weapons of mass destruction (WMD). Yet the need for multiple-agency coordination has never been more evident, and while still the responsibility of fire and policy, an adequate response can no longer be relegated just to public safety personnel. Local government capabilities, critical infrastructure protection needs, and available community resources all must be identified, with a particular emphasis on the ability to set up "command and control" through the incident command system (ICS).

To accomplish this, the Tucson, Arizona, Fire Department/Metropolitan Medical Response System (MMRS) brought together a multitude of organizations in November 2002 for a conference and training exercise. This exercise—entitled the Tucson Metropolitan Medical Response System Bioterrorism, National Pharmaceutical Stockpile, and Mass-Dispensing Site Conference and Statewide Exercise—drew more than 500 attendees from among fire departments, police agencies, physicians, pharmacists, private citizens, and private sector businesses across the nation.

Attendees came from as far away as Hawaii and even the former Soviet republic of Kazakhstan to view this exercise. Agencies involved included the U.S. Centers for Disease Control and Prevention; U.S. Public Health Service; Arizona's state and local emergency-management organizations; and state and local health department officials.

Tucson's exercise was the nation's first large-scale test of a community's ability to receive and mass-dispense federally supplied emergency medication in a bioterrorist attack.

The primary organizer and sponsor was Tucson Fire/MMRS, which is under the direction of the United States Public Health Service, Office of Emergency Response. Tucson is one of the 120 federally funded cities with an MMRS, which is focused primarily on bolstering local response to a disaster for the first 48 to 72 hours, before federal disaster assistance can arrive locally.

Tucson's exercise was the nation's first large-scale test of a community's ability to receive and mass-dispense federally supplied emergency medication in a bioterrorist attack.

Opening the conference was the U.S. Surgeon General Richard H. Carmona, who helped formulate Tucson's terrorism early-preparedness efforts when he was a local trauma surgeon and public hospital administrator. Presentations profiling biological weapons, given on the first day, also outlined both the state and federal government's roles in responding to bioterrorism events; after the presentations, a fictional bioterrorism scenario was described, and the exercise itself began.

What Took Place

The exercise scenario was based both on a covert release of a biological agent in the Phoenix Valley city of Mesa and on an intentional release of anthrax spores at a Tucson hotel and convention center that had contaminated hundreds of people. Combined, these two theoretical events would use up all local, regional, and state resources and require the governor to activate the Federal Response Plan (FRP) to bring the CDC's Strategic National Stockpile (formally known as the National Pharmaceutical Stockpile) to Tucson.

Once notified, the CDC would send the 94,000 pounds of supplies, called a "push package," to a local site that could land a 747 airliner. The push package requires a secure 10,000-square-foot warehouse space and a trained local team to off-load and receive, store, and stage (RSS) all that comes with it. The goal of the RSS team is to set up a sort of super-drugstore that would receive orders and distribute emergency pharmaceuticals and medical supplies to dispensing sites at the affected areas(s).[1]

In this exercise, much as in a real situation, there had to be synchronization of all agencies within the community. As the RSS function is being completed, mass-dispensing sites must be set up throughout a community or state to administer or give out antibiotics to prevent victims exposed to bio-agents (in this scenario, anthrax) from developing infections.

Tucson used volunteers from the Medical Reserve Corps (a part of the citizen corps) to fill logistical positions at mass-dispensing sites. The local emergency operations centers (EOCs) had to coordinate efforts with the state EOC to discern where these pharmaceuticals or other medical supplies were needed. Local officials working within a unified command were asked to coordinate transportation routes for vaccines, blood, or other resources needed, to ensure that delivery was not disrupted. (Security, of course, will always be a major challenge to those emergency managers and other officials who must coordinate these efforts.)

In Tucson, the 162nd Fighter Wing of the Arizona Air National Guard wrote the RSS plan for the Tucson Fire/MMRS and also performed the RSS function. Its members also were assigned the task of organizing a clinic to educate conference attendees on what they would need to do to mirror the RSS function plan in their own local jurisdictions.

In the scenario, once communications had been set up, the RSS function started to receive requests for pharmaceuticals from across the state. The city of Mesa's Fire Department/MMRS, via the Maricopa County Health Department, requested thousands of packages containing hermetically sealed bottles of amoxicillin, doxycycline, and the ciprofloxacin (Cipro), needed at the mass-dispensing sites in both Mesa and Tucson. Mesa's fire department gave more than 3,000 high school students real tetanus titers as a test to help project the real numbers of vaccines that could be given at mass vaccination clinics in an actual emergency.

On the third day, the exercise concluded with a mass medication-dispensing clinic organized and operated by the Pima County Health Department. Held in a 60,000-square-foot arena in the Tucson Convention Center, the clinic focused on registering and screening victims so that they would receive the proper medicines.

Remote pickup sites for the transportation of patients were set up in various quadrants of the city in an attempt to prevent a traffic bottleneck near the dispensing clinic. Tucson's department of transportation provided buses. These sites worked effectively, even though, for security considerations, the required law-enforcement personnel had to be in place to provide security screening of personnel heading to the dispensing clinic. Providing personnel protection equipment for the drivers of these buses is a consideration that cannot be ignored.

Proving that this was a true community effort, the "victims" were drawn from hundreds of volunteers from metropolitan Tucson and were organized by the Volunteer Center of Tucson. Playing the roles of injured patients and the "worried well," volunteers of all ages were processed through the mass clinic. Also part of the exercise was the collection of the victims' personal data so that health authorities could later contact them to follow their progress.

Although too many exercise sponsors and partners took part to note them all in this article, Tucson must pay homage to the members of the MMRS Pharmacy Task Force. Headed by University of Arizona Professor Theodore Tong, a pharmacy doctor, the task force established professional links between pharmacists in the private and public sectors. The task force is a coalition of representatives of pharmacies in retail drugstore chains, public and private hospitals, and health care providers. The county health department also provided training to local pharmacy technicians and pharmacology students.

Dr. Tong's group devised educational guidelines for the pharmacists to prepare them for their roles in the event of a true emergency requiring them to work at a mass-dispensing site. More than 175 such practitioners volunteered and were trained before the exercise. These pharmacists and other professionals were available at the dispensing site to consult on such questions as side effects, drug interactions, and adult versus child doses. Relevant orientation of these pharmacy professionals must be a priority in planning efforts for this kind of response.

Although the health officials' goal was to process 1,000 people during the six-hour mass-dispensing clinic, they met and far exceeded this aim by processing 2,015 "patients." Afterward, Dr. Elizabeth MacNeil, chief medical officer of the Pima County Health Department, noted that, based on her observations, the site could safely and effectively have served 10,000 people in the six-hour period of the exercise.

Overall, the conference and exercise accomplished the majority of Tucson's established objectives. Exercises and drills, however, will always lack the anxious edge that real-life emergencies present for the responder and for emergency managers. This is one component of real-life response that can never be duplicated in an exercise. But we all really do "play as we practice," and local agencies must all practice together.

Tucson Fire/MMRS brought together slightly fewer than 20 agencies, from all levels of government, for this exercise. Each one of these agencies had an opportunity to dust off its plans and do the critical "gap analysis" that should be the end-product of any exercise.

When asked his impressions, U.S. Surgeon General Carmona, who was an active participant in the drill, noted, "We are far more prepared today than we were on 9/11. Are we where we want to be yet [in terms of preparedness]? Probably not. But I think we're going to be better every day, and it's these kinds of conferences, communications, and exchanges of ideas that are going to build that capacity in any community."

Since 2002, Tucson Fire/MMRS has presented three conferences and multiple exercises in the city. As the fire service knows, the process of achieving preparedness is a dynamic progression that can never stop. There is no single institutional solution to the need for preparedness, and communities must work together for the common purpose of getting ready at the local level.

Lessons Learned

Here are some comments and observations on emergency preparedness that were reported by participants in and observers of the exercise:

It's all about relationships. Our daily lives are all about relationships. It established relationships among the federal, regional, state, and local levels that will no doubt lead to better communications and coordination in future exercises and, if necessary, in a real-life disaster. The respect and trust that all participants feel for each other assures them that, if necessary, all partners can and will perform their assigned functions.

Interoperability of communications remains the biggest challenge facing all response agencies. With each local government's public safety agency using a different radio frequency, and with surrounding agencies using yet others, there will be communication problems. The federal government must start to help fund communication infrastructure for local, state, and regional systems that will allow interoperability of responding agencies' communications.

Members of the media, as well as public information officers, must be educated on their roles and responsibilities during a disaster. The media have a responsibility to report the facts and keep from reporting random hearsay, which will only increase citizens' fears. Relationships must be forged with the media to establish ground rules. Communities themselves face the same challenge of providing solid information to the public. Before Tucson's exercise, public information officers from across the state were assembled in Tucson to educate them on their roles in a joint information center (JIC). If mixed messages, instead of one voice, are sent to the public during a disaster, you will quickly lose the public's attention, and create more anxiety or panic.

Tucson had to go through a rigorous evaluation process by the CDC even to be considered as a training site with training, education, and disbursement delivery. Training and educating all those who will be needed for a WMD event is a must. In reality, public safety officials will be on the front lines of any attack, whether terrorism or a natural disaster, so training of all first responders is a no-brainer.

The exercise scenario was based both on a covert release of a biological agent in the Phoenix Valley city of Mesa and on an intentional release of anthrax spores at a Tucson hotel and convention center that had contaminated hundreds of people.

Funding this training is another matter. But a sense of the potential scope of a WMD event is necessary to inspire the realization that educating an entire community and all agencies for such violent acts is essential. Citizens must all learn more about what is in place that will help them, should such an event take place.

Toward this end, in 1999, Tucson Fire/MMRS forged a partnership with Pima Community College's Public Safety Emergency Services Institute to write a curriculum and start more than 30 classes on four different tracks that Tucson has offered free to the community, public safety workers, and health care providers. As of this year, the city has trained more than 5,000 people in the Tucson metro area through these classes.

Public health departments must reestablish surveillance and reporting systems that have been ignored

over the past few decades but now are a necessity to act as "sentinels" for early detection and notification of bioterrorism events. One of the real dangers of bioterrorism is that it is a quiet weapon because it can be released covertly and cause damage before health authorities realize there has even been an attack. Potential bioterrorism agents include smallpox, anthrax, tularemia, and botulinum toxin. Communities must ensure that hospital workers (doctors, nurses, and infection-control staff) and public safety personnel are trained in awareness, as well as in the signs and symptoms of illness caused by WMD agents.

The incident command system (ICS) must be used for command and control purposes and taught to all agencies. This effective system has proven its worth for almost 30 years to fire services and law enforcement agencies. People who do not normally use ICS must learn that it is an extremely disciplined system. Because it was being employed for the first time by several agencies during Tucson's exercise and RSS function drill, those agencies' command personnel often strayed from the command post to view what was going on in the warehouse. These individuals often were missing when critical decisions had to be made by the unified command.

The new ICS students learned that they must stay together at the command post to ensure proper communications and thus maintain command and control during an emergency. ICS must be practiced by all communities and allow a seamless plug-in to the federal assets available through the Federal Response Plan.

Note

1. Although the real National Pharmaceutical Stockpile "push package" is 94,000 pounds of equipment, the CDC has made available for local community exercises a six-ton training, education, and disbursement (TED) package. The antibiotics used in the Tucson exercise were all part of the TED package, which, though a fraction of the size of an actual "push package," still allowed Tucson to set up the massive "drugstore" from which the mass-dispensing site received its pharmaceuticals.

The push package's wide array of antibiotics, vaccines, antidotes, and medical equipment and supplies takes almost 30 minutes per 18-wheeler to unload by forklift, although a community can cut the time to 10 minutes per truck if a truckwell or loading dock is used.

Les Caid is deputy chief in charge of disaster preparedness for the Tucson, Arizona, Fire Department and project manager for the Tucson Metropolitan Medical Response System (lcaid1@ci.tucson.az.su).

How to Make Transit-Oriented Development Work

Number one: Put the transit back.

By Jeffrey Tumlin and Adam Millard-Ball

Even a cursory glance around the country suggests that transit-oriented development is hot; new TODs are on the drawing boards everywhere, from Alaska to Florida. Its advocates tout benefits ranging from more compact development and less automobile dependence to new retail opportunities and improved quality of life.

But the same quick survey raises some basic questions about just how fundamentally different many TODs are from their auto-oriented counterparts. We now have "transit-oriented" big box stores and single-story office parks, set in seas of parking. In many cases, developments with just six housing units to the acre are being advertised as TODs.

"The amount of hype around TOD far exceeds the progress to date, with many transit proponents selling new transit investments on the basis of land-use changes yet to come," writes Hank Dittmar, president of the Great American Station Foundation, in a forward to a discussion paper prepared for the foundation and the Brookings Institution Center on Urban and Metropolitan Policy.

Most often, he continues, "TODs have conventional suburban single use development patterns, with conventional parking requirements, so that the development is actually transit-*adjacent*, not transit-*oriented*."

Instead of branding anything that is built near transit a successful TOD, Dena Belzer and Gerald Autler of Strategic Economics, the principal authors of the paper, suggest that projects should be judged against specific desired outcomes:

Those outcomes include choice (for example, diverse housing and transportation); livability (less pollution per capita); and financial return (for instance, to developers and transit agencies).

First on the list

What can planners do to ensure that TODs actually achieve these outcomes? Robert Cervero, a professor of city planning at the University of California, Berkeley, talks about what he calls the 3Ds, or three dimensions (density, design, and diversity) that are needed for a TOD to work. Of these, says Tom Margro, general manager of the San Francisco Bay Area's BART system, the first is most important. "From the point of view of a transit agency, density is paramount." he says.

In fact, density is a key criterion in the new BART system expansion policy, which was adopted last December. "We're being courted by cities that want BART extensions," says Margro. "The policy helps us reward those communities that make the zoning and land-use changes that we're looking for."

Density is partly a matter of geometry. All else being equal, the more housing and jobs within a short walk of a transit station, the greater the ridership. Nationally, a 10 percent increase in population density has been shown to correspond to a five percent increase in boardings, while doubling density can reduce vehicle travel by 20 percent, according to a 1996 report published by the Transit Cooperative Research Program.

Density has even farther reaching implications. Residents of denser communities are more likely to be able to walk to shops and services and thus to be able to live with just one car—or with none. According to research conducted for Fannie Mae's Location Efficient Mortgage program, vehicle ownership falls rapidly as density increases, reaching an average of just one car per household when density climbs to 20 to 30 housing units per acre.

Many of the best-performing TODs—such as those around Metro stations in Arlington County, Virginia—focus high density immediately around the station.

The Car-Sharing Solution

A promising new addition to the transit-oriented development armory is car sharing. Members of car-sharing programs have access to a fleet of vehicles on a per-use basis, allowing them to live without a second or third car—or to do without a car altogether. In turn, developments need less parking, allowing increased densities and bringing down the cost of housing.

"Car sharing is one of the most practical ways to reduce vehicle ownership," says Gabriel Metcalf, deputy director of the nonprofit San Francisco Planning and Urban Research Association, and chair of City CarShare. "We're not telling people they have to give up their cars," he says. "We recognize that a car is essential for many trips. We're giving them an attractive alternative."

According to Metcalf, surveys show that each City CarShare vehicle takes five to six privately owned vehicles off the road, as members sell or scrap their cars after joining.

CarShare joins forces with Bay Area developers to win approval for reduced parking. The group has negotiated agreements with developers and the city planning department for more than a dozen developments, totaling more than 3,000 units that have been built or approved in San Francisco. A recent approval: a 98-unit affordable housing complex on Folsom Street that will provide just 16 parking spaces. More projects are under way in Oakland, Berkeley, and San Jose, says Metcalf.

According to the San Francisco planning department, the city is now seeking to amend its zoning code to support the development of car-sharing programs, through reductions in minimum parking requirements, and exemptions from planned impact fees and parking maximums for car-sharing spaces.

Adam Millard-Ball

Building height drops rapidly and housing forms change from attached to detached as they approach the existing single-family neighborhoods that surround many of these stations.

The same pattern is seen at the newly built King Farm development in Maryland, close to the Shady Grove Metro station. "We have a gradient away from the village center and a potential future light rail stop," says Neal Payton, director of town planning at Torti Gallas & Partners in Silver Spring, the architecture firm responsible for the King Farm town plan.

"At the center, we have the greatest mix of uses and the highest densities, with town houses and single-family houses appearing as one moves away from the center," he says.

Mixing it up

Not all land uses are equal when it comes to generating transit ridership. Office or retail development tends to employ more workers and thus to produce more riders than industrial uses, for instance.

A less obvious example is affordable housing. Since low-income households tend to own fewer cars and are more likely to use transit, an affordable housing component of a transit-oriented development can add more riders, as well as furthering other public policy objectives.

Is It Really TOD?

What's the difference between a true transit-oriented development, which will deliver promised social and economic benefits, and a transit-adjacent development? A true TOD will include most of the following:

- The transit-oriented development lies within a five-minute walk of the transit stop, or about a quarter-mile from stop to edge. For major stations offering access to frequent high-speed service this catchment area may be extended to the measure of a 10-minute walk.
- A balanced mix of uses generates 24-hour ridership. There are places to work, to live, to learn, to relax and to shop for daily needs.
- A place-based zoning code generates buildings that shape and define memorable streets, squares, and plazas, while allowing uses to change easily over time.
- The average block perimeter is limited to no more than 1,350 feet. This generates a fine-grained network of streets, dispersing traffic and allowing for the creation of quiet and intimate thoroughfares.
- Minimum parking requirements are abolished.
- Maximum parking requirements are instituted: For every 1,000 workers, no more than 500 spaces and as few as 10 spaces are provided.
- Parking costs are "unbundled," and full market rates are charged for all parking spaces. The exception may be validated parking for shoppers.
- Major stops provide BikeStations, offering free attended bicycle parking, repairs, and rentals. At minor stops, secure and fully enclosed bicycle parking is provided.
- Transit service is fast, frequent, reliable, and comfortable, with a headway of 15 minutes or less.
- Roadway space is allocated and traffic signals timed primarily for the convenience of walkers and cyclists.
- Automobile level-of-service standards are met through congestion pricing measures, or disregarded entirely.
- Traffic is calmed, with roads designed to limit speed to 30 mph on major streets and 20 mph on lesser streets.

Patrick Siegman
Siegman is a principal associate with Nelson\Nygaard in San Francisco.

A case in point is Alma Place in Palo Alto, California, where peak-hour parking demand has been measured at just four-tenths of a parking space per unit, even though parking is free. The location of this affordable housing development, just two blocks from the Caltrain commuter rail station in downtown Palo Alto, allowed many residents to sell their cars altogether.

It is mixed use ("diversity" on Robert Cervero's 3D list), however, that has demonstrated some of the highest ridership gains. Dennis Leach, a consultant with the firm of TransManagement is currently researching the performance of TODs in the Washington, D.C., region. "Mixed use is where you get the real payoff in reduced vehicle trips," he says. "It allows residents to walk to shops and services, and it allows employees to take transit to work, since they can do without a car during the day."

TOD Is Working in Suburban D.C.

Readers of *Planning* are surely familiar by now with Arlington County's award-winning efforts to manage growth and encourage transit-oriented development. Less well-known is a recent initiative aimed at making walking in the county's urbanized areas a practical and pleasurable alternative.

Once-rural Arlington has grown rapidly since the late 1960s, with most of the new development centered on the four-mile-long, half-mile-wide Rosslyn-Ballston Corridor. Today, the urbanized strip encompasses over 18.3 million square feet of office space, 3.4 million square feet of retail and commercial space, 3,000 hotel rooms, and 22,500 residential units.

In the early 1970s, county officials made a momentous decision to focus new commercial development in the corridor around five below-ground stations planned as part of the Metro, the Washington area's subway and elevated system. By the time Metro opened in 1979, the county had established a broad set of regulations to guide the shape and form of this development. The plan called for centering the highest density within a quarter-mile of the stations.

Ten years later, when the corridor was half-developed, the county board asked for a "mid-course review" to guide remaining projects. The review made clear that streetscape improvements were needed if the original goal of a walkable urbanized area was to be realized. Arlington's 1997 Pedestrial Transportation Plan picked up on one idea developed in the mid-course review: a landscaped pedestrial walkway along half the corridor, from Ballston and Clarendon. Tom Korns, an Arlington planning commissioner, promoted the concept of an "Arlington Greenway" that would extend the full length of the corridor.

The idea took root when county arts staff, working with the Arlington Commission for the Arts, recognized that it would provide an ideal outlet for developers to incorporate public art and public space into their projects. (Such enhancements are often negotiated during site plan negotiations.) In 1999, a core group of county staff and citizens was formed, and consultants Jennifer McGregor and Todd Bressi were hired to study the idea.

A community design charrette involving more than 100 citizens and officials produced a far more encompassing strategy: a network of walkable streets rather than a fixed greenway. The WALKArlington initiative is the result. It calls for the creation of a variety of pedestrian environments, including civic squares, performance spaces, play areas, and neighborhood gardens—all connected to the county's bike and walking trails.

To implement the initiative the county engaged a project manager and a resident urban designer. Working with the divisions of Cultural Affairs and Public Works, they have started a pilot project for the Ballston Sector of the corridor. Its major goals are to build a sense of place through innovative design and to invigorate the pedestrial environment.

Charles Zucker

Zucker is director of planning for Lee & Associates in Washington, D.C., and WALKArlington's Urban Designer in Residence.

In addition, says Leach, mandating or encouraging mixed use helps to avoid a dull monoculture. "Very high land costs tend to push a single use, such as offices," he notes. "That makes for a dead downtown" at night and on the weekends.

Managing demand

Even the densest mixed-use developments will have only a limited impact if financial incentives discourage residents and employees from taking transit. To achieve the greatest success in reducing vehicle trips, projects need to encompass TOD + TDM, that is, both transit-oriented development and transportation-demand management.

Perhaps the most critical element of a TDM package is parking management. After all, unlimited free (to the user, but not the transit agency) parking is one of the biggest incentives to drive, and also encourages people to own a vehicle in the first place. Conversely, research by UCLA urban planning professor Donald Shoup has shown that ending parking subsidies is an effective way to get people out of their cars, reducing vehicle trips by an average of 25 percent.

Another demand management strategy, used to great effect in Portland, Oregon; Boulder, Colorado; and Santa Clara County, California, is to provide free or discounted transit passes for residents and employees. In 1997, Shoup reported on a survey of Silicon Valley companies that gave their employees Eco-Passes, good for unlimited rides on the Santa Clara Valley buses and light rail. Employee parking demand at these work sites declined by about 19 percent as transit ridership swelled.

Increasingly, parking management strategies are being incorporated into TOD plans from the outset. At San Francisco's Balboa Park BART station, for example, the city's draft neighborhood plan proposes that new development on city-owned land be required to "unbundle" the cost of parking from rents.

"Currently most new ownership housing and some new rental housing has parking included in the base price of a unit," the plan says. "Individuals and families who do not own or may not need a car must pay for the space anyway, needlessly driving up the cost of their housing."

Considering TDM, and particularly parking management, in the earliest stage of planning lets its benefits affect a development's design and allows less parking to be provided. Moreover, if fewer vehicle trips are expected, streets can be designed for lower traffic volume, helping to improve the pedestrian environment.

"TDM is often used as a mitigation strategy," notes Peter Albert, station-area planning manager for BART. "Neighbors and others always use parking as a reason to kill a project. TDM can give local planning commissioners the elbow room to approve a project with less parking."

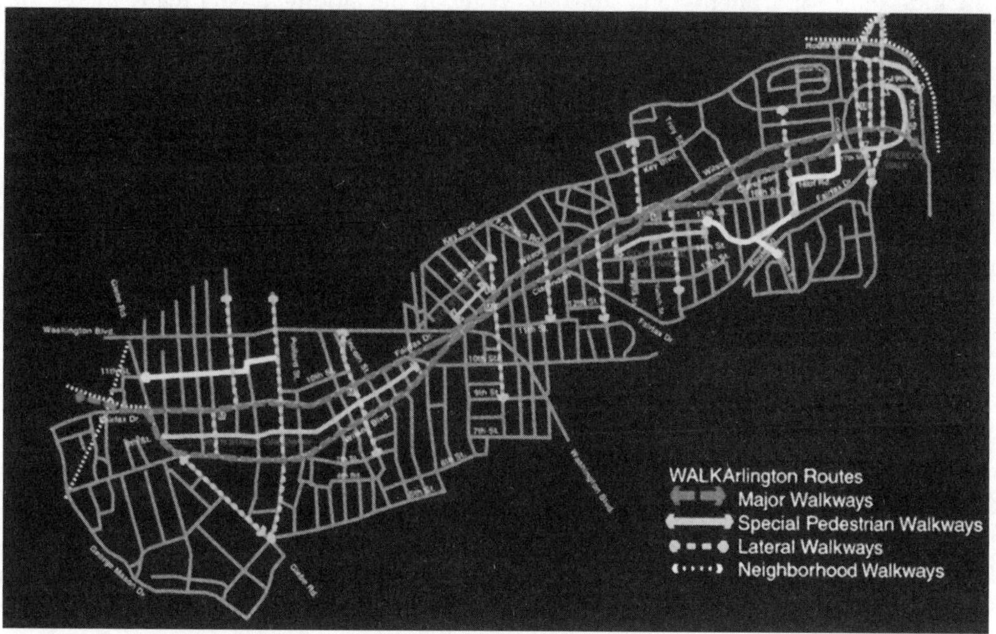

Pedestrian routes proposed by WALKArlington for the Rosslyn-Baltimore corridor.

'Don't even think of parking here'

In the end, TOD and parking are inextricably entwined. "If the parking requirement doesn't reflect the transit resource, it's not TOD," says Albert. "It's just development close to a transit station." Most conventional development, after all, uses parking ratios derived from suburbs that have little or no transit and where everyone is assumed to have a car.

Building projects with reduced parking is another matter. Larger projects are often constrained by the attitudes of developers and lenders. Nevertheless, an increasing number of small-scale developments are selling well with little or no parking. Examples include the 91-unit Gaia Building in Berkeley, California, and the Seaboard Building, where offices have been converted to apartments in Seattle's Westlake Mall.

"In almost every case, parking requirements aren't an issue with local jurisdictions," says architect Neal Payton. "They're willing to provide less parking." Developers are more hesitant. "They don't want to risk not being able to rent a unit because there isn't enough parking."

Transit agencies themselves are often a source of pressure to provide more parking, in the form of heavily subsidized commuter parking for their riders. The surface parking lots owned or leased by these agencies are often a source of conflict. On the one hand, they're prime sites for transit-oriented development. However, the transit agencies often insist that any spaces lost must be fully replaced as part of the project.

"The ability of the market to support development that includes 100 percent replacement parking, with no revenue to support that parking, has been a huge hurdle to TOD," says Peter Albert. BART is now beginning to charge for reserved spaces at many stations, where before virtually all parking was free. The new revenue may be helpful in supporting the construction of parking structures to replace the lots, he suggests.

In other parts of the country, agencies are moving away from a strict one-to-one replacement policy. In the D.C., region, WMATA's Joint Development Policies and Guidelines, revised last year, now allow projects to be approved with less than full replacement parking. In some cases, the agency is even authorized to cover part of the cost of parking garages.

Such a policy makes sense from the point of view of increasing ridership and revenue for transit agencies, as well as promoting TOD. After all, an acre of dense, mixed-use development is likely to generate more transit trips than an acre of surface parking. More important, TOD helps to spread ridership more evenly throughout the day, compared to peak-oriented park-and-ride lots. That's a major concern for agencies facing crushing peak-hour loads.

Looking good

Even better is a transportation-demand policy that invests in alternatives. Pedestrian improvements, bicycle paths, and feeder transit often provide more bang-for-the-buck than parking.

Even with the best of management, however, most TODs still require huge amounts of parking, either in lots or structures. The question then becomes, how can planners reduce its impact?

Neal Payton sees ground-floor uses as key to reducing the impact of parking structures. At Harrison Commons,a planned TOD in Harrison, New Jersey, Payton's firm designed a 2,500-space garage that will accommodate commuters on the PATH commuter rail line. The development will include 3,000 apartments and 100,000 square feet of retail.

The garage will be wrapped on three sides with narrow "liner buildings" containing loft apartments above convenience retail. "You won't be able to see the garage from the street," he says.

In California, liner buildings will wrap around both existing and new garages at Bay Area Rapid Transit's Pleasant Hill station. The garages are part of a transit-oriented development designed by Lennertz, Coyle & Associates of Portland, Oregon.

The location of the parking facility is also important. At Harrison Commons, the mass of the largest garage will serve as a soundwall to buffer neighboring residences from the railroad. Payton warns, however, that this strategy may not be applicable everywhere. "In the New York area, people are used to having their car some distance from their apartment, which gives you a lot of flexibility in the design," he says. "This isn't true in most other places."

Design solutions

Even the third of Cervero's 3Ds—design—comes back to parking. "Reduced parking allows a finer grain of development," says Payton. "With smaller garages, you can achieve smaller block sizes. And small blocks create variety and interest," he says, encouraging walking.

Dennis Leach says the street pattern and other design factors help to explain why some of the most walkable developments are often in established urban areas. He cites Washington's Dupont circle as an example. "The framework of the street and building pattern is extremely strong," he says.

That's less true in suburban neighborhoods like Bethesda, Silver Spring, and Arlington County, where wide arterials, surface parking, and the lack of a fine-grained street grid make walking a challenge. "The framework for urban development isn't really there," he says. "It has to be retrofitted."

All else being equal, walkability is maximized when streets are designed to accommodate lower traffic volumes in the first place. The key, then, is to factor the reduced tripmaking benefits of TOD back into the street design—avoiding the error of widening roads for traffic that never arrives, or worse still, only arrives *because* of the widening.

Many agencies grant generic trip generation credits for transit-oriented development. The Los Angeles Metropolitan Transportation Authority, for example, offers a 15 percent credit for residentially oriented, mixed-use projects that have at least 24 units per acre and that are within a quarter-mile of a light rail station.

An important tool for creating a framework for walkable streets is likely to be the street hierarchy and design standards currently being written by the Congress for the New Urbanism, together with the Institute for Transportation Engineers and the U.S. Environmental Protection Agency. These standards envisage a new hierarchy of streets—from mews and lanes up to main streets and boulevards, rather than local, collector and arterial.

While many of these techniques have been used by new urbanist designers, engineers, and planners—and others—for years, they have generally resulted in one-time exceptions rather than fundamental change. That could change with these new standards.

Resources

The Authors. E-mail Adam Millard-Ball at *amillard-ball@nelsonnygaard.com.* Patrick Siegman is at *psiegman@nelsonnygaard.com.* Millard-Ball's article on parking standards appeared in the April 2002 *Planning*, his viewpoint on TODs is in the December 2002 issue. For a list of resources, see APA's website: www.planning.org

---

Jeffrey Tumlin is a partner of Nelson\Nygaard, a transportation consulting firm. Adam Millard-Ball is a senior associate with the firm..

Article 32

The U.S. Supreme Court's New Federalism and Its Impact on Antidiscrimination Legislation

In recent years, the U.S. Supreme Court has developed a new federalism policy that has eviscerated the powers of the U.S. Congress in favor of states' rights. This article addresses the implications of the Supreme Court's new federalism policy for the Americans With Disabilities Act (ADA) of 1990 and the Age Discrimination in Employment Act (ADEA) of 1967 as amended. It focuses on two recent High Court decisions, Kimel v. Florida Board of Regents *and* Garrett v. the University of Alabama, *which greatly reduced the scope of both the ADA and the ADEA. In light of these decisions, alternative actions for enforcing antidiscrimination laws are provided.*

Keywords: *federalism: civil rights, states' rights; sovereign immunity; discrimination; 14th Amendment; employment legislation*

NORMA M. RICCUCCI
Rutgers University, Campus at Newark

In the past few decades, we have witnessed an accelerated devolution of powers from the federal government to the states, not only by the executive branch but by the judicial branch of government as well. The issue of federalism—or more appropriately, the new federalism—as it pertains to the courts refers to the distribution of power between state and federal courts. At its core is the concept of "state sovereignty," which, through a number of constitutional provisions, seeks to preserve the "immunity"[1] rights of states, protecting them from unnecessary or unwarranted intrusion by the federal government. Recently, the U.S. Supreme Court has brought the new federalism to the forefront of constitutional law.

This article examines the U.S. Supreme Court's role in the new federalism, particularly around two pieces of antidiscrimination legislation: The Americans with Disabilities Act (ADA) of 1990 and the Age Discrimination in Employment Act (ADEA) of 1967 as amended. It begins with a brief examination of the legal framework under which the Supreme Court has been applying and justifying its federalism policy. It then examines the Supreme Court's decisions in two cases involving antidiscrimination laws: *Kimel v. Florida Board of Regents* (2000) and *Garrett v. the University of Alabama* (2001). The implications of these decisions and viable legal responses to them are also addressed.

It should be noted at the outset that the analysis presented here does not address the official or personal immunity doctrines as they pertain to individual government employees (see Rosenbloom, 1994, 1997). These immunity doctrines address whether federal, state, and local government officials or employees who violate an individual's statutory or constitutional rights can be sued and held liable for their actions. However, as will be discussed later in the text, reliance on these doctrines may provide alternative relief to state employees alleging they have been discriminated against based on age or disability.

THE NEW FEDERALISM AND THE U.S. SUPREME COURT

In the past two decades or so, as the U.S. Supreme Court has been faced with opportunities to strike a balance between state and federal power, it has sided almost exclusively with the states. The U.S. Supreme Court's policy of federalism has, in effect, resulted in severe restrictions to an individual's ability to sue a state in federal court for federal rights' violations (Braveman, 2000; Wise, 2001).

In two landmark cases, *Seminole Tribe of Florida v. Florida* (1996) and *Alden v. Maine* (1999),[2] the U.S. Supreme Court expanded the boundaries of the new federalism to extraordinary dimensions.[3] In *Seminole* and *Alden*, a Court majority held that Congress is barred from authorizing individuals to pursue private suits for damages in the federal courts against the states when it does so pursuant to its commerce clause powers.[4] The Court opined that Congress cannot subject an unconsenting state to suit in either federal or (its own) state court, whether the suit is brought by a citizen or noncitizen of that state and whether it is based on federal law or state law. The rulings limit congressional legislation in favor of states' rights, restrict the role of the federal courts in adjudicating claims alleging state violations of federal rights, and ultimately impede an individual's ability to seek court enforcement of their federal and perhaps even state rights against a state (Goodman, 2001; Wise, 2001).

It is important to enunciate the constitutional provisions invoked by the Supreme Court in its new federalism rulings. When we think of state sovereignty, we typically think of the 10th and 11th Amendments to the U.S. Constitution. The 10th Amendment, ratified in 1791 as part of the Bill of Rights, reserves all powers not specifically granted to the United States to the states and to the people, respectively. It seeks to protect state governments from being "commandeered" by the federal government or from being eviscerated as viable political entities (*Printz v. United States*, 1997). In short, its limits Congress's powers to regulate state governments.

The 11th Amendment, which has been more critical than the 10th to the Supreme Court's new federalism policy, gave concrete and specific expression to the abstract or general guarantee of the 10th Amendment. Ratified in 1795, it originally sought to prevent a resident of one state from suing another state in federal court. It was proposed and ratified in response to the U.S. Supreme Court ruling in *Chisholm v. Georgia* (1793), in which the State of Georgia was being sued in federal court by a citizen of South Carolina. Georgia claimed sovereign immunity and refused to appear in court. By a vote of 4 to 1 the Court issued a judgment against Georgia, stating that a state could be sued by citizens of another state.[5]

In an explicit effort to overturn the *Chisholm* decision, the 11th Amendment was proposed and ratified. It was a direct solution that remained unambiguous until Congress enacted the Judiciary Act of 1875, which was part of the post-Civil War civil rights legislation and guaranteed the right of a citizen to sue his or her own state in federal court. As will be seen shortly, it is the 11th Amendment that the U.S. Supreme Court has primarily relied upon in applying its new federalism policy, essentially granting state governments much greater immunity from lawsuits.

Finally, state sovereignty claims also weigh congressional power as defined by the commerce clause of Article I of the U.S. Constitution and § 5 of the 14th Amendment, which grants the U.S. Congress authority to enact legislation enforcing the 14th Amendment.[6] The 14th Amendment essentially applies the Bill of Rights to state governments.[7]

The Supreme Court's reliance on the commerce clause in applying its new federalism policy was first seen in its 1995 *United States v. Lopez* ruling. For the first time since the New Deal, the Supreme Court invalidated a federal statute enacted pursuant to the interstate commerce clause.[8] In *Lopez*, the Court declared unconstitutional a law[9] banning the possession of guns within 1,000 feet of a school, despite the aggregate impact of the regulated activity on the national economy through its effects on education and crime. Turning heavily on whether the law or the activity being regulated affected "economic activity," the Court ruled that "the possession of a gun in a local school zone is in no sense an economic activity that might, through repetition elsewhere, have such a substantial effect on interstate commerce" (p. 549).[10]

Similarly, in the *United States v. Morrison* (2000), the same narrowly divided Court struck down a provision of the 1994 Violence Against Women Act[11] (VAWA) creating a federal civil remedy against the perpetrators of gender-motivated crimes of violence. Again, the Court stressed the noneconomic nature of the regulated activity, stating that Congress does not have the authority to regulate a criminal offense such as rape because it is not an economic issue. The *Morrison* Court stated that "gender-motivated crimes of violence are not, in any sense, economic activity" (p. 598). It said that

> [while] the statute, *is* supported by numerous findings regarding the serious impact of gender-motivated violence on victims and their families, these findings are substantially weakened by the fact that they rely on reasoning that this Court has rejected, namely a but-for causal chain from the initial occurrence of violent crime to every attenuated effect upon interstate commerce. (p. 599)

Broadly interpreted, the *Morrison* and *Lopez* rulings suggest, in effect, that Congress, pursuant to the commerce clause, can only regulate an activity if it is economic and has a substantial impact on interstate commerce.[12]

The *Morrison* Court further ruled that § 5 of the 14th Amendment also does not give Congress the authority to enact the provision of the VAWA creating a federal civil remedy for victims of gender-motivated violence. In so doing, the Court referred to its decision in *City of Boerne v. Flores* (1997), in which it ruled that the 14th Amendment places limitations on the manner in which Congress may attack discriminatory conduct. Foremost among them is the principle that the amendment prohibits only state action, not private conduct. The *City of Boerne* Court affirmed that the states should be unencumbered by far-reaching limitations on their authority, particularly in the absence of clear evidence that they have threatened constitutional guarantees. The *City of Boerne* Court ruled that there was "a considerable congressional intrusion into the states' traditional prerogatives and general authority to regulate for the health and welfare of their citizens" (p. 509). Ultimately, the Court's ruling in *Morrison* further tipped the balance of power toward the states and the judiciary.

In sum, the U.S. Supreme Court has placed severe restrictions on the power of Congress to enact legislation enforceable against the states and has attenuated the ability of individuals to sue a state in federal court. The effects of the Court's expansive new federalism policy can be seen in two recent decisions, *Kimel* (2000) and *Garrett* (2001), in which, for the first time, the High Court held antidiscrimination statutes enacted to protect civil rights inapplicable to the states.

THE SUPREME COURT'S *KIMEL* AND *GARRETT* DECISIONS

In 1967 Congress enacted the ADEA, which made it illegal for private businesses to refuse to hire, discharge, or to otherwise discriminate against an individual, in compensation or privileges of employment, between the ages of 40 and 65. The act was amended in 1974 to apply to federal, state, and local governments. A series of amendments to the ADEA banned forced retirement for all employees, except for public safety officers (i.e., law enforcement officers and firefighters at every level of government).[13] Enforcement authority over the ADEA was originally vested in the Department of Labor but was transferred to the Equal Employment Opportunity Commission (EEOC) as part of the federal service reform of 1978.[14]

In 2000 the U.S. Supreme Court issued a decision in *Kimel v. Florida Board of Regents* that widely reduced the scope of the ADEA. In *Kimel*, the Court barred state employees from suing their employers (i.e., state governments) in federal court to redress age discrimination under the ADEA. The Court ruled that the 14th Amendment's § 5 does not permit Congress to abrogate states' 11th Amendment immunity for violations under the ADEA. Unless a state is willing to waive its sovereign immunity, state employees cannot bring a private cause of action in federal court for discrimination under the ADEA. In effect, state employees do not have the same age discrimination protections as private sector and local and federal government employees under the ADEA.[15]

The *Kimel* case served as another opportunity for the Court to advance its policy of new federalism. The Supreme Court in *Kimel* began by taking as a given the interpretation of the state sovereign immunity doctrine offered in the *Seminole Tribe* (1996) line of cases and proceeded to consider whether the ADEA qualified as an exercise of Congress's § 5 power under the 14th Amendment. To do so, the Court applied the "congruence and proportionality test" from its *City of Boerne* (1997) decision. This test asks whether the legislation in question is congruent and proportional with the constitutional problem identified by Congress. In applying the test, the Court focused its attention primarily on the legislative history of the ADEA and determined that Congress did not identify a serious problem in state and local government sufficient to warrant the protections provided by the ADEA. It said that "Congress had virtually no reason to believe that state and local governments were unconstitutionally discriminating against their employees on the basis of age" (*Kimel*, 2000, p. 65).

The Court arrived at this conclusion without even considering the argument that Congress could have relied on statistics showing widespread discrimination in the private sector and assumed that a similar pattern existed for state employees. The Court's insistence on a showing of explicit documentation of unconstitutional conduct by state employers is rather extraordinary because it indicates that the Court will not permit Congress to infer the existence of a problem and may not even permit Congress to anticipate the future emergence of one. As Ray (2000) observed:

> The strict limitations the Court appears to place on Congress in *Kimel* begs the question of what sort of constitutional conduct Congress is empowered to reach when it passes legislation to deter or prevent unconstitutional conduct by the states, as well as the nature of the basis that the Court will require in order to permit Congress this flexibility. (p. 1767)

The Court went a step further and ruled that the enforcement powers prescribed by § 5 of the 14th Amendment do not permit Congress to determine what constitutes a constitutional violation. It ruled that Congress cannot "decree the substance of the Fourteenth Amendment's restrictions on the States.... It has been given the power 'to enforce,' not the power to determine what constitutes a constitutional violation" (*Kimel*, 2000, p. 81). With the conclusion that there was no constitutional problem respecting age and that Congress, in any event, lacked the power to determine the existence of a constitutional violation, it followed inevitably that the Court would rule that a remedy such as the ADEA was not warranted. The broader implication here is that the High Court is continuing to narrow the nature of the powers it will consider as a valid exercise of congressional authority.

In a second case, *Garrett v. the University of Alabama* (2001), the Supreme Court again accepted an 11th Amendment immunity defense in striking down the applicability of the 1990 ADA to state governments.[16] Title I of the ADA prohibits employment discrimination against qualified disabled persons. It covers nonfederal government employers, employment agencies, labor unions, and joint labor-management committees with 15 or more employees. The federal government, which is excluded from the ADA, continues to be covered by executive orders and the Vocational Rehabilitation Act of 1973 as amended (Lee, 1999; Lee & Greenlaw, 1998–1999).

Interestingly, despite the Supreme Court's rulings in *Seminole Tribe* (1996) and related cases, the U.S. Court of Appeals for the 11th Circuit in *Garrett* (1999) ruled that the ADA is not only valid but also a legitimate use of congressional authority. Thus, the appeals court rejected Alabama's sovereign immunity claim for ADA violations.[17]

In February of 2001, however, the U.S. Supreme Court overturned the appellate court decision in *Garrett*, stating that Congress did not exercise a valid use of power under § 5 of the 14th Amendment in abrogating states' 11th Amendment immunity for violations under the ADA.[18] Consistent with its previous decisions, the Court, in effect, restricted the scope of Title I of the ADA, while at the same time strengthening state sovereignty.

The Court began by examining whether there was "congruence and proportionality" between the injury and the remedy chosen to correct it. Again referring to its *City of Boerne* (1997) decision, the Court argued that this test was appropriate for determining whether remedial legislation such as the ADA is appropriate under § 5 of the 14th Amendment. The Court first ruled that Congress should have made its intentions about the scope of the ADA clear in the record or text of the legislation. The Court majority said that in order to make states liable to private suits for damages, it was inappropriate for Congress to consider general societal discrimination against people with disabilities. Rather, the Court went on to say, Congress must demonstrate a high level of proof that the states themselves had engaged in unconstitutional discrimination.

The *Garrett* Court (2001) thus concluded that the ADA's legislative record failed to show that Congress identified a history and pattern of irrational employment discrimination by the states against the disabled. The Court opined that

> Although the record includes instances to support... a finding [that society has tended to isolate and segregate individuals with disabilities], the great majority of these incidents do not deal with state activities in employment. Even if it were to be determined that the half a dozen relevant examples from the record showed unconstitutional action on the part of States, these incidents taken together fall far short of even suggesting the pattern of unconstitutional discrimination on which § 5 legislation must be based. (p. 959)

The Court went on to say that

> Although "negative attitudes" and "fear" often accompany irrational biases, their presence alone does not a constitutional violation make. Thus, the Fourteenth Amendment does not require states to make special accommodations for the disabled, so long as their actions toward such individuals are rational. They could quite hardheadedly—and perhaps hardheartedly—hold to job-qualification requirements which do not make allowance for the disabled. If special accommodations for the disabled are to be required, they have to come from positive law and not through the equal protection clause. (p. 959)

The Court concluded that the ADA did not exhibit congruence and proportionality between the injury to be prevented or remedied and the means adopted to that end. By applying the rational basis standard to discrimination, the Court has set a very high hurdle for Congress, which must demonstrate that the state choices (i.e., "discrimination") serve no legitimate governmental purpose or are not rationally related to the achievement of a legitimate government purpose. This very heavy burden of persuasion is ultimately placed on Congress.

IMPLICATIONS OF THE *KIMEL* AND *GARRETT* RULINGS

The general effects of the Supreme Court's new federalism on civil rights laws and antidiscrimination legislation are relatively clear. Federal laws are passed to address broad societal issues and problems that the states are either unable or unwilling to address. As many states, particularly those in the South, have historically demonstrated, federal civil rights laws were greatly resisted. And if the states did choose to establish such laws, they differed widely in scope. The question, then, is, Should the states have the power to determine the existence and strength of civil rights laws? If they do, some states will work hard to preserve the civil rights of their citizens, whereas others may be less rigorous in doing so. It is not necessarily the case that state governments would revert to the days of the pre-1960s, wherein pure hate and unmitigated prejudice often governed the actions of policy makers. But rather, state governments today may seek to sidestep employees' civil rights because of the costs that may ultimately be imposed. For example, efforts to achieve pay equity are seen as being very costly to employers, as are efforts to make reasonable accommodations for disabled workers. In seeking to balance the interests of employee's civil rights with economic expenditures, it seems axiomatic that state employers, if given a choice, will decide in favor of cost containment. As a corollary, employees' civil rights could be transgressed.

An analogous situation can be further illustrated in the area of labor relations in the public sector, where there is no national labor law to regulate or oversee collective bargaining in state and local governments.[19] Each state develops its own labor law or policy, resulting in a hodgepodge of regulations or laws in which some states mandate collective bargaining,[20] others permit it,[21] and yet others either have no policy[22] or they prohibit it outright.[23] Moreover, the strength of the state laws varies greatly in terms of scope of bargaining, binding interest arbitration, and striking rights. In the South, several states not only continue to prohibit collective bargaining, but they have developed mechanisms or policies that severely weaken the ability of public employee unions to adequately represent their constituents. In Florida, Georgia, and other southern states, for example, "right-to-work" laws make it extraordinarily difficult to unionize workers, collect union dues, or provide any meaningful protections and benefits to make unionization desirable to public employees (see, e.g., Kearney, 1992; Rosenbloom & Shafritz, 1985).

Another implication of the Supreme Court's devolution of power to state courts is that no national precedents around civil rights will be set. A new body of patchwork case law, expressing the interests of the states, will thus govern the civil rights of the American people. Of course, one might argue the benefits of this, given the conservative majority on the Court. But the issue of the power distribution between federal and state courts, or the federal and state governments, for that matter, goes beyond this concern to the question of which issues should be governed by national interests and, hence, Congress *and* the U.S. Supreme Court and which issues should fall under the jurisdiction of the states. This broader issue surrounding the new federalism goes well beyond the scope of this analysis. So, too, do the numerous other implications of the Supreme Court's burgeoning new federalism. These issues include Congress's concern for individual rights versus the Supreme Court's proclivity toward states' rights, which type of matters the Court sees as the judiciary's exclusive role of constitutional interpretation, and even the less political matter of the workload of the federal courts (see Althouse, 2001).

More specific to *Kimel* (2000) and *Garret* (2001), the Supreme Court's decisions have resulted in nearly 5 million state employees losing their federal protection from age and disability discrimination. Although the decisions continue to allow state workers to sue state governments, they can do so only in state court, and then only if the state agrees to the suit.[24] Moreover, the suit must be brought under state disability or age discrimination laws,[25] which are often weaker, less effective, and narrower in scope. For example, state disability laws tend to be much less rigorous than the ADA around reasonable accommodations (Levinson, 2000).

Kimel and *Garret* may also have ramifications for other civil rights statutes. The Equal Pay Act (EPA) of 1963, the Family and Medical Leave Act (FMLA) of 1990, and perhaps even

Title VII of the Civil Rights Act of 1964, as amended, may fall prey to the Supreme Court's new federalism crusade. In fact, in accordance with the Supreme Court's new federalism policy, many lower courts have recently determined that the FMLA exceeded Congress's enforcement powers under § 5 of the 14th Amendment.[26]

The implications of *Kimel* and *Garrett* for the EPA, however, are less clear. Prior to these High Court decisions most lower courts ruled that the EPA meets the "congruence and proportionality" tests, thus rendering it enforceable against state government employers.[27] But since *Kimel* and *Garrett*, there have been conflicting decisions by lower courts around whether the EPA is a valid abrogation of state sovereign immunity. For example, the U.S. Court of Appeals for the First Circuit, in *Jusino Mercado v. Commonwealth of Puerto Rico* (2000), determined that a nonconsenting state cannot be sued in a federal venue by state employees seeking to enforce the EPA. The *Jusino* court justified its ruling here by pointing to post-*Kimel* Supreme Court actions, which vacated appellate court rulings upholding the EPA's applicability to the states[28] (Murdock, Sezer, & Hodge, 2000; Ray, 2000).

On the other hand, the Seventh Circuit Court of Appeals in *Varner v. Illinois State University* (2000), *on remand* from the U.S. Supreme Court,[29] upheld its initial decision that the state university was not immune from a wage discrimination suit brought by female faculty members under the EPA. The *Varner* court ruled that "Although the Eleventh Amendment grants unconsenting States immunity from suit in federal court, that immunity is not absolute" (p. 930). It concluded with a finding that "the extension of the Equal Pay Act to the States was a valid exercise of congressional authority under § 5 of the Fourteenth Amendment" (p. 937). Thus, despite the Supreme Court's ruling in *Kimel*, as well as its explicit directions to the Seventh Circuit to reconsider its position on state sovereign immunity, at least one circuit court is unwilling to render the EPA inapplicable to the states.

One of the major unresolved issues as of this writing is whether the U.S. Supreme Court will find Title VII, the cornerstone of civil rights laws in this nation, inapplicable to the states, despite the fact that in its 1976 *Fitzpatrick v. Bitzer* ruling the Court upheld Title VII as a valid exercise of Congress's enforcement powers under § 5 of the 14th Amendment. Since *Fitzpatrick*, lower courts have routinely upheld the applicability of Title VII to state governments.[30] *In re Employment Discrimination Litigation Against the State of Alabama* (1999), for example, the U.S. Court of Appeals for the 11th Circuit ruled that "in enacting the disparate impact provisions of Title VII, Congress has unequivocally expressed its intent to abrogate the states' Eleventh Amendment sovereign immunity, and that Congress has acted pursuant to a valid exercise of its Fourteenth Amendment enforcement power" (p. 1324).

However, in recent years some states have argued that the Civil Rights Act of 1991, which amends Title VII to create a remedy of compensatory damages for plaintiffs who proved intentional discrimination, constitutes a separate intrusion on sovereign immunity and therefore requires a separate, independent expression of congressional intent to abrogate sovereign immunity. States have also argued that the increased risk of large monetary awards allowed under the 1991 act calls for a reexamination of *Fitzpatrick*, which was decided when the only monetary remedy available was back pay (Murdock, Sezer, & Hodge, 2000).

A pivotal decision was issued in 1998 by the Seventh Circuit of Appeals in *Varner v. Illinois State University*, discussed earlier in the context of the EPA. The *Varner* case involved a challenge to both the EPA's and Title VII's applicability to states. The *Varner* court (1998) flatly rejected the argument that Title VII, as amended by the Civil Rights Act of 1991, violated the 11th Amendment. It stated that

> The plain language of [the 1991 act] shows that Congress intended to create an additional remedy for Title VII violations, as opposed to a separate cause of action.... Under Title VII, the abrogation of the States' Eleventh Amendment immunity is settled. (p. 718)

Because the Supreme Court vacated and remanded *Varner* (Seventh Circuit, 1998) to the circuit court for reconsideration in light of *Kimel* (2000), questions have been raised as to whether the Supreme Court was implicitly suggesting that states are immune from suits brought under Title VII of the Civil Rights Act of 1991. Murdock, Sezer, and Hodge (2000) argued that this is unlikely, and that it is much more probable that the case was remanded for reconsideration of the EPA issue. First, the 1998 *Varner* court wrote most of its decision around the EPA, and not Title VII. Second, in rendering its decision on the applicability of the EPA to state governments, the Seventh Circuit relied on one of its own precedents, in which it had decided that the ADEA was enforceable against state governments (see *Goshtasby v. Board of Trustees of the University of Illinois*, 1998). But because *Kimel* clearly reversed the Seventh Circuit's ADEA precedent, the Supreme Court had, in effect, eviscerated the Seventh Circuit's rationale for upholding the power of Congress to abrogate state sovereignty rights under the EPA. By remanding the *Varner* case to the Seventh Circuit, the Supreme Court was thus instructing the circuit court to reconsider its decision around the EPA and not necessarily Title VII of the 1991 Civil Rights Act.[31]

It also seems unlikely that the Supreme Court will decide that Title VII is not enforceable against the states, because in its *Kimel* decision, the Court repeatedly relied on race and gender discrimination as examples of the type of discrimination that Congress can appropriately regulate under § 5 of the 14th Amendment. The *Kimel* Court (2000, p. 83) ruled, for example, that "Age classifications, unlike governmental conduct based on race or gender, cannot be characterized as 'so seldom relevant to the achievement of any legitimate state interest that laws grounded in such considerations are deemed to reflect prejudice and antipathy'" (citing its decision in *Cleburne v. Cleburne*, 1985). It further stated that "Older persons, again, unlike those who suffer discrimination on the basis of race or gender, have not been subjected to a history of purposeful unequal treatment" (Kimel, 2000, p. 83).

In short, it appears unlikely that the Supreme Court would actually consider rendering Title VII outside of Congress's purview with respect to applicability and enforcement. However, without a substantive ruling from the High Court on the applicability of the FMLA or the EPA to the states, circuit court decisions, conflicting in the case of the EPA, will govern which states are or are not immune from lawsuits by their employees under the FMLA or the ADA.

ALTERNATIVE ACTIONS FOR ENFORCING ANTIDISCRIMINATION LAWS

Despite the long line of new federalism decisions issued by the Supreme Court, local government employees are still able to file suit against local government employers. Nothing in *Kimel* (2000) or *Garrett* (2001) suggests that Congress did not have the authority to pass the ADEA or the ADA pursuant to its commerce clause power.[32] *Kimel*, for example, held only that Congress did not have the power to pass the 1974 amendment extending the ADEA to state and local government employers pursuant to its power under § 5 of the 14th Amendment (p. 91). In fact, the Supreme Court had already flatly rejected a 10th Amendment state sovereignty defense in *EEOC v. Wyoming* (1983, p. 236–239), when it ruled that the 1974 amendment to the ADEA was a valid exercise of Congress's Article I commerce clause powers.[33]

Moreover, the Supreme Court has never suggested that the 11th Amendment protects local government entities.[34] In its recent decision in *Alden v. Maine* (1999, p. 706), the Court reaffirmed that a core principle of the sovereign immunity doctrine is that it bars suit against states, but it "does not bar suits against lesser entities; it does not extend to suits prosecuted against a municipal corporation or other governmental entity which is not an arm of the state." Thus, Congress need not abrogate 11th Amendment immunity when regulating local governments. Ultimately, local government employees can file suit against their employers (Bodensteiner & Levinson, 2001).

In addition, a disability or age discrimination suit brought under 42 U.S. Code § 1983 claim to enforce the equal protection clause of the 14th Amendment would subject government officials, acting in their official capacity, to suit for prospective relief in accordance with the *Ex parte Young* 1908 doctrine. Section 1983 gives individuals a cause of action for damages and injunctive relief against those persons who violate the 14th Amendment under color of state law. Section 1983 amends and codifies the Civil Rights Act of 1871. Thus, local government officials in their official capacity are subject to lawsuits.[35] Furthermore, state officials may be sued in their personal capacity for damages. Both enjoy qualified immunity, but both are also subject to liability for compensatory as well as punitive damages (see Rosenbloom, 1997).

In addition, neither *Kimel* (2000) nor *Garrett* (2001) precludes the EEOC from filing suit on behalf of an alleged victim of age or disability discrimination. The EEOC, which has enforcement authority over the ADEA and the ADA, can file suit against state or local government employers as well as private sector employers. And suits brought by the EEOC are not barred by the 11th Amendment (Bodensteiner & Levinson, 2001).[36] In fact, the decision in *Kimel* suggests that the EEOC should work more aggressively on behalf of state government employees in order to promote the intention of Congress to eliminate age discrimination by state government employers.

Also, state employees may bring suits against states that have consented to have suits brought against them for certain actions. Some states have specified activities for which citizens may file suit against a state (Wise, 2001), but as of this writing there is no evidence that states have included "civil rights" as one such activity.

Finally, when employees lose their rights they sometimes turn to collective bargaining and unions for protection. Public employee unions have a legal responsibility to fairly represent their constituents and can pursue a number of actions to protect them from discriminatory practices.

Then, notwithstanding the Supreme Court's ardent propagation of the new federalism, there are still avenues for state and local government employees to mount legal challenges in federal courts against states, localities, or government officials for discrimination on the basis of age or disability.

CONCLUSION

For almost 50 years, Congress has sought to eradicate various forms of discrimination in the U.S. workplace. Laws prohibiting discrimination on the basis of race, gender, color, religion, national origin, age, and disability have worked to protect workers and help create work environments free of biases and hostilities. However, the Supreme Court's new federalism decisions, particularly in *Kimel* (2000) and *Garrett* (2001) impose new and substantial restrictions on Congress's power to enact antidiscrimination legislation under § 5 of the 14th Amendment. The Supreme Court's decisions ultimately undermine civil rights and employment legislation enacted by Congress.

It is worth noting in closing that although the U.S. Supreme Court has consistently applied its policy of new federalism in recent years, there is one glaring exception in which the Court struck down the decision of a state court. In *Bush v. Gore* (2000), the U.S. Supreme Court was asked to review a decision by the Florida Supreme Court (see *Gore v. Harris*, 2000), which ordered a manual recount of the state's results in the 2000 presidential election. The U.S. Supreme Court reversed the decision of the state court, ruling that the judgment of the state supreme court violated the equal protection clause of the Constitution's 14th Amendment with respect to the fundamental nature of the right to vote. The Court stated that regardless of

> whether the Florida Supreme Court had the authority… to define what a legal vote is and to mandate a manual recount implementing that definition, the recount mechanisms… do not satisfy the minimum requirements for the non-arbitrary treatment of voters that are necessary to secure the fundamental right to vote. (*Bush*, 2000, p. 530).

At the very least, the decision suggests that the U.S. Supreme Court will continue to devolve authority to state courts, but it will also sit in final judgment of the *merits* of state court rulings.

NOTES

1. There is a wide body of case law addressing personal and official immunity from lawsuits (see, e.g., Rosenbloom, 1994, 1997, and Rosenbloom, Carroll, & Carroll, 2000). In contrast, the research presented here examines the current Supreme Court's decisions around government *employer* immunity.
2. There were two companion cases handed down on the same day of the *Alden v. Maine* (1999) decision. See *College Savings Bank v. Florida Prepaid Postsecondary Education Expense Board* (1999), holding that Congress could not abrogate state sovereign immunity in federal court on a trademark case, even though the federal courts had exclusive jurisdiction, and rejecting the constructive waiver of sovereign immunity via a state's activities in interstate commerce; *Florida Prepaid Postsecondary Education Expense Board v. College Savings Bank* (1999), holding that Congress could not abrogate state sovereign immunity in federal court on a patent case, and congressional power under the due process clause of the 14th Amendment did not give Congress the power to abrogate state sovereign immunity to protect property rights.
3. It may be recalled that in the *National League of Cities v. Usery* (1976), the U.S. Supreme Court ruled that a 1974 amendment to the Fair Labor Standards Act (FLSA) was not applicable to state and local governments. The 1974 amendment extended federal wage and hour requirements to state and local government employees. However, this decision was effectively overturned by the Court's decision in *Garcia v. San Antonio Metropolitan Transit Authority* (1985, p. 546), in which the U.S. Supreme Court found that *Usery* was "unsound in principle and unworkable in practice." See Kearney (1992).
4. The Court held in *Seminole Tribe of Florida v. Florida* (1996) that the Constitution embodies a principle of state sovereign immunity that is not subject to abrogation by Congress. In so doing, the Court majority advanced a two-part test for measuring Congress's ability to abrogate a state's sovereign immunity: (1) "whether Congress has 'unequivocally expressed its intent to abrogate the immunity'" and (2) "whether Congress has acted 'pursuant to a valid exercise of power.'" The *Alden v. Maine* Court (1999) took a significant step beyond *Seminole Tribe* by announcing that this constitutional immunity applies even in state court lawsuits where the 11th Amendment is wholly inapplicable. It should be further noted that in *Alden*, the Supreme Court held that 11th Amendment immunity does not extend to suits brought against municipal corporations or other governmental entities that are not "an arm of the state."
5. The four justices in the majority based their reasoning not on the original intent of the Framers but on the judicial power granted to the Supreme Court under Article III of the Constitution. Section 2 of Article III was revoked by the 11th Amendment.
6. Section 5 essentially permits Congress to enforce, by appropriate legislation, the constitutional guarantee that no state shall deprive any person of life, liberty, or property, without due process or deny any person equal protection of the laws.
7. There is a body of case law, however, addressing whether two of the rights recognized in the Bill of Rights have actually been "incorporated" into the 14th Amendment. They are the right to keep and bear arms of the 2nd Amendment and the 5th Amendment right, "No person shall be held to answer for a capital, or otherwise infamous crime, unless on a presentment or indictment of a Grand Jury." Although the U.S. Supreme Court has avoided taking any cases that would require it to rule on the right to keep and bear arms under the 14th Amendment, it has ruled on the 5th Amendment right noted above. See, for example, the Supreme Court's decision in *Hurtado v. California* (1884), in which it ruled that an individual could be tried and convicted by a jury in the California County Court, because a state is not required to indict by grand jury. The plaintiff contended that under the due process clause of the 14th Amendment, he was entitled to a proper indictment by a grand jury before trial.
8. In response to a political backlash from both the executive and legislative branches, the post-New Deal U.S. Supreme Court slowly began legitimating congressional power to address the social and economic ills of the time. Beginning with its 1942 *Wickard v. Filburn* decision, the Court no longer asked whether a particular statute infringed on state sovereignty but whether it was enacted within the scope of congressional power. Thus, with *Wickard* the Court largely abandoned any efforts to curtail congressional power under the commerce clause (see Merico-Stephens, 2000).
9. The Gun-Free School Zones Act of 1990 forbids "any individual knowingly to possess a firearm at a place that [she/he] knows… is a school zone."
10. Also see *Solid Waste Agency of Northern Cook County v. U.S. Army Corps of Engineers* (2001), in which the U.S. Supreme Court just barely bypassed a commerce clause challenge to the Clean Water Act. In effect, the Court sidestepped the issue of whether Congress's regulating of the environment reaches economic activities and thus operates within its constitutional powers under the commerce clause.
11. The Violence Against Women Act was amended in 2000 to improve legal tools and programs addressing domestic violence, sexual assault, and stalking. The act reauthorizes critical grant programs created by the Violence Against Women Act of 1994 and subsequent legislation, establishes new programs, and strengthens federal laws.
12. See Note 10.
13. However, recognizing that age is not an accurate predictor of a public safety officers' fitness to serve, Congress also included a provision to the amendments stating that if a state or local public safety officer is able to pass a physical fitness exam, he or she cannot be forced into mandatory retirement.

14. In 1990 the Age Discrimination in Employment Act (ADEA) was once again amended to include the Older Workers Benefit Protection Act (OWBPA), which ensures that older workers are not compelled or pressured into waiving their rights under the ADEA.
15. As of this writing, a bill is being proposed that will counteract the Court's *Kimel* (2000) decision, thereby restoring the rights of state employees to sue in age discrimination cases.
16. The state also claimed immunity under the Rehabilitation Act of 1973 and the Family Medical Leave Act of 1993.
17. The *Garrett* Appellate Court also ruled that the State of Alabama was not immune from suits under the Rehabilitation Act, but that under the circumstances before the court in this particular case it was immune from suit under the Family Medical Leave Act. See *Garrett* (1999), p. 1214.
18. The Supreme Court in *Garrett* ruled only on the Americans With Disabilities Act (ADA) aspects of the case and not the Rehabilitation Act or the Family and Medical Leave Act.
19. Of course, some might argue that public sector labor relations is not a matter of great national concern and therefore does not need a uniform national response. It should further be noted that all federal employees, regardless of the jurisdiction or state in which their agencies are located, are covered by Title VII of the Civil Service Reform Act of 1978.
20. New York, Wisconsin, and New Jersey, for example.
21. For example, Louisiana.
22. Mississippi and South Carolina, for example.
23. For example, North Carolina and Virginia.
24. See *Alden v. Maine* (1999), as discussed earlier in the text. It should further be noted that the *Kimel* (2000) and *Garrett* (2001) decisions do not affect private sector employees nor, as will be argued later in the text, local government employees.
25. Although some have argued that litigants will have to research state waiver laws to determine whether they can rely on the ADA or the ADEA to sue their employers in state courts (see Levinson, 2000).
26. See, for example, *Garrett* (1999) addressed earlier in the text and in Note 15. Also see *Sims v. University of Cincinnati* (6th Cir. 2000); *Kilvitis v. County of Luzerne* (M.D. Pa. 1999); *Driesse v. Florida Board of Regents* (M.D. Fla. 1998).
27. See, for example, *Hundertmark v. State of Florida Department of Transportation* (11th Cir. 2000).
28. See *State University of New York, College at New Paltz v. Anderson* (2000) and *Illinois State University v. Varner* (2000).
29. One week after *Kimel* (2000) was handed down, the U.S. Supreme Court vacated a 1998 judgment in *Varner* and remanded it to the Seventh Circuit for reconsideration in light of *Kimel* (see *Illinois State University v. Varner,* 2000). The 1998 *Varner* decision of the Seventh Circuit held that "Congress clearly expressed its intent to abrogate the State's Eleventh Amendment immunity when it enacted the EPA" (Equal Pay Act) (p. 710).
30. See, for example, *In re Employment Discrimination Litigation Against the State of Alabama* (11th Cir. 1999).
31. On remand, the Title VII claim had been waived, and so the *Varner* circuit court did not ultimately reconsider its earlier decision upholding the applicability of Title VII to the states.
32. It may be recalled, however, that the *Seminole* Court (1996, pp. 72–73) interpreted Congress's Article I commerce clause powers *not* to include the power to subject states to suit at the hands of private individuals. Rather, as it made clear in its *Fitzpatrick v. Bitzer* (1976, p. 456) decision and reaffirmed in *Kimel* (2000), it is § 5 of the 14th Amendment that grants Congress the authority to abrogate the states' sovereign immunity. The *Kimel* Court further ruled that the ultimate interpretation and determination of the 14th Amendment's substantive meaning remains the province of the judicial branch.
33. Also see Bodensteiner and Levinson (2001).
34. See *Will v. Michigan Department of State Police* (1989, p. 70). Also see Bodensteiner and Levinson (2001).
35. In *Ex parte Young*, the Supreme Court ruled that 11th Amendment sovereign immunity does not bar federal suits against state government officials for violations of federal rights. It should further be noted, however, that a number of recent U.S. circuit court decisions have limited liability claims under certain statutes, including the ADEA, the ADA, and Title VII to employers only, thus eliminating the possibility of naming state governmental officials in their official capacity. See, for example, *Silk v. City of Chicago* (7th Cir. 1999), holding that the ADA provides only for employer, not individual liability; *Wathen v. General Electric Company* (6th Cir. 1997), holding that individual liability is prohibited under Title VII; *Mason v. Stallings* (11th Cir. 1996), holding that Title I of ADA does not provide for individual liability, only for employer liability. Also see Bodensteiner and Levinson (2001).
36. Also see *Alden v. Maine* (1999), in which the Supreme Court recognized that the FLSA remains enforceable against state governments in actions brought by the U.S. Department of Labor.

REFERENCES

Alden v. Maine, 527 U.S. 706 (1999).

Althouse, A. (2001). Inside the federalism cases: Concern about the federal courts. *The Annals of The American Academy of Political and Social Science, 574,* 132–145.

Bodensteiner, I.E., & Levinson, R.B. (2001). Litigating age and disability claims against state and local government employers in the new "federalism" era. *Berkeley Journal of Employment and Labor Law, 22,* 99–129.

Braveman, D. (2000). Enforcement of federal rights against states: *Alden* and federalism nonsense. *The American University Law Review, 49,* 611–657.

Bush v. Gore, 531 U.S. 98 (2000).

Chisholm v. Georgia, 2 U.S. 419 (1793).

City of Boerne v. Flores, 521 U.S. 507 (1997).

Cleburne v. Cleburne, 473 U.S. 432 (1985).

College Savings Bank v. Florida Prepaid Postsecondary Education Expense Board, 527 U.S. 666 (1999).

Driesse v. Florida Board of Regents, 26 F.Supp.2d 1328, 1332–34 (M.D. Fla. 1998).

Equal Employment Opportunity Commission v. Wyoming, 460 U.S. 226 (1983).

Fitzpatrick v. Bitzer, 427 U.S. 445 (1976).

Florida Prepaid Postsecondary Education Expense Board v. College Savings Bank, 527 U.S. 627 (1999).

Garcia v. San Antonio Metropolitan Transit Authority, 469 U.S. 528 (1985).

Garrett v. the University of Alabama, 193 F.3d 1214 (11th Cir. 1999); University of Alabama at Birmingham Board of Trustees v. Garrett, *cert. granted*, 529 U.S. 1065 (2000); Board of Trustees of the University of Alabama v. Garrett, 531 U.S. 356 121 S.Ct. 955 (2001).

Goodman, F. (2001). Preface. *The Annals of The American Academy of Political and Social Science, 574,* 9–24.

Gore v. Harris, 772 So.2d 1243 (2000); *revised and remanded,* Bush v. Gore, 531 U.S. 98 (2000).

Goshtasby v. Board of Trustees of the University of Illinois, 141 F.3d 761, 765–66 (7th Cir. 1998).

Hundertmark v. State of Florida Department of Transportation, 205 F.3d 1272, 1275, n. 2. (11th Cir. 2000).

Hurtado v. California, 110 U.S. 516 (1884).

Illinois State University v. Varner, 528 U.S. 1110 (2000), vacating Varner v. Illinois State University, 150 F.3d 706 (7th Cir. 1998); *on remand*, Varner v. Illinois State University, 226 F.3d 927 (2000).

In re Employment Discrimination Litigation Against the State of Alabama, 198 F.3d 1305 (11th Cir. 1999).

Jusino Mercado v. Commonwealth of Puerto Rico, 214 F.3d 34, 36 n.1. (2000).

Kearney, R.C. (1992). *Labor relations in the public sector* (2nd ed.). New York: Marcel Dekker.

Kilvitis v. County of Luzerne, 52 F.Supp.2d 403, 408–409 (M.D. Pa. 1999).

Kimel v. Florida Board of Regents, 528 U.S. 62 (2000).

Lee, R. D. (1999). The Rehabilitation Act and federal employment. *Review of Public Personnel Administration, 19,* 45–64.

Lee, R.D., & Greenlaw, P.S. (1998–1999). Rights and responsibilities of employees and employers under the Americans with Disabilities Act of 1990. *Journal of Individual Employment Rights, 7,* 1–13.

Levinson, R.B. (2000). Litigation and administrative practice course handbook series: Discrimination claims. *Practicing Law Institute, 646,* 81–102.

Mason v. Stallings, 82 F.3d 1007 (11th Cir. 1996).

Merico-Stephens, A.M. (2000). Of Maine's sovereignty, Alden's federalism, and the myth of absolute principles: The newest oldest questions of constitutional law. *University of California at Davis Law Review, 33,* 325–388.

Murdock, G.B., Jr., Sezer, K., & Hodge, J.S. (2000). Developments in Title VII and Section 1981: Implications for Title VII. *Practicing Law Institute, 29th Annual Institute on Employment Law, 637,* 597–624.

National League of Cities v. Usery, 426 U.S. 833 (1976).

Printz v. United States, 521 U.S. 898 (1997).

Ray, B. (2000). Out the window? Prospects for the EPA and FMLA after *Kimel v. Florida Board of Regents. Ohio State Law Journal*, 61, 1755–1792.

Rosenbloom, D. H. (1994). Fuzzy law from the high court. *Public Administration Review*, 54, 503–506.

Rosenbloom, D.H. (1997). Public employees' liability for "constitutional torts." In C. Ban & N. M. Riccucci (Eds.), *Public personnel management: Current concerns, future challenges* (pp. 237–252.) New York: Longman.

Rosenbloom, D. H., Carroll, J., & Carroll, J. (2000). *Constitutional competence for public managers: Cases and commentary.* Itasca, IL: F.E. Peacock.

Rosenbloom, D. H., & Shafritz, J. M. (1985). *Essentials of labor relations.* Reston, VA: Reston Publishing.

Seminole Tribe of Florida, 517 U.S. 44 (1996).

Silk v. City of Chicago, 194 F.3d 788 (7th Cir. 1999).

Sims v. University of Cincinnati, 219 F.3d 559, 566 (6th Cir. 2000).

Solid Waste Agency of Northern Cook County v. U.S. Army Corps of Engineers, 531 U.S. 159 (2001).

State University of New York, College at New Paltz v. Anderson, 120 S. Ct. 929 (2000), *vacating* 169 F.3d 117 (2d Cir. 1999).

Stults v. Conoco, Inc., 76 F.3d 651, 655 (5th Cir. 1996).

United States v. Lopez, 514 U.S. 549 (1995).

United States v. Morrison, 529 U.S. 598 (2000).

Varner v. Illinois State University, 150 F.3d 706, (7th Cir. 1998); *vacated and remanded*, Illinois State University v. Varner, 528 U.S. 1110 (2000); *on remand*, Varner v. Illinois State University, 226 F.3d 927 (7th Cir. 2000).

Wathen v. General Electric Company, 115 F.3d 400, 405 (6th Cir. 1997).

Wickard v. Filburn, 317 U.S. 111 (1942).

Will v. Michigan Department of State Police, 491 U.S. 58 (1989).

Wise, C.R. (2001). The Supreme Court's new consitutional federalism: Implications for public administration. *Public Administration Review*, 61, 343–358.

***Norma M. Riccucci** is professor of public administration in the Graduate Department of Public Administration at Rutgers University, Campus at Newark. She has published extensively in the areas of public management, employment discrimination law, affirmative action, and public sector labor relations. Her most recent book is* Managing Diversity in Public Sector Workforces, *published by Westview Press.*

From *Review of Public Personnel Administration,* Vol. 23, No. 1, March 2003, pp. 3-22.

TEA Time in Washington

The debate goes on as Congress faces a September 30 deadline for reauthorizing the nation's surface transportation law.

By Jason Jordan

Looking across the platform at the Chamblee MARTA station in metropolitan Atlanta, riders see boldly printed banners spanning Peachtree Road. The banners advertise new loft apartments and live/work spaces, to be carved out of industrial buildings. Below the platform are various pedestrian-access improvements—new sidewalks and crosswalks, lighting, and landscaping. These enhancements will connect the transit and bus station to the new housing, a nearby business district, and a commercial corridor.

The changes in Chamblee, however modest, represent a new national approach to transportation planning and the legacy of a landmark federal transportation law, the Intermodal Surface Transportation Efficiency Act of 1991 and its successor, 1998's Transportation Efficiency Act for the 21 st Century. The Atlanta Regional Commission used flexible funds authorized by TEA-21 to create its Livable Centers Initiative, which encourages mixed-use development around stations in the MARTA (for Metropolitan Atlanta Rapid Transit Authority) system.

As one of the first communities to take advantage of the program, Chamblee won a $50,000 LCI grant to conduct a planning study and amend the zoning for a 250-acre area around its MARTA station. Additional grants, totaling almost $2 million, were used to plan and fund pedestrian and street enhancements. MARTA's contribution was to designate several surrounding agency-owned parcels for mixed-use, transit-oriented development.

The TOD planning attracted a developer, who is now in the process of creating lofts as part of a $22 million redevelopment project. The larger project includes other loft conversions, new retail, and additional bicycle and pedestrian enhancements.

According to Thomas Weyandt, the director of comprehensive planning for the Atlanta Regional Commission, that's exactly the sort of integrated approach to transportation and land use that LCI was intended to spur. "LCI provides the resources for the community to examine the problem in a new way," he says, "and it's a flexible incentive; it helps solidify the idea of a connection between land use and transportation."

But will it continue? Not if funding disappears, says Weyandt. "We are clearly in a situation where resources are disproportionate to our needs." Now, he says, we need to bolster programs that encourage local decision making, offer more flexibility, and "are backed up by the resources to make things happen."

ISTEA's legacy

Before 1991, the LCI program would simply not have been possible. Now, it seems to most a natural, common-sense approach. The program and the approach to transportation investments it represents are the direct result of a revamped federal policy embodied in ISTEA and TEA-21. This legislation, which in all has provided a record $300 billion for surface transportation, has fundamentally reformed the nation's transportation system.

Ivan Bock, owner of a beauty supply business in Chamblee, sees the results. Half of his 10 or so employees have become transit riders, he says. And now other employees who live in outer suburban areas not served by transit long to be connected.

ISTEA has actually changed public attitudes toward transit, according to former APA deputy director George Marcou, FAICP, who was directly involved in promoting and crafting the law's planning provisions. The act represented a critical step in the "evolution of thinking about public policies and investments in a way that actively links transportation with things like housing, air quality, and land use," he says.

In ISTEA, says Marcou, we can also see the genesis of smart growth as a political movement. In the period leading up to its passage, "planning, land use, and transportation became environmental issues. Air quality concerns led environmentalists to take a broader view and turned an array of groups previously working in relative isolation into a real coalition." This experience not only produced a landmark transportation law but also set the stage for future cooperation and activism.

Deadline

The September 30 deadline for enacting a new surface transportation law has some observers worried. The storm clouds looming over reauthorization (described as a "perfect political storm" by one prominent lobbyist) include state and local fiscal crises, federal budget deficits, security concerns, and global uncertainties.

Such a climate makes some fearful about the future of key programs. "We had hoped reauthorization would be about new innovations," says Deron Lovaas of the National Resources Defense Council. "Now, frankly, preserving the basic framework is the top priority."

Even in the early stages of reauthorization, the White House and leaders on Capitol Hill appear far apart ($128 billion, in fact) on the funding issue. In the Bush administration's draft reauthorization proposal, dubbed SAFETEA for Safe and Flexible Transportation Efficiency Act of 2003, highway and transit spending starts at $37.5 billion in fiscal 2004, and ends at $43 billion in 2009.

Meanwhile, the bipartisan leadership of the House Transportation and Infrastructure Committee is pushing a plan that projects spending moving from $50 billion to $75 billion over the life of the bill. "My committee believes that we cannot afford to merely maintain the status quo," said chairman Don Young (R-Alaska) in February when the administration's budget was released. "The status quo is strangling our economy, limiting our mobility, and affecting our daily lives to an unacceptable degree."

There are key differences as to the sources of funding. Young and the committee's ranking minority member, James Oberstar (D-Minn.), call for retroactively indexing federal gas taxes to inflation, which would mean a tax of 23.75 cents per gallon in 2004. The White House has rejected any tax increase.

Young and Oberstar would also plow interest payments back into the Highway Trust Fund. Under TEA-21, trust fund interest was diverted to the general fund to pay down the national debt. Their plan also directs all revenues from ethanol user fees to the trust fund.

The divide was made clear when Congress adopted the budget resolution for fiscal year 2004. The House, while adhering to the administration's projections, left the door open to increases should revenues be increased through gas taxes or other means. The Senate's budget resolution was $70 billion higher than the administration's proposal.

All of the revenue options face political obstacles. Any policy change affecting the general fund has implications for the growing federal budget deficit, and proposals to alter ethanol or gasohol subsidies are sure to run afoul of farm state lawmakers.

In the Senate, there's a new chair of the Environment and Public Works Committee, that body's key reauthorization panel. Sen. James Inhofe (R-Okla.), whose history as an opponent of some air quality regulations worries many, has responded cooly to the gas tax increases floated by his House counterpart. Oklahoma is a so-called donor state, meaning that it receives less in transportation funding than it pays into the highway trust fund. Whether or not Sen. Inhofe plans to open up the state formula issue is not yet clear.

Roads vs. transit

Advocates for transit and other non-highway spending have particular fears this time around. Even if overall funding levels increase, they worry that the ratio of highway spending to transit spending may tip in favor of highways.

Times were different five years ago when TEA-21 sailed through Congress. "Everybody got fed last time around," notes one lobbyist. Mid-'90s budget surpluses and a strong economy provided ample revenue to smooth out differences in policy. "The transit strategy was basically, if the highway guys eat well, there will be enough crumbs around for everyone else to go home happy. It may not work out that way this year."

Additionally, there is concern that requirements for local matching funds may be increased. The administration has proposed boosting the local match requirement for the main transit program, New Starts, from 20 percent to 50 percent. New Starts provides federal funding for the development of major new transit programs, including subways and light rail.

Transit supporters argue that such a move, which is intended to spread transit funding to more communities, would tilt the scales in favor of highway projects. They maintain that expanding funding for New Starts while considering additional aid for alternate approaches, such as bus rapid transit systems, is a better way to serve more communities.

State budget crises further complicate the funding math of reauthorization. According to the Washington-based Center on Budget and Policy Priorities, state budget deficits for the upcoming fiscal year will total between $70 billion and $85 billion, higher than any point in the last half-century.

Many states are already considering tapping their transportation trust funds to fill the funding gap.

An analysis released earlier this year by the Surface Transportation Policy Project notes that many states have been reluctant to increase gas taxes or user fees to pay their share of the matching funds required under TEA-21. Instead, they have in the past tended to rely on revenues from general funds or increased state borrowing, options not readily available now.

Environmental question mark

Another flashpoint in the reauthorization debate is environmental protection. Last year, legislation was introduced in the House to streamline environmental reviews of transportation projects. This legislation, developed by House committee chair Don Young, was never enacted but may be included in the reauthorization proposal. Also last year, President George W. Bush issued an executive order calling for expedited review of selected projects.

Several interest groups involved in reauthorization have issued their own proposals calling for concurrent reviews by state and federal environmental agencies; fixed timelines for completion of reviews; limits on participation in the review process; and categorical exemptions from reviews triggered by the National Environmental Policy Act.

Environmentalists respond that project schedules can be speeded up without major changes in the entire regulatory review process. They note that an analysis conducted by the Federal Highway Administration found that more than two-thirds of project delays result from insufficient funding, lack of local support, or the complexity of the project—not from environmental review.

Air quality regulations are part of this debate. Currently planners must consider impacts on air quality when drafting transportation plans. In certain cases, if a state falls out of compliance with certain standards, it is subject to restrictions on transportation projects and may even lose federal funding.

But many metropolitan areas are having difficulty meeting the conformity requirements, a situation that is expected to grow worse in the coming years. Critics charge that the regulatory penalties are in fact often counterproductive to the goal of improved air quality.

In hearings now being held in the Senate, various alternatives are being discussed. One amendment would allow projects that don't conform to every requirement to go forward if they can prove that emissions will be lower when the project is completed. Many environmentalists worry, however, that this amendment and others endanger the whole idea of linking air quality to transportation spending.

Also at issue is expansion of the Congestion Mitigation and Air Quality Improvement program, which was established under ISTEA and expanded through TEA-21. CMAQ was designed to help transportation agencies comply with Clean Air Act standards by funding projects aimed at reducing emissions and encouraging alternatives to more polluting forms of travel.

The program's advocates are urging Congress to expand CMAQ's modest funding level, currently about $1.4 billion, and in crease its effectiveness by allowing metropolitan planning organizations serving areas that don't meet federal air quality standards (Atlanta is one) to receive funding directly.

Flexible funding

One vital part of TEA-21, the Transportation and Community and System Preservation program, gives local governments unusual flexibility. The program, which is part of the law's Transportation Enhancements section, funds plans and projects that link land use, livability, and transportation. In the last round of funding, TCSP received $25 million, which was used for a wide variety of projects aimed at linking land use and transportation.

The problem is that the demand for TCSP funding has far outstripped supply, reflecting the growing local desire for transportation solutions that go beyond road construction. Smart growth advocates are pressing for an increase—and for new criteria for awards.

According to planner Tom Weyandt, being able to use flexible TCSP dollars to leverage state and local investments is a key to the success of the Atlanta Regional Council's transit-oriented programs. Those are the funds that have enabled ARC to spur transit-oriented development and various "quality growth" initiatives.

Former Sen. Daniel Patrick Moynihan (D-N.Y.), who died March 27 at 76, was remembered at APA's national conference in Denver as a friend of planning. In 1992, noted APA executive director Paul Farmer, AICP, Moynihan was the first recipient of APA's Legislator of the Year award for his work on ISTEA, the Intermodal Surface Transportation Efficiency Act. Moynihan was a strong supporter of the act's planning provisions. More recently, he played a leading role in the successful effort to revitalize New York's Penn Station. Moynihan, who served 20 years in the Senate, was a former professor of urban studies at Harvard University and a former ambassador to the United Nations. He was also a prime advocate for the revitalization of Pennsylvania Avenue in the District of Columbia.

Watchlist

Among the issues that are sure to be part of the reauthorization debate are these:

- *Social equity.* Will funding be assured for low-income and special needs communities? One program known to be in jeopardy is the Jobs Access and Reverse Commute program, which was established by TEA-21 to help low-income workers make the transition from welfare to work. The administration has proposed that JARC resources be diverted into other programs.
- *Participation.* For planners, a major opportunity in reauthorization is the chance to improve public participation in the planning process. APA and others have urged that the law include language mandating "early and continuous" citizen input and that it provide support for the development of new visualization technologies, which make the planning process more accessible and have the potential to enhance the planning link between transportation and other land uses.

- *MPOs.* As the entities primarily responsible for transportation planning, metropolitan planning organizations have special, and growing, needs. Alex Taft, the executive director of the Association of Metropolitan Planning Organizations, notes that up to 40 new MPOs have been created as a result of the last census. He urges that TEA-21 provide additional planning funds to help deal with increasingly complex requirements. Currently, the Federal Transit Administration allocates .7 percent for planning and the Federal Highway Administration provides one percent. Taft's group is urging Congress to at least double those ratios.

- *Language.* Many also hope that TEA-21 will revise its "planning factor" language. Dan Reuter, AICP, chief of the land-use division at the Atlanta Regional Commission, is among those calling for a specific mention of land-use planning.

- *Context-sensitive design.* Many state transportation departments, with support from the American Association of State Highway and Transit Officials, have already launched context-sensitive design programs that provide alternatives to strict, traditional engineering standards. Advocates like Reuter hope for increased funding for research and training.

For smart growth proponents throughout the country, TEA-21 reauthorization may be the most important piece of federal legislation facing Congress today. In the words of Don Chen, executive director of Smart Growth America, a research and advocacy organization, "Through ISTEA, TEA-21, and now the pending reauthorization, we have an opportunity to use federal policy to empower local communities to build better, smarter futures."

Resources

APA. Last year, APA convened a task force to come up with recommendations for TEA-21 reauthorization. For a complete account, see www.planning.org/legislation. Also on the website: a list of key congressional leaders in reauthorization and tips on effective techniques for legislative advocacy.

On-line. Atlanta Regional Commission, www.atlreg.com. Surface Transportation Policy Project, www.transact.org. Association of Metropolitan Planning Organizations, www.ampo.org. American Public Transportation Association, www.apta.com. American Association of State Highway and Transit Officials, www.aashto.org. Smart Growth America www.smartgrowthamerica.org

---

Jason Jordan is APA's government affairs coordinator.

UNIT 7

International and Comparative Public Administration and Policy

Unit Selections

Key Points to Consider

- Identify and discuss some of the ways in which Holland provides quality housing for its citizens. Also discuss how the Dutch go about national planning. Do you agree or disagree with the way the Dutch conduct their planning and housing activities? Why or why not? Are there any lessons that Americans can learn from the Dutch in these areas?
- Identify and discuss the problems of delivering quality public services to the poor of South Africa. Why is privatization a problem? What are some of the things that can be done to improve the situation?
- Discuss England's experiment with e-Voting. Do you think that the results are successful enough to implement e-Voting in the United States? Why or why not?
- Discuss Ghana's efforts to reform its public service and public administration systems. How do these reforms compare with U.S. reform ideas? Have any of these reforms led to an improved quality of life for Ghana citizens?
- Identify and discuss the innovative use of outcomes in public sector management in the New Zealand public sector. What are some of the things that American public administrators can learn from the New Zealand examples?

Links: www.dushkin.com/online/
These sites are annotated in the World Wide Web pages.

Division for Public Administration and Development Management
http://www.unpan.org/dpepa.asp

European Group of Public Administration (EGPA)
http://www.iiasiisa.be/egpa/agacc.htm

Governments on the WWW
http://www.gksoft.com/govt/en/

Institute of Public Administration of Canada (IPAC)
http://www.ipaciapc.ca

Latin American Center for Development Administration (CLAD)
http://www.clad.org.ve/siare/index.htm

Section on International and Comparative Administration (SICA)
http://www.uncc.edu/stwalker/sica/

UNPAN
http://www.unpan.org

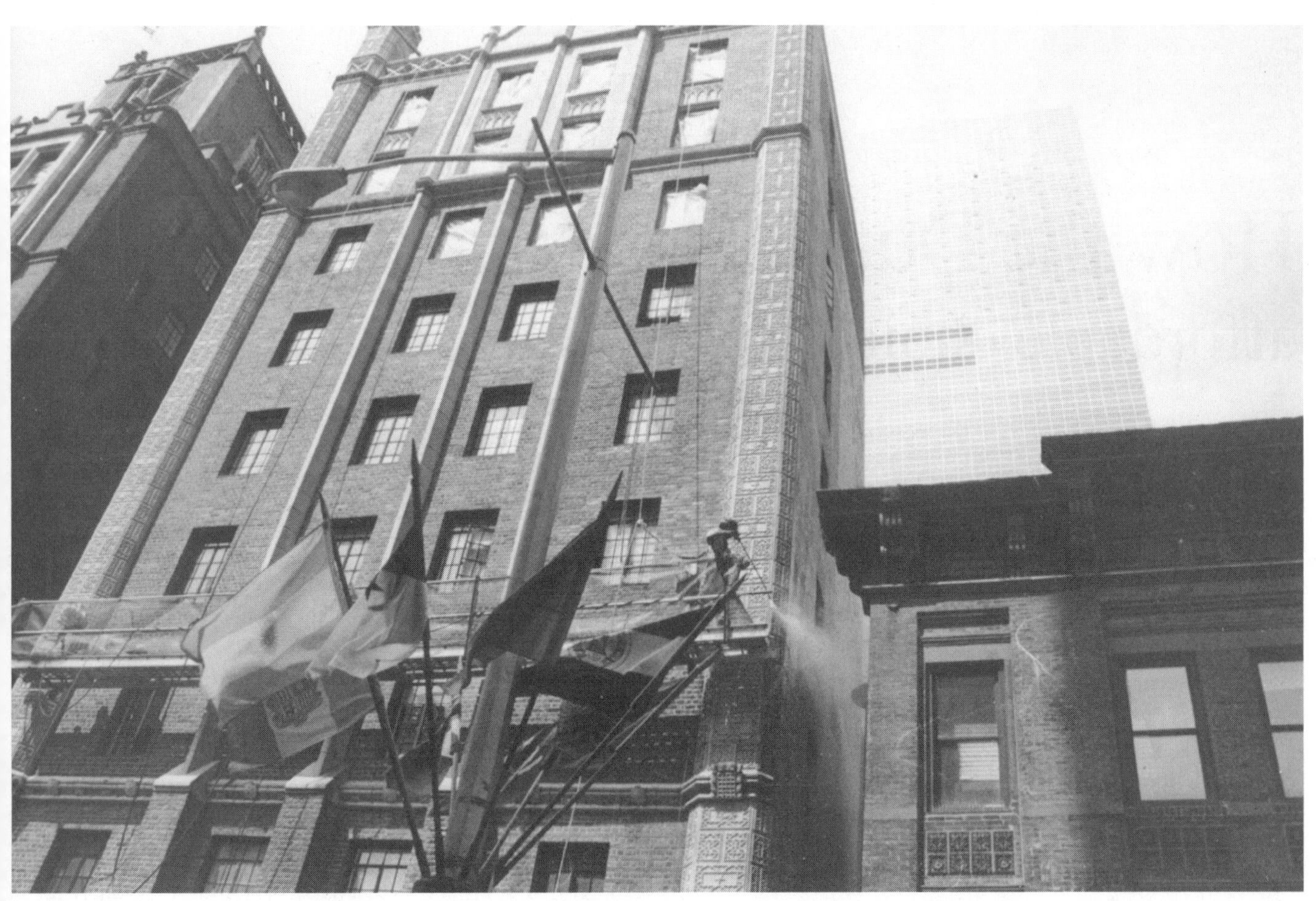

The articles in this unit examine international public administration and public policy issues around the world. They provide the reader with some comparative information in the areas of governance, housing, health, elections, and administration.

In "How the Dutch Do Housing," Jane Holtz Kay states that national planning is required not just for housing but for the conservation of water, land, infrastructure, and forests. Such national planning is essential to Holland's existence and accounts for its progressive reputation. According to the author, the Netherlands does have something to offer to other countries in the way of excellent planning practices in all of these areas.

Ginger Thompson, in her article "Water Tap is Often Shut to South Africa Poor," says that democracy has come to South Africa, but the country has a long way to go in terms of delivering basic public services to its population. According to the author, local governments are not delivering adequate water and utility services to the population. Privatization has also created a special set of problems. In South Africa, access to utility services is limited by the ability to pay, and unfortunately for most of the population, there is no ability to pay for water.

Shane Peterson, in the article "England Tests e-Voting," discusses the fact that England has conducted a series of pilot tests using e-voting over the Internet. According to the author, the results have been successful.

"Reforming Ghana's Public Service: Issues and Experiences in Comparative Perspective," by Peter Fuseini Haruna, addresses how the public service can be reformed to make it relevant to the circumstances and useful to the majority of the people living and working in Ghana. Using Ghana as a case study, the author summarizes and evaluates that country's reform efforts and compares them to mainstream Anglo-American reform ideas in order to provide a better understanding of comparative public administration.

"Outcome-Focused Management in New Zealand," by Andrew Kibblewhite and Chris Ussher, discusses the uses of outcomes in public sector management in New Zealand. The authors describe the overall management system within which governments operate and explain how outcomes are used within the system. In addition, case studies of innovative uses of outcomes in the New Zealand public sector are provided.

How the Dutch Do Housing…
affordable choices in the Netherlands

By Jane Holtz Kay

Holland is a self-made nation.

Smaller than Connecticut, more crowded than Japan,… the country has shaped its housing policies across a waterbound landscape, limited in everything but the need to plan. Both the acres of land reclaimed from the Zuider Zee since the 1930s and the number of housing units built by the government since World War II would dumbfound U.S. planners.

Add the newer designs by Dutch architects, and you have not only aesthetic flair but the "level-headed and pragmatic application of technology and planning," as *SuperDutch*, the aptly titled 2000 book by Bart Lootsmar, observes.

National planning, not just for housing but for the conservation of water, land, infrastructure, and forests, is essential to Holland's existence and accounts for its reputation. So do progressive policies like the postwar plan to set aside some 30 percent of dwelling places for "social" (public) housing.

Amsterdam's newest housing mecca, the Eastern Harbour, built on reclaimed land ("polders," in Dutch), is impressive. After a long planning process and a 1988 referendum to determine the national will, the Dutch transformed the docklands into four communities. The first step was the removal of a slaughterhouse on the industrial island of KNSM in 1988. Development followed on the islands, peninsulas really, of Java and Borneo Sporenburg.

By adroitly massing and individualizing rowhouses and outdoor space, the scheme for the new land set a pattern of unity and diversity. The rowhouses, behind splendid facades, offer light and views from patios and open space. Parking is out of sight. The result: compact but splendidly shaped surroundings that provide 8,000 homes for 17,000 people.

Borneo Sporenburg boasts the unique Scheepstimmermanstratt, an avenue of rowhouses, shoulder to shoulder along the canals. Last fall, it earned its creator, architect Adriaan Geuze of the firm West 8, Harvard's prestigious Veronica Rudge Green Prize for contributing to the public realm and urban life.

The old days

Recent Dutch housing hasn't always held to such high standards. *Spatial Planning and the Environment*, a recently published report by the Ministry of Housing, has the tone of an apologia. Noting the affluence and aging of the population and the shrinking size of the family, the document looks penitently at the last decades, when quantity of housing topped quality. The result, say the authors, was often shoddy, or at the least unfriendly, construction.

"By the late 1970s, it was clear that architecture was hemorrhaging," writes Lootsmar in *SuperDutch*. Plans for city centers languished. A visit bears that out. Like Europe and America, the Netherlands succumbed to Corbusian tower-in-the-park urban renewal, bland high-rise boxes, and sprawling suburbanization and is stuck with it.

Sterile mid-rises from the 1960s are the rule in Rotterdam's old harborfront neighborhood of Kop van Zuid, site of the barracks from which Dutch Jews were deported during World War II. And to walk through the Zuidoost center outside Amsterdam today is to see a grim, wind-whipped Edge City of towers; a drab sports arena; a glitzy, failed theater; and low-scale apartments—many in need of rehabilitation or even uprooting.

Even the supposed core city of Almere, a new town near Amsterdam, offers a grim, car-centered environment. The boxy, mid-rise buildings now under construction are chillingly bleak. Even the pleasant, single-family, canalside houses, designed by the architecture firm MVRVD on Almere's outskirts, and other buildings by well-known architects are devoid of shops and dependent on cars. Despite bike paths and bus-only lanes, such remote outposts give not even a nod to Amsterdam's transportation web.

Dutch architecture has changed dramatically in the last 20 years, with superstars like Rem Koolhaus grabbing the world stage. But housing design has not always kept pace. A decade ago, the national government's Fourth Report on Physical Planning called for new housing districts to be built at countless scattered sites.

The program was criticized for its dispersal and lack of public transportation. Now expanding, it is slated to create a total of 634,800 new dwellings by 2005. The good news is that it will locate roughly two-thirds of that housing in more central, urban zones.

Still, despite these cautionary notes, Holland's planners have an easier lot than their U.S. peers, who are bogged down by complicated and limited federal housing policies, a housing budget diminished by two-thirds in the '90s, and a disdain for city housing needs.

Changing times

For all the Netherlands' planning pluses, its policies are shifting toward more market-oriented housing, as the country as a whole tilts toward the right. Last year's national election reflected this shift.

"Entering the real world of market-driven reality" has lessened government authority, says housing expert Arjen Oosterman. A government that once financed and dictated the course of housing corporations is letting go and loosening controls.

In an ironic twist, this change is occurring just as U.S. eyes turn eastward, seeking to absorb housing lessons from the Dutch, as U.S. planners have studied transportation in France and Germany. "New Design Paradigms for Housing," a program presented at New York's Van Alen Institute by the New Amsterdam Development Corporation, a group of Dutch developers, planners, and architects turning their attention to the city, attracted considerable interest from builders and others interested in the field.

In June, New York's Urban Center will kick off a six-city tour of examples of Dutch urban housing. The models, says Els Verbaken, the exhibit designer who assembled the show, "combine medium or high density with safety, ecology, and tranquility, qualities that are usually found in low-density circumstances."

Verbaken notes that most of the recent Dutch projects were financed by private money, contradicting the assumptions of many Americans about the key role of the government in housing, or at least in high style housing, in the Netherlands.

Who is being served?

In a late fall phone interview, Hans Huijsman, secretary of the Netherlands' central Board of Housing Assistance, looks back 100 years to describe Holland's slums, gradually eradicated by social housing, then skips forward to the last decade's movement toward deregulation. Today, he says, market orientation and financial self-sufficiency are the mode. Government policies that now force municipalities to sell 30 percent of any new development to individual owners for "custom-made" houses are a far cry from earlier public emphases.

"Things are changing quite drastically," he continues. With living space short, jammed cities like Amsterdam (once 80 percent subsidized housing) must shift from serving the hard-pressed to encouraging the comfortable. Today's focus on serving middle- and high-income groups to entice them to stay in cities can slight the disadvantaged. Likewise, stricter proof of legality from immigrants and performance agreements exacted from low-income renters squeeze the less fortunate.

"It was a good system," Huijsman says of the earlier subsidized housing requirements. But he's not opposed to the recent changes: "I think it was high time," he says of the shift in policy.

Others are more skeptical. There's more of a "free-for-all for developers," says Aaron Betsky, Dutch-born head of the Netherlands Architecture Institute in Rotterdam and former director of the San Francisco Museum of Art.

Still, some things haven't changed. The most densely built country in the world still has a pressing need to diagram its future, to look ahead, Betsky feels. "Every plan, every road becomes one giant three-D puzzle," he says. Nevertheless, the shift toward prioritizing private development is troublesome.

Some critics feel that the emphasis on "quality" and "free choice" in the latest Dutch housing survey, conducted by the ministry every fifth year, is a way of kowtowing to developers and serving the affluent. Even at Amsterdam's model Docklands development, planners succumbed to a supermarket developer's demand to exclude small shops for 10 years. And with few transit linkages, residents are left with a choice of 15-minute bike rides to get downtown or a slow crawl through increasing traffic jams.

Unsettled future

How much and how fast will such shifts in thinking alter a nation that keeps 83 percent of its land mass green—for farms (70 percent) and open space (13 percent)? Compact development is still a political dictate in this dense nation, says Huijsman. That won't change, but imperfect implementation will make it hard to check "negative development"—homes heading out of designated central cities.

Harm Tilman, editor of *de Architect*, fears that planning in his country is no more immune to car dominance and polynuclear settlements than it was to the '60s high-rise craze. "We have had a very social kind of development," he says, "but now the old model is in revision." Private housing is promoted, and public spaces and social housing are less assured. A tilt to the right, and to the road, threatens Dutch life. "We have to rethink" what we are doing, he says.

Still, for all such shifts in social policy, the Dutch legacy and achievement in planning are remarkable—socially, quantitatively, and administratively. Spend time in Holland or count the reams of documents and designs, and the model seems alive and well. Factor in that these accomplishments have been achieved for a population of almost 16 million living on 7,000 square miles of mostly reclaimed land—75 percent since World War II—and admiration grows.

Despite the Netherlands' diminishing ratio of subsidized housing to market housing (already down to 30 percent from earlier 50-50 figures), the number of such dwellings would turn a U.S. housing activist green with envy. Equally enviable is the fact that the Dutch have sacrificed neither their social values, nor their urbanism, to that growth. Health care, public universities, and public schools reflect their progressive stance.

Densification

While the U.S. offers minimal direction to settlement or structure, Dutch law demands Bijlmermeur ("bundled deconcentration"), or densification. Thus, two-thirds of the nation's 6.5 million housing units consist of attached houses. Another third are in low-rise apartment buildings. Only a small number are single-family houses.

The Ministry of Housing still restricts half of all new housing to built-up areas within the Randstad—the western conurbation around Amsterdam, Rotterdam, the Hague, Utrecht, and the newer, less urban Almere—in order to preserve its "Green Heart."

The $450 million, 1990 Delta Metropolis plan for the area centered on the deltas of the Rhine, Mense, and Schelder rivers will be reinforced by the construction of some 190,000 homes between 2010 and 2030, all linked to a planned Deltametro light rail line. "It is sustainable development," Allard Jolles, architectural historian in Amsterdam's 75-year-old physical planning department, says of the plan that will add 50,000 new housing units in Amsterdam alone.

In plans for housing released after the United Nations summit conference in Johannesburg last year, the government spoke of "definitive urbanization accords" in 40 to 60 urban districts and 20 urban regions to accommodate an estimated million more people in the Delta Metropolis by 2030.

Always, strict building and design codes will set guidelines for everything from height to sustainability. And, despite change, the system of leasing the land, rather than outright purchase, will remain, benefiting "the community as a whole," says Jolles.

Still, housing advocates worry that the shift from social to speculative housing will drive out Holland's vaunted "polder" model of consensus, based on the historic need to join resources to reclaim a nation, and its imaginative design.Will the country maintain the social policies and tolerance that made it one of Europe's most progressive?

Whatever the outcome, what happens to Dutch housing matters. "If we are concerned about the future of the spatial debate, the Netherlands does have something to offer to other countries," says Betsky, as nations on both sides of the Atlantic look on.

Resources

Reading. *SuperDutch*, by Bart Lootsmar, published in 2000 by Princeton Architectural Press.

On the web. See the work of MVRDV (Maas, van Rijs and de Vries) at www.mvrdv.archined.nl/mvrdv.html.

Jane Holtz Kay is author of *Asphalt Nation* and *Lost Boston* and architecture critic for *The Nation.*

Water Tap Often Shut to South Africa Poor

By GINGER THOMPSON

SHAKASHEAD, South Africa—The afternoon's end brings a rural rush hour of women walking down the dirt road that winds through this village. Many of them barefoot and dressed in rags, the mothers and grandmothers come pushing wheelbarrows or carrying big buckets to fetch water for their families.

But the road quickly becomes a divide between the haves and have-nots. Those with pennies to spend stand in line on one side and buy their water from a metered tap.

The larger group scoops water from a giant, littered mud puddle across the way. Sewage seeps in from leaky pipes nearby. Some of the women said that cholera had stricken their families. Workers at a mobile clinic have reported high rates of diarrhea among children here.

"I know it is not good to take water from this hole," said Nolulama Makhiwa, a 27-year-old mother of two. "But I am not working. I have no money. What else can I do?"

Not long after the country's first democratic government came to power in 1994, putting an end to white minority rule, the new government enshrined the right to "sufficient food and water" in its Constitution, and pledged to make water and sanitation available to every citizen by the end of 2010.

At the same time, the government also began to shift more of the financial burden of those promises to a population in which at least one-third of people live on less than $2 a day. Officials urged municipal water utilities to adopt "cost recovery" policies that require them at least to break even, if not turn a profit.

Municipalities have begun working to turn debt-ridden and inefficient water utilities into profitable operations that could attract private investment. A handful have already granted long-term management concessions to private multinationals.

Advocates argue that such policies have become conventional wisdom, helping governments around the world make ends meet while encouraging conservation. Not only here in South Africa, however, but also in other developing countries like Bolivia, Ecuador and Argentina, privatization and water pricing have met strong resistance and public protests.

"Privatization is a new kind of apartheid," said Richard Makolo, leader of the Crisis Water Committee, which was formed to resist the privatization effort in a township called Orange Farm, 25 miles south of Johannesburg. "Apartheid separated whites from blacks. Privatization separates the rich from the poor."

South African officials say the change in policies has helped expand water services to 8 million of 13 million people who did not have water when apartheid ended. But the statistics have not added up to progress in many poor communities, which have won their first reliable water services but now struggle to pay for them.

The issue of access to services has become an explosive new cause in the same urban townships and rural squatter camps that were principal battlegrounds in the fight against apartheid. During the World Summit on Sustainable Development last August, thousands marched from the tin shacks of Alexandra past the elegant mansions of Sandton to protest, among other things, water and electricity cutoffs and evictions. Their cry: "Water for the thirsty. Light for the people. Homes for the homeless."

Leaders in sprawling townships including Soweto, Alexandra and Orange Farm have encouraged people not to pay electricity and water bills. They have organized teams of bootleg plumbers and electricians to reconnect utilities when they are cut off. Political rallies and demonstrations have turned into street fights.

The highest costs to poor communities have come in the form of disease and mass disconnections. Three years ago, this province on the northeast coast was the center of the country's worst cholera epidemic in recent history, with 120,000 reported cases and nearly 260 deaths. The epidemic spread to seven of the country's nine provinces.

Small outbreaks continue to occur, as those who cannot afford to pay for water in advance from communal meters or have been cut off from services for not paying rising water bills are forced to seek sources in polluted puddles, rivers and canals that carry disease.

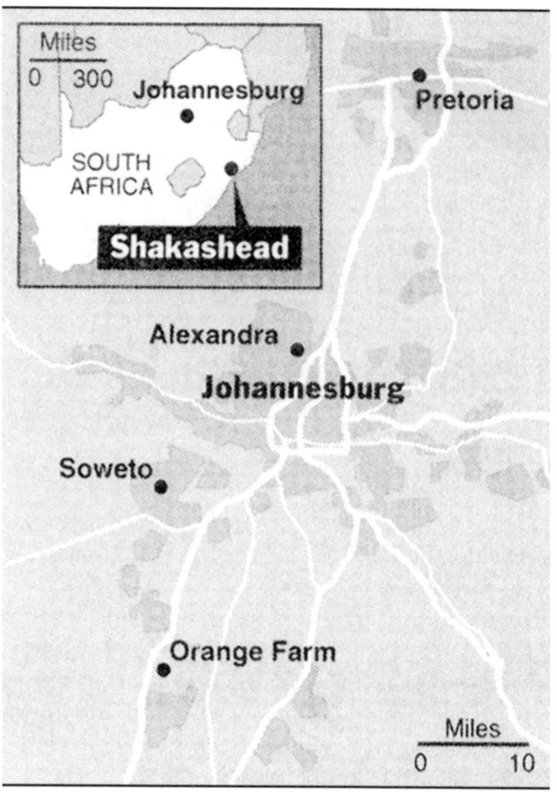

The New York Times

Water divides the haves from the have-nots in Shakashead.

Here in Shakashead, the women, speaking in their native Zulu, explained that only the luckiest among them have jobs at all, in the emerald sugar cane fields that surround their village. Those who work, they said, earn less than $45 a month, not always enough to cover the costs of food and water.

"There is good water here, but you must pay for it," Ms. Makhiwa said. "If you can see the way we live, you can see that we cannot pay." A survey by the government's Human Sciences Research Council for the independent Municipal Services Project found that up to 10 million people have been affected by water cutoffs since the end of white-minority rule.

David McDonald, co-director of the Municipal Services Project, said the government's own reports have portrayed a "crisis of serious proportions." One report, he said, indicated that some 700,000 people were affected by water cutoffs in just the final months of 2001. Meanwhile, he said, surveys showed some 1.3 million people had their electricity cut off, including some 20,000 customers each month in Soweto.

In a telephone interview and e-mail exchanges, a high-level water official rebutted the water cutoff estimates, saying they were "based on a deliberate distortion of very limited survey information."

Mr. McDonald countered: "As far as I'm concerned, you can cut our estimates of water cutoffs in half. The figures are still a serious indictment of post-apartheid cost recovery policies."

In the months following the cholera outbreaks, national water officials started a campaign urging municipalities to provide all households with at least a minimal "lifeline" of free water—some 1,500 gallons a month. Mike Muller, director general of the water department, said that an estimated 76 percent of municipalities had committed to the effort.

"We have had to confront the fact that in a very unequal society like South Africa, a policy of cost recovery, which makes perfect sense in a more equitable society, would exclude the poor from access to that basic commodity, to which they have a right," he said in an interview with the South African press.

But David Hemson, of the Human Services Research Council, said free water still had not been provided to millions living in shantytowns and rural areas who were most at risk for water-borne diseases, like the residents of Shakashead, where no free water was available. Even in communities where a "lifeline" service is provided, water taps are set to dispense a limited amount of water and are then shut down. In others, drip devices have been installed, literally dispensing water one drop at a time.

"The real battle for everyone to understand is how much does it cost to provide water to a nation and how do we pay for it," Mr. Muller said. "This is not privatizing, it is a massive reorganization of a government and how it provides services. We are still working it out."

The KwaDukuza municipality that covers Shakashead, with a population of about 60,000 people that is expected to expand rapidly in the next decade, became the first to sign a long-term management concession with a private company. The agreement, signed in 1999, gave French-based Saur a 25-year control over management of the water utility.

Three years ago, Johannesburg Water signed a more limited management contract with the France-based conglomerate Suez. Among the newest efforts by Johannesburg Water has been the installation of prepaid water meters in townships around the country's business capital. The first prepaid meters were installed last year in Orange Farm, and led to the formation of the Orange Farm Crisis Water Committee, the group headed by Mr. Makolo.

Under the prepaid system, to begin next month and to be expanded to other Johannesburg townships in the next couple of years, families will only get as much water as they can pay for in advance. Their payments will be recorded on digital discs, about as big as a quarter. The disc fits inside the water meter, and activates the taps.

Jean-Pierre Mas, the operations executive at Johannesburg Water, said prepay meters would allow customers to use only the amount of water they could afford, and help the utility avoid clashes over cutoffs.

"Under the old system, people were billed for far less water than they consumed, and still they were not paying their bills," Mr. Mas said. "They had no incentive to lower their consumption. They had no incentives to pay. If we don't do anything about it, it will be an unsustainable setup. We will have a financial disaster."

On the dirt streets of Orange Farm, where state-of-the-art water meters have been installed in front of lopsided tin shacks, people foresee a human disaster. Because of its location, it is known as the "deep south." However, it seems a fitting nickname in other ways.

The township has become a microcosm of the nation's most pressing social problems, including high rates of unemployment, violent crime and H.I.V.-infections.

Officials at Johannesburg Water acknowledged that in communities like these, billing people for water has been like squeezing water from a stone. In addition to the limited resources, a culture of nonpayment lingers from the years when people refused to pay utility bills, usually a flat fee for water and electricity, in support of boycotts against the apartheid regime.

"The problem is not that we do not want to pay for water," said Hilda Mkwanza, a 45-year-old mother of six who lives in Orange Farm. "The problem is we cannot pay."

Interviews with her and other Orange Farm women, who live by doing other people's laundry, said they barely had enough money to pay for food and school fees. Many of them already have prepaid electricity meters in their homes, and they say their families end up in the dark for several days each month.

Mr. Makolo, a veteran of the anti-apartheid movement, urges people not to pay. His motto, he said, is "destroy the meters and enjoy the water."

"The government promised us that water is a basic right," he said. "But now they are telling us our rights are for sale."

England Tests e-Voting

While the United States struggles to merely modernize elections, England experiments with remote electronic voting.

BY SHANE PETERSON

Thirty local governments in England tested various technological improvements to voting or vote counting in May 2002. Some jurisdictions used new technologies for the polling place, such as touchscreen voting machines; others tested techniques for voting remotely.

Nine jurisdictions allowed voters to cast their ballots using electronic methods, such as interactive voice response (IVR) technology, PC-based systems and handheld mobile devices via short message service (SMS). Some of these jurisdictions allowed voters to cast ballots from PCs or kiosks in public places such as shopping centers.

"The central government provided funding and overall strategic planning, and the local officials put it into practice and did all the legwork," said Tom Hawthorn, assistant policy manager of the Electoral Commission, a nonpartisan entity that evaluates and reports on the administration of elections to the UK Parliament, European Parliament, Scottish Parliament, and the Welsh and Northern Ireland Assemblies.

"This wouldn't have happened if the local authorities had to pay for it," said Alan Winchcombe, electoral deputy of the Swindon Borough Council. Swindon tested online voting using PCs, and telephone voting via IVR in19 of its 22 wards. The 19 wards comprised 126,953 voters.

"Swindon was only interested because the central government was paying the bill," Winchcombe said.

Not Just About Turnout

Overall, the pilot tests succeeded, Hawthorn said, although he was careful to define the parameters of success in this instance.

"The big concept for us is multichannel voting," he said. "There is an acceptance that putting in place new ways to vote isn't necessarily going to raise turnout. We're looking at expanding the range of choice voters have of ways they can cast their vote."

In Liverpool, voters could choose to vote over the Internet, with an IVR system or using a handheld mobile device. In St. Albans, voters could use the Net, an IVR system or kiosks scattered throughout the area.

"Voters who have taken part in the tests have been very positive about the choices being made available to them," Hawthorn said. "Remote voting won't be for everybody, and what we're looking at doing is make sure there are a range of options available so people can pick the one that best fits the way they live."

Though increasing turnout is a goal for English elections officials, the May tests were setting the foundation for future electronic voting.

"If we're looking at these pilots as a sound basis for a longer-term, perhaps six or seven year program of development, then they were an excellent beginning," Hawthorn said. "The will is there. The enthusiasm is there. We just have to identify the best technical solutions to the policy aims that we've got. Hopefully, we can put in place procedures that will allow people to vote using whatever technology that we have at the moment or will be developed over the next couple of years."

One Vote, One Identifier

Building confidence in remote electronic voting relies, in part, on the security of voter identity. For the English tests, local elections officials compiled lists of eligible voters and submitted the lists to a vendor that created unique identification measures for those voters.

"Every voter was supplied with a PIN, and they could use the PIN to vote either by the Internet or the telephone," said Winchcombe. "It was a 10-digit PIN that the voters had to enter as two numbers—one block of six numbers and one block of four numbers."

Officials then delivered the PINs to eligible voters.

"They didn't go through the normal mailing system," he said. "We employed people to deliver the PINs to voters' households. The PIN was generated by the vendor. We've got 127,000 registered voters here, and the vendor sent us a random range of 127,000 PINs."

Officials did not want to base PINs on personal information, such as birth dates, to protect against someone guessing another person's PIN and casting a fraudulent vote, Winchcombe said.

eVoting Turnout

LOCAL AUTHORITY	POLLING STATIONS/ POSTAL VOTES	%	INTERNET	%	TELEPHONE	%	TEXT MESSAGING	%
Crewe and Nantwich Borough Council (two wards)	1,839	83.5	364	16.5	—	—	—	—
Liverpool City Council (two wards)	3,957	59.4	1,093	16.4	1,162	17.4	445	6.7
St. Albans City and District Council (two wards)	1,539	49.5	825	26.5	744	23.9	—	—
Sheffield City Council (three wards)	8,881	67.7	2,904	22.1	—	—	1,327	10.1
Swindon Borough Council (19 wards)	33,329	84.1	4,293	10.8	2,028	5.1	—	—
Total 28 wards	49,545	76.5	9,479	14.6	3,934	6.1	1,772	2.7

Use of the different voting options was offered in different areas of England, listed above.

For jurisdictions testing online voting from remote PCs, voters visited a specially created Web site using secure sockets layer protocol, entered their PINs and viewed their "ballot."

"Voters could make their choices, confirm their choices and then send the vote off," said Hawthorn. "In most cases, the voters got a receipt back saying their vote had been cast as they wanted."

That receipt is a printed screen shot of the vote confirmation page, which Hawthorn said is a crucial component of establishing an audit trail. Though remote electronic voting holds much promise, verifying voting data is key to ensuring the validity of a particular election and its electronically cast votes.

The central government and local governments have not yet devised a procedure for deciding which pieces of data will be included in the audit trail, he said, though the pilot tests will provide the opportunity to decide how an audit trail will be established.

"We're here to make sure any system is robust enough to withstand, potentially, quite extensive attacks on the integrity of the system and high user demand," Hawthorn said. "We want to make sure that people have the opportunity—that the access points are kept clear—and the data is counted without having been manipulated by a third party and is not susceptible to attack."

By the Numbers

Remote electronic voting holds promise for other countries because English voters generally didn't shy away from using new methods to cast their ballots. In five of the local jurisdictions, voters had the chance to vote online using their home PCs, PCs at the polling place or a public kiosk.

Usage of the new voting methods varied widely by jurisdiction, according to the Electoral Commission's August evaluation of the 2002 elections, available online at <www.electoralcommission.org.uk/publicationspdfs/pilotreports/modernisingelections.pdf>.

In the St. Albans pilot, approximately 50 percent of votes were cast via the Internet or telephone. Four of 10 Liverpool voters cast their ballots using the Internet, telephone or text messaging. In Swindon, however, only 16 percent of votes were cast using remote electronic technologies.

Overall, the Electoral Commission found that 76.5 percent of eligible voters in the five local jurisdictions that offered multiple methods of remote electronic voting cast 49,545 votes at polling places or via mail-in ballots, by far the most popular way to vote. Approximately 14.6 percent of eligible voters used the Internet to vote, casting 9,479 votes. Voting via IVR accounted for 6.1 percent or 3,934 votes; and 2.7 percent (1,772 votes) were cast using SMS on mobile devices.

Making Voting Better

Both the central government and local jurisdictions were pleased by the results of the remote electronic voting tests, said Thomas Barry, policy adviser in the Office of the Deputy Prime Minister.

"In Sheffield, a woman who is a paraplegic was able to vote for the first time using computer voice-recognition technology," Barry said. "That's just one very extreme instance of how new technology increased the opportunity for voting."

Surveys of those who voted electronically—remotely or at polling sites—indicated voters found the technologies easy to use, Barry said, though a degree of uncertainty did emerge.

"There is a perception that electronic voting isn't as secure as the traditional way of voting," he said, noting that the Electoral Commission contacted each police force in the 30 pilot areas; no reports of fraud or the undermining of security were made.

Combating that perception—and informing voters about remote electronic voting in general—will require some public-relations work.

"The central government and the Electoral Commission and the local authorities have to do more to communicate the new strategy to voters," Barry said. "Certainly, this was evident in the analysis of the pilot programs—we can do more to convey the new ways of voting to not only the electorate, but also to the key stakeholders: political parties, the candidates and elections officials."

Is it **secure**?

To pilot remote electronic voting, Swindon worked with VoteHere, a Seattle-based e-voting company.

Though VoteHere has orchestrated a number of elections for its customers, the UK took a slightly different approach when testing remote electronic voting, said company CEO Jim Adler.

"In private-sector elections for associations, universities and unions, the security requirements are much lower than in the public sector," Adler said. "What the UK really wanted to do was trial the voter experience, and they were really willing to relax a lot of the security requirements for that election to see how the voters liked it."

The UK will be increasing its security requirements over the next several years as the testing continues, Adler said.

"The UK isn't letting security gate the introduction," he said. "They're actually moving usability and security along an evolutionary track as they move through this pilot process. In the United States, you can't make a move unless everything is completely buttoned down."

Adler speculated that several U.S. states are likely to pioneer remote electronic voting.

"If you look at the jurisdictions that are using vote by mail, they're mostly in the West. In Oregon and in Washington, where we're based, 65 percent of the electorate votes by mail," he said. "Those are the areas that are going to move to online voting, assuming that the security can be proven."

The UK is better equipped than the United States to make the transition to remote electronic voting.

"Most of the local authorities [in the UK] vote by pencil on a string," he said. "They really don't have the election technology we have in the United States, so there's not an entrenched industry that serves voting. It's almost like jumping over wire-line communications to wireless. They're jumping over punch cards. They're jumping over optical scanners. They're jumping over computerized voting right to remote electronic voting. They have a much more unencumbered vision of how to move forward."

Swindon's Winchcombe said voters in his borough, when surveyed after the election, reported that they felt safe using the new methods.

"The perception was that it was safe, secure, secret and we wouldn't tamper with it," he said. "They trusted us. If you voted, everything was being recorded in Seattle [by VoteHere, an electronic voting company], and the results were transmitted back to us. When you voted, the server you were talking to was in the United States. We had registered voters from Swindon vote from all over the world—Peru, Brazil, Thailand, Korea."

Vote from Your TV

On the heels of the May pilot, Barry said England already is looking at testing interactive digital TV (IDTV).

One jurisdiction was slated to test voting via IDTV in May, but couldn't due to staffing issues. In the next round of tests, though, officials hope IDTV will be offered as a voting option.

"We will be inviting local authorities to consider using IDTV as another method for remote electronic voting," Barry said. "We conducted some research into the implementation of electronic voting in the UK, and the research concludes that voting by IDTV is possibly one of the most secure ways of transmitting data, and therefore, it's prudent for government to consider this method."

If no local jurisdictions jump at the chance, he said, the Electoral Commission itself has statutory power to create a partnership with a local jurisdiction and submit a joint application to test IDTV, Barry said, adding that next year the pilot test will include many more jurisdictions.

"This year, we had £4 million [$6.2 million] and 16 authorities tested some aspect of electronic voting," he said. "We've managed to increase our funding, so we'll have £10 million for next year. We'll be looking to use it all. Electronic voting doesn't come too cheaply, not initially anyway, so we've got that £10 million and we're confident that it will be sufficient to go around."

Reforming Ghana's Public Service: Issues and Experiences in Comparative Perspective

This article addresses how the public service can be reformed to make it relevant to the circumstances and useful to the majority of people living and working in Ghana. In many public administration journals, reforms in sub-Saharan Africa have received scant attention. Using Ghana as a case study, this article first summarizes and evaluates that country's reform efforts and compares them to mainstream Anglo-American reform ideas. The article comments on the conceptualization of reform based on the notion of community, encompassing the unique political, social, and cultural experiences of the people of Ghana. Finally, the article discusses what a composite formulation of the notion of community might imply for a cross-cultural understanding of comparative public administration.

Peter Fuseini Haruna
Texas A&M International University

Introduction

After nearly two decades of centralized administration, Ghana adopted reforms that instituted a more mixed economy and decentralized public services to improve its mode of governance. One of the considerations was to reduce and restructure the public sector to ensure a more effective public administrative system (Engberg-Pedersen et al. 1996; Adamolekun 1999; Hope and Chikulo 2000). What are the issues and experiences with this type of reform in Ghana? How can public administration be made relevant and meaningful to the circumstances of the people of Ghana?

I argue that a composite framework of reform blending the social and cultural experiences of the people of Ghana with Anglo-American values offers an opportunity for transforming Ghanaian society. Current reform of public administration, which emphasized bureaucratic and managerial values, is skewed toward Anglo-American society. In its reforms, Ghana pursued the goal of linear economic growth. However, this goal was itself a major constraint to reform because the very idea of growth led to neglect of social, cultural, and political realities, which have had much influence on the local understanding and practice of public service. In contrast, the less-than-ideal composite approach is a much better prospect for achieving sustainable reform.

A summary and evaluation of Ghana's reform efforts follows. I argue that Ghana has problems with a centralized bureaucracy similar to that of other countries. Although reforms have been attempted before, they were based on Anglo-American ideas, which do not adapt as fully or as well in a culture based on a different kind of localism, one grounded in hundreds of years of living where the meaning of work and public service are different. Moreover, modern reforms may not work in short order in a country where most of its people can neither read nor write. After comparing Ghana's reform to mainstream Anglo-American reform ideas, a composite framework of reform based on the notion of community is sketched, emphasizing the building of government operations and structures from the bottom up, or at least making compromises between national bureaucratic needs and local conditions in Ghana.

Summary of Reform

Ghana's pursuit of a constitutional, representative, democratic government has led to the creation of political and economic changes that provided a context for reforming public administration. One of the goals was to create a political space for civil society to participate effectively in democratic governance. The changes involved the ideals of political liberty, equality, justice, accountability, transparency, and more (Ayittey 1998; Ayee 1999; Adamolekun 1999). Economic changes included financial and legal reforms that deregulated the centrally planned economy and opened Ghana to international and global competition. Such changes formed the basis for reforming the public service, which initially was concerned with regulating and controlling human behavior. However, reform has not yielded the institutional transformation required for economic development and social progress, an issue of public concern in Ghana (Hutchful 1996; Ayee 1997; Ayittey 1992).

Ghana's reforms focused on the organizational structure and function of the public bureaucracy, comprising all of the government institutions as well as the processes and procedures associated with them. Reform often means creating or expanding such institutions, as occurred in the 1960s (Wereko 1998; Ayee 1994; Adu 1965), or divesting and privatizing such institutions, as occurred in 1970s and 1990s (Divestiture Implementation Committee 1999). As a result, reform is often concerned with structural dimensions—that is, how public institutions such as ministries, departments, and agencies are structured and how they function. Furthermore, the goal of reform is efficiency, focusing on empowering public institutions to work in a transparent, competent, accountable, and cost-effective fashion. Ghana's National Institutional Renewal Program (1994) and Ghana Vision 2020 (1998) provided conceptual frameworks for reform, emphasizing the creation of an enabling environment for accelerated economic growth, as well as the rationalization and decentralization of public administration.

Civil Service Reform

Ghana's civil service, one of the key targets of reform, consists of the ministries, departments, and agencies that form the administrative structure of the local and central government (Ayee 1997). The civil service assists political office holders in formulating and implementing policies. Some problems identified as debilitating to civil service performance included overstaffing, low compensation levels, overcentralization and concentration of powers at the national level, poor infrastructure, and obsolete rules and regulations. The strategies of Ghana's reform involved diagnostic work, institution building, downsizing, identification and redeployment of excess labor, as well as restructuring and decentralizing public administration (Republic of Ghana 1990).

The World Bank's International Development Association provided an incentive package of institutional support to strengthen managerial capability, attract and retain skilled employees, and assist in the implementation of labor rationalization. Reform also focused on labor reduction, redeployment, and the improvement of managerial capacity (Adofo 1990). Labor reduction resulted in the downsizing of 44,838 employees between 1986 and 1993 (ODA 1993). In addition, reforms streamlined salaries, improved infrastructure, and regularized logistics supply (such as computers, printers, and copiers) to improve decision making. These and other measures—limiting the civil service wage bill, implementing compensation reform, decentralizing administration, and introducing a personnel data and management information system—constituted the thrust of civil service reform in Ghana.

The streamlining of salaries and wages was based on a "pay and grading" approach in which grade was related to pay and employees of the same grade received comparable compensation across the public service. Such an approach simplified the salaries and wage structure, consolidated salaries, wages, and allowances into a single compensation package, and reclassified job categories into 12 occupational groupings with each group allotted six separate incremental scales (Republic of Ghana, Gyampoh Commission 1993; Republic of Ghana, PricewaterhouseCoopers Committee 1997). This resulted in decompressing the salary and wage ratio from 4:1 to 13:1 between the lowest-paid and highest-paid employees as a way of improving moral in the civil service.

Decentralization Program

An important aspect of Ghana's reform was decentralization, the process of devolving political and administrative authority and rationalizing the relationship between central government and local authorities. The overall goal was to redress the overcentralization of power at the national level, improve urban-rural imbalance, and enhance local participation in national decision making (Ministry of Local Government 1996; Ahwoi 1992). To achieve this goal, central government ministries, departments, and agencies took more responsibility for policy planning and analysis, while local authorities shared responsibility for policy implementation.

The decentralization program began in 1988 and led to the creation of 10 regional coordinating councils, four-tier metropolitan assemblies, and three-tier municipal and district assemblies (Ministry of Local Government 1996, 11). This reorganization produced three metropolitan, four municipal, and 103 district authorities forming a monolithic structure and unifying departments and organizations at the subnational level. These bodies had responsibility for planning, deliberating, legislating, and executing development policies at the local level, including "the overall development of the District and shall ensure the preparation and submission... for approval of the development plan and budget for the district" (Ministry of Local Government 1994, 8). Decentralization, along with the opening up of the political process for competitive multiparty elections, was intended to enhance participation in Ghana's democratic governance (Adamolekun 1999; Dia 1996).

Divestiture Program

Divestiture was another aspect of reform in which the government divested itself or relinquished some of its responsibility to the private sector. Generally referred to as "load shedding," such reforms aimed to ease government fiscal burden, achieve efficiency in public services, and catalyze economic growth (Gyimah-Boadi 1990; Divestiture Implementation Committee 1999). The process affected government corporations and state-owned enterprises including hotels, industries, banking, manufacturing, transport, and communication companies. The mode of privatization took different forms including outright sale, partnership, deregulation, and contracting. In 1996, for example, the government created the National Communications Authority to set standards for and license privatized communications service providers. Ghana Telecom was privatized by the sale of 30 percent of government shares to Gcom (Telecom Malaysia). Likewise, Ghana Agro-Food Company Limited became a joint venture between Ghana and Industrie Bau Nord AG (Switzerland). By December 1998, about 212 public corporations and enterprises had been divested.

Progress so far has shown that divestiture and privatization have relieved the government of much fiscal burden, a strategy aimed to improve Ghana's economic performance. Divestiture has resulted in increased tax revenues, for example, in the joint venture among Ghana National Trading Corporation Bottling, Coca-Cola International, and the Africa Growth Fund. In terms of employment, Tema Steel Company increased its workforce from 130 during predivestiture to 584 in 1999, while the Tema Food Limited increased its employment from 494 to 1,600 (Divestiture Implementation Committee 1999). However, the withdrawal of the state in the provision of basic utilities such as water, electricity, and medical supplies has affected Ghana's urban poor and its rural communities disproportionately (Konadu-Agyemang 1998; Vehnamaki 1998). The public is concerned that divestiture and privatization are weakening the role of the state and diverting such a role in favor of market forces, private interests, and business firms.

Evaluation of Reform

Most evaluative efforts of Ghana's reform have focused on practical outcomes, highlighting labor reduction, logistics supply, pay raises, tax revenues, block grants, physical infrastructure, and divested public corporations (Konadu-Agyemang 1998; Ayee 1997; Gyimah-Boadi 1990). For example, civil service reform evaluations recognized the streamlining of salary scales and pay differentials, as well as the improvement of office infrastructure. Hutchful (1996, 189) notes that "training in computer skills for junior and middle level (though not apparently senior) civil servants was probably the most successful," although he queried that reform failed to transform "the organizational context and relationships within which this technology is deployed."

In terms of decentralization, some observers agree the process has helped to redress inequities in resource allocation by ensuring that 5 percent of national revenue is reserved for development at the local level. As Ayee (1997) indicates, social and political interest groups have taken advantage of decentralization to integrate state and society in a manner that promotes their own development. Moreover, according to Ayee, decentralization initially created opportunities for ordinary people in rural communities to take responsibility, exercise initiative, and influence the political process for their benefit. These evaluations have some merit because prereform analyses indicated that severe structural weaknesses militated against public administration performance. Understaffing at the professional, managerial, and technical levels produced gross inefficiency, making the government's capacity for planning and analysis weak or unreliable (Marshall 1990).

However, some critics of reform are not overly optimistic about the gains so far. The bureaucracy has been blamed for adjusting too slowly to or resisting the decentralization process (Ahwoi 1992a). More important, according to some observers, decentralization is viewed as an instrument for legitimizing the government's power (Ayee 1997; Crook 1994; Mohan 1996). Ayee argues the government used decentralization for "political purposes" rather than economic and social development interests, while Mohan (1996) asserts that decentralization was used "to deflect pressure from lenders and domestic political forces." In this view, administration remains centralized with local authorities taking directives from the center, a phenomenon that Ayee (1999) refers to as "decentralized centralization."

While these evaluations are useful, they should transcend the narrow technocratic view of reform, provide a comprehensive knowledge, and synthesize both facts and values (Fischer 1995). Fischer argues that evaluation should go beyond the empirical aspects to assess the value judgments infusing public policies and programs. Thus, an evaluation of Ghana's reforms should examine the full range of empirical and normative issues underpinning reform judgment, most notably, is the reform a mark of a good or just Ghanaian society? Does the reform facilitate accepted or desired Ghanaian values, goals, and purposes? At the core of such an approach is a concern for democratic governance in which consultation, dialogue, and consensus are sought across a wide range of political, social, economic, and cultural issues. Specifically, such an approach is necessary for creating broad-based support to sustain reform for the benefit of Ghanaian society.

Society and Administration

The conception of reform reflects a clear misunderstanding of both public administration and the structure of Ghanaian society. By focusing on the managerial values of competence and efficiency, reforms reinforced an existing administrative framework that was almost incompatible with Ghana's predominantly poor, rural, and ethnic society. As a result, there is a mismatch between the lived experiences of the people of Ghana and their government operations. True, a viable polity requires a public service with basic bureaucratic criteria, that is, large-scale organization, functional specialization, and qualification (Heady 2001, 77). However, bureaucratic adaptation and innovation is necessary to make public administration relevant to the context and meaningful to the living conditions of the people.

Far from considering the relevance and meaning of administration to local conditions, the ultimate goal of Ghana's reform was to improve administrative performance, which glossed over the practical difficulties of nationally centered bureaucratic decision making in Ghana. Poor means of communication, inadequate transportation, low literacy rates, and incompetence contributed to making bureaucratized administration almost impracticable. Several communities, for example, are inaccessible, while interregional communication is inadequate (Ayee 1997). The requirement of competence is often difficult to meet in Ghana, where adult literacy is only about 60 percent, despite the growth and expansion of education at all levels in the past 43 years (World Bank 2000). As Woode (1989) argues, one of the challenges of public administration is finding qualified personnel with the requisite education and training to staff local government jurisdictions. From such a viewpoint, there was some dissonance between the social and spatial reality of Ghana and the administrative structure and process, which worked to exclude the majority of the people living and working in the rural communities.

In addition, bureaucratic administration raised equity concerns, which current reform has been unable to address (Vehnamaki 1998; Konadu-Agyemang 1998). Vehnamaki argues that reform favored the "golden triangle" or the southern urban regions, while Konadu-Agyemang points out that poverty in Ghana's rural communities was higher than the prereform level. In other words, those benefiting from the merit-bureaucratic reform included mainly urban residents and not the rural people to whom the administrative process was both largely inaccessible and incomprehensible. As part of the political changes, Ghana's constitution mandated a regional balance in appointments to the top echelons of the public service, as well as the transfer of at least 5 percent of national revenue for district and regional development. While these measures aimed to minimize inequity and enhance redistribution, the bureaucratic and managerial reform worked to the disadvantage of the poor rural people.

Reform took the moral, social, cultural, and political context of public administration for granted while overlooking social-cultural differences, the role of community and indigenous institutions, as well as women and gender differences in the public service. The fact that Ghana's population comprises several ethnic groups should be an important reform concern because the arbitrary demarcation of regional boundaries by ex-colonial rulers constituted a source of conflict between and among Ghana's social-cultural groups. In particular, public service should be sensitive to the predominance of some ethnic groups in public affairs and how such predominance affects public trust and national integration. Further, reform should grapple with the effects of indigenous social and political institutions (for instance, chieftaincy) that compete for individual and group loyalty (Ayittey 1992; Busia 1967). To the extent that the constitution recognizes and protects such indigenous institutions, they should be included as part of the overall administrative reform.

In spite of the creation of the National Council on Women and Development and the 31st December Women's Movement, reforms have failed to address women's and gender concerns in public administration. The Women in Public Life report suggests that women's role in Ghanaian society remains underrecognized in the public service (WPL 1998). While women's workforce participation has improved since the introduction of the Industrial Relations Act (1965) and the Equal Pay Act (1967), biased cultural attitudes toward females persist.

The Women in Public Life report (1998, 4) found that most of Ghana's public institutions were inclined toward "masculine" work environments, where women were underrepresented, less educated, and less competitive. Specifically, "women constitute only a fraction of the management and leadership of their organizations." Indeed, women form only about 18 percent of the middle to top public-sector executives in Ghana (Haruna 1999), a situation that is inconsistent with global and international efforts to improve the economic and social status of women. Important as these findings are, the issue is not only creating women's organizations and appointing women to top positions, although those were necessary first steps for addressing the problem. The central issue is to embark on reforming Ghana's public administration in a manner that enhances equity, taking into consideration the peculiar circumstances of women and other minority populations in the country.

Human Resources Management

Reform of human resources management persistently has emphasized material aspects at the expense of deeper human motivational concerns. Such a materialistic approach revolves around periodic salary and wage adjustment and occasional tinkering with training in management techniques and the provision of facilities (Republic of Ghana 1967; Republic of Ghana, Gyampoh Commission 1993; Ali Committee 1984). Nonetheless, compensation levels remain low, and the highest-paid executives receive an annual gross equivalent of about $2,500 (Haruna 1999). The result has been that public service is viewed as a job (means of survival) or a career of last resort in which absenteeism, turnover, disinterest, and lethargy are pervasive (Indome 1991). Paradoxically, public service not only constitutes the single largest source of employment for many Ghanaians, it is also the main provider of basic services to most people (Office of the Head of the Civil Service 1993). In fact, Ghana's public service is considered one of the oldest and most professional fields of public administration in sub-Saharan Africa and a training ground for most of the top administrative corps (Hyden 1983; Huq 1989; Werlin 1994).

While pay and grading have eliminated distortions and improved equity in compensations, they are not the most effective means of addressing motivational concerns among Ghana's public employees. For example, Indome (1991, 4) identifies political intrusion and threats to tenure of office as factors contributing to what he sees as "lethargy and apathy" in the civil service. In interviews conducted with mid- to top-level Ghanaian public-sector executives, politicization of the civil service was one of the most frequently cited sources of concern (Haruna 1999). The weakening of civil service protections, reduction of labor, and fear of victimization have contributed much discomfort among the personnel and, in many cases, devastated morale within the public service. Ironically, reform has not helped the problem by making political officeholders responsible for hiring, supervising, and terminating public employees (Republic of Ghana, Gyampoh Commission 1993).

It is somewhat understandable that reform emphasized the instrumental at the expense of the social and psychological motivation of public employees. Given the extent of poverty in Ghana, this type of orientation is inevitable, and people regard their jobs not as ends in themselves or as a central life interest, but as the means to other ends. However, the psychological needs of esteem that are achievable through promotion, participation, and autonomy in decision making are equally important and applicable factors among public employees in Ghana (Haruna 1999).

Beyond these concerns, a serious reform defect was the failure to consider the meaning of work and public service in a predominantly rural society, where indigenous social and cultural values are important for understanding work behavior. In such a society, work often is considered an avenue for helping kith and kin, ethnic groups, and regions, which reflects parochial interests (Isamah 1991). In particular, ethnic loyalty exerts a strong influence on Ghanaian public employees, most of whom are first-generation government workers (Haruna 1999). Such employees often are identified both by their formal grades and ranks and by their ethnic and regional origins. Culturally, people in government positions are expected to be of help to relatives and protect ethnic and regional interests in matters of national policy. Thus, an important reform issue is how to balance such a strong feeling of ethnicity with the objectivity and neutral competence required of the bureaucratic administrative process.

Some studies have chronicled the prevalence of maladministration, inefficiency, misconduct, absenteeism, tardiness, and discontent in Ghana's public service without relating them to the social, cultural, and psychological challenges entailed. Such studies lament the turnovers in government ministries and departments and inefficiency among public employees (Gyimah-Boadi 1990; Hyden 1983), while others note frequent industrial action among workers' unions and professional associations. Although these occurrences raised public interest concerns, and were difficult to justify in some cases, individual employees may not necessarily be blamed. In short, the public bureaucracy could be a national asset if it is suitably reformed and adapted to the underlying local circumstances in Ghana.

The attempt to decentralize and encourage local participation raised more questions than answers, despite the fact that the idea is consistent with indigenous African political institutions (Ayittey 1992). The often-cited problem was either the lack of government political will or the bureaucracy's unwillingness to cede administrative authority. However, the problem of decentralization centers on two issues that are ill-understood and poorly addressed by current reforms. The first concerns the failure to understand and appreciate the complexity of the concept itself, which is frequently associated with the provision and administration of financial and material resources. The implementation of the program focused on creating districts, constructing office buildings, and recruiting officers (Ministry of Local Government 1996), with little effort to advance the deeper understanding of the concept of decentralization.

The second issue dealt with the fact that insufficient attention was paid to developing local leadership with the required knowledge and professional competence to bear responsibility for devolved administrative tasks. It is true that the creation of districts and the transfer of financial and material resources were necessary, but they were insufficient conditions to guarantee the long-term sustainability of the reform program. In fact, it did not take long, as Crook (1994) points out, for people to realize the leadership and managerial competencies of personnel at the local level were low, contributing to poor performance in Ghana. As Rondinelli (1981) argues, leadership, responsibility, and service are sine qua non for decentralization to advance the cause of economic and social development. Thus, one of the central issues of decentralization in Ghana is how to develop community capacity, including leadership that can be leveraged to solve collective problems and improve community well-being.

The Role of the Public Sector

In regard to the public sector's role, reform has taken a managerial perspective that has limited the government's intervention in the economy. This resulted in a much smaller public sector with a lessor role than in the past. For example, civil service employment was reduced from 143,237 employees in 1986 to about 79,000 in 1997 (Office of the Head of the Civil Service 1993). Likewise, there have been steady withdrawals of government subsidies for petroleum products, agricultural inputs, and health and educational supplies and equipment, with considerable negative consequences for the rural poor communities and the urban working people (Rimmer 1992; Rothchild 1991; Brydon and Legge 1996). Public policies, programs, and projects based on development need have been replaced by businesses concerned with economic efficiency, and the government has found it difficult to legitimize its active role in the public interest.

The size of the public sector is only a part of the problem because the government cannot bear the entire burden of development. However, as Rasheed and Luke (1995) argue, Asian countries grew with large, not small public sectors. Ironically, by reducing the size of the public sector, reform somewhat paralyzed the state in Ghana as an arbitrator between competing and conflicting interests in society. For example, Ghana is losing its grip on Ashanti Goldfields Corporation, one of the richest mining companies in the world. The crisis facing the company reflects the loss of government control, and with it the loss of adequate guarantees to protect Ghana's public interest. The issue is that Ghana needs to find an appropriate balance between the public, private, and nonprofit sectors in its socioeconomic development efforts in order to avoid falling into the trap of all-or-none government.

Comparison with Anglo-American Reform

How do Ghana's reforms compare with mainstream Anglo-American reform ideas? Although several broad categories of Anglo-American reform initiatives may be discerned from the literature, not all have any measure of applicability in the Ghanaian context. On the one hand, bureaucratic and managerial reforms have modest applicability, although these are predominant in Ghana. On the other hand, while the growing "new public service" perspective (Denhardt and Denhardt 2000) has not been tried, it seems largely applicable. Bureaucratic reform is unsuitable, not because it is necessarily evil, but because it is incompatible with the structure of Ghanaian society: predominantly rural, low literacy, multicultural, low infrastructure, and ethnic loyalty, to name a few.

The socioeconomic and political uniqueness of Ghanaian society is important to this discussion because, as Albrow (1970, 43) indicates, rational bureaucracy has been considered the most important element of the social process in Anglo-American society, involving "growing precision and explicitness in the principles governing social organization." It is well-known that a combination of factors—industrialization, urbanization, written tradition, the constitutional and legal system, mass communication, and well-developed physical infrastructure—have contributed to enhance the rationalization, formalization, codification, and mathematicization of Western civilization, including Anglo-American society.

However, this observation neither means that bureaucracy works perfectly well in Anglo-American society, nor that it necessarily suits the public business. To be sure, political and management scientists, sociologists, and public administrationists have questioned and provided perceptive critiques of bureaucracy over the years (Bendix 1947; Peters and Waterman 1982; Hummel 1994).

In fact, by 1992, all levels of government in the United States had installed quality management systems to reinvent their bureaucracies (Gore 1993; Osborne and Gaebler 1992). Nonetheless, it can be argued that the nature of Anglo-American society affords a meaningful conduct of official record keeping, accounting of various kinds, official reporting for a variety of purposes, and community relations. Under the material conditions in Anglo-American society, it makes sense to talk about transparency, the rule of law, and public accountability, although the bureaucracy continues to be discredited (Pollitt 1990; Hummel 1994; Fox and Miller 1995; King and Stivers 1998; Box 1998; Stivers 2000).

Similarly, the managerial movement sweeping the world has Anglo-American cultural roots (Pollitt 1990; Terry 1998). While the public management philosophy involves quantitative approaches (Lynn 1996), liberation management (Light 1997), and neoclassical economics (Peters 1996), its ultimate goal includes efficiency and effectiveness. Philosophically, both bureaucratic and managerial approaches are associated with what White and Adams (1994) see as Western society's belief in the power of money, science, and technology to free humankind from physical and social constraints. Many Anglo-American reforms have pursued the modernist dream, emphasizing the material aspects of humanity, especially economic and practical outcomes as the purpose of human development.

In contrast, Ghana's predominantly rural and semirural society is patriarchal and patrimonial, dominated by extended families, clans, and ethnic communities (Takyi and Oheneba-Sakyi 1994). Although Ghana's national law is supreme, acceptable public conduct tends to be what the ethnic community says it is, often based on unwritten but acknowledged tradition and cultural values. These traditions and cultures vary from region to region, but they all tend to have similar magnitudes and effects across the country. Neil Henry observes, "While the power of Ghana's governing political institutions has proved ephemeral during the nation's first three decades of independence, the popular influence of village chiefs has never waned… they remain virtually indispensable to the fabric of Ghanaian culture and society… the power and respect they command from their followers seem to derive from their intelligence and wisdom and the model of behavior they set for the community" (cited in Ayittey 1992, 73). The reason that ethnic community leaders are obeyed is not difficult to trace rationally because their activities and behaviors are largely consistent with culturally and socially prescribed duties, functions, and roles.

In much of Ghanaian society, there is no distinction between the public and private domain or between work and home. Often, work is carried out as a sense of personal obligation derived from one's conscience, focusing on family and community development. The fulfillment of social, economic, and political duties depends on everybody working cooperatively and relying mainly on experience, not expertise. There are no systematic written rules describing jobs or work, although private and public conduct are regulated according to certain established codes. Responsibilities may be delegated, though hardly systematically, and they may be subject to change. The absence of standardized rules, especially in Ghana's rural communities, makes it difficult to find a uniform application of laws and the existence of the same economic conditions.

Table 1 indicates the sharp contrast between Anglo-American and Ghanaian society, which may be characterized roughly as premodern, transitional, precapitalist, underdeveloped, and developing as opposed to urbanized, modernized, industrialized, and developed society (Heady 2001; Hyden 1983; Riggs 1964). Despite this distinction, public-service reform in Ghana has hardly paid much attention to it, adopting uncritically bureaucratic and managerial models of administration that are better suited for industrialized societies. However, if one took such a distinction seriously and considered the apparent incompatibility of both the bureaucratic and managerial approaches with the structure of the so-called premodern societies, it may be necessary to conceptualize reform differently. This undertaking needs to proceed cautiously, delineating and integrating values from both Ghanaian and Anglo-American society in a manner that reinforces, not undermines, community capacity.

Community Reform

The argument so far is that bureaucratic and managerial reform approaches are problematic in Ghana and should not, therefore, be expected to lead to meaningful institutional transformation there. However, reform that is based on the notion of community, which has received continued emphasis as an important alternative model of public service, has better prospects of succeeding because it is closer to Ghana's unique political and social conditions. This is not to say that community necessarily means the same thing in Ghana as it does in Anglo-American society. Nonetheless, community-based reform has been justified on the basis that it largely meets both the practical needs and the theoretical demands of public service. The notion of community also has historical roots in both societies, and it has helped to focus the values of citizen participation and democratic control in the United States (Gardner 1991; Selznick 1992; Etzioni 1995; Putnam 1995; Box 1998; King and Stivers 1998; Denhardt and Denhardt 2000).

The idea of community in American society is associated with the historical town meetings and the promise they hold for realizing direct participatory democracy (Barber 1984; Bellah 1991; Zimmerman 1999). Beginning with the Pilgrims and the Puritans from England, the early town meeting was the distinguishing feature of

Table 1 Comparing Ghana and Anglo-American Society

Dimension	Ghana	Anglo-American Society
Nature of society	Mostly rural	Mostly urban
Nature of the economy	Mostly agricultural	Mostly industrial
Worldview	Mostly communal	Mostly individualistic
Nature of learning	Listening and observation	Question and argument
Source of authority	Traditional/legal	Legal-rational
Nature of knowledge	Tradition and science	Science and technology
Nature of governing	Traditional/legal	Legal-rational
Nature of organization	Community-centered	Hierarchical
Loyalty	Lineage-centered	State-centered
Decision making	Consultation and consensus	Competition and compromise
Nature of leadership	Collaborative	Hierarchical
Goal of reform	Growth and development	Goodness, prosperity, and justice
Reform since 1980s	Privatization	Reinventing and devolution
Meaning of work	Help kith and kin	Live a good life
Nature of education	Informal/formal	Mostly formal

town government, which considered "all mundane matters, major or trivial, affecting the town" (Zimmerman 1999, 35). This implies civic activism and participation in local affairs, reflecting Jefferson's "little republics" and his "vision of governance for America centered on small local governments" (Box 1998, 6). For Dewey (1985, 218), "democracy must begin at home, and its home is the neighborly community," where people can realize their full potential and dignity as individuals. From this perspective, the communitarian ideal is essential to the understanding of human beings as active social and political animals, whose development occurs in a well-ordered community.

In the wake of growing alienation among the U.S. working and middle classes, there has been a resurgence of the themes of the self and the community aimed at recovering the values of local control and small and responsive government (Barber 1984; Box 1998; King and Stivers 1998). Public administration scholars argue that citizens should be more involved in decisions that affect them, not only for the sake of social justice, but also for developing their full potential. For example, King and Stivers argue that in a community-based reform, public administrators relinquish control, become facilitators, and collaborate with citizens in the production and delivery of public services. They also suggest that public administrators should seek greater responsiveness toward building the integrity and legitimacy of public institutions. From this perspective, public administration is not simply a passive policy or a managerial instrument, nor a static organization of rules, regulations, and procedures, but a dynamic process seeking to advance the common good.

How does this Anglo-American idea of community fit with the local, social, and political experiences of Ghana? It can be argued that the U.S. understanding of community, which is based on local control and small responsible government, has general applicability in Ghana. For example, community is the organic unit of cultural, social, economic, and political organization in Ghana (Boamah-Wiafe 1993; Ayittey 1992; Wright 1984). Community consists of families sharing the same lineage and identification with a village, constituting "the most powerful and effective force for unity and stability" (Ayittey 1992, 38). Each lineage is governed primarily by a council of elders whose responsibilities include the spiritual, social, political, and economic welfare of the community. For example, a meeting of the council of elders often considers issues relating to community development through resource mobilization and arbitration, with each elder participating in a decision-making or issue-solving dialogue until unanimity is reached.

According to Mensah-Sarbah, "the village council represented the fountainhead of the common life, and its determination found expression in the popular voice" (cited in Langley 1979, 20). The village council of elders represents the broad mass of the people, advises their heads, and assists in the general administration of the lineage or tribe. Periodically, lineage heads summon village meetings to deliberate issues of communal interest until a consensus is reached (Boamah-Wiafe 1993). Ayittey (1998, 86–89) argues that the governing concepts of community in African society include participation, consultation, and consensus, with the aim of advancing political unity and social cohesion in the solution of community problems.

While differences exist between Ghanian and Anglo-American society regarding the notion of community, there are similarities that make this comparison interesting. For example, the community of Pilgrims and Puritans evolved around the written "town charter," whereas community in Ghana relies on informal oral traditions. Moreover, community governance in Ghana emphasizes lineage and village. However, there is a sense in which the village meeting in Ghana is similar to the New England town meeting: promoting direct popular participation in public affairs. Likewise, the ideas of home rule, local control, and responsible government are inherent in both societies, and their potential for strengthening the legitimacy of democratic governance makes community-based reform more appealing than other administrative models.

Critics of the community perspective point out weaknesses, however, often raising the practical, theoretical, and philosophical difficulties that such a perspective entails (Fox and Miller 1995). Aside from the definitional difficulty of whether community should be defined geographically, sociologically, or politically, Fox and Miller (1995, 35–39) emphasize idealism, "totalitarian tendencies," and "citizen apathy" as some of the major obstacles to community democratization. To them, existing notions of community have little or no relevance "in the mass societies inexorably created by advanced and postindustrial capitalism." In spite of these limitations, Fox and Miller agree that community can be refined to create a communitarian medium "where full ethical citizenship flourishes." The starting point is to conceptualize community in "pluralistic, associational terms," which serve as a mediating institutional structure between "legal citizens and government."

Nonetheless, community-based reform is more an exception than the rule in U.S. society, despite its potential for engendering an active citizenry that can stem the tide of discontent and alienation. Anecdotal evidence suggests that community spirit is alive and that citizens are ready to collaborate in coproducing and codelivering public services (Timney 1998; Foley 1998; Gray and Chapin 1998). Gray and Chapin use the "targeted community initiative" in Orange County, Florida, to showcase community capacity and the possibility of shared governing. This initiative reached out to neglected poor communities, drawing from citizens' lived experience and highlighting some of the related challenges (1998, 175–92).

Paradoxically, while the United States seeks to recover its past sense of community, Ghana's reform draws little from its communities. Ghana relies instead on what may be described as the "managerialization" of public services, where expertise, rationality, and material foci replace experience: It is more like catching up with industrialized society, according to Hyden (1983). As a result, the informal network of social, cultural, and economic activity that facilitates the pursuit of common purposes is largely lost in Ghana. This is not to suggest that all of Ghana's community values should be embraced. In fact, Ghana's community has been criticized for promoting tribal and parochial interests at the expense of the broader national good. As Gyekye (2000, 280) argues, reform should encourage a transcultural ethos, one that makes acceptable compromises between modernity and localism on the one hand, and bureaucratic needs and community values on the other, toward the enhancement and fulfillment of human life.

Conclusion

Ghana's experience provides hard lessons and choices about the nature of reform, public service, and the role of public administration. First, the government needs to recognize that institutional reform is difficult and slow to achieve, but that gradual and partial progress has been made. Reform seems to work if it grows out of the cultural, social, and political experiences of the people of Ghana. In criticizing current reform, one should be careful not to throw away the baby with the bath water, that is, one should recognize the potential benefits of bureaucratic and managerial approaches. For example, instrumental rationality associated with bureaucratized administration should be broadened and carefully adapted to suit the local and community-based values of collaboration, consultation, and consensus.

Second, the government needs to make a judgment about the appropriate role and size of its public administration in order to bring in and nurture local participation. Current reforms have pursued restrictive goals involving internal reorganization to achieve efficient and effective policy implementation. With international and global trends of fiscal austerity, it is reasonable for Ghana to emphasize managerial efficiency, but this is problematic because it fails to consider the socioeconomic and political uniqueness of Ghanaian society. In addition, public-service motivation is based on a carrot-and-stick policy while ignoring autonomy and participation, which are equally important for achieving public purposes.

Third, the reforms offer a notion of public administration that is insufficient for meeting the challenges of a culturally and politically diverse society. More than anything, public service faces the challenge of making itself relevant and meaningful to a poor rural society, such as that in Ghana. Thus, the government needs to find a way to protect the public interest and ensure a measure of equity in sharing the burden and benefit of reform. One of the government's major roles will be to strengthen public institutions by building relationships based on human dignity and by bridging the gaps between the different sectors of the polity while nurturing collaboration between and among administrators, citizens, and the disadvantaged segments of Ghanian society.

Fourth, the case study of Ghana provides useful suggestions for comparative purposes, targeting and identifying issues that comparativists often frame broadly as North America versus all others or industrialized versus nonindustrialized societies (Welch and Wong 1998; Riggs 1998; Haque 1998; Heady 1998; Brinkerhoff and Coston 1999). While these broader analyses enhance our cross-cultural understanding of public administration, other more specific national and social-cultural differences are diminished. This article has focused on Ghana's experience with reform, whose uniqueness conditions and is conditioned by administrative practice there. Such uniqueness makes certain Anglo-American ideas such as the new public service perspective more applicable than bureaucracy and public management.

Fifth, such a comparison explores the possibility of developing a composite framework that blends the Anglo-American idea of community with Ghana's unique localism, primarily to ground public-service reform in the people's daily experience. Such a formulation would enable reformers and public administrators to move beyond the big "T" truths and pay attention to the context in which they are working (Follett 1924). In addition, such a community approach constitutes a more viable alternative to the rhetorical propositions of structural adjustment and accelerated growth (World Bank 1981), and instead creatively builds on local institutions and capacities to ensure steady and sustainable progress (Jun 2000; Callaghy 1994).

Finally, the present comparison is useful for developing a curriculum for a global and international education to prepare younger generations of African and Anglo-American origins for living and working cooperatively in a rapidly changing world. This will reinforce participation in cultural exchange programs that enhance the education of "world citizens" (Pires 2000, 44). Although such programs tend to be few, they promote an awareness of broad cross-cultural knowledge that is capable of equipping people to work in an interdependent world (Burn 1985, 48). Such a global and globalizing education should consider and include learning from and about Africa and Africans, for which this essay focused on Ghana as one way of enhancing the understanding of comparative public administration.

Acknowledgments

This article was presented at the 24th Annual Conference on Teaching Public Administration held at Arizona State University, Tempe, Arizona, February 4–5, 2001. The article is based on my dissertation research, and I wish to thank my advisor, Dr. Nancy Grant, and members of my committee at the University of Akron for their guidance. I also would like to thank Dr. Julia Beckett and anonymous reviewers for helpful suggestions and comments on earlier drafts of this article.

References

Adamolekun, Ladipo, ed. 1999. *Public Administration in Africa: Main Issues and Selected Country Studies.* Boulder, CO: Westview Press.

Adu, Amishadai L. 1965. *The Civil Service in the New African States.* London: G. Allen Unwin.

Ahwoi, Kwamina. 1992. The Constitution of the Fourth Republic and the Local Government System. Address delivered at the 5th Annual Workshop on Decentralization in Ghana, September 1, School of Administration, University of Ghana, Legon.

Albrow, Martin. 1970. *Bureaucracy.* London: Pall Mall Press.

Ali Committee. 1984. Report of Committee on Civil Service Salaries and Wages. Accra: Government of Ghana.

Ayee, Joseph R. 1994. *Anatomy of Public Policy Implementation: The Case of Decentralization Policies in Ghana.* Aldershot, UK: Avebury.

——. 1997. The Adjustment of Central Bodies to Decentralization: The Case of the Ghanaian Bureaucracy. *African Studies Review* 40(2): 37–57.

——. 1999. Ghana. In *Public Administration in Africa: Main Issues and Selected Country Studies,* edited by Ladipo Adamolekun, 250–74. Boulder, CO: Westview Press.

Ayittey, George B. 1992. *Africa Betrayed.* New York: St. Martin's Press.

——. 1998. *Africa in Chaos.* New York: St. Martin's Press.

Barber, Benjamin. 1984. *Strong Democracy: Participatory Politics for a New Age.* Berkeley, CA: University of California Press.

Bellah, Robert. 1991. *The Good Society.* New York: Knopf.

Bendix, R. 1947. Bureaucracy: The Problem with Its Setting. *American Sociological Review* 12(5): 493–97.

Boamah-Wiafe, Daniel. 1993. *Africa: The Land, People, and Cultural Institutions.* Omaha: Wisdom Publications.

Box, Richard C. 1998. *Citizen Governance: Leading American Communities into the 21st Century.* Thousand Oaks, CA: Sage Publications.

Brinkerhoff, Derrick, and Jennifer Coston. 1999. International Development in a Globalized World. *Public Administration Review* 59(4): 346–61.

Brydon, L. and Legge, K. 1996. *Adjusting Society: The World Bank, the IMF, and Ghana.* London: I.B. Tauris Publishers.

Burn, Barbara. 1985. Does Study Abroad Make a Difference? *Change* 3(4): 48–49.

Busia, Kofi. 1967. *Africa in Search of Democracy.* New York: Praeger.

Callaghy, Thomas. 1994. Africa: Falling Off the Map? *Current History* 4(1): 36–45.

Crook, Richard. 1994. Four Years of the Ghana District Assemblies in Operation: Decentralization, Democratization, and Administration Performance. *Public Administration and Development* 14(3): 339–64.

Denhardt, Robert B., and Janet Vinzant Denhardt. 2000. The New Public Service: Serving Rather than Steering. *Public Administration Review* 60(6): 549–59.

Dia, Mamadou. 1996. *Africa's Development Management in the 1990s and Beyond.* Washington, DC: World Bank.

Divestiture Implementation Committee. 1999. Annual Report. Accra: Ghana Publishing Corporation.

Engberg-Pedersen, Poul, Peter Gibbon, Phil Raikes, and Lars Udsholt, eds. 1996. *Limits of Adjustment in Africa: The Effects of Economic Liberalization, 1986–94.* Copenhagen, Denmark: Center for Development Research.

Etzioni, Amitai: 1995. *The New Communitarian Thinking.* Charlottesville, VA: University of Virginia Press.

Fischer, Frank. 1995. *Evaluating Public Policy.* Chicago: Nelson-Hall.

Foley, Dolores. 1998. We Want Your Input: Dilemmas of Citizen Participation. In *Government Is Us: Public Administration in Anti-Government Era,* edited by Cheryl King and Camilla Stivers, 140–57. Thousand Oaks, CA: Sage Publications.

Follett, Mary Parker. 1924. *Creative Experience.* New York: Longmans, Green and Co.

Fox, Charles J., and Hugh Miller. 1995. *Postmodern Public Administration: Toward Discourse.* Thousand Oaks, CA: Sage Publications.

Gardner, John. 1991. *Building Community.* Washington, DC: Independent Sector.

Gore, Al. 1993. *From Red Tape to Results: Creating a Government that Works Better and Costs Less.* Washington, DC: Government Printing Office.

Gray, Joseph E., and Linda Chapin. 1998. Targeted Community Initiative: "Putting Citizens First." In *Government Is Us: Pub-*

lic Administration in Anti-Government Era, edited by Cheryl King and Camilla Stivers, 175–94. Thousand Oaks, CA: Sage Publications.

Gyekye, Kwame. 2000. *Tradition and Modernity: Philosophical Reflections on the African Experience*. New York: Oxford University Press.

Gyimah-Boadi, E. 1990. Economic Recovery and Politics in PNDC's Ghana. *Journal of Commonwealth and Comparative Studies* 28(3): 328–43.

Haque, M. Shamsul. 1998. Impacts of Globalization on the Role of the State and Bureaucracy in Asia. *Administrative Theory and Praxis* 20(4): 439–51.

Haruna, Peter F. 1999. *An Empirical Analysis of Motivation and Leadership among Career Public Administrators: The Case of Ghana*. PhD diss., University of Akron.

Heady, Ferrel. 1998. Comparative and International Public Administration: Building Intellectual Bridges. *Public Administration Review* 58(1): 32–40.

——. 2001. *Public Administration: A Comparative Perspective*. 6th ed. New York: Marcel Dekker.

Hope, Kempe R., and Bornwell Chikulo, eds. 2000. *Corruption and Development in Africa: Lessons from Country Case-Studies*. London: Macmillan.

Hummel, Ralph. 1994. *The Bureaucratic Experience: A Critique of Life in a Modern Organization*. New York: St. Martin's Press.

Huq, Mozammel M. 1989. *The Economy of Ghana*. London: Macmillan.

Hutchful, Eboe. 1996. Ghana: 1983–94. In *Limits of Adjustment in Africa: The Effects of Economic Liberalization, 1986–1994*, edited by Paul Engberg-Pedersen, Peter Gibbon, Phil Raikes, and Lars Udsholt, 143–214. Copenhagen, Denmark: Center for Development Research.

Hyden, Goran. 1983. *No Shortcuts to Progress: African Development Management in Perspective*. Berkeley, CA: University of California Press.

Indome, James A. 1991. Apathy and Lethargy in the Ghana Civil Service. Address delivered at the Ghana Military Academy and Staff College, July 11, Accra, Ghana.

Isamah. A. 1991. *Social Determinants of Labor Productivity in West Africa*. New York: Hanszell.

Jun, Jong S. 2000. Transcending the Limits of Comparative Administration: A New Internationalism in the Making. *Administrative Theory and Praxis* 22(2): 273–86.

King, Cheryl, and Camilla Stivers, eds. 1998. *Government Is Us: Public Administration in an Anti-Government Era*. Thousand Oaks, CA: Sage Publications.

Konadu-Agyemang, Kwadwo. 1998. Structural Adjustment Programs and the Perpetuating of Poverty and Underdevelopment in Africa: Ghana's Experience. *Scandinavian Journal of Development Alternatives and Area Studies* 17(2/3): 127–43.

Langley, Oyo J., ed. 1979. *Ideologies of Liberation in Black Africa*. London: Rex Collins.

Light, Paul C. 1997. *The Tides of Reform: Making Government Work, 1945–1995*. New Haven, CT: Yale University Press.

Lynn, Laurence E., Jr. 1996. *Public Management as Art, Science, and Profession*. Chatham, NJ: Chatham House.

Marshall, Gary. 1996. Deconstructing Administrative Behavior: The "Real" as Representation. Proceedings of the Ninth National Symposium on Public Administration Theory, 292–306.

Ministry of Local Government. 1994. *The New Local Government System*. Accra: Ministry of Local Government and Rural Development.

——. 1996. *The New Local Government System*. Accra: Ministry of Local Government and Rural Development.

Mohan, Giles. 1996. Neoliberalism and Decentralized Development Planning in Ghana. *Third World Planning Review* 18(4): 433–55.

Office of the Head of the Civil Service (Ghana). 1993. *The Civil Service Management Handbook*. Vol. 1. Accra, Ghana: Universal Printers.

Osborne, David, and Ted Gaebler. 1992. *Reinventing Government: How the Entrepreneurial Spirit Is Transforming the Public Sector*. New York: Plume.

Overseas Development Administration (ODA). 1993. *Evaluation of ODA Project in Support of the Ghana Civil Service Reform Programme*. London: Her Majesty's Stationery Office.

Peters, B. Guy. 1996. *The Future of Governing: Four Emerging Models*. Lawrence, KS: University Press of Kansas.

Peters, Tom, and Robert Waterman. 1982. *In Search of Excellence: Lessons from America's Best Run Companies*. New York: Harper and Row.

Pires, Mark. 2000. Study Abroad and Cultural Exchange Programs to Africa: America's Image of a Continent. *African Issues* 28(1/2): 39–45.

Pollitt, Christopher. 1990. *Managerialism and the Public Services: The Anglo-American Experience*. Cambridge, MA: Blackwell.

Putnam, Robert. 1995. Bowling Alone. *Journal of Democracy* 6(1): 65–78.

Rasheed, Sadiq, and Fashole Luke, eds. 1995 *Development Management in Africa: Toward Dynamism, Empowerment, and Entrepreneurship*. Boulder, CO: Westview Press.

Republic of Ghana. 1967. *Mills-Odoi Commission Report*. Accra, Ghana: Republic of Ghana.

——. 1990. *Report of the Committee on Public Administration Restructuring, Decentralization, and Implementation Committee*. Unpublished report.

Republic of Ghana, Gyampoh Commission. 1993. *Civil Service Law, PNDC Law 327*. Tema, Ghana, Republic of Ghana.

Republic of Ghana, PricewaterhouseCoopers Committee. 1997. *PricewaterhouseCoopers Report*. Accra, Ghana: Ghana.

Riggs, Fred W. 1964. *Administration in Developing Countries: The Theory of Prismatic Society*. Boston, MA: Houghton Mifflin.

——. 1998. Public Administration in America: Why Our Uniqueness is Exceptional and Important. *Public Administration Review* 58(1): 22–32.

Rimmer, D., ed. 1992. *Staying Poor: Ghana's Political Economy, 1950–1990*. Oxford, UK: Pergamon Press.

Rondinelli, David A. 1981. Government Decentralization in Comparative Perspectives: Theory and Practice in Developing Countries. *International Review of Administrative Sciences* 47(7): 22–47.

Rothchild, Donald. 1991. *Ghana: The Political Economy of Recovery*. London: Lynne Rienner.

Selznick, Philip. 1992. *The Moral Commonwealth*. Berkeley, CA: University of California Press.

Stivers, Camilla. 2000. Resisting the Ascendancy of Public Management: Normative Theory and Public Administration. *Admistrative Theory and Praxis* 22(1): 10–23.

Takyi, Baffour, and Yaw Oheneba-Sakyi. 1994. Customs and Practices about Marriages and Family Life in Ghana. *Family Perspectives* 28(4): 257–81.

Terry, Larry D. 1998. Administrative Leadership, Neo-Managerialism, and the Public Management Movement. *Public Administration Review* 58(3): 194–200.

Timney, Mary M. 1998. Overcoming Barriers to Citizen Participation: Citizens as Partners, not Adversaries. In *Government Is Us: Public Administration in Anti-Government Era*, edited by Cheryl King and Camilla Stivers, 88–101. Thousand Oaks, CA: Sage Publications.

Vehnamaki, Mika. 1998. The Economic Geography of Ghana's Structural Adjustment. *Scandinavian Journal of Development Alternatives and Area Studies* 17(2/3): 127–43.

Welch, Eric, and Wilson Wong. 1998. Public Administration in a Global Context: Bridging the Gaps of Theory and Practice between Western and Non-Western Nations. *Public Administration Review* 58(1): 40–49.

Wereko, Theophilis B. 1998. Role of the Management Development Institution in the Reform Process in Ghana. Paper presented at the Workshop on the Role of Management Development Institutions in the Reform Process, February 2–6, Maseru, Lesotho.

Werlin, Herbert. 1994. Ghana and South Korea: Explaining Development Disparities. *Journal of African and Asian Studies* 3(4): 205–25.

White, Jay, and Guy Adams, eds. 1994. *Research in Public Administration: Reflections on Theory and Practice*. Thousand Oaks, CA: Sage Publications.

Woode, Samuel N. 1989. *Making the District Assembly Work*. Accra, Ghana: Ghana Publishing Corporation.

Women in Public Life in Ghana (WPL). 1998. Research Report submitted to the Department for International Development, Development and Project Planning Center, University of Bradford.

World Bank. 1981. *Accelerated Development in sub-Saharan Africa: An Agenda for Action*. Washington, DC: World Bank.

——. 2000. *World Development Report*. Washington, DC: Oxford University Press.

Wright, Richard A. 1984. *African Philosophy: An Introduction*. Lanham, MD: University Press of America.

Zimmerman, Joseph F. 1999. *The New England Town Meeting: Democracy in Action*. Westport, CT: Praeger.

Peter Fuseini Haruna** is an assistant professor and MPA program coordinator at Texas A&M International University. Dr. Haruna has published in the African Studies Review and is the coauthor of* IMF and World Bank-Sponsored Structural Adjustment Programs in Africa: Ghana's Experiences from 1983–1999 *(Ashgate 2001). His research interests include leadership, governance structures, public finance, and comparative administrative systems.* ***Email: pharuna@tamiu.edu.

Outcome-focused Management in New Zealand

by ***Andrew Kibblewhite*** *and* ***Chris Ussher****

1. Introduction

This paper discusses the uses of outcomes in public sector management in New Zealand.[1] It begins by describing the overall public management system within which government departments operate, and how outcomes are used within this system. It then outlines some work that is underway to improve the focus on outcomes, and the way that outcomes are used within the system. The remainder of the paper is a series of case studies of innovative uses of outcomes in the New Zealand state sector.

2. Overall approach to outcomes-focused management

2.1. *New Zealand's public management model: An overview*

New Zealand's public sector management system has been in place for over a decade. The intent of the reforms of the late 1980s and early 1990s was to shift the focus from how much was spent, to what it was spent on and why.

The core of the model underlying the reforms involves ministers specifying the outcomes they wish to achieve and the outputs (and other interventions) they wish to pursue to achieve these outcomes. Policy advice informs this process.

When ministers have agreed the outputs to be supplied and the parameters[2] they should be supplied within, with departments and other providers, the departments and other providers have freedom to manage the resources allocated to them to produce the desired outputs. The other element of the system is accountability for performance: A requirement for managers to be held to account for their performance managing the allocated resources to produce the desired outputs. Policy managers, for example, need to be held accountable for the quality and responsiveness of the advice they provide to ministers.

To make the model work, decision-makers needed better information than was available previously. In particular, as ministers began to focus on outputs rather than inputs, there was a move from cash accounting to accrual accounting so that ministers, Parliament and other stakeholders had better information on how much it actually cost to produce the desired outputs. At the same time, government budgets began to be presented to Parliament in output terms rather than input terms. Although the government is required to state in the budget papers how the purchased outputs are linked to its desired outcomes, Parliament still appropriates explicitly for outputs.

An explicit part of the reforms, which relates to the output/outcome distinction, was to outline the separate responsibilities of ministers and chief executives. Scott, Bushnell and Sallee state:

> *The approach taken in the New Zealand financial management reforms is to require chief executives to be directly responsible for the outputs produced by the departments, while the ministers choose which outputs should be produced and should therefore have to answer directly themselves for the outcomes.*[3]

This vision has not been realised as completely as was originally envisaged. It illustrates, however, the central role that outcomes played in the financial management reforms and play in the public management system. Conceptually, the New Zealand system focuses on outcomes. There have, however, been difficulties integrating outcomes into public management, principally because it is hard to specify, measure and manage for outcomes. Work continues to address these difficult issues.

2.2. *Strategy setting*

2.2.1. *Whole-of-government strategy*

The government sets the highest-level outcome goals. The Fiscal Responsibility Act (1994) required the government, in the Budget Policy Statement, to:

> *specify the broad strategic priorities by which the government will be guided in preparing the budget for that financial year.*[4]

Since the mid-1990s, this requirement has been met by various sets of strategic priorities under a variety of names. There have been *Strategic Result Areas* and *Strategic Priorities and Overarching Goals*. Currently, there are *Key Government Goals to Guide Public Sector Policy and Performance*, which are attached as an annex.

In general, these strategic priorities have not been goals as much as statements of broad direction. They are not tightly specified, and no targets or quantifiable measures have been developed to monitor progress against them.

2.2.2. *Outcomes in the budget process*

The high-level strategic priorities have been used as a prioritisation tool in the budget process. As noted above, Parliament appropriates for outputs. The Public Finance Act, however, requires ministers to identify in the estimates (ministers' requests to Parliament for appropriations):

> *the link between the classes of outputs to be purchased by the Crown and the government's desired outcomes.*[5]

Current practice at making this link is variable. For the most part, it has been done in a cursory fashion merely by asserting that output *a* contributes to outcome goal *b*. Ministers are not required to demonstrate the link or to provide targets for outcome performance. Also, because there is a relatively high number of ministerial portfolios and departments, few key goals are the responsibility of a single minister or department.

The requirement to link outputs to outcomes in the estimates is not the only way outcomes feature in the budget process. Most ministerial scrutiny of expenditure in the budget process is of new spending proposals and that scrutiny explicitly addresses whether the new expenditure is likely to contribute strongly to achieving outcomes.

Priorities for new spending are managed using a fiscal management tool called the fiscal provisions. The Fiscal Responsibility Act (1994) requires the government to be transparent about its short-term fiscal objectives, so each year it must outline how much more it intends to spend for that year and the two following. Informally, this statement of fiscal intentions is built upon a fiscal provisions framework that sets the level of additional discretionary government expenditure (there are separate provisions for capital and operating expenditure). The fiscal provisions limit the amount the government can spend on new policy decisions.

The combination of the fiscal provisions framework and the broad strategic priorities is a powerful prioritisation tool. Together, they set a transparent budget constraint, and outline what the highest priorities are within that constraint. Since demand for funding exceeds supply, there are incentives for ministers to demonstrate that proposed new expenditure is worthwhile and will contribute to the government's outcomes. Ministers are required to indicate how the proposed new intervention will be evaluated. This is a new requirement, and so can be expected to yield more useful information as time passes.

Few formal processes exist to assess the value for money of baseline expenditure (as opposed to new spending proposals), although that is changing. In 2000, and again in 2001, Treasury has run a *Value for Money* process to identify opportunities for reprioritisation within existing departmental baselines for high spending portfolios. In particular, this is a chance for ministers to work with officials to identify spending that may not fit closely with their priorities. Lower priority expenditure within a portfolio then becomes available for funding higher priorities.

Parliamentary scrutiny of the budget and of departmental performance, *ex post*, is principally performed in select committees through the Estimates Review and the Financial Review processes. The standard questionnaire that departments are required to answer for select committee examination asks for information on how outputs contribute to outcomes.

In summary, outcome goals inform the budget, particularly for the allocation of new expenditure, but increasingly for expenditure within baselines too. These outcome goals are not usually accompanied by outcome measures in the budget documents themselves.

2.2.3. *Departmental strategic planning*

The government's high-level goals have been translated into departments' planning through a small number of "key priorities" (previously known as "key result areas"). Since the high-level goals have generally been broadly defined, most departments can tie their key priorities back to them. Departments choose their key priorities, but central agencies[6] have some input, both to perform a quality assurance role and to gain a whole-of-government picture.

Previously, key priorities have formed a key part of chief executives' performance agreements and were driven down into the departments' businesses effectively.

Key priorities were supposed to be SMART—Specific, Measurable, Achievable, Results-focused and Time-bound. Since chief executives were held accountable for delivering on these key priorities, they tended to be outputs rather than outcomes although the better ones included accompanying outcome goals and targets that indicated how progress was being made achieving the goal the key priority contributes to. Although key priorities are not currently part of the formal architecture of the system, departments are still required to link their activities back to the government's broad strategic priorities. Central agencies review departmental plans to ensure that departments are collectively doing the right things to achieve the government's high-level goals.

Initiatives are underway to improve the quality of departmental strategic planning and to make it more outcomes-focused. This should be reflected in improved *ex ante* reporting to Parliament. For example, five departments are piloting a new approach to strategic planning in the Capability, Accountability and Performance (CAP) pilot. The new approach encourages agencies to take a more consultative approach to departmental planning. In particular, it seeks to ensure that agencies take explicit account of:

- the outcomes the agency is aiming to achieve;
- the capability it will require both now and in the future to achieve those outcomes;
- the environment within which the agency operates;
- risks that the agency must take account of.

The planning process culminates in a Statement of Intent, which is a high-level summary of an agency's internal planning, with a multi-year focus. The Statement of Intent will be tabled in the House of Representatives and will be an important external accountability document.

2.3. *Translating strategy into action*

Both the budget and departmental planning documents translate strategy into action. The budget contains general output information but more specific information is contained in an Output Agreement[7] which describes the outputs a department is producing within one or more years. The Output Agreement generally contains relatively little information on the outcomes an output contributes to. Departments are being encouraged to include more contextual information about how the outputs will contribute to outcomes.

This apparent focus on outputs at the departmental level has to be understood in the context of the sharp distinction made between the responsibilities of chief executives and ministers. The distinction is closely linked with the way accountability is thought of in the New Zealand system. In an accountability relationship, performance may attract rewards and sanctions so managers must have control over the performance dimensions for which they are held accountable.

Outcomes are generally beyond the control of individual managers[8] so managers are not usually held accountable for them. Of course, decision-makers can be held accountable for the decisions they make and they can be held accountable for managing emerging risks and opportunities to the extent of their management authority to maximise the likelihood of the outcome being achieved. There are areas, of course, where experience shows it is possible to hold managers accountable for outcomes. For example, the Governor of the Reserve Bank has authority to set monetary policy and is held accountable for holding inflation within a specified target.

Although outcomes have some uses (but also some well-known limitations) in an accountability relationship, they have a far wider and more important role in departmental management. Information on outcomes is essential for direction setting, making intervention choices, improving co-ordination and identifying and building the capability needed to achieve the outcomes.

We have already noted the importance of outcomes in departmental strategic planning processes shaping a department's direction. In addition to their use in the formal machinery of the system, however, outcomes are critical to the effective day-to-day operation of the state sector. Both in strategic planning and in day-to-day management, outcomes information focuses prioritisation choices about where to intervene, and trade-offs between different interventions. These choices and trade-offs need to be made in all levels of the system: Teachers need to decide which children require remedial reading programmes and ministers must decide whether they can best meet their education objectives by increasing early childhood education funding or tertiary education funding. Information on what outcomes are desired and whether government is achieving them must influence decisions and judgements throughout the state sector.

In summary, a key benefit of retaining a focus on outputs within formal management systems is that this ensures a better understanding of what is done by the public service. This is a prerequisite for assessing value for money. There are other parts to that value for money puzzle, however, including robust outcome information about whether the outputs had the desired impact. In other words, good outcome information is an addition, not a replacement, for good output information.

2.4. *Improving outcome information*

A key focus for improving outcome information is the policy advice process. After all, the key function of policy advice is to identify what the problem is and how to solve or mitigate it. This involves making judgements, based on evidence and sound reasoning, of how outputs contribute to desired outcomes. This can go hand-in-hand with a more sophisticated understanding of risk management as part of output specification. The biggest contribution to improved government performance in achieving outcomes is likely to come from improved policy advice, based on better information. Several initiatives are underway in this area, which are principally focused on improving the quality of information available on outcomes. This includes work on state indicators at a whole-of- government level and work within departments to define and measure outcomes better, and to ensure that outcomes information is used in decision-making.

2.4.1. *State indicators*

There are several different types of indicators that are relevant for outcomes-focused management, including (in increasing order of sophistication):

- *state indicators* which provide a snapshot of the world or aspects of it—*e.g.*percentage of children sitting and achieving School Certificate in five subjects:
- *effectiveness indicators* which attempt to measure the success of particular interventions—*e.g.* percentage of offenders in a target risk band re-offending within 12 months of release, following a particular intervention, compared with a matched-pair control group;
- *risk indicators* which suggest where interventions should be targeted—*e.g.* risk of imprisonment within five years.

States' information differs from effectiveness information as it does not rely on causal inference about the relationship between the intervention and the way the world is. By collecting comparable information across time and across location, policy-makers and decision-makers can see how the world is changing. States' information has a number of uses:

- it can guide prioritisation choices, by showing where the serious problems are;
- it can guide evaluations of effectiveness by providing an information base against which change can be assessed. Analysts can then use this knowledge about the world to make inductive judgements about the effectiveness of various interventions.

Some departments have already developed relatively comprehensive sets of state indicators. Fewer departments, however, have specific effectiveness measures that are intended to reflect the success of various interventions. This reflects the complexity of the public policy environment where many outcomes are reflected by a wide variety of interventions and environmental factors.

In particular, work is underway to develop whole-of-government or sector-wide sets of state indicators. For example, the Ministry of Social Policy has recently published *The Social Report* 2001, which contains around 35 indicators of the state of New Zealand's social health. Other projects are looking at reporting indicators of environmental health and sustainable development.

2.4.2. *Defining, measuring and using outcomes*

Although improving information about outcomes is an essential part of integrating outcomes into public management, it is only part of the picture. The achievement of outcomes requires decision-making processes to take account of information about outcomes. Treasury and the State Services Commission have recently set-up the Pathfinder Project to build management capability to develop outcome measurement frameworks and outcome management tools and approaches that can be used to improve outcomes across the state sector.

The Pathfinder Project, which seeks to demonstrate that it is possible to manage for outcomes in parts of the state sector, is a network of eight agencies, which, while working individually to define, measure and use outcomes in management, are actively sharing lessons learnt in the process. At the same time, Treasury and the State Services Commission are working to capture the lessons learned from the Pathfinder Project so that they can be shared more widely across the state sector.

2.4.3. *Evaluation*

In an outcomes context, by evaluation we mean impact evaluation. *Ex Ante* analysis and assessment of proposed interventions is part of the core policy advice process, but the *ex ante* analysis needs to be backed up *ex post* by evaluation of the effectiveness of the intervention, when cost-effective. Impact evaluation may involve more than just setting and monitoring effectiveness indicators. It can also include some more in-depth analysis of causes and effects, and so seek further opportunities for greater value for money.

Impact evaluation is coming into sharper focus in the New Zealand public sector and we are beginning to evaluate the outcomes of policies/programmes/projects more systematically. The government has investigated requiring all policy proposals going to Cabinet to have evaluation criteria stated, but this was seen as impractical. In particular, there was a risk that agencies would develop a compliance attitude towards evaluation, rather than focusing on it when it adds value. Central agencies are focusing on improving evaluation criteria when discussing policy proposals with departments. A systems-wide approach to evaluation is actively being considered.

Budget initiative bids are required to include evaluation criteria. Ministers must outline if the proposal has been evaluated, and if so, what the results are. If not, ministers must outline how they will measure the success of the initiative. For example, if a minister proposes to purchase more special education services programmes to improve educational outcomes for a group of special needs children, that minister is required to outline in the bid how the success of those programmes will be evaluated. This information has only been required since the 2000 Budget so it is not yet clear how effective this will be at increasing the value that evaluation adds to the policy process.

2.5. *Co-ordination and outcomes*

Outcomes are the key focus of government activity, around which government co-ordination should be managed. To enable such co-ordination, there need to be shared high-level strategies and shared outcome targets. Shared outcome targets make explicit what the government is trying to achieve, and allow trade-offs to be made among different means of achieving the target.

Co-ordination is required beyond just the planning phase however. Managers also need to be aware of risks that can arise to hinder the achievement of the outcome. In a complex system, an intervention from one department can have a negative effect on the effectiveness of an intervention from another. There are many and varied interrelationships between interventions and outcomes in most social policy areas. For example, housing, education, welfare, environment, food safety and economic policies—the responsibilities of a range of ministers—will impact on public health, which is within the purview of the Minister of Health. Thus being aware what the outcomes risks are, and how they can be managed, is critical both at the policy advice phase and the implementation phase. Work is underway at present to consider ways of improving co-ordination both at a policy and at an operational level.

3. Case studies

These examples illustrate some of the ways that outcome goals, measures and targets are used in New Zealand.

3.1 *Integrated Offender Management (Department of Corrections)*

3.1.1. *Context*

New Zealand's Department of Corrections has been developing a set of outcome measures on the effectiveness of rehabilitative programmes delivered to convicted offenders. The government spends around NZ$32 million per annum on rehabilitative programmes for convicted offenders both in prison and in the community. The programmes are intended to reduce re-offending and so reduce the future cost of re-offending. This contributes to the government's goal of building safer communities.

The aim of the outcomes management project is to identify the effectiveness of specific rehabilitative programmes at reducing offending among a targeted group of offenders. Prison officers and probation officers will then be able to place offenders on programmes that are statistically most likely to be effective, given the offender's risk profile. Senior managers will be in a better position to advise the Minister of Corrections which programmes should be offered where and to whom, and, significantly, ministers will be in a better position to trade-off spending on offender rehabilitation programmes *vs.* other spending priorities based on robust cost-benefit data.

3.1.2. *The Outcomes Measurement Model*

The model is built around a cost-benefit equation that takes into account both the societal costs of crime and the cost-effectiveness of rehabilitative programmes. The basic cost-benefit equation is:

$$BCi = (CPHi * RQi)/RCPHi$$

Where:

- BC is the benefit—cost ratio for a specific intervention;
- CPH is the future cost per head of untreated offenders, which is defined as the average direct cost or total seriousness score of all offences committed over the next five years by individuals within the primary target group;
- RQ is the actual (or expected) Rehabilitation Quotient of a given intervention, as measured on the primary target group;
- RCPH is the rehabilitation cost per head given a rehabilitative intervention; and
- *i* indicates that the calculation's inputs (and thus output) are specific to a particular intervention and the particular target group it is delivered to.

It is relatively easy to determine cost of delivering a rehabilitation programme per head. The more sophisticated measures are the future cost per head (CPH) and the rehabilitation quotient (RQ).

- **Future Cost per Head**

This measure takes account both of the direct cost to the police/courts/corrections systems plus an estimate of the cost to society of an offender's re-offending over a five-year period. The future cost per head data was determined by following 28 000 criminal careers from 1993 to 1998 and counting the total length of sentences and numbers of offences in each offence class. Separate counts are completed for each risk bank. Risk of imprisonment (RoI) and risk of reconviction (RoC) rates are determined for each of 10 target groups into which offenders are grouped. A profile is thus established for each of the target groups which is used to calculate the average future cost per head for individuals within the target group.

- **Rehabilitation Quotient**

The rehabilitation quotient (RQ) quantifies the reduction in the re-offending rate, as a percentage, due to rehabilitative interventions delivered to the target group. The RQ is measured by comparing an intervention group with a statistically valid, matched pair control group. Statistical demands mean that identifying RQs has been the most difficult data set to gain, given the relatively small size of New Zealand's offender population. However, the department plans to have robust RQ measures for its current set of programmes by February 2001. The mean RQ for a good adult programme is around 10–15%, while RQs for some youth programmes have approached 40%.

When RQs are available, a cost-benefit ratio can be determined that indicates how benefits compare to costs for a given intervention targeted at a given target group of offenders. Cost-benefit ratios of 1.8 to 30 have been obtained using RQ data from separate evaluations and from literature sources.

3.1.3. *Applying the model*

The cost-benefit model gives an accurate picture of the effectiveness of specific interventions targeted at specific groups. When the department has sufficient data to calculate the RQs for its current (core) programmes, it will be in a position to calculate the cost-benefit ratios for those core programmes. Thus it will be directly able to prioritise programmes and target programmes better at offenders.

The department will also calculate cost-benefit ratios from pilot programme results. Existing CPH and RCPH information can be combined with RQs based on overseas research or best estimates to determine the likely cost-benefit ratio. The estimated cost-benefit ratio can then be tested in the pilot. If predictions are borne out, the pilot can then become a core programme, competing for core funding on the basis of its cost-benefit score. Pilot information can continually be fed into the core programme prioritisation system to ensure that ministers get best value for the money they spend.

The cost-benefit ratio information has also been used to determine how much expenditure is justified on rehabilitation programmes. Ministers may determine a minimum cost-benefit threshold and fund everything within that threshold. Since there will always be constraints on government expenditure, funding limits will see continuous improvement as the best pilots displace programmes in the core.

Data will continue to feed into the system through time, so that continuous evaluation can occur. The department will continue to operate matched pair control groups to recalculate RQs.

3.1.4. *Governance and decision-making*

The outcomes management project will have a significant effect on the way that the department manages its rehabilitation programmes. Initially it will provide information to aid decision-making: managers and case workers will continue to be held accountable for delivering their outputs, rather than outcomes. Continuation of funding will, however, be increasingly dependent on delivering outcomes.

3.2. *Outcomes-based funding for employment programmes (Department of Work and Income)*

This example, which is still at the pilot stage, shows the potential use of outcome measures and targets in managing contracts with non-department providers. It is an explicit example of accountability for outcomes in the New Zealand public service, which illustrates the value of thinking carefully about output specification.

The Department of Work and Income is responsible both for assisting job-seekers find work and for assessing and paying benefits. A significant part of its business is contracting employment programmes and services from third-parties to minimise unemployment.

In the past, these programmes have been funded on an activities or outputs-basis: The provider is paid based only on the number of programmes they deliver. Because the contracts for services with employment programme providers needed to be specified up front, case managers were constrained over the choice of programmes they could suggest customers enrolled on.

The department currently contracts with individual providers for training and/or other programmes (*e.g.* Work Confidence, ESOL and industry-based training programmes). It is piloting contracts that combine some sort of payment for activity with payment for achieving an outcome or output. If successful, such output contracts, with outcome performance measures, could show that it is possible to incorporate rich outcome measures that matter for accountability into output contracts. There are also, to date, some examples of contracts that are solely outcomes-based, although there is obviously a risk here that a provider can be paid for doing nothing, if the contract is not well specified. The long-term success and impact of these approaches is still to be determined.

3.2.1. *Progress to date*

In line with international trends, the department is about to pilot an outcomes-based approach in New Zealand that strengthens the focus on achieving specified employment outcomes, and provides support to this process through increased programme and funding flexibility. The pilots will take place in seven regions, and around 12 providers and 500 job-seekers will be involved. The pilots will test issues around:

- appropriate target groups for the initiative;
- specification of outcomes that should be achieved;
- costs to the department of specific groups for a set period as a basis for setting a "price"; and
- funding formulae and accountability frameworks that are appropriate to the local delivery environment.

If the pilots are successful, they could inform the development of an outcomes-based approach in relation to the department's mainstream delivery of employment programmes. There may also be potential in the longer-term for extending this approach to other core services.

In some regions, the department has been contracting for services with pay for performance-based on achieving the desired outcome. Third-party providers are paid an up-front fee for service, but the bulk of the payment comes later when the customer finds and remains in a job. For example, the provider may get a fee upfront, an incentive or performance payments when the customer gets a job, a further payment if the customer stays in the job for 13 weeks, and a further payment when the customer has stayed in the job for 26 weeks. Research suggests that after six months or so, the relationship between the employee and employer assumes greater importance than the relationship between case manager/trainer and customer.

There have also been some contracts where providers receive no upfront fee, but are paid only performance payments as the customer successfully finds and remains in a job.

3.2.2. *Future directions*

In line with the aim of devolving responsibility for choosing programmes to the most appropriate level, the department is looking at developing the use of outcomes-based funding contracts further. One option is to contract out case management services to local providers. Contracts could focus on the outcomes to be achieved, without limiting the programmes that the funding could be used for. The department would specify an outcome or a hierarchy of outcomes such as:

- the client is placed in stable unsubsidised employment;
- the client has been placed in stable employment for three months;
- the client is in unsubsidised employment;
- the client is in subsidised employment.

The provider would be paid as the client achieved each of those outcomes and so funding would not follow programmes, but individual clients. Contestability should see a culture of continuous improvement develop so that the funding goes to the most effective providers and programmes.

An outcomes-based funding approach will only be effective, however, when:

- there is a clear statement of the desired outcome;
- providers have the capability to manage service delivery on an outcome-based funding model;
- outcome payment is targeted to client risk and need, so that providers to not have incentives to concentrate on short- term temporary unemployed who could find jobs by themselves;
- there are incentives to ensure that the provider has an interest in the person remaining in the job for a certain period; and
- there is sufficient demand in the job market.

3.2.3. *Evaluation*

The goal of funding employment assistance on an outcomes basis is to reduce the persistence and incidence of unemployment. Short-term unemployed pose far fewer costs to society than a core of long-term unemployed, who are likely to be the hardest to get into jobs. As a result, work is underway to develop better tools to assess risk.

An evaluation of the success of the outcomes funding model will need to focus on success at reducing the rate of persistent unemployment among the pilot groups.

3.2.4. *Comments*

It is possible to contract for these services and measure aspects of performance on an outcomes basis. The accountability issues are more complex in an outcomes-based approach and require robust measures and monitoring of performance against outcomes. There are risks of providers under-performing or undertaking undesirable activities that are not picked up by an outcomes-based performance framework.

In order to fund on an outcomes basis, however, robust prices are needed to ensure both that the government is getting value for money and that providers (many of which are not-for-profit) remain viable. In running the pilots, the department will need to determine the cost of specific target groups for specific periods as a basis for setting the "price". The report collects historical data on length of benefit receipt of its clients, and this can be accessed for particular groups.

3.3. *Road Safety Strategy (Land Transport Safety Authority, lead agency)*

3.3.1. *Context*

The National Road Safety Committee has recently released "Road Safety Strategy 2010". The strategy outlines options for reducing the social cost of crashes on New Zealand's roads and seeks public feedback on which option to choose.

The previous road safety plan—*National Road Safety* 1995—aimed to achieve a level of road safety equivalent to the safest countries in the world. The updated plan has a more modest target. The goal is to achieve current (*i.e.* 2000) world's best practice by 2010. At present, New Zealand has around twice as many deaths per 100 000 persons and deaths per 10 000 vehicles as the safest countries in the world.

There are three interesting aspects of this work from the perspective of outcomes-focused management. One is the manner in which the actual outcomes targets will be set. The second is how these targets are translated into interventions at minimum cost. The third is how people are held accountable for achieving the targets.

3.3.2. *Setting the targets*

As noted above, the overall outcome goal is to achieve current world's best practice by 2010. This high-level goal, measured in terms of social cost is built upon a hierarchy of targets. Social cost is underpinned by final outcome targets such as the road death toll (target 2010 = fewer than 295 deaths). Beneath this are intermediate outcome targets—targets like proportion of drunk drivers, the average speeds on various types of roads. Underneath these are output targets such as the number of police traffic patrols, the number of anti-drink driving or anti-speeding advertisements shown or the number of passing lanes. Some of the targets can also be broken down by region and by road user groups—cyclists, pedestrians and older drivers, for example.

The targets are set using a mathematical model that predicts road safety outcomes. The model is built upon a set of assumptions derived from a wealth of historical crash and roading information. This snapshot of New Zealand road safety is the base from which a set of mathematical functions predict how various interventions and other factors should affect road safety outcomes.

For each of around 12 000 categories of casualty type, the current outcome is taken from the historical datasets. The current outcome is then adjusted to a 2010 baseline level. This adjusted baseline takes account of factors outside road safety agencies' control such as increased traffic volumes. The 2010 baseline outcome provides a benchmark against which predicted improvements can be measured.

Interventions are now added to the mix. For each of the 12 000 casualty types, the predicted effectiveness of various interventions is calculated. The calculation is based both on the rate of effectiveness for an intervention and the number of times the intervention is used. Thus we are left with predictions of how using specified amounts of specified interventions would affect the road safety outcomes for each category of casualty type. These results can then be aggregated to produce a full picture of how a mix of interventions can be expected to affect road safety outcomes.

The mix of interventions can also be costed to give a robust cost-benefit ratio for any given mix of interventions. Officials are still working to determine appropriate costings for different interventions.

Thus policy-makers and decision-makers have relatively good *ex ante* information, based on historical data and transparent assumptions, on which to base decisions on future interventions. The information can also be used to set targets. For example, the predictive model may suggest that an extremely costly set of interventions is likely to produce the lowest absolute reduction in the social cost of accidents. An intervention mix such as lowering the open speed limit to 20km/h and policing it strictly would probably lower the social cost of accidents near to zero. However, given the total costs this poses on society, this is unlikely to be a viable option. Hence a target based on that intervention set is unlikely to be a credible one.

3.3.3. *Choosing interventions*

When the public consultation process is completed, ministers will choose the targets. They can then use the cost/benefit information to determine which interventions are most likely to achieve the desired road safety outcomes at the least cost. Throughout the life of the strategy, the outcomes predicted by the model can be tested against the outcomes actually achieved and the intervention mix can be altered accordingly. Thus a feedback and evaluation loop is effectively in place. New data will also help modellers refine the functions that predict how interventions affect outcomes.

3.3.4. *Accountability*

A number of agencies contribute to these outcomes, especially the road safety agencies and the Police. The aim is for the National Road Safety Committee to take collective responsibility for the overall achievement of the social cost and final outcomes targets. Outcomes performance monitoring will continue on a quarterly basis with annual reviews, while formal reviews will be held every three years.

It is likely that the Land Transport Safety Authority, as the lead agency, will continue to be held accountable for these final outcomes, as in its current performance agreement. However, individual agency accountabilities will be more clearly specified within the performance management framework set out by the final strategy.

The envisaged accountability arrangements will "bite" harder than the current ones because they are based on a more rigorous and transparent analytical base. Certain difficulties associated with linking specific outputs to final outcomes will not disappear, but performance expectations will be more clearly defined and tracked across the full suite of road environment, vehicle and road user interventions. Regular review and *ex post* evaluations will sustain the outcomes-focus. Specific output targets will highlight key agency implementation accountabilities.

3.4. *New Zealand Biodiversity Strategy (Department of Conservation, lead agency)*

3.4.1. *Context*

The New Zealand Biodiversity Strategy (NZBS) was released in March 2000 and aims to halt the decline of New Zealand's indigenous biodiversity. The strategy has a 20-year timeframe and establishes a framework of goals, objectives and actions that are required to halt the decline. Priority actions have been identified and are currently being implemented that will lead to the greatest gains in biodiversity in the next five years. The strategy covers terrestrial, freshwater and marine biodiversity. A key feature of the strategy is that it does not focus solely on biodiversity on the Crown-owned conservation estate, but seeks to halt the decline in biodiversity nation-wide, including on private property. Partnerships are needed to ensure that the strategy is successful, allowing the participation of all New Zealanders, not just central government. Other key participants are local government, the private sector, iwi (Maori tribal groupings) and local communities.

The strategy includes a wide range of initiatives. Some are designed to halt the decline in biodiversity, while others, such as information gathering programmes, are to ensure that outcomes can be measured. The strategy is still at an early stage, so reporting on outcomes in relation to the strategic goals in the strategy is some years off. The major report after the first year (in October 2001) focused on auditing the implementation of the priority actions in the strategy. The report after the second year will include some preliminary intermediate outcome related directly to those actions (*e.g.* number of possums killed). There will not be reporting against outcomes relating to the strategic goals in the strategy (*e.g.* reduction in rate of deforestation, change in number of key species) until the end of the third year.

- **Outcomes measures in the strategy**

Outcomes measures and targets are used in the strategy to determine priorities for funding and to determine the effectiveness of interventions. There is a wide variety of projects, some involving information gathering for monitoring and evaluation purposes. Outcome measures have been developed for some programmes and are still being developed for others. Nevertheless, it is useful to give some examples.

- **Offshore Island Eradications**

New Zealand has a number of offshore islands that are sanctuaries for protected species. A project is underway to eradicate pests or to manage them at sustainable levels so that they do not pose a threat to each of the islands' unique environment. This involves both eradicating pests, and ensuring that they do not come back. The key intermediate outcome measure fore these projects is the presence or absence of target pests on the islands two years after the operation is completed. This is measured by sophisticated trapping and monitoring programmes. Longer term, the desired outcome is to halt the decline of biodiversity by ensuring the protection and recovery of at-risk species.

- **Increasing Protected Areas on Private Land**

The goal of this programme is to purchase, or support the effective management of, private lands with high biodiversity values. The programme aims to apply increased funding to existing mechanism to ensure that a wider range of natural habitats and ecosystems are protected. Results will be measured using ecological criteria and other appropriate measures. Longer-term measures for assessing the contribution of the programme to the goals in the strategy are still being developed.

- **Terrestrial and Freshwater Biodiversity Information System**

The aim of this project is to develop awareness of and access to existing information, as well as gathering and providing new information. The intermediate outcome is to have developed systems for gathering and accessing information, to improve knowledge about biodiversity and to increase public awareness about the state of New Zealand's biodiversity.

Initial targets are focused on the development of appropriate systems to collect, manage and disseminate the information. Longer-term targets are still being developed.

3.4.2. *Using the measures*

The primary purposes of collecting the outcomes information is to increase our understanding of New Zealand's biodiversity and to halt the decline of indigenous biodiversity. The information will be used to assess the effectiveness of various projects and to determine priorities. It can inform both what the desired outcomes should be and how they should change across time, and which interventions should be used to achieve those outcomes. Measuring the extent to which the desired outcomes have been achieved is also a useful information base for evaluating the overall success of the strategy from a process perspective.

The 20-year strategy has a funding plan for the first five years. Reprioritisation can begin when outcome results start to emerge. A major review after five years will assess success and direct new funding to the highest priorities.

3.4.3. *Managing the strategy*

As is usual practice in the New Zealand public service, managers are held accountable for managing the particular programmes. This can include assessing their success at managing risks that arise, including outcome risks.

A ministerial group is responsible for developing and implementing the New Zealand Biodiversity Strategy. This group is supported by a central government co-ordinating group, comprising the chief executives of the relevant agencies. Accountability for the overall management of the strategy is being bedded down through each agency's purchase and chief executive performance agreements.

3.5. *Maori Education Strategy (Ministry of Education)*

3.5.1. *Context*

One of the government's key priorities is to reduce inequalities in health, education, employment and housing. Maori—New Zealand's indigenous people—and Pacific peoples, as a group, fare worse than the population as a whole in these areas. A co-ordinated effort is underway to reduce these disparities and to ensure that all New Zealanders have the opportunity to participate fully in society.

Three areas, in particular, are being targeted: Education, employment and health. Outcome measures and targets have been developed for all of them. The nature of the social inequalities means however that a long-term timeframe is required to see if the desired outcomes are achieved. Significant educational outcomes especially can only be assessed after 10 or even 15 years of the intervention.

This paper focuses on the definition, measurement and use of education outcomes within the Maori education strategy.

3.5.2. *Reducing education inequalities*

It is well recognised that education achievement is a key determinant of achievement later in life. As a result, much of the early focus has been on improving Maori educational performance.

The outcome indicators developed do not cover the whole ambit of the education system. Instead, a set of key indicators has been chosen, which research suggests are the best indicators of ongoing improvement and success in Maori educational achievement and reducing inequalities between Maori and non-Maori.

The desired outcomes are broken down into participation and achievement goals for early childhood, school and tertiary education. Some of the outcomes, and indicators for them, are outlined below:

- **Early Childhood Education**

Goal	Measure	Target
Increase Maori participation in early childhood education.	Percentage of Maori aged 0-4 enrolled.	65% by 2006.

This target was set by comparison with the rate of participation among non-Maori.

- **School Education**

Goal	Measure	Target
Increase rate of Maori participation in school education.	Rate of Maori suspensions per 1 000 students.	Reduce rate to five per 1 000 by 2008 and to three per 1 000 by 2016.
Increase the achievement rate of Maori students in senior secondary education.	Rate of achievement of A, B and C grades in School Certificate and University Bursary.	Increase by 12% by 2010 and to parity by 2020.

These goals are derived from the non-Maori participation and achievement rates.

- **Tertiary Education**

Goal	Measure	Target
Increase participation of Maori students in tertiary education.	Percentage of students who are Maori.	13.8% by 2002, up to 16.7% by 2006.
Increase achievement of Maori students in tertiary education.	Percentage of graduates who are Maori.	15.1% by 2002, up to 18.2% by 2006.

3.5.3. *Using the outcome measures*

A variety of products have been developed in addition to the goals, measures and targets. In particular there are regular monitoring reports, which assess progress across the board, and evaluation reports, which assess the effectiveness of specific programmes.

Each goal is supported by a strategy to achieve it. For example, alongside the goal to increase Maori participation in early childhood education are a number of strategies including:

- examining ways of removing barriers;
- promoting the benefits of early childhood education; and
- expanding the availability of early childhood services.

Progress against the goal will be informative, but will not indicate which interventions are effective and which are not. Across time, it will become apparent where progress is being made and where continued efforts should be focused, but the outcome indicators will not show which interventions offer value for money. Hence, evaluation of programmes is critical at the micro-level of resource allocation as well as the policy development and planning stages of the cycle. The goal is to ensure that budget decisions and intervention decisions are based on outcome information.

3.5.4. *Managing and reporting outcomes*

The outcome goals and targets in the Maori education strategy have considerable political buy-in. Although the eventual goals are often long-term ones, achievable two- to three-year intermediate goals have been included. This enables ministers to focus on delivering tangible results within the electoral cycle.

At a departmental level, departments are required to report in their annual reports on their effectiveness in reducing inequalities. The annual report needs to include information on amount of expenditure spent reducing inequalities, and information on the effectiveness of that expenditure. In addition, departmental material is aggregated into a whole-of-government report, which is audited and tabled in the house.

4. Conclusions

New Zealand's public management reforms were designed to move the focus from what resources were being used, to what was being produced and what outcomes were achieved as a result. Considerable gains have been made, particularly in understanding what is being produced and how much it costs. Further work is underway to develop outcome management systems. The Pathfinder Project, in particular, may produce some tangible gains in this area.

Considerable effort is being applied to move outcomes into the core of the practice of public management in New Zealand. The five case studies illustrate that this process is well underway, and that it is possible to make progress despite the often-mentioned difficulties in managing for outcomes. One of the lessons that can be learnt from the New Zealand experience is that creating an environment that enables outcomes-focused management is unlikely to be enough. It is difficult to define, measure and manage for outcomes, and in some areas of government activity it is probably too difficult. Central agencies must balance the need to be responsive to the constraints that specific agencies face, with the need to provide impetus and leadership from the centre. This makes it difficult to drive outcomes-based management from the top-down. If agencies are to use outcomes-based systems, they need to have a sense of ownership and so need to develop the tools and systems themselves to fit their businesses.

It is important to focus on outcomes in both the formal and informal parts of the public management system. While outcomes may have some value in an accountability relationship, greater gains are likely to be realised from outcomes in planning, budgeting and decision-making processes. The key is good quality information: Information on what works and what does not is essential for effective public management. Similarly, outcome objectives need to be clearly stated and meaningful for both ministers and managers.

A third lesson that can be drawn from the New Zealand experience is that moving the focus to outcomes forces government to rethink its attitude to risk. The Corrections example shows that agencies need to be open to the possibility of programme failure if they are to improve the effectiveness of government expenditure. Corrections deliberately allocates a portion of its rehabilitation programmes budget to test new interventions to assess their effectiveness. Thus, the department can continually improve the value of its expenditure by taking risks and being open to failure.

New Zealand's public service has a large number of specialist agencies. As a result, co-ordination is critical for effective policy advice and service delivery. Outcomes can play a critical role focusing agencies on the same issues, and since outcomes cross organisational boundaries, effective outcome management also requires agencies to co-ordinate. The New Zealand Biodiversity Strategy is a good example of outcome co-ordination in action, as is the Road Safety Strategy. Joint initiatives like these are needed to address the critical public policy issues facing New Zealand.

---

* The Treasury, New Zealand.

Notes

1. This paper was originally prepared as a background paper for an OECD experts' meeting on outcomes-focused management.
2. The key parameters are quality, quantity, timeliness, location and cost.
3. Scott, Bushnell and Salee, *Reform of the Core Public Sector: New Zealand Experience*, p. 157.
4. Fiscal Responsibility Act (1994) Section 6, Part 3(a).
5. Public Finance Act (1989) Section 9, Part 2(a).
6. Central Agencies are the Department of the Prime Minister and the Cabinet, the State Services Commission, and the Treasury.
7. Previously called a "Purchase Agreement".
8. Commonly cited reasons for this include the difficulty of determining causality accurately, the time-lags between intervention and outcome, and information difficulties.

Annex I

Terminology

Outcomes—The Public Finance Act (1989) states: *"Outcomes" means the impacts on, or the consequences for, the community of the outputs or activities of the government.*

Judgements about outcomes depend upon judgements about causal relationships between interventions and the final results.

Outputs—The Public Finance Act (1989) states: *"Outputs" means the goods or services that are produced by a department, Crown entity, Office of Parliament, or other person or body.*

For an output to be meaningful as an accountability tool it must be described in ways that enable the producer of the output to be held to account for its delivery. To this end, output performance measures have traditionally been thought of in terms of quality, quantity, timeliness and cost. More sophisticated measures of output quality may well make reference to the outcomes the output contributes to.

Government can intervene via other activities such as regulation, funding, making grants or investing.

Annex II

Key Government Goals to Guide Public Sector Policy and Performance

Strengthen national identity and uphold the principles of the Treaty of Waitangi

Celebrate our identity in the world as people who support and defend freedom and fairness, who enjoy arts, music, movement and sport and who value our cultural heritage; and resolve at all times to endeavor to uphold the principles of the Treaty of Waitangi.

Grow an inclusive, innovative economy for the benefit of all

Develop an economy that adapts to change, provides opportunities and increases employment, and while closing the gaps, increases incomes for all New Zealanders.

Restore trust in government and provide strong social services

Restore trust in government by working in partnerships with communities, providing strong social services for all, building safe communities and promoting community development, keeping faith with the electorate, working constructively in Parliament and promoting a strong and effective public service.

Improve New Zealanders' skills

Foster education and training to enhance and improve the nation's skills so that all New Zealanders have the best possible future in a changing world.

Reduce inequalities in health, education, employment and housing

Reduce the inequalities that currently divide our society and offer a good future for all by better co-ordination of strategies across sectors and by supporting and strengthening the capacity of Maori and Pacific Island communities.

Protect and enhance the environment

Treasure and nurture our environment with protection for eco-systems so that New Zealand maintains a clean, green environment and rebuilds our reputation as a world leader in environmental issues.

From *OECD Journal of Budgeting,* Vol. 1, No. 4, 2002, pp. 85-109.

Index

Index

Test Your Knowledge Form

We encourage you to photocopy and use this page as a tool to assess how the articles in *Annual Editions* expand on the information in your textbook. By reflecting on the articles you will gain enhanced text information. You can also access this useful form on a product's book support Web site at *http://www.dushkin.com/online/*.

NAME: DATE:

TITLE AND NUMBER OF ARTICLE:

BRIEFLY STATE THE MAIN IDEA OF THIS ARTICLE:

LIST THREE IMPORTANT FACTS THAT THE AUTHOR USES TO SUPPORT THE MAIN IDEA:

WHAT INFORMATION OR IDEAS DISCUSSED IN THIS ARTICLE ARE ALSO DISCUSSED IN YOUR TEXTBOOK OR OTHER READINGS THAT YOU HAVE DONE? LIST THE TEXTBOOK CHAPTERS AND PAGE NUMBERS:

LIST ANY EXAMPLES OF BIAS OR FAULTY REASONING THAT YOU FOUND IN THE ARTICLE:

LIST ANY NEW TERMS/CONCEPTS THAT WERE DISCUSSED IN THE ARTICLE, AND WRITE A SHORT DEFINITION:

We Want Your Advice

ANNUAL EDITIONS revisions depend on two major opinion sources: one is our Advisory Board, listed in the front of this volume, which works with us in scanning the thousands of articles published in the public press each year; the other is you—the person actually using the book. Please help us and the users of the next edition by completing the prepaid article rating form on this page and returning it to us. Thank you for your help!

ANNUAL EDITIONS: Public Administration 04/05

ARTICLE RATING FORM

Here is an opportunity for you to have direct input into the next revision of this volume.
We would like you to rate each of the articles listed below, using the following scale:

1. **Excellent: should definitely be retained**
2. **Above average: should probably be retained**
3. **Below average: should probably be deleted**
4. **Poor: should definitely be deleted**

Your ratings will play a vital part in the next revision.
Please mail this prepaid form to us as soon as possible.
Thanks for your help!

RATING	ARTICLE
________	1. Time of Turbulence
________	2. In Memoriam: David O. "Doc" Cooke
________	3. Doc Cooke's Reflections on Effective Public Management
________	4. The Odyssey of Senior Public Service: What Memoirs Can Teach Us
________	5. Predictable Surprises: The Disasters You Should Have Seen Coming
________	6. Is Silence Killing Your Company?
________	7. Wireless Interoperability: A Key Element of Public Safety
________	8. Does Government Need a Sarbanes-Oxley Type Reform Act?
________	9. Underestimating Costs in Public Works Projects: Error or Lie?
________	10. Roadblocks in Reforming Corrupt Agencies: The Case of the New York City School Custodians
________	11. Is Your Performance Evaluation Fair for All?
________	12. Preventing Workplace Harassment: A Fact Sheet for Employees
________	13. Drug and Alcohol Testing in the Workplace: An Overview and Practical Guide for Cities
________	14. Double-Dip Dilemma
________	15. Dealing With Uncertain Budget Forecasts
________	16. How Congress Divides Our Money
________	17. City of Austin's Budget Crisis
________	18. The Budget Game
________	19. Deferrals: Gimmick or Usual Budget Math?
________	20. "Smart" Government Online, Not Inline
________	21. All Rise (and Power On)
________	22. The Price of Progress?
________	23. Doing the Right Thing
________	24. Wi-Fi Anxiety
________	25. The Twin Challenges That Immigration Brings to Public Administrators
________	26. Deadly Strains
________	27. Winning the Water Wars
________	28. A Mighty Wind
________	29. Like Go-Go 1990s, Smart Growth's Time Had Passed
________	30. Tucson Fire Department's MMRS Exercise: A Bioterrorism Response Plan
________	31. How to Make Transit-Oriented Development Work
________	32. The U.S. Supreme Court's New Federalism and Its Impact on Antidiscrimination Legislation
________	33. TEA Time in Washington
________	34. How the Dutch Do Housing
________	35. Water Tap Often Shut to South Africa Poor
________	36. England Tests e-Voting
________	37. Reforming Ghana's Public Service: Issues and Experiences in Comparative Perspective
________	38. Outcome-Focused Management in New Zealand

(Continued on next page)

ANNUAL EDITIONS: PUBLIC ADMINISTRATION 04/05

BUSINESS REPLY MAIL
FIRST-CLASS MAIL PERMIT NO. 84 GUILFORD CT

POSTAGE WILL BE PAID BY ADDRESSEE

McGraw-Hill/Dushkin
530 Old Whitfield Street
Guilford, Ct 06437-9989

ABOUT YOU

Name Date

Are you a teacher? ❒ A student? ❒
Your school's name

Department

Address City State Zip

School telephone #

YOUR COMMENTS ARE IMPORTANT TO US!

Please fill in the following information:
For which course did you use this book?

Did you use a text with this ANNUAL EDITION? ❒ yes ❒ no
What was the title of the text?

What are your general reactions to the *Annual Editions* concept?

Have you read any pertinent articles recently that you think should be included in the next edition? Explain.

Are there any articles that you feel should be replaced in the next edition? Why?

Are there any World Wide Web sites that you feel should be included in the next edition? Please annotate.

May we contact you for editorial input? ❒ yes ❒ no
May we quote your comments? ❒ yes ❒ no